# TEXAS BLOOD

## Seven Generations Among the Outlaws, Ranchers, Indians, Missionaries, Soldiers, and Smugglers of the Borderlands

## ROGER D. HODGE

"In *Texas Blood*, Roger Hodge takes the reader on journeys through intricate maps of the past and present, through politics and luck and greed and death, but always returns to the beautiful, unforgiving land of his heritage."　—Susan Straight, author of *Highwire Moon*

"Imagine finding out that the land where Cormac McCarthy set one of his most brutal novels was your family's ranch. . . . I've read loads of books about Texas but rarely encountered one so deeply of it, so deep the story escapes and becomes a treatise on the twisted American past and the force exerted by that on our complex present."
—John Jeremiah Sullivan, author of *Pulphead*

"A fusion of historical narrative, memoir, exposé, and lament, *Texas Blood* is a rigorously researched, compassionate examination of one of our country's most polarizing states. Hodge casts an unflinching eye on the violence of the borderlands yet does so with the tender lyricism and spiritual acumen of the best Cormac McCarthy. *Texas Blood* is a timely, important work: in grappling with Texas, Roger Hodge is holding America's own deeply troubled feet to the fire."
—Jamie Quatro, author of
*I Want to Show You More*

"Hypnotically written, deeply researched, profoundly elegiac—the adverbs pile up and with good reason. Roger D. Hodge has written a wonderful book about our most vexed and peculiarly American state, with an eye for detail and anecdote that's as loving as it is merciless."　—Tom Bissell, author of *Apostle*

"*Texas Blood* blends the personal and the historical to create a vivid portrait of a place unable to transcend its violent past. Roger D. Hodge is a very gifted writer, and he tells his story with the energy of a perfectly paced novel."　—Ron Rash, author of *Serena*

"Roger Hodge has crafted a masterful alloy of memoir and reportage, of social criticism and regional history. *Texas Blood* is an unforgettable foray into our most mysterious, violent, myth-soaked state, a portrait of enormous talent and skill that reveals precisely what America is."　—William Giraldi, author of *Hold the Dark*

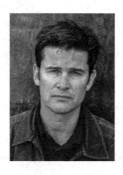

## ROGER D. HODGE
# TEXAS BLOOD

Roger D. Hodge is deputy editor of *The Intercept* and the author of *The Mendacity of Hope: Barack Obama and the Betrayal of American Liberalism.* Formerly he was the editor of the *Oxford American* and *Harper's Magazine.* Hodge's writing has appeared in many publications, including *Texas Monthly,* the *London Review of Books, Popular Science, The New Republic,* and *Harper's Magazine. Texas Blood* received the 2017 Texas Institute of Letters Award for Best Book of Nonfiction. He lives in Brooklyn.

www.texas-blood.com

ALSO BY ROGER D. HODGE

*The Mendacity of Hope:*
*Barack Obama and the Betrayal of American Liberalism*

# TEXAS BLOOD

# TEXAS BLOOD

SEVEN GENERATIONS AMONG THE OUTLAWS,
RANCHERS, INDIANS, MISSIONARIES, SOLDIERS,
AND SMUGGLERS OF THE BORDERLANDS

## ROGER D. HODGE

**VINTAGE BOOKS**
**A Division of Penguin Random House LLC**
**New York**

FIRST VINTAGE BOOKS EDITION, SEPTEMBER 2018

*Copyright © 2017 by Roger D. Hodge*

All rights reserved. Published in the United States by Vintage Books, a division of Penguin Random House LLC, New York, and distributed in Canada by Random House of Canada, a division of Penguin Random House Canada Limited, Toronto. Originally published in hardcover in the United States by Alfred A. Knopf, a division of Penguin Random House LLC, New York, in 2017.

Vintage and colophon are registered trademarks of Penguin Random House LLC.

The Library of Congress has cataloged the Knopf edition as follows:
Names: Hodge, Roger D., author.
Title: Texas blood : seven generations among the outlaws, ranchers, Indians, missionaries, soldiers, and smugglers of the borderlands / by Roger D. Hodge.
Description: First edition. | New York : Alfred A. Knopf, 2017. |
Includes bibliographical references and index.
Identifiers: LCCN 2016053188
Subjects: LCSH: Texas—Description and travel. | Texas—History, Local. |
Mexican-American Border Region—Description and travel. |
Mexican-American Border Region—History, Local. |
Hodge, Roger D.—Travel—Texas. | Hodge, Roger D.—
Travel—Mexican-American Border Region. |
Hodge, Roger D.—Family.
Classification: LCC F391.H755 2017 | DDC 976.4—dc23
LC record available at https://lccn.loc.gov/2016053188

**Vintage Books Trade Paperback ISBN: 978-0-345-80260-6
eBook ISBN: 978-0-307-96141-9**

*Maps by Mapping Specialists
Book design by Soonyoung Kwon*

www.vintagebooks.com

Printed in the United States of America
10  9  8  7  6  5  4  3  2  1

*For my father*

Life is but a motion of limbs.

—Thomas Hobbes

# CONTENTS

# TEXAS BLOOD

# SOUTHWEST TOWARD HOME

The boy wears a cowboy hat and boots, his jeans tucked in. He carries a gun, and a knife, and sometimes a sword. He can't be older than five or six. He stalks small birds, rabbits, lizards, and longs for a snake to show itself. Feral house cats, some lacking tails and ears, maintain a wary distance. The boy played no part in that mutilation, but the cats avoid all human contact. He wanders in and among dusty pens, spying on enemies, then out into the mesquite and cedar brush, wary of Indians lurking on the hilltops above.

He carefully avoids the prickly pear, lechuguilla, and other spiny desert shrubs that grow all around him. Sotol and Spanish daggers and yucca entice him with their tall woody stalks. Always looking for better guns, knives, and swords, he tests each stick with earnest concentration. He searches among fragments of chert for arrowheads, knives, ax heads, overlooking the mortar holes that pock limestone outcroppings, the stone wickiup rings and trash middens, all of which bear witness to thousands of years of human struggle in an unforgiving desert landscape.

Heat drives him back into the shade of the barn. Generators rumble, turning the long driveshafts of the shearing rig. Dusty men speaking Spanish, caked with sweat and grime, wearing dungarees black with lanolin, bend over bleating ewes, rapidly running clippers through the oily wool, over the belly, and inside the legs. They tie legs together and clip the wool from backs, haunches, necks, heads. Too fast and bright red lines appear, then blood. A foreman steps over with a needle and thread and stitches the wound. Untied, a shorn ewe leaps twice and scrambles back to her sisters just off the shearing floor. The boy watches from the shadows, sees his father deep in conversation with another man who wears a broad straw hat. They speak of breeding, stud rams, market prices, the never-ending drought. The boy slinks farther back into the barn, the crepuscular gloom broken by slashes of light glinting through old boards, and climbs a haphazard mountain of burlap sacks stuffed with wool, at least five hundred pounds each, and disappears into his game.

One afternoon a few years later the boy and his brother prowl about with their pellet guns, looking for something to shoot. They discover dozens of small birds, some brightly colored and others dull and tan but all of them lively and chattering, captives of an old wire shed that might once have been a chicken coop. They kill every one of them. When the boys finish with their game, small carcasses litter the floor of the shed; others hang upside down by their feet from wires and perches. On this ranch and others like it the boys grow used to the sight of blood. Blood from the lambs whose ears they mark, whose severed tails shower them with gore. Kid goats must be marked and calves branded and castrated. A colt's ears might be spared but not his testicles. Varmints they hunt down without mercy, for they compete for resources. The foxes and the coyotes and the bobcats and the mountain lions. The coons and the ringtails. Rabbits perish by the hundreds; they eat the grass, which is more precious than blood.


My childhood ended when I was twelve years old. Not so much because I began sampling my father's liquor, but because that year I went to work, in the summer after seventh grade. Of course I had labored in one way or another for as long as I could remember, because my father believed a boy's day should be filled with chores. We lived on a little piece of land just outside the Del Rio city limits, on ten acres among a patchwork of irrigated fields and homes, adjacent to a chicken farm, a trailer park, and a private rodeo ring where older kids practiced their calf roping. The old Border Patrol station for the agency's Del Rio sector was one road over, and the international bridge across the Rio Grande was just a few miles away. On a clear day I could see the low hills of Ciudad Acuña through my bedroom window. My childhood chores had been simple drudge work, and I hated them. I filled wheelbarrows with rocks from the fill dirt that had been spread around our house to make a proper lawn out of what was previously a field. I was lazy, and the job seemed endless. In my young eyes the yard was vast. After a pipe fence was built on the property, I had to prime and paint the fence with Rust-Oleum and collect the heavy leftover pipe segments that the welders had left lying everywhere. Somewhat more interesting was the care and feeding of the sheep, goats, horses, and the occasional calf that populated our pens out back, on the other side of an irrigation ditch. I would much rather have been splashing about in that ditch with my dogs, catching crawdads or snakes, and so I would somehow forget about my chores and lose myself in that tiny wilderness. Until I heard my father coming up the driveway, and then I'd make a desperate run for the wheelbarrow.

But in the summer of 1980, I began to work for hire, for a boss other than my father. I can't recall how it was decided, though I do remember sitting in the office of the Southwest Livestock and Trucking Company, before the intimidating figure of Darrell Hargrove. Darrell agreed to take me on, working in his stock pens with a motley gang of other boys more or less my age. I would make $37.50 a week.

Such work was good training for country boys who had ambitions as ranch hands. In those days I always assumed that I was destined to be a rancher, that it was my duty to carry on the family business, so I was proud of my new job. Every morning we showed up at Hargrove's pens on the north side of the Southern Pacific railroad tracks. All day we loaded and unloaded sheep, goats, and cattle from eighteen-wheeled tractor-trailer rigs and gooseneck trailers pulled by six-wheeled "dually" double-cabbed pickups and every other imaginable vehicle that could be kitted out to haul stock so that the animals could be counted, weighed, handled, assessed, fed, watered, then sold or traded and shipped on down the line.

Sometimes the livestock went right back on the truck, destined for a buyer in Mexico or some more distant market. Other times the animals were driven into pens where they awaited their indeterminate fate, milling about and bawling in their various brutish dialects. We put out alfalfa hay for feed and washed water troughs, threw rocks and knives at lizards, swatted flies and wasps and bumblebees, tortured crickets and grasshoppers, peed on ants, and sketched diagrams of naked women in the dust with sticks. We dipped Copenhagen snuff, strutting around the pens and feeling superior to the boys who spent their summer hanging out at the pool just up the road at the San Felipe Country Club.

I suppose I showed some promise as a hand, because after a few days of such work I was chosen to help with a special project. Hargrove had leased much of the Babb ranch in Terrell County and was grazing thousands of sheep in the rough canyon lands out there along the Rio Grande. The time had come for shearing, so he sent a team of cowboys out to do the gathering. The ranch was more than an hour west of Del Rio, so Darrell's teenage son Frank would pick me up at home every morning at 3:30 for the long drive through the outer dark. Frank had longish blond hair that emerged from under a baseball cap and covered his ears, and a large beak-like nose. He was funny and bragged constantly about his exploits with girls. I did my best to stay awake with my wad of Copenhagen lodged against my gums, but the drive inevitably blurred into a half-waking nightmare of fanfaronade, loud music, and the aroma of rank tobacco spit in nasty makeshift spittoons.

At 4:30 or 5:00 a.m. we would pull up at the ranch in front of Smokey Babb's trailer house. I remember sitting inside around a table, visiting. Smokey was skinny with wild black hair, and his wife, whose name I've forgotten, was quite fat. She wore a dirty terry-cloth housecoat. I have a strong memory of being given a rubbery piece of steak to eat that was cooked in a microwave.

Then we would saddle up and ride through the predawn darkness for what seemed like hours so that we'd be in the back of the pasture by daybreak. I was given a mule to ride, and on the first morning, like a fool, I immediately drifted to the head of the group, though I had no idea where we were going. Darrell's son-in-law, a wise young cowboy named Carl, spoke quietly to me that first day. He advised me never to ride at the front of a party, but always to hang back, where I could watch the other men and perhaps learn something. Then we had arrived, and I was sent off, taking my portion of a pasture of several thousand acres, riven by canyons and choked with brush, with little real sense of what I was supposed to be doing.

I hooted and hollered in imitation of my elders, driving sheep out of draws and off the top of what seemed like mountains, pushing them in what I hoped was the desired direction, toward a fence where they'd bunch up and settle down for the long walk to the barn. My mule, with its choppy gait, was torture to ride, but at least it was sure-footed as we climbed up and down the slick limestone outcroppings and made our haphazard way through the day. At one point, when it seemed like hours since I had seen another cowboy, I began to wail and cry out for help. I was sure that I would be lost forever in that desert. No one heard me, or if they did, they were too embarrassed by my shameful behavior to even tease me about it. Perhaps my cries of distress were indistinguishable from those we directed at the sheep. Eventually, I saw another cowboy making his way along the caprock and realized I'd never been lost at all.

I remember sitting on my mule at the cusp of an impassable jumble of rock and brush dropping down toward the thin brown ribbon of the Rio Grande, slowly carving its way in broad meanders through the stone landscape. I remember thinking how easy it would be to cross.

The morning's gathering ended with a huge flock of sheep clumped together, balking before a gate, hesitating until one or two leaders, pressed forward by the fearful mass of their ovine comrades, leaped through the gate, as if expecting a coyote to spring out from behind the cedar picket fence. After we ran the sheep from one pen to another, carefully counting two by two, the shearing commenced. The days were long and hot, with temperatures above one hundred degrees, and at noon all work stopped. Then the men told stories in Spanish and joked about subjects I pretended to understand. One day an older man, an Anglo cowboy who seemed to dislike me, took me aside and chewed me out for some imaginary offense. He told me he'd kick my ass if I ever did it again, and then he'd kick my daddy's ass. I took the abuse in silence and walked away, mostly because I was fighting back the urge to bawl like a baby. Carl looked on from the shadows and nodded his head in approval of my silence.

After a few days of this routine I called in sick. I was tired of dragging myself out of bed at 3:30 a.m. and getting home at 9:00 p.m. I lost my place in the cowboy crew and went back to the dreary monotony of work in the stock pens, where at least I could get a decent night's sleep. One of the chores we boys performed every morning in the stockyard involved hauling out the carcasses of animals that had died overnight, from being either crushed or otherwise injured in transit, or simply from the stress and terror of the experience. Typically, we'd find a handful of dead sheep or goats every morning. We collected them using a small tractor with a front-end loader. On what turned out to be my last day working for Darrell Hargrove, a boy named Mike and I went out to fetch some dead sheep. I remember standing in the front bucket of the tractor tugging on the carcass of a dead ewe when Mike started joking around, moving the bucket back and forth. I remember laughing, and then I lost my balance. My butt slipped between the tractor's front end and the bucket of the loader, which closed on my body with crushing force. I heard a loud crack and tumbled to the ground. As I lay facedown in sheep dung, I heard Mike ask if I was all right.

I tried to tell him he'd broken my back. Mike must have run for help, for after some time I heard voices. Someone said to just get me up and walk me around, that I'd be okay. I'm not sure what happened next, but I remember screaming with pain.

Though my back wasn't broken, that was the end of my first summer job. After two weeks in a hospital, my broken pelvis had healed enough that I was able to hobble about on crutches. A few weeks later I went to see Darrell Hargrove. He wrote me a check for seventy-five dollars.

Six months later I enrolled at Texas Military Institute in San Antonio. I had taken to running with an unruly crowd, drinking Coors around campfires in weedy overgrown lots or out at the cliffs of Amistad Reservoir, a huge lake formed by the dammed waters of the Rio Grande, the Pecos, and the Devils River. We wore cowboy boots and Wrangler jeans hitched around our skinny waists with braided belts and rodeo belt buckles and fought with other aspiring tough boys who called themselves *cholos*. One day in science class the girl sitting next to me flashed a lighter, so I stuffed my desk with paper and lit it just as the bell rang. I heard later that the fire was three feet high. When the vice-principal called me into his office that afternoon, I denied everything. Why would I start a fire in my own desk? I argued. He had no evidence against me, but the teacher wouldn't let me back in the class. I went to see him after school and assured the man that I didn't know who had started that fire but I'd be sure to find out and tell him.

No doubt I was getting a reputation around town as a hellion. My father grew alarmed and sent me off to school. At TMI, I learned to smoke pot and drop acid and drink ever greater quantities of alcohol. The music of Rush, Cheap Trick, AC/DC, and Black Sabbath provided the soundtrack to an education in delinquency. When my friends and I were spotted smoking pot behind the science building, the school's prefects—seniors who maintained order in the dorm—took us down into a subbasement and gave us swats with a paddle until our bottoms were black with bruises. They weren't opposed to drugs but had no tolerance for stupidity. We were more careful from then on.

When I came home for high school, I went back to work, this time for my father, spending summers at our family ranch in Juno, along the upper Devils River, about fifty-five miles northwest of Del Rio, and weekends working at the Sycamore Creek ranch just east of town. I bunked with the ranch manager at first, a fair-haired bachelor from East Texas named Pete. He had a degree from Texas A&M in agricultural economics.

I brought my new habits home with me from military school and introduced my friends to marijuana. My friend Scott liked it too much. His parents had died in a car accident, and eventually he came into some insurance money and bought a white Chevy Camaro. We all thought he was lucky until he crashed the Camaro and damaged his brain. I went to see him at the hospital in San Antonio. He looked so small in that bed—skinny, broken, with his jaw wired shut and a catheter on his penis. His eyes were open, though he was still in a coma, and he babbled incessantly. He was never quite the same.

All of us were lucky we didn't end up like Scott. At Juno when I was fifteen, I rolled a ranch pickup. I was driving too fast on a stretch of highway along the banks of the Devils River. It was Sunday, and Pete was away, so I decided to drive up to a nearby country store to see a girl who was staying there for the summer. One of our heifers had gotten through the fence, and I took my eyes off the road, and then I was rolling and tumbling. I kicked my way out of the vehicle and caught a ride back to the house. Somehow I never crashed when I was drinking. Pete died on that road a few years later after flipping his pickup at a low-water crossing.

When I wasn't out at the ranch, I went to Mexico every weekend, to bars with names like Boccaccio's and Ma Crosby's and Lando's. We drank flaming tequila shots, bourbon and coke, and endless beers and fought with boys from other Texas towns who we thought were invading our territory. Sometimes I made the drive to Acuña from the ranch, along the old U.S. Cavalry route along the Devils River.

Cocaine started showing up among some of my friends in 1984. I ran into my neighborhood drug dealer one night in Acuña, and he suggested we go for a ride. He directed me to a quiet spot under some trees in the shadow of Acuña's bullfighting ring, and we shared a couple of lines. Snorting coke in a car in Mexico was probably the single stupidest thing I've ever done. My dealer friend later sold me a baggy of what was probably baking soda for a hundred dollars, thus ending what might have been a dangerous infatuation.

The drug war was escalating all along the border at that time, but I didn't really have the wit to notice it or to connect it to my cravings for stimulation and release. My father began to grow more agitated about our outings to Mexico. Rumors of kidnappings and killings on both sides of the river were circulating. Bodies and body parts began to turn up in border towns. Not all the killings were drug related.

On Friday, January 27, 1984, a customs inspector named Richard Latham was abducted from the international bridge at Del Rio. He was one of my father's best friends, practically an uncle to me. I was at home alone the next day when I got a call that Richard was dead. A man collecting firewood along the highway near Eagle Pass found his body facedown in a ditch. He had been bound with his own handcuffs, shot twice in the back with his own gun.

Richard's killers had robbed a jewelry store in Acuña. They crossed the river at around 4:00 p.m. in a gray 1978 Pontiac Grand Prix. In those days the port of entry at Del Rio was very low-tech and casual, with just a few inspection lanes and no video cameras. Agents entered license plate numbers by hand as cars approached. They used to just wave me through when I was headed home at 1:00 a.m. The agent on duty that day had some questions about the robbers' papers, so he pulled them over for a secondary inspection, and Richard was working secondary. No one saw what happened. It was an hour before anyone noticed that Richard was missing.

The killers were soon caught, two of them within a day. At Eagle Pass they had crossed the river into Piedras Negras, where they sold the Pontiac. Rafael Calderon and Jesus Ramirez crossed back into Eagle Pass and hired a man to drive them to Presidio, a border town about 350 miles to the west. They were west of the Pecos River, between Langtry and Dryden, not far at all from our Cinco de Mayo ranch, when a state trooper pulled them over. During the stop, Ramirez shot himself dead, perhaps by accident. Richard's gun and a bag of jewelry were found in the car. Calderon blamed Ramirez for killing Richard.

Ricardo Cortez was arrested a week later in El Paso. He and Samuel Olguin-Mato had separated from their compadres in Piedras Negras and caught a bus to Juárez. Cortez said that Calderon had pulled the trigger. Olguin-Mato later surrendered to police on the Santa Fe bridge between El Paso and Juárez. He also testified that Calderon was the killer. Cortez and Olguin-Mato were convicted of kidnapping and sentenced to twenty-three years in prison. Rafael Calderon was convicted of murder and received a life sentence.

Richard Latham was one of my favorite people. He was funny in a way that no one else was. He teased me without mercy, about the music I listened to, about girls, and about my longish hair, but he made me laugh when he was doing it. He had big ears and a big nose and ironic eyes. He snored like a chain saw. These fragmentary impressions and decaying memories are all that remain of him, for me, that and some newspaper clippings and an episode of *The FBI Files*.

My father told me that Richard had never wanted to take a job that would require him to carry a gun; he was afraid of developing a lawman's swagger. But good jobs are hard to come by along the border, so he became a lawman in the end, though he never let the gun on his hip change him.

I can't explain why, but I have dreamed about Richard's death off and on for thirty years. I've tried to imagine what went through his mind during that last hour of his life as his kidnappers drove south toward Eagle Pass. I have sought to picture the killing itself, to feel what he felt as the life drained out of him into the dry rocky ground where he lay. I guess you could say his death scarred me, because all these years later I'm still haunted by it. If you talk to Border Patrol and customs people nowadays, everyone knows who Richard Latham was. His portrait hangs in the new state-of-the-art port of entry at Del Rio. Other agents who were on the bridge that day blamed themselves for his death. Some never got over it.

When I was eighteen years old, I packed up my car and left Texas forever. Maybe not forever, but I'm still gone. I spend as much time there as I can, and its landscapes inhabit my imagination, but since that bright sunny day in 1985 when I drove off to college in Tennessee, unconsciously reversing my family's long-ago westward migration, I haven't lived in my home state for more than a few months at a time. The Texas that I keep in mind is largely defined by the Rio Grande and from my hometown perspective stretches westward from Del Rio—which sits at a crossroads of Texas geography, on the northern shoulder of that intermittent stream that we insist on calling a big river, where the rolling grasslands of the Edwards Plateau give way to the great Chihuahuan Desert—through Comstock and beyond the Trans-Pecos creosote flats and the steep draws along the canyons of the Rio Grande and the wide volcanic vistas of the Big Bend to the barren sandy waste-lands of El Paso. But also and especially it includes the rugged canyons of the western Hill Country that drain into the Devils River as it winds its way toward the Rio Grande. Beyond the immediate range of my boyhood domain, that long riverine landscape drops below the Balcones Escarpment to encompass the flat savannas and harsh Tamaulipan thorn brush of South Texas and the fertile lowland *vegas* of the lower Rio Grande valley. Beyond the Hill Country to our northwest, the Llano Estacado rises up and opens the infinite expanses of the high plains, whence the Comanches came down their raiding trails toward the rivers, where they preyed on their ancient enemies the Apaches as well as the precarious settlements and ranches of Texas and northern Mexico.

Above all, I think of Juno, now just a name on a map, a spot on a perilous winding road, no longer a town. The post office and the

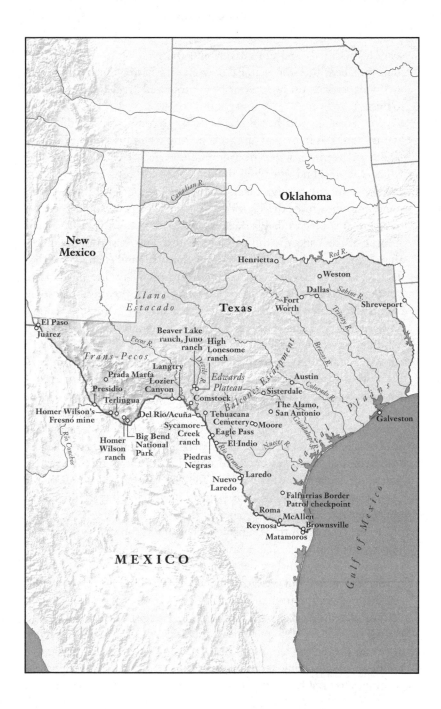

school, the hotels and the saloons and the old country store are all long vanished, the stones and the lovely old hardwood washed away by floods, carried off by interior decorators and "reclaimed," or gone to dust.

My great-grandfather B. E. Wilson, Byron Earl (called Dandy by his grandchildren), was just a young boy when his father, T.A. (for Thomas Austin), brought the family in a wagon to the Juno country. When I was a child, spending my summers working sheep and goats and cattle on my family's ranch, the house Earl grew up in was still standing, miles from the highway, near a set of pens and a shearing barn called the Murrah Place. As I recall, it was in that barn that I sheared my first sheep, a difficult job that I did my best to avoid thereafter. Near that ruined house I shot my first deer and changed my first flat tire. I did my best to experience what it would have been like to live out there at the end of the nineteenth century, in that high lonesome country, traveling by horseback every morning to a remote schoolhouse where a teacher, in awesome solitude, taught the children of a handful of ranching families.

My ancestral home, as I've always thought of it, is that ranch in Juno, where an expanse of bone-white gravel marks the remnants of what we still call Beaver Lake, along a historic stretch of the Devils River. Ancient live oak trees shade the banks. Ponds covered in green scum, the remnants of flash floods that can fill the mile-wide valley, dot the old lake bed, and the gnawed leavings of a recently departed beaver colony lie scattered over the dried mud. I see it in my mind's eye. Up the road a few miles, where the old Juno store used to be and not far from where my cousin lies buried, the beavers are still working, taking down cottonwood trees and stripping them of bark.

I never expected to be a professional Texan, one of those writers who wear the lone star like a brand, who play up the drawl and affect pointy boots or a cowboy hat with a tailored suit. Even as a child I never had much of an accent, and people still express surprise when I tell them where I'm from, for Texas to New Yorkers and other lifelong eastern city dwellers is a terrifying land of racism and violence and retrograde politics. Of course, eastern cities like Baltimore and New York and Boston can also be places of racism, violence, and retrograde politics. Yet something about Texas and the epic violence of its history continues to mystify, to attract and to repel the American imagination.

In 2006, when I came to occupy the editor's chair of *Harper's Maga-zine*, I was interviewed by a colorful *New York Times* media reporter who was dressed head to toe in black. When he learned I was from Texas, he immediately asked whether I owned a gun. I told him I did, whereupon he asked if I was a good shot. Once more I answered in the affirmative. And so was born the fleeting public image of a cowboy editor with a "gimlet eye."

I was a little surprised by the discovery that I was a "Texan," yet I had to accept the judgment. As it happened, I had just published an essay on Cormac McCarthy and the puzzling reception of *No Country for Old Men*, his great novel of the low-intensity warfare that has been consuming the borderlands for a generation. McCarthy's fiction had long been the primary medium through which I indulged a stubborn nostalgia for my lost Texas landscape. No other writer has so perfectly captured the sublimity of that rough country, its subtle beauty and deceptive power. McCarthy's prose comforted me in my spiritual exile and helped make bearable the collapsed horizons of life in a small New York apartment above a troll-like neighbor who regularly protested my toddler's heavy footsteps with broomstick blows to her ceiling.

Then, several years ago, when I was suddenly free from both the troll and, for a time, the responsibilities of running a national magazine, my thoughts quickly turned to my lost Texas landscape. My young sons required instruction in handling a rifle, and it had been too long since my soul was refreshed by the sight of a limestone countryside dotted with mesquite and prickly pear. We met up with my family in Juno, where my father taught my boys to shoot and my grandmother told my children stories of the town's heyday, of saloons and stagecoaches, Indi-ans and outlaws. On the hill above the rock house my grandfather built from native stone, I showed my wife and sons ancient Indian metates, bedrock mortars ground in the limestone shelves overlooking the val-ley, where meal was made from mesquite pods and perhaps from the acorns of those gnarled oak trees along the riverbank, over the course of hundreds if not thousands of years. Right next to the metates was a mysterious concrete receptacle, about four feet high, clearly unused for decades. I'd been on horseback in that pasture so many times, but I'd never given it any thought; there were always so many inexpli-cable ruins, remnants of my grandfather's adventures farming hay or onions or who knows what in the fertile bottomlands along the river.

My father told me, as we watched my sons searching for arrowheads, that the tank had been used in the fight against screwworm flies in the 1930s. When I was growing up, Rambouillet sheep and Angora goats populated the pastures of that ranch, along with Brangus cattle. Today they are all gone, replaced by Spanish goats, which are exported to places like Detroit and Brooklyn, to be eaten.

Nowadays the neighboring ranches are mostly empty of livestock, predator populations are booming, and exotic creatures like aoudads and axis deer have invaded. They aren't the only invaders. Now we have tobacco lawyers and oil tycoons buying up land, while drug mules paid by Mexican drug cartels play cat and mouse with various armed functionaries of the Department of Homeland Security. Beaver Lake, once a stop for stagecoaches and mail riders, a refuge to overland emigrants and ragged cavalrymen harried by hostile Indians on the southern road to California, is now merely a picturesque bend in the road. Like all American landscapes, that of West Texas is a palimpsest of lost

Beaver Lake

and vanishing lifeways. Yet the aura of a potent mythology lies heavily upon the land and exerts a fascination that defies easy analysis; it draws new blood, new life, to refresh the thorny countryside.

As I stood there, surveying the vistas of my birthright, standing in a place where seven generations of my family have gazed over the same hills and valleys, I realized that my knowledge of the lives of my forebears and their contemporaries, their motivations and their passions, was pathetically thin. So much had happened in this place that I was ignorant of, but even more mysterious to me was the route that had brought my people here. I wasn't even sure what year they had arrived in the border country, or even when they had come to Texas. It's not that I never asked. I was vaguely aware that we had come from Tennessee, or maybe it was Virginia, like many of the early Texas settlers, but that was about all I could say for sure. I was always told we were Scots-Irish, but I'd read enough nonsense about that fabled tribe to be skeptical of what it meant. So much about the history of my family and my home remained hidden. How was it that my forebears had come to settle along the Rio Grande, just beyond the 100th meridian, engaged in one of America's most iconic vocations?

Of course I knew the official version of the settlement of Texas. Like all Texas schoolkids, I had spent a year on my state's glorious history in seventh grade, studying the deeds of Stephen F. Austin and Sam Houston, the treachery of the dictator Santa Anna, the great tragedy of the Alamo, and the eternal victory over Mexico at San Jacinto. In the years since I moved away, I had read a long bookshelf of the standard works, of which T. R. Fehrenbach's *Lone Star* stands as the most magnificent and problematic example. But such epic histories sweep high above the hard ground of lived experience. Fehrenbach and others make their grandiose arguments and synthesize the material of human history into broad streams of migration and triumphant inevitabilities. The singularities of human striving and affection, which are far weirder than an epic "rise of a people," tend to fall by the wayside. No historian could answer my questions.

The outsized Texas of popular lore is the "Lone Star State," the cauldron of ugly politics that spawned George W. Bush, Rick Perry, and Ted Cruz. It's the state you don't mess with, the land that always remembers the Alamo but maybe not so much the slaughter of peaceful Cherokee and Mexican farmers. It's the land of longhorn cattle, bull riders, calf ropers, Aggies, the oil patch and J. R. Ewing, and the Dallas Cowboys Cheerleaders; the land of the big river and an even bigger sky.

This Texas was settled by genteel southern planters, whose slaves cleared the eastern forests, and conquered by fierce Scots-Irish hill men, rough-and-tumble pope haters, borderlanders from the ancient war zone in the north of merry intolerant ole England, Scots Lowlanders, and Ulster brawlers, who in a great spontaneous migration swarmed out of the British Isles like termites into Appalachia. Yet the coves and sinkholes and eroded picturesque stubs of those ancient mountains could not contain them; the Scots-Irish longed for new borderlands, for the bleeding edge of civilization, for blood and soil and conquest. They needed more room, so they pushed westward, the most warlike of all warlike tribes. To Texas! Where the most vigorous and restless and violent specimens of the Scots-Irish were drawn southward as if by geographical and temperamental gravity, leaving behind their more sedentary brothers and cousins to raise a patch of beans or maybe some corn and a couple head of cattle. GTT! Gone to Texas! That was the sign they nailed on their empty cabins by way of explanation to their creditors and forsaken wives. They didn't know it yet, but a cattle kingdom awaited. There was a whole new country to be liberated from the red savages and effeminate Spaniards in tight pantaloons. Coahuila y Tejas was a dark-eyed beauty longing for a real man to set her free. Texas would grow to become a rich man with murder in his eyes.

As I reread the conventional histories, I remained dissatisfied by their generalizations and hoary meditations on Texas "character." Much of it struck me as self-congratulatory nationalistic rubbish. I read those fat tomes mostly for the footnotes, the infinite forking paths of primary sources and archives. The revisionist historians, the borderlands scholars, and the ethnohistorians were far more useful, but even so I was more drawn to the first-person accounts of exploration and contact and Indian captivity; the travel memoirs of fur traders and scalpers, soldiers and profiteers and pioneer wives; the apologetics of utopian visionaries and confidence men; the letters home of sheep farmers and cowboys, the travelogues of nineteenth-century journalists and architects. I immersed myself in the stories of the first Europeans who penetrated the wilderness of the border country, and that study led me to the Native peoples who were displaced by the arrival of the Spanish, then the Mexicans, the Tejanos, and the Anglo Texians.

The official story of Texas is not false, but there is another Texas, every bit as violent but perhaps more tragic and thus far more interesting. This Texas is a land of Apaches and Comanches and Kiowas, but also the Jumano, the Ervipiame, the Bobole, and the Gueiquesale. Explored by unlucky Spanish conquistadors like sad Coronado and misfortunate Cabeza de Vaca, who walked barefoot and naked from the Gulf of Mexico to the Gulf of California. This Texas, sparsely populated by missionaries and lonely ranchos, menaced by American filibusters, freebooters, and buccaneers and French pirates, was invaded by the Scots-Irish, yes, but also by Quakers and German liberals and utopian Frenchmen and Poles who sought to create a New Jerusalem but instead simply added to the entrepreneurial energies of Dallas.

It should be obvious enough if you stare at the old maps, but it's too often overlooked that the history of Anglo Texas up through the latter years of the nineteenth century is largely the story of East Texas, because during those early decades the Anglos were pinned down in precarious settlements along the lower reaches of Texas's rivers in the gulf plains, with a few border settlements on the central plains and in the fringes of the Hill Country along the Balcones Escarpment. Austin was such a border town, as was San Antonio, exposed and vulnerable to the depredations of Texas's great western neighbor, the Comanche empire. West Texas was unconquered, largely unsettled, until years after the Civil War, when the U.S. Army finally chased the last bands of Comanches off the caprock and into the dreary reservations of Oklahoma. Apaches were still raiding into the late 1880s. The military outposts farther west were mostly just primitive camps along the mail routes to El Paso and beyond.

My questions about the history of my family and how my ancestors had come to settle along the international boundary with Mexico soon broadened into an obsession with the character of the southwestern borderlands, the nature of the peculiar ranching society that had sprung up there in the nineteenth and early twentieth centuries,

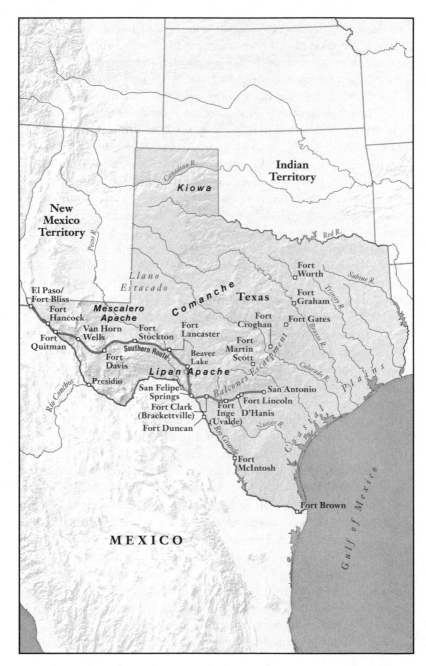

**THE MAIL ROUTE FROM SAN ANTONIO TO EL PASO, 1850s**

and the whole history of human habitation in this hard country. But it wasn't just the region's past that came to preoccupy me. I felt that I was beginning to see, at least in outline, the whole arc of my particular American subculture's life and death. There had always been something wild and dangerous about life along the border, but it seemed that a darker violence had overtaken us. Or perhaps an older darkness had returned.

I remember hearing talk in Del Rio about the bloody head that was found in a dumpster one day, and other body parts were rumored to have shown up across town. A drug-smuggling cult in Matamoros had carried out human sacrifices and made jewelry from its victims' bones. Rising violence in Mexico, fueled by the perverse cycles of drug prohibition and insatiable market demand, had destroyed the local economies on both sides of the river. Piles of bodies, usually mutilated, often with messages carved in them, were routinely dumped in Mexican border towns. Hundreds of women had been murdered in Juárez, across from El Paso, where my mother lived for decades after she left my father. On the American side, an enormous law-enforcement presence had descended upon the region. All outbound traffic from Del Rio on Highway 90, heading both east and west, was stopped at Border Patrol inspection stations. People were routinely questioned about their destinations and private business. Helicopters and drones buzzed overhead. Sinister sedans with darkened windows raced along the highways. The border country was being transformed into an armed camp, and this militarization and the anxieties it heralded seemed to echo and recapitulate the history of the region in curious and unexpected ways. Down on the border, we were playing cowboys and Indians, cavalry and Comanches all over again.

Borderland narratives, like the water that falls so infrequently in the great Chihuahuan Desert or the mine tailings that leach into the local groundwater, all eventually flow toward the Rio Grande. That drift can lull the observer into an easy complacency, metaphorical or not. I've done my best to resist those complacencies, to think through the seeming inevitabilities of technological and economic determinism. Hundreds of years passed before the border solidified along the meandering and shifting course of the Rio Grande; for generations the borderlands began a few miles southwest of Independence, Missouri.

Migrants, traders, mountain men, outlaws, scalpers, buffalo hunters, speculators, and prairie tourists quickly entered the Indian territories and made their overland crossings at the sufferance of the Osage, Pawnee, Kiowa, Apache, and Comanche nations.

The Spanish discovered the Rio Grande again and again, eventually finding that the Río de Nuestra Señora and the Guadalquivir and the Río Turbio and the Río del Norte and the Río Bravo were all one great river that flowed southward from the mountains of Tiguex and through the deserts and wastelands of the north to the lush valley and into the sea at Boca Chica with its palms and savage river people. Three Englishmen who came upon the river in 1568 called it the River of May and, once they had walked all the way to New Brunswick, reported the wonders they had witnessed in that land of "Furicanos" and "Turnados" and "great windes in the maner of Whirlewindes."

Likewise, I have sought to rediscover the border and its rivers of water, people, data, and capital from different thematic and geophysical angles, sometimes journeying upriver, like the Spanish castaway and explorer Álvar Núñez Cabeza de Vaca, and sometimes downriver, but always moving aslant, both physically and metaphorically, cutting against the currents of institutional, governmental, and industrial momentum with side trips and excursions, historical and literary and personal interludes, as well as digressions and dalliances with a broad cast of characters. Their interpretation will serve to place our contemporary strivings in a broader context of history, landscape, and memory. I can offer no definitive answers to the most existential of my questions, but my hope is that a significant pattern will rise to the surface as I sift the remnants of the vanished world that nurtured my family from the time my great-great-great-grandfather led his family into the canyon lands north of the Rio Grande.

What was it that brought my people to this particular place? Why would *anyone* attempt to settle in this unforgiving landscape? What were they searching for that was found here, in the devil's own country, alongside his namesake river? My attempt to resolve these questions has resulted in many long journeys, in thousands of miles of travel all across my home state and beyond, and in untold hours of research, in archives both dusty and digital. I have followed the trails of my ancestors through six different states and at least fifteen Texas counties, tracing their habitations and professions and places of final rest. In tracking and describing my family's migrations and peregrinations along the constantly shifting western borders of settlement in the Southwest, I have tried to create a portrait of the borderlands. Along the way I have marshaled the eloquence and insight of fellow travelers, those who followed similar paths and byways, as witnesses to my family's passage. I have sought out the testimony of contemporary border dwellers, hoping to understand what has become of my native landscape under the watchful and unblinking stare of the border-industrial complex. Each of these journeys seeks to discover some kernel of the primordial fascination, the lure of the rough country, but also the impulse that drove people to forsake all that they had known and enjoyed and push off into the wilderness of a thousand sorrows, the Great American Desert.

No reckoning with Texas history, however personal, can ignore the foundational experience of the journey, the expedition, *la entrada*, the filibuster, the crossing. As with many historical adventures, digression emerges as the dominant trope, with each turning from the definitive path leading us farther afield. Growing up in Texas, especially rural Texas, entails long drives to get anywhere at all, and the longest stretch of any transcontinental road trip is always the one that passes through Texas. Whether in the nineteenth century or the sixteenth or the twentieth, Texas was far away, no matter where you were going, and getting there was always hard. Even so, my nineteenth-century ancestors and their fellow travelers never stayed in one place for long. Their lives were but a motion of limbs.

My grandmother Anale Hodge, born in 1920, and I were sitting on the front porch of her house overlooking the Devils River. We were talking about my sons, while her son, my father, was shooting with them at a range he had set up in a small pasture near the house. They fired hundreds of rounds from his elegant bolt-action Sako .22 rifles. Leelee, as we call my grandmother, had come out earlier that day and shot with us as well. She refused to sit at my father's portable shooting bench, as we did, preferring instead to fire standing up. She wore a kerchief, knotted below her chin, to protect her hair, carefully permed and set, from the relentless wind that whipped down the canyon across an old caliche

Targets

airstrip, now grown up with prickly pear and mesquite. We shot toward a large earthen berm, at targets and little steel figures of rams, pigs, quail, and turkeys. It was mid-February and the weather was warm and mild, and we were enjoying the rare pleasures of being all together, at the ranch, as a family. My sons and I had been prowling around down by the lake looking for varmints, and now Leelee was curious to know whether there was any water in the riverbed, which is obscured from the house by enormous ancient live oaks. Only a few green puddles in the gravel, I told her, not quite stagnant, home to minnows and frogs. We saw all kinds of scat along the edges.

Leelee told me about fishing for bass in that lake when she was a girl, about riding her horse through its shallows and swimming there in the summers. She wasn't allowed to go in the water by herself, of course, so when she was on her own, she'd creep right up to the edge and dig a little channel, line it with rocks, and let the water trickle in to wet her toes. When she caught fish, she'd take them to the cookhouse. "Mother didn't like to cook them, and she sure wouldn't clean them," she said. "There was always a cook there. He cooked for the men. And he always had camp bread that he cooked on top of the old woodstove, and I loved it." She grew up riding these ranches with the men who worked them. She'd go out gathering livestock in the mornings whenever she was allowed.

Earl, her father, bought the Beaver Lake ranch when she was a girl of eight or ten. He was raised here in the Juno country but was born in Frio County, in South Texas, near the town of Moore. I asked her, not for the first time, how they came to settle out here. You never know when new details will emerge from a story, no matter how many times it's been told.

"Granny always said they were passing through. They stayed in a little rock house—it's not there anymore, it was washed away years ago in a flood—down by the lake. Granddad was a great one to want to go look at some other area. He did that," she paused, as if weighing her words, "too frequently."

Such understatement! Somebody told T. A. Wilson to go look at the Devils River country, and then, a few years later, in about 1891 as far as I've been able to determine, he packed up the family in a wagon or two and came west. My father remembers approaching our south fence through a neighbor's ranch, along a dirt road in the 1960s, driving his father and grandfather, ascending a steep switchback, when Earl remarked that he remembered climbing that exact switchback in a wagon, when he and his family first moved out to the Juno country.

"Daddy never said this," Leelee continued, "but Mother said that anytime a good friend or somebody that Granddad particularly liked would come to him and ask him to co-sign a note, he would do it, and then he'd end up paying for it. That happened several times." Again, that pause. "And it *broke* him several times.

"He lost the Murrah ranch that way. Somebody named Murrah bought it, and Daddy bought it back."

But they lived out at the Murrah Place for years before her grandfather—T.A.—lost it, and the children went to school at High Lonesome, another ranch just to the east of the Murrah Place that her daddy later bought as well. There were eight of them, five girls and three boys: Earl was the oldest, then Amy, Beula, Homer, Callie, Beatrice, and Edna; Ernest was the youngest, born in 1900, when Granny moved to town. "She told Mother she was tired of having babies." T.A. never moved to town. After he lost the Murrah Place, they moved to another ranch, closer to Juno, the Cully Place. But in those early years, in the last decade of the great century of the American continental empire, the Wilson children had to travel for school. They camped for weeks at High Lonesome, where children from other nearby ranches also came and stayed with the teacher. High Lonesome is up on the divide between portions of the Devils River watershed, an uneroded remnant of the great Edwards Plateau. It isn't flat exactly; the terrain is rolling grassland savanna, dotted with invasive cedar, bounded to the north, south, and west by the meanders of the Devils River, with steep canyons dropping off on all sides. It was, and remains, fantastically inaccessible.

While they were camping at High Lonesome, Earl watched out for the younger children. Once, when they were sitting around a fire, a little fox darted into the light from the outer dark and bit Homer. Well, that was a true emergency, for surely a fox that would invade a fire circle was rabid. Of course there was no rabies vaccine in those

Anale shooting

days, or any vaccines for that matter, but there was frontier medicine, folk medicine, and people made do with that. Back then everyone on the frontier lived in terror of rabies, which was common, and they kept mad stones as a remedy. A mad stone is an enterolith, a calcium deposit formed in the stomach of cattle and deer and other animals, that resembles a stone but is really more like a pearl that forms around a hair ball or some other indigestible object. The most desirable mad stones came from the stomach of a white deer, and a white mad stone was best of all. Usage was strict; mad stones could not be bought or sold; rather, they had to be found or received as a gift. The wounded person had to be brought to the mad stone, which was boiled in milk and then applied to the wound, which must be open and bleeding, where it would adhere and draw out the poison. When the stone was released from the wound and dropped off, its work was done, and the stone was again boiled in milk, which was supposed to turn green as the poison was released. Mad stones were also used for snakebites. The Wilsons had one back at the house, so Earl took Homer home on horseback, riding long through the dark night, to apply the remedy. Fortunately, the chances of contracting rabies from a single bite are far from certain. Homer lived.

I got this story not from my grandmother but from her cousin Patricia. Leelee might have heard the story, but she isn't one to dwell on the colorful details of frontier life. She is the most sensible person I have ever known. She is not sentimental. She does not dwell on the past. She is tough and practical, and she gets on with life when tragedy befalls her. And yet she is full of laughter and joy. In fact, she is probably the most consistently joyful person I have ever known. Her husband, Roger, for whom I am named, died in 1972, when I was five years old. Everyone called him Wally. Anale and Wally were married in 1940; she has been a widow for a decade longer than she was a wife. For those forty-four years she has remained the matriarch of our family and our family ranching business.

When I was a child, I spent countless afternoons playing in Leelee's big yard on Losoya Street in Del Rio. My grandmother's yard was a private world, enclosed with high tan brick walls, scarred and pocked by fig ivy removed when I was very small. Within those walls stood tall, majestic pecan trees and a building we called the party house, which contained a precious pool table. Bird feeders always hung from a pecan branch outside her big kitchen window so she could watch the little songbirds as they darted in and out, squabbling and fussing at one another as hummingbirds buzzed and hovered like huge bees. Behind the party house and my grandmother's plastic greenhouse were corners and shadows and hiding places. Her yard seemed so vast, the walls that bounded it so high. I had my ways of scaling them, and I patrolled that perimeter endlessly, usually with some kind of makeshift weapon, a plastic rifle, a sword, or an improvised stick pistol. When I came to a wooden gate, I would leap down and scramble up again on the other side. Standing on a gate was a terrible sin, for it would ruin the hinges and earn me some grievous punishment from my father, who was likely to come striding suddenly into the yard, shattering my private world, if Leelee spotted me misbehaving and gave him a call.

Next door was my great-grandmother's house, slightly scary, unwalled, with big white columns out front and what seemed to my young mind to be an enormous grove of magnolia trees. The magnolias were mysterious, and they could be climbed, though I was not permitted to do so. Yet climb I did, because I was a reckless child who never failed to find ways to injure himself. I never fell from those particular trees, though I climbed so high that the slender branches swayed and bent and threatened to break. The terror of falling made my body tingle. The pleasure was intensely sensual. The thrill of that fear was something I never mentioned to anyone. I could not explain it; I had no vocabulary for such feelings. When I threw rocks at hornets' nests until the angry yellow and black demons attacked me—their stings, to which I was allergic, causing my arm to double in size with the swelling, or my cheek to balloon and sag as if I were chewing a gigantic wad of tobacco, or my eyes to swell shut like a matching pair of hairless puffy alien vaginas—or when I came running with cuts, gashes, scratches, punctures, and other bloody wounds acquired from falling off walls, falling into irrigation ditches, or stepping on rusty nails, my cautious, careful, reserved father would just stare at me and shake his head. He could not fathom such behavior. My recklessness was always a mystery to him. He was convinced early on that I possessed a death wish.

But we were not talking about my errant childhood. I was trying to coax my grandmother into reminiscence, which was never easy.

I asked her when the big rock house at Beaver Lake had been built. Although I had plied her with questions about the past before, this was something that I had never asked. She had to think. Well, the house in town, by which she meant her mother's house with its white columns and magnolia trees, was finished in 1940. She and Wally were married on November 30, and by Christmas, when they came back from their honeymoon, that house was finished. "Mother was furious with me, because we wouldn't wait," she said, slightly mysteriously, and did not elaborate. "There were no carpets in the house." The house at the lake was not finished when my father was born, in 1942, but it was by 1945, when his sister Luralee came along. Leelee was eight or ten years old when my great-grandfather bought the Lake ranch, so it was probably 1930. That date brought me up short, because for me the Beaver Lake ranch had always seemed like the center of my world, but it was a relatively late addition to Earl Wilson's country.

"Daddy started out at the Juno ranch," Leelee said, "buying acreage a little bit at a time." His parents' ranch was nearby, but he went out on his own. This would have been just after he returned from Galveston, where he had enrolled at a business college. He was in Galveston during the great hurricane of 1900. Everyone thought he had died, Leelee told me once. Of course, communication was slow, and it wasn't easy to get word about who had survived and who had perished. Eight thousand people died in that storm, which is still the deadliest in American history, and Galveston, then a major port and the largest city in Texas, was leveled. Earl just showed up one day a few weeks later, to everyone's surprise and delight. He leased his country at first, running sheep and goats, and slowly started buying rangeland near Juno. Eventually, he was able to buy the Murrah Place, the ranch where he had been raised, and he bought the High Lonesome ranch, where he had gone to school, and the Beaver Lake ranch, a historic and beautiful site where soldiers and Texas Rangers and stagecoach passengers had sojourned in the mid-nineteenth century. By the 1930s, he was running the largest operation in the county, with more than thirty thousand sheep and more than one hundred hired men, who worked livestock, built fences, fought the brush, and farmed the fields in the fertile Devils River valley.

Leelee couldn't say much about Moore or why T.A. and Bettie had left Frio County. She went there as a child many times. They'd be driving to San Antonio and her daddy would take a right-hand turn at Hondo, and then she knew they were going down to Moore to see family. "There are lots of Wilsons down there," she said. "They had the look. Big and tall." During the Depression various Wilsons and Crains (Bettie Wilson was a Crain) came to the ranch at Juno to work. "Daddy was a great one for hiring relatives. Wylie Crain lived over in the little house over there. Jesse Crain was working at the Juno ranch. Later Daddy hired Warner, and he drove the big trucks to haul the wool to town. Daddy always said he was the best truck driver he ever had, because when something breaks, Warner doesn't try to fix it!

"The young man that I just adored, I guess I was just in junior high, was named Dick Edwards, from down around Moore. He had graduated from high school, was a football player, and he was a big husky fella. And he wanted to come out and work. Granny's father died, I don't know when, and her mother remarried an Edwards. So this young man was in some way related. And he was good help. He'd been here several years, three or four, everybody liked him. He was a hard worker, and he died out here. They said he had a bad heart or something.

"On Sundays, there at Baker's Crossing, after you pass the big house on the road, two story, on up a little ways, are lots of these big ole live oaks, and there's a little house set back there. And at one time the Altizers had that place leased. And on Sunday, all the surrounding ranch people would go down there and everybody would take something for lunch and afterward they'd have roping. The Altizers were big ropers. Sometimes Mother would take a pie or a cake, we'd stop there and visit. Of course all the men were down in the pens watching the roping. And all the men from here would go down for the Sunday roping. We had a whole bunch who always went.

"I always wanted to go swimming. And Mother always said I couldn't go unless someone went with me. She didn't swim, so she wasn't crazy about going with me, but I could always find Warner. He'd be around. He'd go. We'd walk down there, and he'd say, 'All right, Anale, don't drown, because I'm going to take my boots off before I come in after you.' And I could swim. That was his favorite story. 'If you're going to drown, take it slow, I'm going to take my boots off.' Oh, he was a character.

# AN ABBREVIATED FAMILY TREE

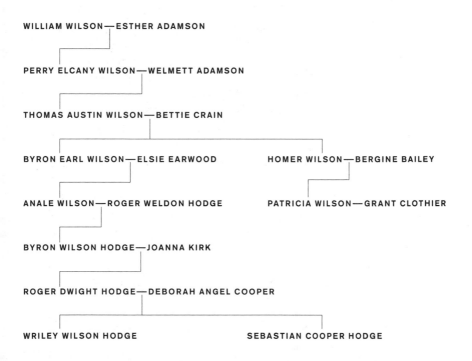

WILLIAM WILSON — ESTHER ADAMSON

PERRY ELCANY WILSON — WELMETT ADAMSON

THOMAS AUSTIN WILSON — BETTIE CRAIN

BYRON EARL WILSON — ELSIE EARWOOD          HOMER WILSON — BERGINE BAILEY

ANALE WILSON — ROGER WELDON HODGE          PATRICIA WILSON — GRANT CLOTHIER

BYRON WILSON HODGE — JOANNA KIRK

ROGER DWIGHT HODGE — DEBORAH ANGEL COOPER

WRILEY WILSON HODGE          SEBASTIAN COOPER HODGE

"We'd come out for the weekend, because Daddy would stay out most of the time. If he had a bank meeting or a wool house meeting or something like that, he was always in town for that. He preferred the ranch."

Earl's father was the same way. T.A. hated going to town and would do anything to avoid it. Earl would tell him that he needed to go to town for some reason, and T.A. would put it off and put it off until finally he would load up his wagon and set off. Today, with paved highways maintained by the state, the drive from Juno through Comstock to Del Rio takes just over an hour. In the early years of the last century, the trip might take all day. T.A. would take his time. He'd get just out of sight of the house, and then he'd stop and make camp. The rest of the family would see his fire off in the distance. That's how I imagine him, along the bank of the Devils River, leaning up against a mesquite tree, perhaps burning an old dried sotol bush, shadows flickering on limestone. For more than ten thousand years people have been sitting by fires in that landscape.

Leelee says that she never once saw T.A. lying down, not until he was laid out dead. His allergies and asthma were so bad that he couldn't breathe unless he was standing or sitting. So he slept in a chair, in front of a fire, covered in blankets. T.A. came by his condition honestly. His father, Perry, like so many westering emigrants, had come to Texas in 1854 searching not only for his fortune but for a healthy climate, a place where he might be able to breathe freely.

Six months later I was back, again with my sons in tow. It was a summer of floods, one year before a summer of fire. Heavy rains generated by Hurricane Alex had drenched the vast watershed of the Rio Grande and the Río Conchos in the Mexican state of Chihuahua, causing the desert to bloom and filling Amistad Reservoir, just west of Del Rio, beyond capacity. Dam officials, fearful of testing the resilience of their fifty-year-old structure, were forced to open all fifteen floodgates; the resulting floods ravaged the communities downriver, tearing up hundred-year-old oak trees and upending homes and businesses all the way to Brownsville, four hundred miles downriver, where the Rio Grande pours its liquid cargo of silt and sewage, tires and nitro-

View of the Rio Grande and Mexico from a bluff in Roma, Texas

gen runoff, into the tepid waters of the Gulf of Mexico. The surviving trees as well as the eternal brush and river cane would for years display countless fluttering plastic bags as a testament to the high-water mark in places like Eagle Pass and Laredo and Roma, where on a bluff far above the river, a short distance from mysterious crumbling circular ruins bounded by barbed wire, you can visit the World Birding Center to learn about Plain Chachalacas and White-Collared Seedeaters.

We flew into El Paso to see my mother, who for decades lived in that strange and historic community where the Rio Grande flows out of its rift valley, through the Paso del Norte between the Franklin Mountains and Mount Cristo Rey, and assumes its geopolitical role as an international boundary.

Traveling east through the pass, my sons and I were sticking close to the river, visiting family and ancestral landmarks along the way. We soon left behind the blasted and grassless landscape surrounding El Paso and passed quickly through the checkpoint at Sierra Blanca, a town that for years was known as the prime destination for trainloads of New York sewage sludge that were spilled without ceremony upon the barren ground. I rolled down the windows to see if my boys could catch a whiff of their hometown. "There's a little piece of you out there!" I yelled over the roar of the wind whipping through the cabin of our rented minivan.

We were headed for a place that the Spanish used to call *el despoblado*, the land without people. I felt uneasy as we continued southeastward. Something was bothering me, but I couldn't say what it was. At first I told myself it was the checkpoint and the intrusive questioning of the Border Patrol, who rarely fail to ask a driver where he might be going. My father always makes a point of answering, "I didn't say," but I had no desire to subject my boys to a confrontation with *la migra* or to endure a prolonged search of our rented minivan, so I simply answered, "Big Bend." Still, the ever-encroaching gaze of federal law enforcement, as obnoxious as it might be, was unable to account for my psychological agitation. Finally, I realized what was bothering me: the color of the grass. *It was green.* It was July in the Big Bend—July in West Texas—and the grass in the Chihuahuan Desert was green.

No one could know that the next summer wildfires would sweep across that very landscape to threaten the towns of Marfa and Fort Davis, as well as our family's ranch in Juno.

We stopped briefly at the enigmatic and quietly brilliant art installation called Prada Marfa, a modest simulacrum of a big-city boutique, patronized by scorpions and flies and flanked by barbed-wire fences extending toward the horizon. It's really closer to Valentine than to Marfa, but nobody in L.A. or Brooklyn has ever heard of Valentine, Texas. I decided to skip Donald Judd's austere minimalist steel boxes, on display at the Chinati Foundation, in favor of maximal exposure to the Big Bend's infinite basin-and-range vistas.

The Marathon Basin opened before us, a large depression bounded by the Glass Mountains to the northwest and the Del Norte Mountains to the west, various ridges and escarpments rising off to the east. Poking out of twenty-five thousand feet of fossil-laden Paleozoic limestone and shale were hard sharp ridges, known as hogbacks, composed of a variety of chert called novaculite. In places this chert emerged as scalloped white outcroppings called flatirons. Geologists have matched

Prada Marfa, near Valentine, Texas

these deposits with Arkansas novaculite, which I've read is traditionally used to make whetstones for sharpening knives; they believe the rocks are one and the same formation and that they and the surrounding strata, containing matching fossils of the same age, are the roots of the Ouachita Mountains, a range of Himalaya-sized mountains long ago eroded into sand. Some geologists believe that the Ouachitas were part of the original Appalachian mountain system, bringing together, in this warped, folded, compressed, stretched, and deformed landscape, the bones of the Appalachians with the southeastern vestiges of the Rockies, far younger mountains formed in a completely different episode of mountain building. Thus east meets west at the Big Bend of the Rio Grande.

The Ouachita formation, moreover, traces a long arc from its namesake mountain remnants in Oklahoma and Arkansas down through Texas via Austin, San Antonio, and Del Rio, to the Marathon Basin, a path that limns, through much of its route across Texas, the Balcones Escarpment, which neatly divides the coastal plains of South and East

Texas from the stepped plateaus and uplifts that gradually open into the Great Plains. The Balcones scarp corresponds to a wide fault zone, both geographically and culturally. Before the late nineteenth century, when the Plains Indians were finally pacified—that is, conquered and exiled to reservations in Oklahoma—west of the Balcones was the Comanche empire; east toward the gulf lay the Anglo settlements in thin bands along the rivers. And as I was eventually to discover, that fault zone also happened to trace, with uncanny accuracy, a partial map of my ancestors' nineteenth-century peregrinations.

Our destination was the great basin of the Chisos Mountains in Big Bend National Park, which was part of a large ranch formerly owned by Homer Wilson, my great-granduncle, who tried and failed to make his fortune there as a rancher and quicksilver miner in the 1930s and 1940s. At the time, all I really knew about Homer was that he and his family had lived up there together in a Sears, Roebuck mail-order house. I knew there was a Homer Wilson ranch exhibit in the park, but I had never gotten around to visiting it, and I quickly discovered that I was unable to answer even the most basic questions from my children about Homer's life. I assumed that Homer had been raised on our family's ranch near Del Rio, but I didn't even know that for certain. I could tell my children that their great-great-grandfather Earl was Homer's brother, but I couldn't tell them much about his life or how he and his family came to settle and build a ranch along the Devils River, not far from the Mexican border.

From Tornillo Creek, we ascended some three thousand feet up Green Gulch, navigating the looping switchbacks of a road originally built by Civilian Conservation Corps workers in 1934, to Panther Pass and into the Chisos Basin, a very large depression eroded into the center of the Chisos Mountains, which achieve elevations up to seventy-eight hundred feet. We drove through a fog so thick we could hardly see the road or the cliffs just beyond it. Rooms had not been hard to come by at the Chisos Mountains Lodge, because the July heat tends to discourage park visitors, yet there we were, shivering in our thin jackets, sitting on the front porch of our cabin, listening to the strange catlike barks of little gray desert foxes. That night I finally read *Beneath the Window*, a memoir by Patricia Wilson Clothier, Homer's daughter and my grandmother's cousin, whom I could not remember meeting, though I must have known her when I was a child. Homer was a geologist who dreamed of mineral riches in the Big Bend; he sold his share of a sheep and goat ranch near Del Rio and in 1929 began buying land in and around the Chisos Mountains. He married the young widow of his best friend, a fellow geologist who died in an explosion at the Humble Oil Company in East Texas, and in 1930 carried his new bride, Bergine, a city girl who had never ridden a horse or shot a firearm, to live in glorious isolation in what was still the most inaccessible and remote corner of the Texas border country.

Homer ranched about forty-four sections, about half of the old G4 Ranch, a large operation that got started in 1885 with a herd of six thousand cattle ranging across fifty-five thousand acres. Some were shipped by rail to the nearest train station in Marathon. About two thousand were driven overland, more than three hundred miles, from Uvalde through Del Rio, Langtry, Dryden, Sanderson, and Marathon. By the early 1890s the G4 was running some thirty thousand head. It's

The Window, Chisos Mountains, Big Bend National Park

hard to imagine the Big Bend country supporting that many cattle, and in fact it couldn't. Herds of buffalo migrated through from time to time, and the Comanches drove their stolen horses and cattle from Mexico along their great war trail, but these were sporadic and seasonal passages. Sustained heavy grazing was something else. But the grasses were abundant on the virgin pasturage, so at first the cattle thrived. Most ranchers in those days let their livestock drift, because fences were uncommon. They worked the cattle when they had to, when branding or marking calves, and when it was time to drive them to market. Drought came in 1885, and by 1895, when the G4 stock was liquidated, only about half the herd could be located.

Patricia and her parents lived in a two-story wood-framed Sears, Roebuck mail-order house that was purchased by the ranch's previous owner, Harris Smith, who hauled his residence some eighty miles to Oak Creek by wagon in pieces from the train station in Marathon. Oak Creek, in Patricia's telling, was a lovely oasis of willows and oaks enlivened with the sound of running water and the bleating of Angora nanny goats, in the lower reaches of the Chisos Mountains below the Window, an eroded pour-off gap that drains the entire basin, which is three miles across and almost three thousand feet deep at the lip of the Window, its lowest point. During wet weather the waterfall can be thunderous as boulders, carried by Oak Creek at flood, roll and bounce through the opening, dropping seventy-five feet to a jumble of debris below. Casa Grande, capped with a monumental lava formation, stands framed between the Ward and the Pulliam intrusions, two massive igneous formations that compose the poles of the Window gap and enclose the basin to the north and west with their high walls.

Homer raised sheep and goats on his ranch and prospected throughout the Big Bend. Both Ross Maxwell, the first superintendent of Big Bend National Park, and Patricia report that Homer once found a small gold nugget in the Chisos Mountains, but it turned out that the most promising mineral resource in the area was cinnabar, a red crystalline mineral containing mercury. Ferdinand von Roemer, a German scientist who traveled throughout Texas in the 1840s and published the first survey of Texas geology, once traded a rope with some Indians for a small bit of cinnabar. Commercial mercury mining in Terlingua and nearby Study Butte began in the 1880s, which just added to the strange character of the bizarre moonscape of that area. Homer was a partner in the Fresno mine, eleven miles north of Terlingua, that began production in 1940 and supplied mercury to the military during World War II.

Nothing is harder on the land than mining and smelting. The scars seem to last forever, at least in human terms, but the landscape of the Big Bend continually reminds us that even high mountains are cast down in time and deep valleys and basins fill with the eroded debris.

Mining was Homer's passion, but he seems to have spent most of his time ranching, which was never easy in the Big Bend, or anywhere else for that matter. To reach market, cattle, sheep, and goats had to be driven almost a hundred miles to the nearest rail station, in Marathon. Ranchers like Homer spent their days, which were always too short, fighting predators and improving their property: putting up fences, building water tanks, blasting roads out of the rock with dynamite. Homer took advantage of low sheep and goat prices immediately after the crash of 1929 to stock his ranch, but prices didn't improve for years. The 1930s were hard for ranchers all over, but they seem to have been especially hard for a sheep and goat man in the Big Bend.

Patricia spent her first fourteen years in the Chisos Mountains. She tells stories of depredations by bandits and mountain lions and coyotes, the perils of flash floods and driving along poor mountain roads. She remembers the challenges of cooking, cleaning, and homeschooling while living many hours' journey from the nearest paved road. She records the sorrows of Depression-era agricultural economics and the joys of visiting her friend Julia Nail, who lived several miles away with her family on a neighboring ranch. The Depression dragged on; money was tight and the banks were tough on a rancher, demanding detailed accounts of every head of livestock and expense, but at least the Wilsons and their neighbors could grow fruits and vegetables and slaughter a goat or a steer for meat. Ranch work was difficult and dangerous; working horseback in rocky country could lead to death by dragging, when a man, unhorsed, cannot free his boot from his stirrup. Men fell into canyons and suffered broken bones. One man, Patricia remembers, lost an eye to a cow's horn. Medical help was far away, and when Homer suffered his first heart attack, he was lucky his doctor, visiting for a hunting trip, was standing nearby. Homer never fully recovered.

Meanwhile, the state was forcing ranchers to sell their land for the national park. Some resisted, but Homer knew the state would take the land one way or another. He did his best to secure a fair price. Patricia found him dead on the screened sleeping porch one morning in July 1943. A small bird, trapped on the porch, was flying back and forth trying to escape. She had gone out on the porch to set it free.

Our cousin Jack Ward came home from the army and along with his brother Bill and my grandfather Wally helped Bergine gather and sell off the livestock. In 1945, Bergine left the Sears mail-order house beneath the great Window of the Chisos Mountains and said good-bye to the Homer Wilson ranch for the last time. She and Patricia and little Homer and Thomas moved to Alpine and then to Del Rio. Bergine never returned to the Big Bend.


In my family it has always been said that when the park officials came in and forced out the ranchers, they also killed off the wildlife by removing all the waterings—the header tanks and water troughs and windmills the ranchers had spent years building. Patricia tells a version of this tale in her book, and she said much the same to me personally when I spent time with her and Grant, her husband. She shook her head in disbelief at the rudeness of a park ranger who aggressively challenged her with the accusation that the early ranchers had all overgrazed the land and permanently damaged it. As Patricia remembered it, there was always much more grass on the Wilson ranch in the 1930s than she has ever seen in the park in later years, and she recalled seeing more deer and turkey and other wildlife as well. Two strikingly opposed value systems come into conflict here. The ethos of the rancher, a businessman who always seeks to improve his property and believes that wildlife is a resource that requires careful management, just like any other feature of the land, cannot easily be squared with the ideology of the modern environmentalist, with his dream of a wilderness unmodified by human culture, who seeks to heal the damage committed by thoughtless agriculturalists, miners, and others who exploit the land and seek to extract value from it. At his prudent best, a rancher is a steward of the land, a conservationist who cherishes his property and everything in it; at his worst, he is everything the earnest environmentalist, who strives to re-create an ecosystem that has not existed for more than fourteen thousand years, fears and loathes.

Wildlife thrives where water abounds and cares not whether that moisture comes from a man-made receptacle or a limestone pothole. I have spent time in the Big Bend during dry spells and hardly saw a living creature. That summer with my sons, damp and green as it was, we saw many dozens of deer and uncountable species of birds, including a magnificent black hawk perched in an old pecan orchard along the banks of the Rio Grande. My boys were hoping to see an owl, and we had heard owls haunted that abandoned farm. Driving slowly back toward the basin at sunset, bathed in the last vestiges of a light that can only be called divine, we watched in awe as a great horned owl swooped across our path and landed, wings flapping dramatically, on a thorny stalk of ocotillo, silhouetted against the pale light of the vanishing sun. The next day we hiked down from the Chisos Lodge to the Window, hoping to see either the bear or the mountain lion that were both said to be active in the area. Water alternately seeped and poured down the craggy faces of reddish-brown cliff walls, set off in striking contrast by the almost radioactive green of the grateful grasses and desert shrubs clinging to small patches of volcanic soil, and tumbled down the winding bed of the creek toward the pour off. Mist wreathed the upper reaches of the mountains, winding in and among towering hoodoos, pillars of rock carved by water and wind. One group of hikers we spoke to had seen the bear. Insects buzzed and swarmed, and lizards scrambled out of our way. No one really expected to spot the great cat, because those animals move like ghosts through this country. Spike deer, still in velvet, watched us from patches of brush. Every plant capable of flowering was bursting in a vegetal frenzy of reproduction.

Down in the lowlands, on another day, at one of the few remaining windmills in the park, we played peekaboo with javelinas as they snuffled about in a thicket of mesquite and huisache that had grown up around a water trough and an old leaky concrete reservoir. Driving one bright sunny afternoon, I spotted a coyote as it dashed across the macadam. I pointed it out to my sons, and we pulled over to take a photograph. Oddly, the coyote paused halfway up the barren hill and commenced yapping and barking. This strange behavior continued until we drove on, and that must have been fifteen or twenty minutes. No one I spoke to later, among park workers or my family, had ever seen or heard such a thing before. We could only conclude that the desert canine was calling out a warning to a litter of pups, perhaps in the care of its mate.

The old crossing to the village of Boquillas del Carmen, probably the safest town on the entire Mexican side of the border, had been shuttered by the Department of Homeland Security, in its infinite bureaucratic wisdom. So my sons, who longed to cross the border into Mexico, threw rocks across the Rio Grande into our sister republic at the head of Boquillas Canyon. Later we left a few dollars in a tin can for enterprising Boquillas residents, who fashion simple handcrafts, such as lovely painted sotol walking sticks, dart across the border, and write messages for the tourists, encouraging them to leave money in exchange for their goods at trailheads. We stopped and contemplated a message left on a rock by Jesús the Singing Mexican, a famous character who sings sad songs for hikers from across the river. There was no sign of Jesús himself; business was very bad for singing Mexicans.

Homer Wilson ranch, Big Bend National Park

We seemed to have the entire park to ourselves. One afternoon we drove into the nearby town of Terlingua to watch the World Cup Final between Spain and Holland in a little watering hole called the Boathouse. The barkeep was a friendly Brit, a fan of the Dutch who didn't hold it against us for being partisans of Spain. A motley assortment of local river guides, Big Bend outlaws, refugees from the wide world, and local country singers befriended my towheaded sons, who sat at the bar, before an enormous television, underneath a lovely old kayak suspended from the ceiling, and watched the great Andrés Iniesta as he made his magnificent and immortal world-championship goal.

It was a misty, foggy afternoon with low clouds slipping in and among the surrounding mountains and escarpments when we hiked into the Homer Wilson exhibit at Blue Creek. Situated just below a butte called Signal Peak, Blue Creek was the headquarters of the Wilson ranch, but it was not where Homer and the family lived. No trace now remains of the mail-order house at Oak Creek, which was demolished by the park. Homer and his men built the house at Blue Creek from local flagstones, and a foreman typically lived there with his family. Homer kept an office in the house, and he and the family would stay there from time to time. Homer employed up to a dozen hands on the ranch, depending on how many he could afford. Those men helped him construct this small flagstone cabin with its reed ceiling and concrete roof, instead of the traditional adobe, covered in corrugated steel; the window and door frames were made from knotty pine; and its long porch, with open windows showing no trace of a screen, opened to the jaggy vista of Signal Peak. The steel on the roof appears to have been replaced, and presumably the blue paint on the wood surfaces was applied more recently than 1943, when Homer died. An application to place the house on the National Register of Historic Places, filed in 1975, mentions an outhouse and a chicken coop. I saw no sign of those structures. All that remains of this ranch, the fruit of Homer Wilson's life and labor, was this small stone building, with its ruined storehouse and rainwater cistern, and a circular cedar picket pen for halter-breaking horses. The desert had reclaimed this place. The Wilson ranch was now truly *despoblado*.

# CHAPTER 2

# PARABLES OF FIRST CONTACT

I set out from El Paso on a rainy September morning. I was returning to the *despoblado*, the grand canyons and basins and ranges of the Big Bend—110 miles to Van Horn, then south on 90 to Marfa, where a single right turn would take me down the Comanche trace to old Presidio del Norte, La Junta de los Ríos. My plan was to wander around Presidio and try to imagine what the unfortunate Spanish castaway Cabeza de Vaca and his companions had seen when they stood in that ancient riverine settlement in the 1530s. I thought I might go in search of Homer Wilson's old cinnabar mine.

Another hurricane was dumping huge amounts of rain on West Texas. This time it was Odile sweeping across northern Mexico after hammering Baja California, pushing moisture eastward into the Chihuahuan Desert and beyond. I had flown in the night before and slept at my mother's house, listening to the wind and thunder and lightning as the storm blew in across Chihuahua, southern Arizona, and New Mexico. I awoke before dawn, checked the weather, and saw there had been flash flooding overnight.

El Paso was weirdly green, I could see, even in the dim light of dawn; the omnipresent dun-colored stone was everywhere wet and dripping. Driving my gigantic rented 4x4 white Ford F-150 pickup over the ridge on McRae Boulevard, I could see the lights of Juárez sprawling out over the valley, dotted with green instead of the usual dull brown. It was almost pretty. Thunderclouds massed in the west, beyond the Franklin Mountains, whose peaks were shrouded in mist. An electronic billboard, with flashing orange bulbs, warned El Paso drivers, who I suppose are decidedly unused to driving in wet conditions, to beware water on the roadways. Slippery conditions were to be expected. Bob Dylan was singing "Desolation Row" through my USB-equipped car stereo, a particularly fitting soundtrack, I thought, as I gazed across the river at what was still the most dangerous city in North America: Ciudad Juárez. Even better was the next song, "Beyond Here Lies Nothin'," the phrase taken from Ovid's *Tristia*, a poem of despair and loneliness written on the shores of the Black Sea, where the poet languished in exile, spending his last years along the empire's rim. Behind the clouds, off to the west, I knew that a concrete Jesus, his arms spread wide, was standing watch over us from high atop the peak of Mount Cristo Rey.

Flying down the interstate in my huge white truck, I was again transfixed by the site of grass, *green grass*, in the outlying areas around El Paso. A monsoon season had descended, and the sandy wastes sprouted in response. Last night's rain, moreover, had caused all the draws to run, so water stood in all the culverts and creek beds along the way. The terraced fields and orchards along the river, which normally stand out in almost radioactive contrast to the bare reddish ground, seemed far less lonely amid the creosote, white brush, catclaw, and occasional sotol that populate this stretch of country. The mountains of Sierra Blanca were gorgeous in their wispy white cotton-candy mantles.

After dodging an errant box spring shed by a pickup hauling furniture piled up high like something out of *The Grapes of Wrath*, I stopped at the Van Horn truck stop, where a loud voice informed shower customer number 29 that shower number 2 was ready for his ablutions. Turning south, I passed Hereford Street, Brahman Street, and a few old horses and rusty trailers, but no actual Hereford or Brahman cattle. They would have found little to eat thereabouts among the cast-off vehicles and other agricultural debris, unhidden by the flat brushless terrain, amid bare dirt and greasewood in pastures so abused that not even a season of Pacific cyclones would yield a crop of grass.

Conditions improved rapidly as I pushed southward, and the grass was soon embarrassing in its proliferation. The old spring known as the Van Horn Wells, about twelve miles south of town, was used by Indians long before it was "discovered" in 1849 by Major Jefferson Van Horne while searching for a shorter route to El Paso. The spring served stagecoach travelers, mail riders, and soldiers throughout the nineteenth century. Now adjacent to a large pecan orchard and the ruins of Lobo, Texas—as well as a striking orange tractor-trailer rig sitting idle, year after year, in a large pasture—the neglected old spring was once fiercely contested, with Indians burning the adobe buildings of the small garrison that stood there. The town of Lobo came later, originating as a land swindle that lured investors west to a nonexistent community furnished with bathing springs and a luxury hotel. Lawsuits followed, and the hotel promised by the speculators was eventually built, only to be destroyed by an earthquake in 1929. In recent years three Germans bought what was left of the Lobo country store and have sought to promote a film festival called Desert Dust Cinema. Patrons, a sign advises, should bring their own chairs.

A few miles down the road, the air force's expensive radar blimp, now ceded to U.S. Customs and Border Protection, was sitting on the ground. In all the years I've been driving this road, I've never seen it aloft (though shortly after I arrived home I read that the CBP had

Surveillance blimp near Marfa, Texas

finally succeeded in getting the aerostat back in service). I stopped in Marfa for lunch and eavesdropped on beautiful young people complaining about L.A. while I ate a delicious kale salad.

From Marfa the road undulated and wound its way through rolling hills, steep draws, damp drainages, and narrow defiles. Down in the bottoms the grass was tall, yellow with numberless bright wildflowers, sunflowers; dead cedar dotted the hills, testaments of fire or drought or both. Roadrunners popped out from wide-gauge fence wire, and hawks perched on telephone poles, one eating a snake, as if enacting the Mexican flag. The hills, with their jagged outcroppings, appeared at sharp angles and loomed close to the road. A jumble of hoodoos—called Elephant Rock by an official-looking sign—appeared to thrust upward from the plain. Astonishing vistas opened suddenly as a canyon revealed itself around a curve, the road hanging along the edge on a terrace blasted into the picturesque hillside. Alas, a hideous high-capacity power line ran right down through the middle of the canyon, spoiling the view.

Twenty miles from Presidio I came upon Shafter, an old silver-mining town. I thought perhaps the town was named for a hole in the ground, but in fact it was a colonel in the U.S. Army, based in Fort Davis, who gave the place its name in the 1880s. The mine closed in 1942, after producing thirty-five million ounces of silver, and only about two dozen people still lived there, in a pass cut through the southeastern fringes of the Chinati mountain range by Cibolo Creek. A few years of production in the late 1970s and early 1980s yielded another twenty-four million ounces, and in 2008 a small Canadian mining company called Aurcana reopened the mine, chasing after another forty-seven million. The aim was to make it one of the largest primary silver mines in the world. Jobs were created and taxes were paid, and overnight the mine became the county's largest taxpayer. But the little company's timing was off: the silver market dropped 38 percent in 2013, and Aurcana shuttered the mines once again. A large church or mission with a shiny new metal roof and a bright red statue of the Virgin adorning its facade stood near the side of the road; limestone ruins crumbled on the adjacent hillsides, near an enormous black satellite dish, surrounded by ocotillo, that occupied the yard of a modest white house. Jagged Chinati peaks directed my eyes toward heaven.

On down the road an enigmatic sign declared, PROFILE OF LINCOLN.

I confess I could not see the resemblance on any of the various mountain silhouettes, and I very nearly ran off the road in my attempt.

Descending into the valley of the Rio Grande, an undulating, barren, eroded expanse of badlands to my east, I saw before me the cities of the floodplain, Presidio and Ojinaga. Junkyards littered the outskirts of town, busted-up school buses and tractor trailers, mobile homes and RVs, old cars, bails of wire, rusting pipe, old pickups from the 1930s—all smashed and twisted, the slowly combusting detritus of industrial society.

The road into Presidio proceeds along the edge of a mesa formation apparently composed, like the eroded badlands to my east, of volcanic tuff. From this vantage I could just make out the meandering track of the Rio Grande to my west, and what I took to be the converging green line of the Conchos as it captured what remains of the younger river's pathetic northern stream. I could see no obstacle to floodwater.

Descending to the plain, I entered what at first looked much like any other impoverished West Texas settlement. Desert towns wear everything out in the open. No sizable trees grew along the fringes of garbage pits; weedy instances of mesquite and huisache served only to accentuate the clutter. An Alco discount store greeted me, followed by a sad little Radio Shack, isolated and lonely, far from its natural habitat in a strip mall. Empty gas stations, modest little homes, the lowest possible reaches of motel life; architectural desolation punctuated with struggling dusty palm trees. Trailer homes nestled in among antique vehicles and neat frame houses; two-story buildings abandoned and windowless; adobes slowly melted back into the mud whence they came; shacks atop hills that might even hide a dugout room in the traditional Indian style.

I turned down O'Reilly Street, downtown Presidio's main drag, and parked across from a Family Dollar. I could see the small city hall, its galvanized metal roof glinting in the sunlight, just up the block. There wasn't much foot traffic or many cars moving about town. My eyes fell on a Dollar Tree and a Payless ShoeSource, a diner called El Patio, a small lumberyard. I stood in the middle of the street and took photographs, then climbed back into my pickup and drove on. A crumbling storefront caught my eye. It was brick, partially stuccoed, with half of a broken sign reading MID-WAY in green letters. Around back,

Presidio, Texas

behind the remnants of a fence, there was what looked like a small rock well house next to the remains of a pump and some old pipe, in a yard littered with small mesquite bushes, tall clumps of green grass, rubbly piles of stone, and a large earthen mound.

Brown-stained plywood covered the front windows. Someone had scratched the anarchy symbol on the board covering the left window, under which I could barely make out the word "Fireworks." Adjacent to the Mid-Way building was a sturdy cement storm-water culvert with walls about two feet high. A steel pedestrian bridge, with steel railings, spanned it. On either side of the bridge, attractive stone walls lined the sidewalk for about six feet, then stopped. The culvert opened directly onto the street. It was all very mysterious to an outsider, and strangely beautiful.

Down the road a few hundred feet, past a small grocer, I could see a large sign for a small Bealls department store. When I was a child, I used to get my school clothes at the Bealls in Del Rio. Palm and cypress trees held the skyline, and I thought I could see Mexico in the hot, hazy distance.

I drove around for a while, trying to find a way to the river without venturing too near the port of entry. I found a dirt road perpendicular to O'Reilly Street, and it seemed to lead toward the river, so I followed it across some railroad tracks that had not seen recent use, through old grown-up fields lined with neglected fences clotted with brush. I was searching for intimations of the ancient peoples who once inhabited this narrow fertile crescent where two rivers deposit their silt and sweep all else before them. What I found was an agricultural ruin scattered with shacks, collapsing barns, forlorn homes stripped and salvaged and bare of copper or any metal worth scrapping, defunct tractors and farming implements, curling barbed wire. A land ill-used, disrepaired, fertile yet fallow. Fence posts soaked in creosote will long outlast the rusting steel alloys of this ruin, but they too will give way to the rushing waters. This land has been farmed, irrigated, and largely abandoned to idle panting dogs and bored horses swatting flies with their tails, one of whom rubbed his cruel halter on a post as he stood, lonely and hopeless, his back nearly bald with scars of long-ago travails, staring vacantly at the overgrown rail line as if waiting for the mild diversion of a passing train.

People will tell you that the fields around Presidio and Ojinaga have been under continuous cultivation for thousands of years. I've seen claims that farmers were here as far back as 1500 B.C. And perhaps they were. Archaeologists who study such things tend to be more circumspect. We know that humans came into the Trans-Pecos region of West Texas more than fourteen thousand years ago, but they were hunters following the great herds of Paleolithic megafauna. They hunted the elephants, giant bison, and horses into extinction. Farmers began cultivating the rich alluvial deposits along the juncture—*la junta*—of the Rio Grande and the Conchos at least eight hundred years ago, that much we can say. La Junta was a confluence not only of rivers but of peoples. Villages naturally sprang up and then pueblos, close towns made of adobe. Patarabueye settled here, and Jumanos came and went. They traded with one another and with the travelers who were always passing through. Cabeza de Vaca and his companions made an appearance, and over the next two hundred years the Spanish several times established presidios and missions here, and so the town came to be known as Presidio del Norte. With the Spaniards came the horses, forever transforming the culture of the Plains Indians. In time the raiders came. But more fearsome than the horse Indians, the Comanches and Kiowas and Apaches, were the rivers.

That seemed to be the point of a very long disquisition by David Lewis, a park ranger at the Fort Leaton State Historic Site just west of Presidio, one of the welcome centers for Big Bend Ranch State Park.

"What was the life span of a Native American ten thousand years ago?" he asked me. Probably thirty years, I responded. "Exactly," he said. "Twenty-five maybe thirty years. Well, these floods happen every twenty-five years like clockwork. They call 'em hundred-year floods, but they're about every twenty-five. Grandma saw it, and then she dies, and the kids have never seen a flood. Most of the generations, once they'd seen it, they didn't build down there on the river."

He was talking about the flood of 2008, when a big storm got pulled in off the Pacific and dumped thirty inches of rain in Chihuahua over five days.

"The Conchos drains the entire state of Chihuahua, did you know that?" I had to admit that I didn't. "Texas has seven rivers that drain it. Chihuahua has one."

All that water came roaring down and took out the levees. Fortunately, there's that big wide floodplain, so that spreads the floodwaters out a bit. Over the millennia, those floods have scraped away much of the archaeological evidence for human agriculture here. There are still sites going back eight hundred years, but they're well back from the river, and there are sites in the state park that are far older. Lewis estimated there were five to ten thousand archaeological sites in the park, and only a very small fraction have been studied.

Lewis, who like me graduated from Del Rio High School, kept going on about that flood in 2008, pulling out scrapbooks and showing me photographs he took. At Lajitas, about fifty miles east, the photo showed twenty-two feet on the flood gauge. "Had some of our river rafters thought it'd be cool, so they put in at Lajitas. They ended up in Boquillas, in something like eight hours. That's a three-day boat ride normally." He paused for dramatic effect. "I didn't say they were smart." Then Lewis laughed his wild laugh and assured me that these guys were friends of his, that he didn't mean any harm, but you know what they say, he said, "Terlingua's the world's largest outdoor asylum."

I thanked Lewis for his time and nosed around the historical exhibits. I eyeballed the displays about the Jumanos and Cabeza de Vaca and the Apaches, then I left the shade and cool of the old adobe structure and walked out into the triple-digit heat.

Fort Leaton was built in the late 1840s, just after the Mexican War, by a desperado named Ben Leaton and his wife, Juana. Doña Juana, surname either Pedrasa or Pedraza, depending on the source, held a disputed title to the land, and she had some money. Leaton was a former scalp hunter turned trader—which is to say that he was a trader who once also trafficked in scalps. He'd been running wagons between Santa Fe and Chihuahua, and during the Mexican War he rode with Colonel Alexander William Doniphan and his Missouri Mounted Volunteers. Leaton thought La Junta would be a good location for a trading post, because it was on one of the old roads to Chihuahua, and he hoped that the new road from San Antonio to El Paso would pass through here as well. Ben and Juana set up housekeeping and built an adobe compound. Ben sold guns to the Apaches and attempted to set himself up as a lawman. The authorities in Chihuahua weren't happy about his activities, and they complained to the Americans. The San Antonio–El Paso road ended up bypassing La Junta for a more northerly route, but Leaton didn't live long enough to suffer many regrets.

Various legends circulate about the circumstances of Leaton's demise. One story has it that he was murdered by his neighbor, a rancher named John Burgess. Another story says he died of malaria in New Orleans. Yet another story, supposedly based on documentary evidence, has him expiring in San Antonio in 1851. Regardless of the where, when, or how, Leaton's friend Ed Hall ended up marrying Juana and raising his sons. A feud developed with John Burgess, and a series of murders followed, with sons and grandsons of Burgess and Leaton killing one another in vengeance.

I left Presidio and was headed east toward Terlingua, passing through a tiny village called Redford, when I noticed that I was driving on the Esequiel Hernández Memorial Highway. Esequiel was a teenager, a high school student who was shot and killed by U.S. Marines in 1997. He was out tending his goats when the marines, who were on patrol as part of a military-civilian joint task force, tracked him, targeted him, and shot him dead. It never occurred to the marines, apparently, to learn about the community they were supposedly protecting from Mexican drug smugglers. The marine who killed Esequiel was never tried; investigators concluded he was just following orders. Local Border Patrol agents would never have made that mistake; they knew Esequiel and they knew that he had a habit of carrying his old .22 with him when he was out herding his family's goats. The politicians who pound their podiums and scream for troops to patrol the Mexican border, to protect the "homeland" from economic refugees and Honduran and Salvadoran children who just want to be reunited with their parents, should think about Esequiel Hernández in his last moments, dragging himself along the gravel, after an American soldier put a bullet through his body.

Just then I saw something that caused me to pull over and grab my camera. It was a ramshackle house along the side of the road with a broad awning across the front. Across the awning the word "JUMANO" was spelled out in cedar branches, then two words I couldn't make out. I was excited, because here was the first sign of the Jumanos, aside from the Fort Leaton museum, that I had come across in the La Junta area. I knocked on the door, but no one answered. Later, after studying my photograph and digging around online, I realized that the branches spelled "JUMANO APACHE PEOPLE."

The Jumano people were probably first encountered by Europeans in 1535, by Álvar Núñez Cabeza de Vaca, right here at La Junta de los Ríos, after he walked barefoot and naked from the Gulf of Mexico along with his three surviving companions from the 1527 Narváez expedition. After years of slavery and misfortune, Cabeza de Vaca and his companions, including an African slave named Estebanico, walked some twenty-four hundred miles, surviving on pecans, prickly pear fruit, and the occasional dog. Whenever the Indians gave him a piece of meat, he writes, he ate it raw; when they gave him skins to scrape, he ate the scrapings. The land was extremely rugged, and all the plants had thorns, which tore his flesh and caused him to bleed whenever he gathered firewood. Cabeza de Vaca writes that he shed his skin twice a year like a serpent. His only consolation was the thought that Jesus had suffered far worse.

Cabeza de Vaca's account of his journey, published in 1542, stands

Jumano Apache People, Redford, Texas

as the greatest of all first-contact narratives, and he is an eloquent witness of the West Texas landscape. His *entrada*, though involuntary, established the pattern of suffering that would mark almost every subsequent overland journey through Texas. The first wetback, illegal alien, undocumented migrant, and *mojado* was also the first European invader. His countrymen followed with their horses and their crosses and their maps, with their guns and knives and Bibles. They ministered the souls of the people they found and administered their bodies.

Cabeza de Vaca's narrative is a treasury of geographical and ethnographic detail. He describes crossing a great river coming from the north that sounds very much like the Pecos, after which he and his companions crossed fifty leagues of dry, rugged, and uninhabited country. They crossed a deep river, possibly the Rio Grande. Eventually, they came to a settlement that he says "looked like houses," which probably belonged to the Patarabueye, a pueblo people who lived at La Junta de los Ríos, where the Río Grande del Norte flows into the larger Río Conchos at present-day Presidio. Several distinct groups lived at this fertile crossroads, through which passed a major Native highway connecting the peoples who lived south along the Conchos and far down into the interior of Mexico with the pueblos in the upper Rio Grande valley, the Great Plains, and beyond. Here Cabeza de Vaca describes meeting a group of Indians he calls *la gente de las vacas*, the people of the cows, because they were such accomplished hunters of buffalo. The Cow People had no pottery, and they cooked by filling a pumpkin with water, heating stones in a fire, and placing the hot stones in the pumpkin, causing the water to boil. He marvels at "how diverse and strange human ingenuity and industriousness are."

Finally, Cabeza de Vaca and his companions came to a permanent settlement where the people raised corn, squash, and beans and possessed cotton blankets. These Indians wore clothes and treated their women with kindness. And they described bearded men who came from the sea, men with horses and lances and swords, who had raided their villages, killed their people, and taken many people as slaves. Cabeza de Vaca and his companions rejoiced, for surely these men were Christians.

Some scholars seek to quibble with the identification of the Jumanos with the Cow People, but we know from later Spanish accounts that the Jumanos were buffalo hunters and they were often found at La Junta. Historians also disagree among themselves about Cabeza de Vaca's route, as they do about most questions concerning the Jumanos. In fact, this mysterious Native people has been an object of particular scholarly debate. In the literature, which is highly specialized and technical, one often sees reference to the "Jumano problem."

Whether or not Cabeza de Vaca's Cow People were Jumanos, they do enter the historical record *by name* with the expedition of Antonio de Espejo, which in 1582 passed through La Junta on its way to the pueblos of New Mexico. The people Espejo encountered at La Junta said they remembered a group of naked Spaniards who had passed that way long ago.

Espejo was a cattleman who moved to Nueva Vizcaya, as the Mexican state of Chihuahua was then known, to avoid paying a fine for murdering one of his workers. He was thus an ideal borderlander and proto-Texan. Espejo had some difficulties with the natives. His chronicler, a man who probably had not bathed in months, wrote that the pueblo Indians did not stink quite as much as other Indians they had encountered, and he observed that the pueblo women were whiter than the Indians in Mexico. Espejo found it necessary to burn a town; he also garroted sixteen Indians for insolently mocking him and refusing to provide food for the expedition. Indians were not supposed to mock Spaniards. Here is a sentence found in the expedition diary, one that could serve as epigraph for any number of Spanish *entradas* in the New World: "The Lord willed this that the whole land should tremble for ten lone Spaniards, for there were over twelve thousand Indians in the province with bows and arrows." On his return trip the following year Espejo traveled south along the Pecos River, mistakenly believing that the river would lead him back to La Junta. After several days in which they saw buffalo without number, Espejo and his men traveled for almost three hundred miles without seeing any buffalo or natives whose food they might appropriate. They were "greatly troubled," and probably quite hungry. Near the confluence of Toyah Creek and the Pecos, they came upon three Jumanos, who kindly guided the Spanish back to their *ranchería* and fed them catfish and "sardines" as well as squash and prickly pear. "The food," wrote the expedition's diarist, "was delicious." Unlike the reception Espejo had received among the pueblos, the Jumanos celebrated the coming of the Spanish and greeted them with dancing and song. Then they led the hapless tourists by a familiar and level trail back to La Junta.

Over the next century and a half, the Jumanos remained closely associated with the Pecos River, but it's also clear that the Jumanos were well traveled. They followed the buffalo and made frequent appearances at the eastern pueblos of the people who were called the Humana, because they were very friendly with the Jumanos, with whom they seem to have intermarried. The Jumanos, also called the Juman, Jumanes, Jumanas, Xumanos, Xumanas, and Xoman by the Spanish (the *J* and the *X* being interchangeable, as in Tejas/Texas) were also called the Choumane or Chouman by the French, who encountered them in East Texas, among the Hasinai, a Caddoan people who were also called the Tejas, which means "friend." The Jumanos were *rayados*, or "striped," which is to say that they wore tattoos on their faces and thus were distinctive in appearance. The inhabitants of the Humana pueblos also decorated their faces with the ray-like tattoos. Sometimes the Spanish referred to any Indian with such markings as a Jumano, thus providing grist for more than one doctoral dissertation.

Jumanos are known to have attended the great summer trade gatherings in Central Texas. They were found along the Pecos and along the Concho River, a tributary of the Colorado River of Texas, near contemporary San Angelo. They apparently ranged down the Devils River, along the Rio Grande from Del Rio and Eagle Pass into South Texas and northern Mexico. They hunted buffalo in the eastern plains of New Mexico and the Big Bend and across the Edwards Plateau into Central and East Texas. No other group of Indians, prior to the Apache invasion, appears to have ranged so widely across the Texas landscape during the first two centuries after contact.

Other Spaniards penetrated north into Tejas and crossed the stream called Río Bravo or Río Grande del Norte in brief sorties and *entradas:* Franciscan friars with their crosses and catechisms, and enterprising soldiers with manacles. Slave raids were often the most common mode of first contact. Because the slavers were not subject to the king's Laws of Settlement, because their activities were officially illegal, records of such raids are scarce. Northern Mexico, rich in minerals, was quickly if sparsely settled with small mining camps, and missionaries began to penetrate farther northward. Slavers pushed even faster, seeking labor for the mines. Applications were submitted from ambitious would-be conquerors of the north for permission to found the colony that all believed to be inevitable. The king's council was taking its time, though by 1586 the viceroy of New Spain was instructed to "endeavor to carry out the discovery, pacification, and settlement" of the north. Gaspar Castaño de Sosa, the new lieutenant governor and captain general of Nuevo León, had his own plans, and he provides some of the best and earliest descriptions of the Devils River and the Juno country.

Because he had "a proud heart" and wanted to make a great discovery, as a Spanish historian wrote fifty years later, Castaño, after he heard about "a country to the north with people who wore clothing," tricked the people of the mining village of Almaden into believing that a fabulous new silver mine had been found. So the villagers took everything they had—oxen, plowshares, tools, weapons, food—and left the town deserted. Castaño marched north out of Nuevo León in 1590 with more than 170 colonists and soldiers, wagons loaded with supplies, and beef on the hoof. After revealing his true plans and, using

Pecos River, west of Comstock, Texas

both persuasion and threats, prevailing upon the skeptics in his party to follow him, Castaño, with his expedition, continued north, crossing the Rio Grande near Del Rio. Castaño's plan was to follow the Pecos River, known to him as the Río Salado, north to the pueblos of New Mexico that had been described by explorers such as Coronado and Antonio de Espejo, who followed the Pecos south to the Rio Grande. What Castaño did not realize, however, was that Espejo had left the Pecos before it entered into the steep canyons of its lower reaches. Nor was he aware of the Devils River, which also presented an intimidating canyon at its juncture with the Rio Grande. At last, after finding a place to ford the Devils, which he called the River of Rocks, Castaño was confronted with the great canyon of the lower Pecos.

Castaño had no choice but to follow the Devils River, which was far from easy but at least provided some access to water. His men repeatedly tried to find a way across the Pecos, losing twenty-five dozen horseshoes in their various attempts. One group of scouts came upon a large group of Indians who were friendly and gave them buffalo and antelope hides and shoes, as well as meat. Finally they succeeded in finding a good route to the Pecos and a passable ford, possibly striking what became known to westering Texas Rangers, adventurous mail carriers like Bigfoot Wallace, U.S. cavalrymen, and stagecoach customers as the Southern Road, one portion of which happens to cross the divide between the two rivers on my family's ranch at Juno, after leaving the Devils a few miles south of Beaver Lake.

After crossing the Pecos south of what would later be Fort Lancaster, the members of the expedition followed the river north. They came upon empty *rancherías* and occasionally met natives, such as one group that was traveling with "loaded dogs." The Spaniards had never seen a dog dragging a travois, so they were delighted, "as it was a new thing." A group of Indian warriors killed one of the expedition members; another stole some cattle, which led to a battle in which several of the thieves were killed. Two were captured and hanged; three youths were taken as "servants" but later escaped with an ox.

Eventually, Castaño and a small group of scouts came to the Pecos pueblo, a fortified adobe town of four or five stories with a central plaza. It was not the first time these people had encountered Spaniards (both Coronado and Espejo had paid visits, which did not go well), and they were not disposed to be friendly. Castaño ordered his men to blow trumpets, and he attempted to make peace. The Indians threw stones and fired arrows and slingshots at their visitors. Castaño walked around the building and attempted to communicate his peaceful intentions. He gathered his men and held a conference. Perhaps he was concerned about the 1574 Law of Settlement, which forbade making war on the natives. Whatever his motivations, Castaño asked his secretary to record that their intentions were peaceful and the fact that the pueblo insisted upon presenting a hostile face to their entreaties. Then he attacked. Two cannons were set on a high place, and they were fired at the pueblo. Harquebuses were fired and Indians were shot. Castaño's Indian guides fired their arrows, which apparently did more to frighten the residents of Pecos than the explosions of gunpowder. Eventually, the Indians surrendered and became friendly, even though they had suffered casualties, and the Spanish entered the pueblo. They were amazed at how much corn was stored inside the buildings and at how comfortable and well-appointed the dwellings were. They made note of the underground kivas and other structures as well as the complex and interesting methods used by the pueblo Indians for processing their corn and beans. These Indians wore cotton blankets and buffalo hides and robes woven from turkey feathers, and they stockpiled stone and wood in addition to corn and water.

The next day the Spanish were astonished to find that every single inhabitant of the pueblo had slipped away during the night, especially because the weather was very cold, with severe wind and snow. Even the rivers were frozen. Castaño and his party were very sad and disappointed, and they resolved not to harm the pueblo or take any of the people's belongings, though they did help themselves to the pueblo's precious stores of corn and bean flour. When the Spaniards went among other pueblos, they sounded their trumpets and fired guns to proclaim their arrival; they erected crosses and appointed mayors and governors; they forbade the natives to carry bows and arrows in Castaño's presence, and they feasted on tamales and tortillas, beans and squash and turkeys. The Indians were mostly friendly, and because Castaño was gentle, for a Spaniard, and did not take their turquoise jewelry or other belongings, they humored him and swore allegiance to his mysterious God and to his equally mysterious king beyond the sea. Some of Castaño's men wanted to pillage the pueblos, and they were very unhappy with his refusals. They plotted to kill him; the plan was discovered, but Castaño took mercy on the conspirators and did not execute them in the traditional Spanish manner, by affixing an iron collar, called a garrote, around the neck and tightening it with screws until the condemned person was strangled.

Castaño de Sosa pursued his expedition under an interpretation of the laws that was not shared by the Spanish crown and its agents in New Spain. He did not have the proper authorizations, and so the king disbanded his colony and sent soldiers north to arrest him. When the soldiers arrived, they informed Castaño that the king had ordered his arrest. Castaño submitted and said that the arrest was very welcome if that was the will of his king. Castaño was tried, found guilty, and banished to China. Later, Spanish authorities had occasion to revisit his case, and his sentence was voided. The reprieve came too late, for he was dead, having been killed by pirates.

．　．　．

It was Don Juan de Oñate who at last received the royal charter, in 1595, to establish a colony in the north. Oñate was a rich man, and his *entrada* was largely financed out of his personal funds, which had been greatly increased by his marriage to Isabel de Tolosa Cortés Moctezuma, the granddaughter of Hernán Cortés and great-granddaughter of the emperor Moctezuma. Three years later Oñate crossed the Rio Grande at El Paso, marched across a desolate stretch of ground known as the Jornada del Muerto, Dead Man's March, into the northern Rio Grande valley, and subdued the many pueblos he encountered there. He founded the river kingdom of New Mexico. He searched for gold and silver—traveling as far as the Gulf of California to the southwest and Kansas in the east—but found only Indians, mountains, deserts, and seas of grass on the high plains. When the Indians rebelled, Oñate was brutal in suppression. After the revolt of Ácoma pueblo he ordered that all male prisoners over the age of twenty-five forfeit one foot by amputation and serve twenty years of what was euphemistically called personal service. Women were also sentenced to twenty years of slavery; they were permitted to keep both feet.

Oñate was eventually called back to Mexico City, in 1606, after King Philip III ordered a halt to all exploration in search of treasure in New Mexico. He said the colony was profitless. The king told his viceroy in Mexico to find some sufficient pretext for recalling Oñate, "so that he may come without disturbance; as soon as he has come you will detain him in the City of Mexico, disband whatever military force he may have, and appoint a satisfactory governor." On his way back to Mexico, in a skirmish with some Indians, Oñate lost his only son, whom he buried on the Jornada del Muerto. He continued down the Camino Real to the capital, where like so many great conquistadors he was convicted of committing crimes against the Indians as well as adultery.

The friars who lived in New Mexico and the other northern reaches of New Spain continued to harvest the souls of Indians with Christian zeal. The Christian brothers were often abused, sometimes fed tortillas made with dead mice and urine, and occasionally martyred. They came into contact with the Apaches. They taught the Indians to make adobe;

they taught them to use whitewash and to work hard, like European peasants; they instructed them in Christian dogma. The friars, assisted by the Indians, cultivated grapes for Communion wine and planted fruit trees. Churches were raised.

One day in 1629, fifty Jumano Indians showed up at the Isleta pueblo and begged for the friars to come to their *rancherías* across the wide plains and convert their people to Christianity. It was not the first time such a request had come from the Jumanos. The Spaniards were impressed by this distant people who so desired to be instructed in the one true faith, and there was great interest among the religious of New Mexico in bringing these earnest natives into the faith. But there were so few priests and so many souls to attend there in New Mexico. At about the same time, a supply train, the first to be received in four years, arrived from Mexico City, and with it came thirty new padres, who brought word from Spain about a miraculous phenomenon involving a Franciscan nun from northern Castile named María de Jesús de Ágreda. María de Jesús was a remarkable young woman who had become famous for her trances, in which she claimed to travel to the Orient and to New Mexico, where she appeared to the natives and spoke to them in their own language. Religious officials in Mexico were asked to investigate these mysterious "bilocations."

When a friar asked the Jumanos how they had come to learn about Christianity, they responded that it was the Lady in Blue who came among them and was always preaching. They pointed to a painting of a nun and said that she was dressed like that one, except her face was young and very beautiful. The Spanish were stunned, because the nuns of the Convent of the Immaculate Conception, where Sister María de Jesús was abbess, wore a distinctive blue cloak over their habits. Friars were sent east from New Mexico to the Jumanos, who were camped along a river called Nueces, which was probably the modern Concho River near San Angelo, Texas. At that time, according to a Spanish memorial of 1630, the Jumanos were suffering from a drought that had dried up their water sources and caused the buffalo to move away. They were planning to move their *rancherías* to find new sources of food, when the Lady appeared to each of the Jumano captains personally and told them that the Spanish fathers were coming near, so they sent out a party to meet them. The padres and the soldiers who traveled with them were greeted by a procession of the Jumanos, led by two men holding crosses. More than ten thousand people assembled in a field, and the padres asked if they wished to be baptized. The captains of the Jumanos responded that it was only for this purpose that all the people had gathered together. The padres asked that everyone who wished to be a Christian raise up his arm, and in response, "with one great cry, all uplifted their arms, rising to their feet, asking for the holy Baptism." Even mothers with suckling babies took them by their little arms and held them upward. And so they were baptized and indoctrinated, and before the fathers left the Jumanos, they healed their sick and their infirm, the blind, the lame, and the dropsied, of all their pains and afflictions.

The religious custodian of New Mexico, Fray Alonso de Bena-vides, was so amazed by all the miracles that had transpired that he undertook a great journey, traveling down the Camino Real from Santa Fe, across the Jornada del Muerto to El Paso, and thence to Chihuahua and southward to Mexico City, to make a report to the archbishop of Mexico. Then he sailed to Spain, where after some time he obtained permission from the head of the Franciscan order to visit Mother María de Jesús herself in Ágreda. María de Jesús was a spiritual vir-tuoso, a religious prodigy who took a vow of chastity at the age of eight and entered the Convent of the Immaculate Conception at seventeen, with her mother, the same year that her father and brother entered the Franciscan order, very much under her influence. The pope made her abbess when she was twenty-five. When Fray Benavides appeared before her in 1631, she was twenty-nine years old and very beautiful, with large black eyes and pale white skin and rosy cheeks. María de Jesús told the padre of her travels among the heathens and the savages who did not know the one true God, transported by guardian angels, among them Saint Francis. She described to him the pueblos of New Mexico and told how she had been present when he himself had per-formed various baptisms among them. She described his appearance when he was a younger man and that of the Jumanos and the friars who had gone among them. The padre was greatly moved and wrote down an account of what he had learned and showed it to her, and she signed it with her own hand. Fray Benavides sent this account in a letter to the friars in New Mexico and said that he had been convinced absolutely of all that she had told him. Included also was a message from Mother María, who charged them to work tirelessly and gently to bring the Indians out of darkness and blindness into the immaculate, tender, and delightfully radiant law of God.

In later years, Mother María de Jesús published a book titled *The Mystical City of God, Divine History of the Virgin, Mother of God*, which includes detailed descriptions of her mystical flights to the New World in addition to the life of the Virgin, as well as an account of the nine months that Mary spent in her mother's womb, during which time, already infused with the holy light of reason, the Virgin Mother commenced her great work of mediation, intercession, and reparation. The book was condemned for indecency and heresy by the Roman Inquisition in 1681, though the king of Spain, who was an active correspondent with Mother María, insisted on an exemption within his domains.

In 1658 a group of Babane and Jumano Indians petitioned the local Spanish captain at Saltillo for the right to form an autonomous pueblo in Coahuila; they were seeking a legal remedy to their predicament, which was not much better than slavery. The Native peoples of the region had been rounded up and put to work; children were taken and imprisoned so that the parents would work on the *encomiendas*, in the farms and mines of settlers who were *entrusted* (for that is the meaning of *encomendar*) with the bodies and souls of the Native peoples, who were to be instructed in the ways of civilization, the Spanish language, and the one true faith. The Spanish called this *reducción*. In practice, the reduction of the Indians, whether as part of the *encomienda* system or not, typically meant they were subjected to forced labor without contract or payment. The petitioners pointed to a precedent, which was the agreement between the Spanish and the Tlaxcaltecans, who had previously established a pueblo there. The *encomenderos* were not happy; the haciendas and the mines needed workers, and their labor force was parlous. Indians tended to die when forced to work. The petition was rejected.

Sixteen years later a businessman from Saltillo by the name of Don Antonio de Balcarcel was appointed mayor of Coahuila. He soon reestablished a settlement at Monclova that had fallen victim to frontier hazards. Large groups of natives began to appear before him, asking to be taken under his protection. The political situation was remarkably complex, with different nations vying for position and various coalitions trying to ally themselves with the Spanish. In the documents one finds wonderful names of vanished peoples. The Bobole coalition included the Xicocosse, Jumane, Bauane, Xupulame, Yorica, Xianco cadam, Yergiba, and Bacaranan. Another coalition included the Gueiquesale and the Hueyquetzale, as well as the Manos Prietas, Bacoram, Pinanacam, Cacaxte, Coniane, Ovaya, Tetecora, Contotore, Tocaymamare, Saesser, Teneymamar, Codam, and many others. A third comprised the Mayo, Babusarigame, Bamarimamare, Cabesa, Bauiasmamare, Igo quib, and others. The Catujano led a coalition that included the Masiabe, Madmeda, Mabibit, Ape, Pachaque, Xumez, and Garafe.

In one report, a Spanish soldier complains that the Indians were always starting wars with one another, killing and eating one another. Managing all the possible enmities was daunting. One group in particular, the Ervipiame, who might have lived near the Devils River, were fighting with the Gueiquesale coalition and the Yorica. The Spaniards, good imperialist bureaucrats, were diligent with their paperwork. They took notes and they took names. Ethnohistorians, mining Spanish archives, have identified more than six hundred different Native groups living in Texas alone.

Balcarcel officially established a pueblo under the leadership of the Bobole and their allies, which included groups of Jumanos. Other groups were there as well, and soon many more arrived. The Native population swelled, and alarmed Spanish settlers began to flee. Balcarcel, fearing that he would be overrun, sent a group led by Father Juan Larios and Fernando del Bosque to count the people living north of the Rio Grande and to urge them to stay put. Although the territory of Coahuila already included the lands north of the Rio Grande, at least nominally, those lands had not been explored, and the Spanish evidently viewed the river as a convenient administrative boundary. There is no reason to believe the Indians did so, and some groups defended territory on both sides. All were hunter-gatherers; they lived in one area for a brief time and then moved on when they had exhausted local resources, just as they had when Cabeza de Vaca came among them some 150 years previously. When the buffalo appeared in South Texas every year, some of the Indian groups fought wars over hunting rights.

All that began to change as the Apaches came under pressure from the Comanches and started to move south out of the Great Plains. The Apaches had been raiding pueblos in New Mexico for decades and were beginning to pressure the nations in Texas, which could explain the eagerness of so many groups to ally themselves with the Spanish. The Apaches themselves would do the same a century later.

The Bosque-Larios expedition set out in May 1675. Wherever the Spanish went, they took possession of the land in the name of their king. When they encountered Indians, according to the expedition diary, the natives asked for baptism, and Fray Larios taught them doctrine. When they came to the Rio Grande, it was very full; the riverbed was more than eleven hundred feet wide. They found Indians drying buffalo meat who complained about the depredations of their enemies, the Ervipiame. Everywhere the expedition went, they counted the numbers of warriors and women, girls and boys. On May 15, the expedition came to a river that the natives called Ona, which in their language meant "salty." Bosque took possession in the name of the king, erected a tall wooden cross, and named the place San Isidro Labrador. (The ethnohistorian Maria F. Wade, in her definitive study on the Indians of the Edwards Plateau, suggests that the location was probably Elm Creek, between Brackettville and Del Rio.) The Indians came to them, and their leaders were questioned individually. All declared that they were ignorant of God and the way to salvation but they now wished to be baptized and to settle in a pueblo as Christians under the authority of King Carlos. Bosque welcomed them under Spanish dominion and ordered them to be peaceful. The new converts kissed the robes of the friars and left offerings. "One placed on the ground a piece of animal fat, and another a piece of rendered fat." The next day more Indians arrived, and they asked to be baptized but were told they must learn the doctrine first. The friars baptized fifty-five suckling babies. A Gueiquesale leader presented a twelve-year-old Spanish boy who had been raised by the leader's own mother; he said that he loved the boy like a brother but that he would give him back as a sign of friendship. "The boy was tattooed with a black line that ran from the forehead to the nose, and one row of round designs in the shape of the letter O on each of his cheeks. The boy had several rows of Os on the left arm, and one line of Os on the right arm."

Under questioning, the man revealed that his mother had received the boy from a group of Cabesas, who had taken him along with some other captives, including a girl. Another young boy had been killed with arrows. "When the boy realized he was about to die," the diarist recounts, "he picked up a cross which he held while he prayed. He prayed until he died." The Cabesas kept the Spanish girl as a slave. After some of their warriors were killed in a raid, they killed the girl with arrows. Two years passed, and they returned to the place where they had left the girl's body and discovered the body just as they had left it, uncorrupted and unmolested. That was all he knew, "except that the girl had long hair." He affirmed that all he said was the truth.

In 1680, the pueblos of New Mexico rose up and drove out the Spanish; those who did not escape were slaughtered. The Apaches, who had been raiding the pueblos and harassing the Spaniards, took part. The colonists and their Native allies fell back across the Jornada del Muerto to El Paso del Río del Norte. It was sixteen years before the Spanish were able to reconquer New Mexico.

Three years after the uprising, in 1683, a Jumano captain named Juan Sabeata came before the governor of New Mexico in El Paso. It's no exaggeration to say that he was the first great political leader of early Texas. Not one in a million Texans have heard his name.

Sabeata reminded the governor of the long friendship and trade relations between the Spanish and his people since the time when they first came to New Mexico and that Spaniards came every year from New Mexico to trade in their *rancherías*. He said that he had come to find out whether it was true, as the Apaches claimed, that because of the rebellion of the apostate Indians in New Mexico the Spanish were finished. Sabeata was very happy to learn that his Apache enemies were lying. He offered to help the Spanish people in El Paso, who were suffering from great want and hunger. He offered to bring food to the Spanish, and he invited the Spanish to come visit the Jumano *rancherías* and to help them against their mutual enemies the Apaches. He said that within six days' travel there were Indians who were growing wheat, corn, and beans in abundance and that they had deer and buffalo hides that they would give to their friends the Spanish. He also said the Jumanos' friends the Tejas would come and that the Tejas, who lived in the east, had brought news of other Spaniards who were very white with red hair and came over the sea in wooden houses that walk on water. These other Spaniards had brought earrings and other marvels and traded with the Tejas and the Jumanos for deer and buffalo skins and other goods. He also spoke of a River of Nuts where shells containing pearls could be harvested.

In October, Sabeata returned and spoke of ten thousand souls who were asking for baptism. He asked for Spanish settlers to come and live among them and for Spanish soldiers to protect them from the Apaches. He spoke of other nations as well, and he praised the quality of the nuts that are so numerous they will feed many nations. And buffalo were there as well. And he spoke of "the nation of the long penis which is a very widespread nation without a number," and the nation that grinds, and the nation of the ugly arrows, and those who are called the people of the fish, and the people of the dirty water, and those who make bows, and many others, including the people of the great kingdom of the Tejas. He said that he had no doubt that all these nations would come to the friars to be baptized, because all the nations have been waiting for them to come. He said that in the kingdom of the Tejas, where the Spaniards with the wooden houses that walk on water have been trading, there are acorns the size of large eggs and abundant grapes. Sabeata said there is a king there who never travels and that his land is so rich with food that even the horses, of which there are great herds, feed on corn.

The strange white Spaniards were actually French, led by René Robert Cavelier, Sieur de La Salle, who in 1685 had established a colony in East Texas, but the Spanish did not pick up on this important piece of intelligence. For the Native people of the Texas borderlands, all Europeans were Spaniards.

Juan Sabeata apparently knew his audience, so he told the story of a miraculous event. Four years previously, he said, when his people were sitting peacefully in their houses and in their fields, they saw a cross coming down from the sky, floating in the air. The people were amazed and understood that the God of the Spanish wanted them to be Christians. His people painted the cross on their bodies and carried the cross into battle before them and defeated their enemies, and it was the greatest victory the Jumanos had ever enjoyed. Since that time nothing bad had happened to them.

Except of course now there were Apaches moving into their territory, and Sabeata very much wanted to enlist the power of Spain against these new invaders, who were pushing down out of the high plains of the Llano Estacado.

The Spanish governor was sufficiently impressed by Sabeata's story to order an expedition into the Jumano lands. It did not go particularly well. He sent a disaffected and troublesome New Mexican refugee named Juan Domínguez de Mendoza, who had lost a fortune during the 1680 uprising, along with Friar Nicolás López. Both men were unhappy with the situation in El Paso and were interested in finding new areas for settlement. Mendoza, who had traveled through the Jumano lands before, took twenty men with him, including three friars. They traveled southeast along the Rio Grande and found large numbers of the Suma people, who were very poor and drank a great deal of mescal and asked for help against the Apaches, who they said would not leave them alone. Mendoza left crosses for the Suma and promised to return and help them, but he never did.

As they traveled, the Spaniards found plenty of good land and abundant supplies of water from fresh springs running into the river, and they left a cross on a hill that resembled a church. They met with Julime Indians who already had many crosses planted on the hills around their *ranchería*. More than one hundred Julime were baptized. After arriving at La Junta, the expedition turned north toward the Jumano lands. In early January, about one month into their journey, they came upon the first buffalo tracks. Three days later they killed three bulls, which greatly relieved everyone's hunger. Soon they crossed the Pecos River and arrived at the *ranchería* of a Jumano group called the Gediondos, the Stinking Ones.

In what appears to have been a carefully choreographed encounter, the Gediondos fired harquebus shots in salute, and Juan Sabeata fired his harquebus in answer. The Spanish returned the salute. These Indians had horses as well as European weapons, but they were afraid the Apaches were going to raid them and take their horses. They begged the Spanish to protect them. There were people here from other nations as well as the Jumanos. A large, heavy wooden cross was revealed, evidently made some time ago, painted yellow and red. Attached to it was a flag made from white taffeta that bore two crosses in blue. This was the cross that was supposed to have fallen from the sky. The friars dismounted and kissed the cross, but the soldiers remained on their horses. The women and children from the *ranchería* came forth and kissed the frocks of the friars. The expedition stayed at the *ranchería*, which they named San Ygnacio de Loyola, camped for seven days a prudent distance from the Indians, and killed twenty-seven buffalo.

A meeting was called by the Indian captains from all the different nations who were present. Juan Sabeata spoke for the group, and he asked Mendoza, "for the love of God, to make war on their common enemy, the Apache." Mendoza agreed to do so. The next day Sabeata presented Mendoza with seventeen deerskins. Mass was celebrated, and buffalo were slain. It seemed that a bargain had been struck.

Over the next several months, the Spanish traveled through the Jumano country east of the Pecos, apparently following the buffalo, which they slaughtered in great numbers. They passed through land that had been burned and land that was filled with good pastures and abundant game. Sabeata told Mendoza that his spies were tracking Apaches who had stolen some horses. They found the tracks of an Apache *ranchería* and met a group called the Arcos Fuertes, or Strong Bows. They ate catfish and turkeys and wild grapes and mulberries and pecans and other wild game on the wing. And of course buffalo. On some days they killed as few as seven; on others they killed as many as two hundred and then celebrated Mass. Apaches stole more horses. The Spanish came to what the Indians called the River of Pearls.

During this time, the Spaniards grew to distrust Juan Sabeata. They did not believe what he was saying about the Apaches. Finally, Mendoza expelled Sabeata from the camp and continued hunting as they traveled toward the great gathering of nations that had been promised. In mid-March, the expedition came to a particularly lovely spot on the San Saba River, near Menard, Texas, where they stayed for forty-six days. This country was bountiful, with abundant game, including bear and antelope, and wild grapes, mulberries, and plum trees. "The buffalo were so many that only God could attempt to count them." The expedition killed 4,030 buffalo, but those were only the ones that were brought to camp. Others were simply skinned and left in the field.

Here the Spanish waited because they were expecting people from forty-eight different nations. Not all showed up. Mendoza said he would return in a year, and he built a small fort on a hill that included two rooms, one of which was used as a church. The Spaniards celebrated Easter, and all the natives who were there asked for baptism.

Apaches attacked three times, as did another group called the Salinero. The expedition diary states that Juan Sabeata tried to enlist some of the nations who were gathered there to kill the Spanish but that the conspiracy was unsuccessful.

No great alliance was cemented at this gathering, but Mendoza and López returned to El Paso convinced that Texas should be settled. Meanwhile, the Suma, Patarabueye, and other natives along the Rio Grande rebelled. Conditions at El Paso continued to deteriorate, and the colonists sent petitions to the viceroy asking for permission to leave or to settle in Texas. Both Mendoza and López traveled to Mexico City and attempted to persuade the viceroy to authorize a settlement in the lands of the Jumanos and their allies. López wrote in his petition that he had made friends with seventy-five Indian nations; he described the great numbers of buffalo; he explained that he had learned the Jumano language and was able to preach in it. He intimated that an alliance with the Jumanos and a settlement in their country would be useful to prevent the hated French from gaining influence there. Nothing came of it.

Despite his failure to secure an alliance with the Spanish against the Apaches, Juan Sabeata continued to lead the Jumanos and their allies. He surfaces again in documents connected with the French in East Texas. The records of the La Salle party reveal that the "Choumans," allies of the Tejas, were "always at war with New Spain." The account describes Chouman ambassadors who demonstrate their knowledge of Christianity by kneeling, clasping their hands, and kissing the habit of a French priest. "One of them sketched me a painting that he had seen of a great lady, who was weeping because her son was upon a cross. He told us that the Spaniards butchered the Indians cruelly, and, finally, that if we would go with them, or give them guns, they could easily conquer them, because they were a cowardly race, who had no courage, and made people walk before them with a fan to refresh them in hot weather."

Sabeata and his allies were apparently playing a complex game, attempting to set these strange invaders against one another and strike a profitable alliance. Their home range, which encompassed much of the Trans-Pecos and the Edwards Plateau, extending eastward off the Balcones Escarpment and down the Pecos and the Devils River through Del Rio and Eagle Pass into the coastal plains of South and East Texas and northeastern Mexico, was being pressed on all sides—by Apache aggression from the northwest, by the Spanish from the west and the south, and by the French from the east. It is a pity that we do not know what Sabeata was telling the Apaches during this time. The picture that emerges, however fragmentary, is of a sophisticated foreign policy, orchestrated by the Jumanos and their Native confederacy, aimed at preserving their continued autonomy in a complex and highly mobile society based on foraging, hunting, and trade. Their homes and their whole way of life were under mortal threat. American anxieties over immigration pale somewhat in comparison.

By the time the Spanish had finally caught on to the presence of the French along the Gulf Coast, the La Salle expedition had ended in disaster; mutineers had murdered its leader. Those who remained at Garcitas Creek were massacred by natives in 1688. The Spanish did not know this, however, and they did their best to obtain intelligence through their friends the Jumanos, who were highly selective with their news and chose not to reveal the presence of a surviving Frenchman who had assumed leadership of a sizable *ranchería* not far north of the Rio Grande in South Texas. He was taken into custody by soldiers sent north from Monclova about the time General Juan Fernández de Retana was sent into Texas to investigate the reports of the French colony. Retana was in contact with Juan Sabeata, who eventually brought him word that the French settlement had been wiped out; he brought with him papers written in French and a drawing of a ship on parchment, all wrapped in a lace scarf.

In 1691, the Spanish established eight missions among the Caddos, whom the Spanish called Tejas, in a short abortive push into East Texas. Again Sabeata and his allies tried to persuade the Spanish to stay with the Jumanos. He was unsuccessful, and so were the Spanish. The Tejas were not friendly to the Spanish, and even though they were already farmers and slept in proper beds, they were not inclined to be converted and reduced.

Juan Sabeata disappears from the historical record after 1692. By 1693, there were rumors that the Jumanos were planning to attack

The River Road, looking west toward Presidio, Texas

Spanish soldiers, and that was the year the Spanish essentially abandoned Texas and withdrew to the Rio Grande. By 1716, when the
Spanish returned to Texas, the Jumanos were allied with their former
Apache enemies. Apache raids commenced on the new Spanish settlements along the San Antonio River and elsewhere as soon as they were
established. By the 1730s, the Jumanos had been absorbed into the
Apaches; thereafter, one sees references only to the Apaches Jumanes.

Whatever happened to the Ervipiame or the Yorica or the Bobole,
all of whom were associated with the Jumanos at one time or another?
Or the Gueiquesale, a large group of foraging people (also known as
Coetzale, Gueiquesal, Gueiquechali, Guericochal, Guisole, Huiso-
cal, Huyquetzal, Huicasique, Quetzal, and Quesale) who lived in the
southern Edwards Plateau and the canyon lands along the Pecos and
the Devils River? The enormous diversity of peoples with their mel-
lifluous and peculiar names who inhabited Texas and northern Mexico
came to an end as groups were reduced and lost their cultural identity.
Most of those who remained free either perished of disease, died in

battle, or were absorbed into greater Apachería. Soon the Comanches would arrive.

I was musing on the Jumanos, the Apaches, and the Comanches as I pulled out of Redford and continued eastward. I had rented a small cabin in Terlingua and hired a guide with a Jeep to take me into Fresno Canyon, on the east side of Big Bend Ranch State Park, to seek out Homer Wilson's old mercury mine. In front of me lay one of the most sublime stretches of roadway in North America, Texas Farm-to-Market Highway 170, known as the River Road. Winding through the many canyons that open onto the Rio Grande, FM 170 runs between a small ghost town called Candelaria, on the west, through Presidio and Redford to Terlingua and Study Butte in the east. The road sticks close to the meanders of the muddy Rio Grande for the most part, occasionally rising over the mountains to provide spectacular views of the river canyon. I stopped along a wide bend in the river to gaze at magnificent hoodoos made of volcanic tuff that stand like giant mushrooms or biomorphic sculptures fashioned out of wet sand. I hiked Closed Canyon, a stunning narrow slot canyon formed by a stream that cut right through a mesa on its way to the river. It was barely wider than the trail, with vertical walls more than a hundred feet high. The temperature at the trailhead was 102 degrees, according to a handy thermometer posted there; inside the canyon it dropped at least 15 degrees. Closed Canyon wasn't a good place to ride out a sudden thunderstorm, though, and I knew more rain was likely, so I was slightly nervous until I reemerged and continued on my way.

I pulled in to Terlingua and located my lodgings. My key was taped to the front door of the office of the local outfitter, Far Flung Outdoor Center. I found my cabin out back, a pleasant little casita with a red metal roof, one of several arranged in a compound surrounded by a desert garden, barbecue pits, and picnic tables. I was hot and tired from hiking and desperate for a shower. I stripped off my clothes and turned the shower knobs. A gasp of air and a few tablespoons of water trickled out. Then nothing. I tried the bathroom sink and the kitchenette. No water. I went outside and wandered around. I found an ice machine, and it was working, so that was something.

A few minutes later I was sitting on the back porch of my casita, watching an approaching line of thunderstorms over the mountains in Mexico, sipping a bourbon. I was filthy but content.

I walked next door to a Mexican restaurant and discovered that the entire town of Terlingua was without water. I ate tacos under a metal awning (and tried not to think about how the kitchen staff was washing their hands) as a wild desert storm blew in, then I walked slowly through the rain back to my casita, my boots crunching the gravel, my ears still ringing from the airborne liquid attack on the aluminum shelter. That was the closest I came to a shower. I opened the windows on both sides of the cabin and let the wind blow through my room. The next day, I learned that the problem was a broken pipe. Terlingua's water originates from a very deep well, and the water comes out of the ground hot, with a high sulfur content, so it's hard on the pipes and other equipment. Nobody I spoke to in Terlingua seemed all that surprised to be without running water for a day or two. Just part of life in the wildest little corner of the Big Bend.

In the morning I met up with my guide, Randy De La Fuente, and we climbed into a Jeep for our trip out to the Fresno mine. Our route took us over many miles of washed-out ranch roads, through several locked gates, into the back country of the state park. We wound our way up the great expanse of Fresno Canyon, bound by mesas and jagged hills topped with reddish outcroppings of rhyolite, a good sign of mercury, to what's called Buena Suerte, a mining village that grew up in the 1940s around the Fresno mine.

Homer Wilson bought his ranch in the Chisos Mountains from Harris Smith, who then bought a ranch and raised his family in Fresno Canyon. Homer and Smith went into business together in the 1930s, after Smith noticed that the red outcroppings on his ranch had the same shiny character that he had seen in the Terlingua mining district. Homer was a mining engineer by training, and Smith had access to the land and plenty of water in Fresno Creek. The two partners pooled their capital and began acquiring more land and filing mining claims. By 1937 they had moved from prospecting and testing to actual mining. They were making a profit by 1940. Because the partners had access to good water, they first built an experimental flotation mill to process the ore; then, after a few years, they moved the mining camp closer to their primary mine shaft and built a rotary furnace, houses for workers, a school, and a store. For a few years, the village even had a post office. Everything was hauled in over that rugged country. Labor was cheap in those days.

Now I was standing in the ruins of the mining community that Smith and Homer fostered. The old store, constructed out of flaggy limestone, was still standing, with a roof and windows and two long stone tables topped with massive cottonwood planks within. The walls were plastered with local bentonite clay, Randy told me, and he should know, because he used to work in a bentonite mine nearby. Nowadays bentonite, used for cat litter, he told me, as well as for drilling mud and cement, seems to be the only real mining action in the area. Randy said the park had done some restoration work on the old store and that the stable in Lajitas brings people in on horseback to camp. There was a picturesque cedar corral for horses, or for mules, which were used to draw ore up out of the mines, though I suspect it was constructed more recently, perhaps for the horseback tourists.

Other buildings of the village were slowly crumbling, their metal roofs peeling back under the force of decades of high winds. Most of the workers' quarters had been reduced to mere walls. They resembled something from ancient Greece or the cliff dwellings of Mesa Verde. In other structures, piles of slowly corroding roofing material provided good homes for rattlesnakes. Aside from crickets and a few scurrying lizards, the only visible inhabitants of Buena Suerte were creosote bushes and ocotillo.

At one point Randy pointed out a waxy candelilla plant, which has long been used in wax camps in the Big Bend and throughout northern Mexico. Wax production was big business. In 1923, a wax camp here in Fresno Canyon reportedly produced $100,000 worth of wax. Wax smuggling was a big business as well, because it was illegal to export wax from Mexico, though perfectly legal to bring it into the United States. One burro could carry up to $200 worth of wax, and sometimes trains of a hundred or more would come across the Rio Grande near Boquillas. Homer might have been in the wrong line of work.

About a mile from the village we came to the ruins of the processing facility, where the cinnabar ore was crushed into pebbles and then heated in the rotary furnace to separate the mercury from the rock

Fresno mine, Buena Suerte, Texas

waste. Collapsed ventilation stacks, mysterious tubes, ducts, and the old rotating kiln itself stood their ground against the encroachment of mesquite and huisache bushes. Old diesel generators, pumps, and other abandoned equipment littered the area. A bright yellow tractor rusted near an overturned Buick and the remains of a 1940s pickup.

Homer died at his ranch in the Chisos Mountains in July 1943. Harris Smith abandoned the mining operations a year later. Seems he and Bergine Wilson didn't get along. Other individuals and mining companies dabbled with the Fresno claim over the years, but prices were never again high enough to justify full-scale production. The primary use of the mercury had been for munitions, and in times of peace the market would collapse. Eventually, bomb technology changed, and the mercury wasn't needed anymore. Buena Suerte was abandoned and so was Terlingua, remote and obsolete outposts of the military-industrial complex. Years later, Terlingua rose again from the ashes of a world-famous chili cook-off.

Towering over the abandoned village of Buena Suerte was a red-capped mesa, and behind that mountain was the Fresno mine. A long trench, once the cradle of a rail track, ran up to the shaft's entrance, which had partially collapsed. Along the hill to the right of the main shaft other shafts were visible. They were covered by wire mesh, apparently to prevent errant hikers and history buffs from falling in. One elevator shaft remained, capped with a steel grate and a rotting timber structure. I peered into the darkness. I don't know what I hoped to glimpse down there.

# CHAPTER 3

# THE TEXAS ROAD

No one in my immediate family could tell me very much about how or when or why our ancestors originally came to Texas, so I went in search of my great-great-great-grandfather Perry Wilson, father of T.A., grandfather of Homer and Earl, who came to Texas from Missouri with his young bride, Welmett, in 1854.

Perry was a wanderer, a restless cattleman and Indian fighter who followed the southern road to California more than once. For decades he and his brother Levi drifted their cattle along the western margins of Anglo Texas, first along the Red River in northwest Texas and later on the Devils River and points south and west. I became obsessed with this enigmatic ancestor. He left no letters or diaries that I ever found. Property records, passing references in oral histories, and a few entries in old archives were the only written traces of his passage through history. Yet he seemed in some indefinable way to hold the answers to my questions. In time, I logged thousands of miles as I tracked his movements along the western border and beyond.

My grandmother's cousin Patricia, the one who had grown up in the Big Bend, was the family historian and genealogist. Everyone kept telling me that I needed to talk to Patricia about the Wilsons. Patricia lived in a suburb of Kansas City called Prairie Village.

I arrived in Missouri on a dreary late January day, dreaming vaguely of barbecue and the commerce of the prairies. If I wanted to understand Perry Wilson, and indeed early Texas in general, I needed to understand Missouri, because in the middle of the nineteenth century, this corner of Missouri was border country, the primary staging area for western migration.

All the trails—the Oregon Trail, the California Trail, the Santa Fe Trail, the Butterfield Stage, the Texas Road—originated in western Missouri. Liberty, Independence, Smithville, Fort Leavenworth, Weston, Westport. I read Josiah Gregg's *Commerce of the Prairies*, Mark Twain's *Roughing It*, *The Oregon Trail* by Francis Parkman, *With the Border Ruffians* by R. W. Williams, and Washington Irving's *Tour on the Prairies*. I read Bernard DeVoto's *Year of Decision: 1846* and *Annals of Platte County, Missouri, from Its Exploration down to June 1, 1897: With Genealogies of Its Noted Families, and Sketches of Its Pioneers and Distinguished People*, by William McClung Paxton, who opened his learned volume with a discussion of what he called the "evidence of a prehistoric race" that had inhabited the neighborhood. Paxton did not seem to think these vanished people were Indians, because, he said, they made houses in the Egyptian style, with bricks. By the time President Thomas Jefferson purchased the Louisiana Territory from Napoleon, and Captain Meriwether Lewis and Lieutenant William Clark passed through with their Corps of Discovery, the settlement of Missouri had been under way for half a century, financed largely by the fur trade. French influence was strong. Among such traders was the Chouteau family, who established the Missouri Fur Company and lent their names to nature trails and highway rest stops throughout Missouri, Kansas, and Oklahoma.

Missouri was a rough neighborhood, outlaw country, swarming with a wild mixture of every conceivable American frontiersman and borderlander: trappers and fur traders and mountain men and pioneers, Indians and half-breeds wearing blankets, peddlers and prospectors, gamblers, whores, politicians, bankers, and land speculators. There were foreigners and journalists and other tourists, explorers, Mormons, boatmen, settlers, bushwhackers, claim jumpers, privateers and thieves and hunters, slaves and freemen and runaways.

The earliest American settlers, out of Kentucky and Tennessee, came the hard way, by wagon. The pioneers fashioned rude cabins from round logs, pointed with mud and floored with split logs called puncheons. Clapboards were a luxury. Once sawmills were built and lumber was available, log cabins were succeeded by proper houses, with chimneys of native stone and plank floors. Stoves eventually came up the river to warm the houses. Farmers avoided the prairie and set about clearing woods and forests, preferring to stay near the streams and minor tributaries, in the uplands. Land was cleared by felling smaller trees, which were cut for fence rails; larger trees were girdled. Once they rotted, they were rolled and burned, sometimes with rocks to make lime, sometimes with earth to make charcoal. Timber along the river was sold to the steamers, who would stop at a convenient riverside woodpile, load up with fuel, leave a note, and settle up later. Once corn and other grains were planted, quail and prairie fowl followed. Otters and minks, beavers and muskrats, lurked in the rushes along the rivers. Perch and catfish and buffalo fish, bass and campbellites, were found in great numbers; fishermen could stand by the falls and spear the fish with sharp sticks. The spawning of the fish was interrupted by the water mills, which settlers built so they might have flour, and whose wheels sometimes were jammed by the fish, but as years passed, the number of fish dropped off.

Rattlesnakes and blacksnakes plagued the homesteaders. One pioneer told a story of sleeping in a little mud-daubed cabin, the cracks covered inside with clapboards, that he had built in order to secure his preferment claim to the land. He made himself a bed with four poles and some trestles covered with hazel brush. In the middle of the night a noise behind the clapboards awakened him, and he lit his candle. Expecting to find rats, he pried back a board, and two entwined blacksnakes fell out, landing in his bed. He crushed their heads with a pole, grabbed an ax, and started peeling off other boards. His walls were infested with snakes.

Game was more common on the west bank of the Missouri. Bears were few, though wolves would cross the frozen river during the winter in large numbers to feast on rabbits. "They did little harm," wrote a witness, "but their dismal howling made the night hideous. Though their presence was unknown to the sleeping family, the morning disclosed their tracks at their very door." Deer declined as the number of settlers rose. Hunters would find bare spots in the prairie where the deer would lick for salt. They'd set up blinds on poles, twenty feet high, and lie in wait to assassinate their salt-craving prey.

Canoes, pirogues, bull boats, Mackinaws, and keelboats populated the rivers, all carrying their loads of peltries and supplies. Prior to the advent of the steamer, the river settlements along the Mississippi and up the Missouri were supplied largely by keelboat, attended at docks and levees by boatmen, who were known for their red shirts and blue jackets. They wore leather caps, woolen trousers, and stiff-backed high Suwarrow boots. The first steamboat to dock at the St. Louis levee, in 1817, was appropriately named the *Zebulon M. Pike*. The steamers began to make their way up the treacherous Missouri in 1819. One, the *Jefferson*, sank that first year. They were plagued by mechanical problems, sprang leaks, blew out pistons, ran aground on shoals and sandbars. They hit *snags*, which were trees caught on shoals, lying in wait, traps for the unwary steam captain with his tight pants, high boots, and ruffled shirt. *Planters* were what boatmen called trees standing on the bottom of the river. Worse were the *sawyers*, submerged trees that floated free, appearing and disappearing like phantoms.

By 1825 one or two steamers would reach Liberty landing every season, and in 1827 Colonel Henry Leavenworth and his Third Infantry landed there, having been charged with the task of establishing a permanent military cantonment near the mouth of the Little Platte River. Because there was no suitable place on the left bank of the Missouri, Leavenworth established the fort on the west side, in the Rattlesnake Hills. Thereafter the farmers of the neighboring counties profited by supplying the soldiers based in the cantonment of Leavenworth with beef, bacon, lard, firewood, and vegetables. A pioneer named Zadock Martin in 1828 was given authorization to settle at Platte Falls and maintain a ferry there and one across the Missouri. He came out of Kentucky with his stalwart sons and his Negro slaves and built a two-room log house on the eastern bluff above the Platte, where he and his handsome wife and three pretty daughters kept a saloon. No one lived within fifteen miles, but all who traveled west on the military road to Leavenworth and back were happy to have it there, a bright light along a dark road.

Martin was tall and brawny and well made to be a ferryman and tavern keeper. He wore a broad hat and carried a stout hickory walking stick and with his bright eyes and loud voice commanded respect from all men. He grew corn and maintained a sugar camp and cut his hay on the prairie. His cattle grazed the fertile bottomlands along the Missouri, and his hogs wandered the woods, feeding on abundant acorns, pecans, and hickory nuts. "His hog killing was done with dogs and guns," Paxton tells us. "When pork was wanted, he shouldered his rifle, called his dogs, and went game-hunting." Nine years after establishing his ferries, Martin built a large dam and a mill above the Platte Falls. The next year he acquired a pair of French millstones, which he shipped up the river. Martin used oxen to do his hauling and plowing. His cattle were primitive and fed on native grasses at night after their hauling and grinding; he possessed a buffalo steer that he took when it was a calf and raised with his herd; his hogs were called wind-splitters, and their fat, it was said, yielded oil instead of lard. Years later, when towns and counties were well established and municipal government had descended on that wild territory, the local worthies of Weston, then a thriving river port, decreed that a free ferry across the river be established. Martin lost a good business, and his lawsuit of protest went nowhere. *Annals of Platte County* fails to mention whose nephew or cousin was hired to maintain the new public utility.

Patricia and her husband, Grant, were kind and generous with their curious young cousin who came begging for family lore. Over the course of many decades, Patricia had pieced together an impressive genealogy of the Wilson line, which intertwines with other names such as Adamson, Routh, Covey, Williams, Nelson, and Crain. For years she published a genealogical newsletter, *The Wilson/Adamson Links*, in which she dutifully reported the discoveries she made in dusty basements of courthouses across the old border South. Grant did the same for the Clothier family, and like Patricia he published a family memoir, in his case about pioneer ancestors in Kansas. The Wilsons seem not to have left much in writing; they were practical people who farmed or raised livestock; at least one branch of the family were blacksmiths. Property records are the most prolific evidence of their passage through history.

In 1829 or 1830, William Wilson and his wife, Esther, came up the Missouri River from Tennessee and got off the boat in Bluffton, which was settled in 1816 by families from Virginia, Tennessee, and Kentucky. Or perhaps they traveled by wagon, like the earliest settlers of Ray and Clay Counties, who came in trains up the left bank of the Missouri, groups of families bound together by kinship and ambition, hauling

Bridges over the Missouri River, Kansas City

their precious keepsakes and china, with barrels of salt and flour and meat on the hoof. The river would have been the faster road. Peddlers had long come down the wagon road or in keelboats, hauling their carts of dry goods; now on the steamers came heavy cargo in large quantities: bolts of cloth in calico, gingham, and cotton checks; tin cups, iron spoons, coffeepots, spools of thread and paper and pins; horn buttons, cakes of soap, ribbons, boxes of pepper, tablecloths, knives and forks and razors and sausage stuffers, along with neckerchiefs, hose, boots and shoes, wax dolls, oysters canned in milk, bottles of pickles, kegs of whiskey, hammers and saws and firearms and Jew's harps.

Following the trails of pioneers and settlers came wave after wave of entrepreneurs, artisans such as blacksmiths and cobblers and tailors as well as preachers, medicine men, and traveling photographers, not to mention gamblers, bankers, highwaymen, and whores. The Santa Fe Trail was outfitted first at Franklin, Missouri; then, as the river began to eat away at the banks, the trailhead moved across the river to Boonville, which saved a ferry ride. From a pathetic co-location of huts, Boonville grew into a thriving den of vice. The levee at Boonville became a clearinghouse as muddy clerks received the goods from the *riverains* and deckhands—enormous hogsheads of sugar orbited by bees and plundered by small boys wielding slender spoons whittled from thin reeds, which they inserted, like great featherless hummingbirds, through triangular openings meant to ventilate the great barrels.

Bluffton was the county seat for seven years, and the local citizenry built a fort on the bluff because they were expecting an Indian attack. The Missouri Indians had mostly died out by that time, ravaged with diseases caught from trappers, and the Kansa, who still inhabited the area when Lewis and Clark passed through, had departed as well. No doubt it was the Osage who worried them. Bluffton was eventually abandoned after the river altered its course, leaving in its trace an oxbow lake.

By the middle of the 1840s, hundreds of steamers were landing every year at the major river ports; it became fashionable to take evening cruises on the most sumptuous of them, known as packets. Large side-wheelers lit up the murky night, crowded with dancers and music played by brass bands. They bore names such as *Clara, Alert, Pocahontas No. 1, Cumberland Valley, Oceana,* and *Elk.*

Indians often took passage, such as when a party of Sioux, Cheyenne, Arapaho, Crow, and Snake boarded the fireboat *Clara* in Westport, later known as Kansas City, so that they might walk on the waters to their audience with President Fillmore. A spring menu of the *Clara* offered calf-head soup, roast beef with gravy sauce, roast mutton with chili sauce; roast chicken and pork were both available with a ketchup sauce. Boiled ham, corned beef, mutton, tongue, and codfish were also offered, the last "ala Rain Egg Sauce." Gooseberry pie, rhubarb pie, sago pudding, and blancmange were all available for dessert, as well as selections of Madeira, sherry, port, claret, and malt liquors (quarts of London porter, "do do pints," and Tennent's Scotch Ale). Champagne was available in Heidsieck quarts, "Do pints," "Irroy Cabinet Wine," and "Do do do pints." A note at the bottom of the menu warned that "Gentlemen ordering Wine from the Bar without designating the kind or price, will be furnished with Madeira at two dollars per bottle."

Many steamboats sank. The *Iowa* sank after it hit a snag. The *Otoe* suffered various mishaps, sank and was raised, and sank again; then, in 1837, its boiler blew up in St. Louis while parked at the levee; ten people died; four months later it sank forever at Euphrasie Bend. Steamboat races were held at Jefferson City in 1838; the *Edna* blew up in 1840, killing fifty-five German immigrants.

Esther Wilson was born an Adamson, and other Adamsons traveled with her and William. The Wilsons and the Adamsons had come together, in that generation, in northeastern Tennessee, among a circle of Quakers who met in silence at a place called Lost Creek, in Jefferson County, not far northeast from what is now Knoxville. William's Wilsons came from Grainger County and before that were in North Carolina, and so too did the Adamsons come out of North Carolina and like the Wilsons were previously in Bucks County, Pennsylvania, and western New Jersey, along with the Rouths and other families in our lineage. Patricia believes that William and Esther were married at the Lost Creek church, though records from that period are spotty and their names do not appear on the rolls. We know Esther's father was a member of the local Meeting, but I find no evidence that the Wilsons were members of the Society of Friends, and it could be that in that first union of Wilson and Adamson, two great immigrant streams from the British Isles, the Quakers and the Scots-Irish, come together.

Another Adamson genealogist compiled a volume titled *Lost Creek Memories*, which records the names and dates of dozens of branching lineages. I found a copy in the New York Public Library. A curious code accompanies the lists. Entries include notations such as "con," "dis," "ltm," "mbr," "mcd," and "mou," which signify, in order, "condemned," "disowned," "leave to marry," "member," "married contrary to discipline," and "married outside of unity." Marriage regulations were strict among the Society of Friends, as were social restrictions. In those days many sons were disowned for pursuing the wrong vocation or the wrong wench. A son or daughter who married a Methodist or a Baptist had turned away from the way of truth and was lost to the community, cast out of the Meeting.

The Wilsons might have been Quakers or Quaker sympathizers

Lost Creek Quaker Church, New Market, Tennessee

or the descendants of English borderers or Lowland Scots or Ulster Orangemen. Whatever their lineage, they married into the Adamsons, who were undoubtedly Quakers, at least until then. When the Adamsons and Wilsons left Tennessee for Missouri, they seem also to have abandoned the Friends, though their austere folkways and fierce moralism left an imprint that can still be felt in their descendants.

Patricia and Grant gave me a tour of the ancestral Wilson properties in Missouri. I piloted their car while Patricia navigated and Grant, in the backseat, made jokes about heaven. We drove out of Prairie Village, north through Kansas City across the river into Missouri and east on Missouri Highway 210 through empty plowed fields patchworking the broad fertile floodplain of the Missouri River. We stopped briefly in a hamlet called Orrick, where I admired the tiny brick city hall, an array of hulking grain elevators, and the picturesque remnants of the RRICK FARM SERVICE, whose sign had gone to rust and lost its initial *O*. We drove on, passing a floral cross memorializing someone named

Bubba who met his end on that road, to Bluffton, Missouri, which no longer exists, outside Camden, and read the historical marker, found next to some corrugated-aluminum sheds and two squat grain storage buildings. The marker said that the town was founded in 1816 by families from Virginia, Kentucky, and Tennessee and that Meaders Vanderpool founded the county's first school in 1819, the same year the first steamboat ascended the Missouri River. A train sat idle on a sidetrack, loaded with farm equipment. The river meandered several miles to our south, across a barren field. I didn't see any bluffs.

Patricia, who wasn't at all shy, rolled down her window as we wandered around the town of Richmond and asked a scruffy young man who was wearing a dirty wifebeater and torn jeans, his belly poking out from under his shirt as he walked, where we could get a good sandwich. He directed us to his favorite diner, which to my relief was closed, because from the outside it didn't look very appealing. We had passed another place up the road, and its lot was full of cars, so we stopped there. We were hunting for a small farm that William and Esther Wilson had owned in the 1830s, and Patricia was worried about finding her landmark, a small white church on a hill. She asked the chubby blond waitress, who knew it immediately. Patricia was skeptical, because you can't see the church from the road, but the waitress said, "Yes, that's exactly right." She and her friends used to drive up that steep hill to the little church when she was in high school. They would hang out in the boneyard on Halloween.

She remembered the road being pretty bad, and I imagined the sorts of things I would have done on a lonely hill, late at night, in a graveyard, when I was that age. The menu would have included alcohol and much more. The waitress directed us toward Excelsior Springs and said the turnoff for the church would be about five miles up the road. Her directions were perfect. The sign said, TODD'S CHAPEL. We parked near the quaint white clapboard chapel and admired its simplicity: a sharply peaked roof and even sets of lancet windows, four on each long side and one by the front door.

I hiked down a rutted double-track road that plunged off the back of Todd's Hill, climbed over a fence, and stood in a field that William Wilson owned until about 1830. It was a stock field, well trod and fertilized by cattle, stretching over a modest bulge at the base of the much steeper hill, surrounded by scrubby trees at the fence line. Dry straw-

Site of William Wilson's farm, near Todd's Hill,
outside Richmond, Missouri

colored grass crunched beneath my feet. Beyond the trees lay almost
identical fields and then another hill. Possibly William and Esther and
young Perry had lived on this property, after clearing it by hand and
burning the timber to make charcoal or lye, and attended the nearby
church, which to judge from the dates on the grave markers was standing even then. Patricia told me that somebody's Wilson sister was buried there, but I didn't find the grave. Probably they were too far from
the river to have sold the timber to the riverboats. I lingered in the old
field for a time, listening to the ugly sound of a lonely bird, and tried
to feel the weight of nearly two centuries of history on that land. All I
could imagine was the weight of 182 years' worth of cow shit.

In 1836, under pressure from white settlers, the Ioway Indians, along
with the Sac and the Fox, agreed to sell their lands, which lay west of
the Platte River and east of the Missouri, opening more than three

thousand square miles to development. The Platte Purchase signaled the unraveling of the Missouri Compromise. The Wilsons and the Adamsons were attracted by the new prospects and moved west, settling first in the area of New Market, named for their old Tennessee home, in what became Platte County, then in Weston, which was then one of the busiest ports on a busy river. Following Patricia's directions, I drove through charming hills splattered with farms, some with showy white fences fashioned of split rails intended, perhaps, to evoke Kentucky horse country. Other nearby residents decorated their properties with cast-off farm machinery and less than picturesque household appliances. We pulled off on a dirt road and peered at a parcel that once belonged to Simon Wilson, Perry's uncle. I got out and took a photograph of a bare stubbly field in gray light, bounded by tree-grown fence lines serving as windbreaks. In the distance I could see the peaks of an industrial facility of some kind. Returning to the macadam and turning north, I soon discovered that a strip mine and processing plant had sprouted atop the Wilson farm.

One fine April day a few months later I returned to New Market. The fields had sprouted up green with new growth, and leafy trees obscured the views between them, but there was no hiding that strip mine. A large yellow apparatus, a conveyor belt it seemed, stretched across the highway to transport material from the plant to great uniform piles on the west side of the road. I could hear the grinding of machinery crushing its material. I was alone this time, so nothing prevented me from pulling in to the plant's parking lot and taking photographs. Apparently, some workers grew alarmed at my curiosity and alerted their superiors. Out strode a striking fellow named Michael Puffinbarger. He was a quality-control engineer, and he told me all about his plant. Puffinbarger and his colleagues were mining the Weston shale and crushing the ore down to what he called a four-inch top size. Then they put it all in a big rotary kiln, 175 feet long by 11 feet in diameter, and fired that crushed gray Weston shale at twenty-two hundred degrees Fahrenheit for about an hour. What came out at the end was Haydite, an expanded shale used as a lightweight substitute for limestone in making concrete and asphalt. Haydite was named for Stephen J. Hayde, who developed the process in the early 1900s in Kansas City, and this plant was built on the former Wilson farm more than sixty years ago.

I stood listening politely, genuinely interested in what the friendly Mr. Puffinbarger was telling me about his product, but really I couldn't get over his appearance. His hair and scalp were caked with a dark black material. I couldn't tell whether it was dust from the plant or if he had smeared shoe polish or some really old Just for Men black dye all over his hair. The stuff was plastered all over his scalp, and his hair was inky black. He was a large man, wearing a bright red T-shirt and blue jeans, with a ruddy face, a healthy beer belly, and a small tobacco stain near the corner of his mouth. I left New Market feeling rather well informed about the usefulness of Haydite and proud to know that the substrate of an ancestral homestead was saving taxpayers money and keeping motorists safe throughout Missouri, Kansas, and Nebraska.

I spent a few days exploring northwest Missouri. Rolling hills and pretty old fields alternated with gigantic mown lawns surrounded by wrought-iron steel pickets and rock pillars. Bored cattle stood idly swishing their tails at flies in muddy old stock ponds of captured rainwater. Drowning traps for careless schoolchildren. A hobby farm with

Simon Wilson's former farm, New Market, Missouri

longhorn cattle flew the rattlesnake "Don't Tread on Me" flag on a low hill. The country looked productive and fertile, though little real agricultural production was in evidence. I lingered at Weston Bend State Park and learned about the region's bygone tobacco industry as dozens of carpenter bees burrowed into the weathered boards of a grand old barn.

On one of our drives Patricia and Grant took me to Liberty, where they lived during the 1970s and raised their children. We drove up a tall hill to see their beautiful old house, which now shared its yard with a monstrous rusty hulk of a water tower more than three times its height. A Hallmark cards shipping facility had come to town, and the city decided that the Clothiers' yard was the perfect place for a new tower, which for some mysterious reason was required by the new plant. The Clothiers fought the condemnation all the way to the Missouri Supreme Court. When they lost their case, Patricia took out an ad in the paper putting the house up for sale, and it was bought by the attorney who had represented the opposing party in their lawsuit. He apparently didn't mind sharing his yard with a gigantic steel spider just thirty-nine feet away.

In the evening I sat with Patricia and Grant and watched Fox News. Grant asked me with a sly grin if I thought it was true that Obama hated America: "You don't think he's a dedicated Marxist?" We talked about the Wilsons and Perry's trips to California, and Patricia said that she thought he might have gone around the cape on one of his trips. They discovered gold in 1848, she said, and he got married in 1854, so you've got six years in there. Grant said he saw a program on television the other night, *Nova* or something; it showed huge mountains with glaciers, and fifty-foot waves off Tierra del Fuego. They don't have any big land predators down there, he said, but in the ocean they have orca whales.

I said I thought you'd have to be crazy to go down there in a ship when you could cross the isthmus. "They've got no predators," Grant said, chuckling in his deep gravelly voice, "in heaven."

When we sat down for dinner, Grant gave one of his wonderful blessings. "Father, we thank you for the night of rest. We're grateful for the privilege of this day. And we're so thankful for the fellowship with Roger. We pray, Father, you'll be with him as he travels. And with his family. We thank you now for this food, and we pray for the one who's prepared it, for her health and well-being. We ask, Father, that you watch over and keep our loved ones. We pray that you will be with your people everywhere. Help us to choose wisely those who would lead us, and we pray for the well-being of those who defend us. Guide us today and keep us, we pray. In Christ's name, Amen."

At dinner we talked about the civil unrest of the 1840s. It wasn't yet the period we call Bleeding Kansas, but there was plenty of bloodshed. The Kansas-Missouri border country, even before the arrival of Old John Brown, was a rough territory in those days, with pro-slavery border ruffians marauding through the countryside and civil unrest over the Mormon question. In Liberty, I came across a stately antebellum residence, recently pressed into service as a frat house, that once belonged to Alexander William Doniphan, a hero of the Mexican War. During the 1838 Mormon War, the occasion of the famous extermination order of Missouri's governor, Lilburn Boggs, Doniphan refused to execute the prophet Joseph Smith after a court-martial found him guilty of treason. Smith was locked up for five months in the Liberty Jail, which has now been reconstructed inside a museum by the Latter-day Saints, before escaping to Illinois, where he was eventually murdered.

In the historic town of Weston, where William Wilson was slain by a mob in 1841, the former port long since abandoned by the fickle Missouri, I stood where the docks would have been, next to a railroad track at the edge of the quaint downtown, gazing out into the alluvial plain, trying to guess how many miles away the river flowed. I wondered about the mob that had taken poor William's life. Perhaps he was mistaken for a Mormon.

In 1849, my great-great-great-grandfather Perry Wilson made his first trip to California. He was the child of Quakers who had fallen away from the Truth; raised on a farm in a frontier society, he was surrounded by a clan of relatives who were ambitious and responsible members of their communities. His uncle Jacob Adamson was among the founders of New Market and was elected justice of the peace in Green township on June 22, 1839, and we find Larkin Adamson's name listed among the first citizens of Weston. Yet the call of the West had brought his clan to Missouri from Tennessee, and before that from North Carolina, Pennsylvania, and New Jersey. No one can ever know exactly what brought his ancestors to the colonies. They were restless people, and soon even Larkin and Jacob would pull stakes and move on.

Perry's family never settled for long, though it's likely he knew John Strode Brasfield, born in Clark County, Kentucky, in 1825, who came with his family to Platte in 1838 and settled in the Great Bear Rough along Todd's Creek, not far from Todd's Hill and the Wilsons' farm. Perry and John were five years apart, and their lives followed similar paths. As a child Brasfield caught four bear cubs and walked three miles to attend school. He raised a sow and a litter of pigs and sold them at a profit of two dollars. He purchased a fiddle. Later he borrowed money from his family's old slave Aleck and bought four calves, which he broke and used as oxen. In 1842, John signed on as a cook and hunter for a party of traders and went to Santa Fe. He encountered Comanches and was nearly captured and made it home with a mule and fifty-five dollars in his pocket.

Then came the news from Sutter's Mill, and in the spring of 1849 John and his brother William and three friends set off to California to make their fortunes. They almost perished in the Humboldt Desert, and one of his companions went mad with thirst, but they made it through and spent the winter in Hangtown, a mining camp near Coloma that was known for its lynchings. Food was dear in the goldfields, and men grew as rich trading in groceries as they did from digging, with far less effort. Potatoes went for a dollar a pound and eggs for that much apiece. A dozen eggs brought the same as the twelve hundred pounds of young pork John had raised in Missouri. After clearing fifteen hundred dollars in the mines, John engaged in the mercantile trade and made a great profit in San Francisco. His brother William died, perhaps of cholera, and John went home to Platte, discouraged.

Another lapsed Quaker named Charles Pancoast set out from New Jersey in 1840, the year before Perry was orphaned by that mob, and made his way to Missouri. Years later he wrote down his adventures, and through his eyes we can see the world Perry Wilson inhabited. Pancoast traveled by rail and mule-drawn packet boat, then took the steamer *Boston* down the Ohio to Cincinnati and from there took a western boat to St. Louis. Although the waters were often shallow, the great boats were able to jump sandbars by running full steam, bucking and twisting until clearing the obstacle. A young pharmacist out to make his fortune in the drug trade, Pancoast was naive and trusting and soon fell victim to sharpers. He went bust and started anew, traveled up and down the Missouri and the Mississippi and even the Osage on his mercantile adventures, narrowly escaping a Mormon mob at the baptismal pool in Nauvoo, Illinois. Pistol shots were exchanged, and stones were flung, but no one perished.

Practically all business activity at that time was speculative: Gamblers made their bets with cards and dice, and so with the tools of their trade did slave traders, farmers and planters, merchants and boatmen. Every transaction was a wager, because credit was uncertain and the exchange value of banknotes was in constant fluctuation, with notes from the State Bank of Illinois or perhaps the Shawneetown Bank of Illinois being discounted against those of the Dubuque Bank of Iowa, or some other wildcat bank, at one time or another. Bad money and good money were engaged in a constant war of depreciation.

Religion itself was closely allied with commerce. Mormons tended to keep to themselves, nursing their grudges and preparing their exodus, and they had a reputation for sharp, some might say dishonest, trading. Hard-shell Baptists, Campbellites, and Presbyterians all preached the dogma of the heaven-born institution, declaring both love and slavery to be divine. Methodists tended to waver on that point. Morals were said to be poor in Ray County, home to Jesse James and other wild children who were raised on farms by pioneer wives, fed from the land. Many had never seen a town or store or even the Missouri River. Regulators and "slickers" and kindred vigilante groups roamed the counties with their bowie knives. Townspeople had no theaters, but they were able to make a fair sound with the banjo, mouth organ, fife, or tambourine.

After settling for a time in Warsaw, a pro-slavery township that was nonetheless burned by rebel mobs in 1862, Pancoast sold his shop and became a partner in a steamboat in 1846, moving freight up the shallow Osage. He became a prolific river pilot and freight speculator. Small fortunes could be made and lost in the course of a single run. On one trip he carried a thousand barrels of pork at a dollar per barrel from Weston to an army warehouse in St. Louis; upon arrival, an officer came aboard and shipped it back to Fort Leavenworth for $1.25, thus shipping one load of pork twelve hundred miles for a net distance of five. Pancoast and his partner cleared $2,000 on the trip.

In the spring of 1849, when America's argonauts began massing in Missouri, preparing their wagon trains for the long overland journey to the goldfields, Pancoast, broke again, resolved to go with them. After a harrowing trip up the river to St. Joseph aboard a cholera boat laden with westering emigrants, Pancoast joined a ragged group of Peoria pioneers and left Fort Leavenworth in late April as part of a train of forty-four wagons, two hundred men from many different states and countries, together with women and children and thousands of animals. Among the party were preachers, doctors, lawyers, druggists, pilots, farmers, Mexican War veterans and West Point graduates, mechanics, farmers, laborers, and sailors. It's possible that Jacob Adamson and Perry Wilson were among them. A Millerite preacher used the Sabbath to undermine the gold fever, sending more than one man homeward, only to be killed by Indians on the plains. One gold seeker weighed three hundred pounds when they set out; he was not so heavy when they arrived in California.

By the end of the first day the train had already passed through villages of Wyandot and Delaware Indians, who raised scrawny pigs and ponies and scratched at the prairie to bring forth a few vegetables. The prairie was lovely in spring, a gently rolling landscape of flowing grass cut by gentle streams and small hollows filled with rocks and woods. The argonauts lunched on antelope and jackrabbits and paid $2.50 a wagon to a ferryman on the Kansas River who was making his fortune off Santa Fe traders, the U.S. Army, and the argonauts. The Mexican War had brought him very good business indeed. Pottawatomie Indians might appear before them suddenly, stepping forth casually from the tall grass, curious about their purposes. They came upon graves of men they had met in Missouri just a few days before, a pair of consumptives hoping to find a healthier climate in the West.

At Council Grove they met degenerate white men as well as Delaware and Wyandot, but also fierce, proud Pawnee with painted faces, nose and ear rings, adorned with bear and wolf teeth.

As a guide the company hired a mountain man named James

Kirker, giving him a good horse and a fifty-dollar deposit, with a hundred dollars to come when they arrived in California. Kirker persuaded his clients to follow the southern route, which dropped south along the Rio Grande from Santa Fe and westward along the Gila River, claiming he had taken the shorter northern trail with John C. Frémont and that water and grass would be a problem for so large a train. He was probably lying, for there's no evidence he ever traveled with the Pathfinder or that he had taken that route. He would not have been much of a guide on a trail he had not traveled, and men naturally stuck to the trails they knew. The same was no doubt true for Perry, and we know he took the southern route in 1858 and again thirty years later. Kirker had spent decades in New Mexico and northern Mexico, so he knew that southwestern country well. He could track errant livestock at a gallop and was an experienced Indian fighter, but he was not necessarily an asset to the forty-niners, as they soon discovered.

According to custom, the members of the company elected a captain and a lieutenant, and they passed rules requiring men to walk if they were able instead of riding in a wagon, in order to preserve the teams of mules and horses and oxen. Walking also conveyed the benefits of exercise and good health. At night they made a circle with the wagons and drove the cattle and other livestock inside for protection. Cattle guards were named and camp guards, and so they passed along the prairie, usually without incident. Indians were met occasionally; small bands who would appear suddenly and seek to trade. Buffalo were seen as they passed westward, and they were pursued with a great galloping, and some were shot by these amateur pioneers and eaten with enjoyment. Only Kirker was experienced with prairie life, and on the first buffalo chase one of the greenhorns managed to put a rifle ball through his own shoulder; another shot his horse through the neck. One day, in the vicinity of a stream known as Cow Creek, one of perhaps ten thousand so named in the American West, the pioneers spotted a row of poles from which a number of caps dangled in the breeze. Upon closer inspection, the caps turned out to be scalps, left by Pawnee after a battle with Arapaho and Cheyenne.

The identity of the scalps was revealed several days later when they came upon an army of fifteen hundred Arapaho and Cheyenne warriors traveling east to fight the Pawnee. The pioneers were terrified at the spectacle of the warriors and prepared for battle. Fortunately, Kirker was there to advise the pioneers, and he cautioned them not to fire; the Indians were carrying peace blankets. A meeting was arranged, and the Indians' leading men assembled; all cried out "Kirker!" when the old scalper let himself be seen. He was among the most hated of all white men.

James "Don Santiago" Kirker was born in Antrim, north of Belfast, Northern Ireland, on December 2, 1793, into a family of refugee Lowlanders from the borderlands of southern Scotland. The Kirkers, like many of their fellow borderers, had suffered under both the English and the Highlanders, prey to rustlers and reivers as well as soldiers, and their migration was part of that great eighteenth-century movement of the Scots-Irish, as we call them, over the sea to America. Kirker left his family's grocery business in Northern Ireland at age sixteen to avoid the British draft and arrived in New York harbor in 1810. He took a familiar job as a grocery clerk but soon sailed aboard the *Black Joke*, a privateer, during the War of 1812. Upon the conclusion of the war, Kirker returned to find his old employer dead, so he married his boss's pregnant young widow. More Kirkers arrived from Ireland, and soon James left his wife and children for the West, descending the Ohio and arriving in St. Louis by 1817. He went to work for the McKnights, an Irish family with interests across the western and Spanish borderlands.

Within a few years, Kirker established his own business, first as a grocer and then in partnership with the McKnights in the Santa Fe trade. Kirker's interests soon expanded into the fur trade, and he was spending most of his time trapping in New Mexico, though he would occasionally reappear in Missouri on business. In 1826, he showed up at Fort Osage with a young Kit Carson, headed for Mexico. He passed through Santa Fe, turned south, and soon found himself in Apache country, trapping along the Gila River and establishing his headquarters at the copper mines, owned by Robert McKnight, of Santa Rita del Cobre, about fifty miles west of the Rio Grande. The Mexican government strictly regulated trapping, and Kirker had no license, so although he had a permit to carry on trade between Santa Fe and Chihuahua, he was obliged to smuggle his furs.

Relations between the Mexicans and the Apache nation, which had rarely been peaceful—Spanish friars complained of Apache raiders as early as 1672—were deteriorating rapidly, and Kirker began providing security for the mining trains on their way from Santa Rita to Chihuahua. He acquired a reputation. Before long, he lent his name to a style of warfare that was nothing if not genocidal and of which he was the consummate practitioner: *quirquismo*, or Kirkerism. *Quirquismo* was bounty warfare, a war of extermination directed at the Apaches. Borderland historians sometimes refer to this period as the War of Apache Scalps.

Kirker did not start the War of Apache Scalps. In 1837, an American mercenary named John James Johnson did so with an ambush near Santa Rita. Johnson operated a trading post in Sonora, and he fell in with a group of Missourians who were looking to purchase some mules, but the only mules to be had were in the possession of the local Mimbreño Apaches, who were led by a chief named Juan José Compa. Compa was a clever bandit who had spent time in a Spanish school and could read. He and Johnson were on friendly terms, so he suspected nothing when Johnson invited Compa and his men to share a meal. Johnson fired on them from a hidden cannon, variously described as a "blunderbuss" and a "six-pounder," loaded with shrapnel, killing about twenty men, including three chiefs. One account says four hundred were killed. Ben Leaton, who later settled at La Junta, was there as well. Johnson, Leaton, and their compadres scalped the dead Indians instead of simply taking their ears, as was then required for bounty payment under Mexican law, an innovation that led to legislation in Chihuahua, a *proyecto de guerra*, a law or plan of war, financed by the state's leading men, offering a bounty of a hundred dollars for each male Indian scalp, fifty dollars for each female, and twenty-five dollars for each child prisoner. The *proyecto* called for establishing "a permanent company for hunting Indians and making the activity lucrative so that it may be effective." Kirker was well known in Chihuahua for his work along the copper road from Santa Rita, and it was hoped he would take charge of the plan.

Several months later, the national government declared the *proyecto* unconstitutional and immoral, yet the idea of a scalp bounty remained popular along the frontier. Kirker, meanwhile, had taken up arms trading with the Apaches, finding it more profitable than fur trapping or security work. The next year, Apaches overran the mines in southern New Mexico, and Kirker, apparently with the backing of Mexican authorities, took steps to reestablish the proper order of things. In Missouri he assembled a company of Shawnee warriors, including a chief named Spy-Buck, and brought them down the Santa Fe Trail to New Mexico. They came upon a village called Galeana, where they found 247 Apaches, and totally destroyed it. They killed fifty-five warriors, took nine women prisoners and four hundred head of livestock. The Apache wars were now commenced and would not end until 1891.

In Chihuahua City a group of wealthy citizens formed the Society for Making War Against the Barbarians and authorized a new campaign against the Apaches. Its inaugural conference called on "Don Santiago Kirker, a citizen of the United States of the North and a resident of El Paso," to make a contract "about the method, expenditure, gratifications and other matters relative to the campaign which he and some Shawnees are going to make for the Society." Kirker was promised 100,000 silver pesos to solve Chihuahua's Apache problem. The society was responsible for raising the money, and a pamphlet was circulated promising a "war unto the death of the Apaches."

The authorities in Chihuahua appointed a committee to examine the mercenaries' scalps, which were required to pass certain tests. Each scalp had to be about one hand wide, with two ears naturally attached; each had to be positively identifiable as an Indian. This business was complicated. The Mexicans also entered into bounty agreements with Indians; they paid Apaches for Comanche scalps, and they paid Comanches for Apache scalps. "The appearance of the scalp itself depended on whether the taker intended for it to be a trophy for display or a *pieza* for reward," writes Ralph Adam Smith in his strange and disturbing biography of Kirker. "Comanches took both kinds. For a trophy, one of the warriors would take the crown or the center of the head skin about the size of a silver dollar or peso. After stretching it on a circular willow twig to the size of a saucer, he would allow it to dry. Not being consistent scalpers, Apaches took scalps only for revenge."

Kirker was not a reliable ally and in that sense was a typical mercenary, and his clients in Mexico seem to have been almost as worried about his behavior as they were about the Indians'. Over the next several years Kirker slaughtered hundreds of Apaches—he told a newspaper in 1847 that he had killed 487 Apaches "in the service of the state of Chihuahua"—though he often seemed to ignore them, or to travel outside the boundaries of this contract to hunt Comanches and Kiowas, and before long it was rumored that he was submitting counterfeit scalps from Mexican peons. His activities, as far as can be determined by the historical record, make little strategic sense, except insofar as he was always pursuing whatever seemed to be his own narrow material interest at any given time. George Wilkins Kendall, editor of the *New Orleans Picayune*, who was imprisoned with a group of Texas filibusters and authored the two-volume *Narrative of the Texan Santa Fé Expedition*, repeats the story but suspects, for no good reason that he mentions, that it was fabricated by Kirker's enemies. The governor of Chihuahua had his own suspicions and put Kirker on a per diem rather than a bounty. Disputes arose, and Kirker quit. It is telling that when Kirker was absent from the borderlands for three years, the Mexicans and the Apaches were able to establish a fragile peace. When the raids worsened, and the Mexican authorities grew desperate, they hired Kirker once again, despite deceptive whispers that he was now the supreme chief of the Apache nation.

When the Mexican War came upon the southwestern borderlands in 1846, Kirker abandoned his former clients and his adopted country and entered into a conspiracy with a Santa Fe trader named James Magoffin, who had been recruited by President James Polk to facilitate the quick and easy conquest of northern Mexico. Magoffin succeeded in engineering the bloodless surrender of New Mexico to General Stephen Kearny's Army of the West, which had marched from Fort Leavenworth, Missouri, directly to Santa Fe. Then Magoffin traveled to Chihuahua, ostensibly as a trader, to attempt the same feat. He was arrested and very nearly executed. The Chihuahuans were hoping that Kirker, a naturalized Mexican citizen, would lead the defense against the yanqui invaders; instead, he left his Mexican family behind and slipped out of Chihuahua, riding north through the wilderness to avoid Mexican troops, and joined the Missouri Mounted Volunteers under Colonel Alexander William Doniphan in Santa Fe. The governor of Chihuahua put a ten-thousand-dollar bounty on Kirker's head.

Kirker knew the border country better than any non-Apache; he knew all the trails and all the water holes and where shelter and forage could be found and when. He led the Missouri Mounted Volunteers south to El Paso, where he had often resided, and entertained them there with the local "pass wine" and charming young señoritas. Then he guided Doniphan south to conquer Chihuahua, serving again as an advance scout and guide. According to his biographer Smith, who seems strangely concerned to rehabilitate the historical reputation of the most prolific scalp hunter in North American history, Kirker was a model of bravery and patriotism. Through his feats of daring and especially a courageous charge at the skirmish of Sacramento, Kirker led Doniphan's forces to their victory in Chihuahua City.

Kirker continued eastward with the Americans across Mexico and eventually joined the main body of troops. At the completion of the war, he took passage to New Orleans. He was on his way back to New Mexico from Washington, D.C., where he had lobbied Senator Thomas Hart Benton for payment for his war services (and almost succeeded in getting legislation introduced in Congress to appropriate funds for that purpose), when he joined up with the band of forty-niners that included Charles Pancoast.

The Arapaho permitted Kirker's forty-niners to pass without molestation, but only after trading for paints, moccasins, buckskin clothing, tobacco, whiskey, and looking glasses. They wanted to trade for horses and weapons, but the pioneers refused; they had none to spare. Indians and forty-niners competed in footraces, and a blacksmith from Illinois was able to outrun every Indian who challenged him. The chiefs were so impressed they asked to keep him as a pet.

The pioneers continued on to Bent's Fort, and then to Santa Fe, braving stampedes of buffalo and long days of blistering sun and prairie thunderstorms that flooded their camps. Pikes Peak appeared, shining on the horizon, and Pancoast was caught up in the magnificence of the scenery, when suddenly all the animals in their train bolted and began a wild rush, a stampede, as if some magic signal had been given. Men and goods were thrown here and there, and a wagon was smashed before the emergency passed and the beasts were brought under control. Other stampedes vexed them as they traveled; men and animals died as a matter of course. A fat man suffered and lost weight. Mountain lions fed on cattle. Like most pilgrims on the great overland trails, the forty-niners amused themselves on occasion by shooting prairie dogs, marveling at their coexistence with rattlesnakes, which also invaded the men's tents. Horses disappeared at night, probably taken by Ute Indians. Cattle were lost to some poisonous weed, which caused them to swell up and die, splitting their sides and spilling their guts in the dust. Men gave up and turned back to Missouri, only to be murdered on the plains by Indians. Others followed a Delaware Indian who promised them a faster route through the mountains for fifty dollars and a good horse. They were abandoned in rugged mountains after twelve days. They wandered southward and then quarreled and divided. A few made it to California eventually, and so their story became known. Others perished, miserable and alone.

They stopped over at the ranch of Kit Carson, whose buckskin outfit, moccasins, and sombrero did not disappoint their expectations. He was attended by a motley entourage of Mexicans and Indians and degenerate Anglos, and he told stories and sold them some horses. In Santa Fe, Pancoast found friends he knew from Missouri and attended a fandango, where he spoke to a beautiful, bright-eyed young Spanish woman who asked whether he had ever met her husband, Joe, who married her and fathered a pretty little girl during the Mexican War. She was hoping he might have sent word about the date of his return. One of the gamblers in his company managed to get beaten, shot, and stabbed for cheating at monte by some Mexican vaqueros wearing tight trousers, lace shirts, and silver buckles.

After several days waiting for Kirker to reappear at camp, the pioneers realized they had been abandoned by their guide, to whom they had paid too much up front, so they continued on to California without him. Probably he had planned to ditch them all along and had used their train simply as a convenient escort across the prairie. Because Kirker still had a ten-thousand-dollar bounty on his head, he was wise to avoid venturing too close to Chihuahua, especially because the latitudinal blunders of the Treaty of Guadalupe Hidalgo had left the international boundary west of El Paso so uncertain. Much of the southern route west through the lower reaches of the Mimbres Mountains and along the Gila River, not to mention much of southern Arizona, remained legally part of Mexico until the Gadsden Purchase of 1853.

Kirker had probably not revealed as much, but he had led his greenhorns into a combat zone, for the War of Apache Scalps was very much alive and was becoming ever more so. In May 1849, *quirquismo* was ascendant again in Chihuahua, and the state congress renewed the bounty on Apache scalps. It was known as the Kirker bill and, once passed, was called the Fifth Law. A bounty of two hundred dollars was placed on each "barbarous Indian" killed. The law did not specify age or sex. By that time, however, there were plenty of other prospective scalp harvesters in the neighborhood, drifters and adventurers left over from the Mexican War, including John Joel Glanton, whose works and days were immortalized by Cormac McCarthy in his great borderland novel *Blood Meridian*.

Although Kirker was unable to collect bounties in person, he could easily have discounted them through intermediaries. Certainly he would have learned of the new law as soon as he arrived in New Mexico. The atmosphere in New Mexico might not have been very welcoming. An old Indian trader named Daniel Jones reports in his autobiography, *Forty Years Among the Indians*, that he ran into Kirker in Santa Fe in 1849 and that people there wanted to lynch him for his part in stirring up the Apaches. All decent men despised him, Jones writes, and for years anytime an Anglo was killed by an Apache, people would remark, "There is another of Kirker's victims."

Kirker shows up in San Francisco by October 1850. He died peacefully on his ranch at nearby Mount Diablo in 1852, an old man at fifty-nine. Driving west from Pittsburg to Oakland today, you can take Kirker Pass Road through the low, grassy dun-colored hills.

Pancoast and company made it to California in decent time, passing through Apache country mostly unscathed. They took note of the copper mines of the Mimbres Mountains near Santa Rita, held their noses and drank from scum-covered water holes, marveling at salamanders as they scooted across the mud. Like all wayfarers passing through that country, including the Glanton Gang, Pancoast and his Peoria Pioneers rested at the mission of San Xavier del Bac, south of present-day Tucson, and beheld the elaborately sculpted and painted figures that adorn the great monument even today. Ruins attracted their curiosity, and they wondered at the lives that were led in such a desolate place, now occupied by poisonous insects, owls, and wolves.

For all who made the journey west along this route, the most difficult passage was through the Sonoran Desert up to Yuma, across the Colorado River, then the perilous crossing through the sands of southern

California. Tormented by the sun, teased by mirages, argonauts trudged forward. Progress was slow, because forage for the teams was scarce, so the animals were permitted to range widely at night. Half of the next day would be spent gathering strays. Men grew weak; exhausted women and traumatized children crouched in the shade of their wagons, eyes wide and hollow. Cattle failed, as did mules and men.

Once arrived in California, in San Diego or the dreamy old Spanish town of Los Angeles, argonauts found a most salubrious climate and much California wine to refresh their weathered constitutions. Most made their way north to the goldfields, where they engaged in a frenzy of prospecting, digging, and panning, as well as claim jumping, robbing, and the occasional cold-blooded murder. A device known as a rocker was used to sift dirt and stone from the diggings. If gold was found, a claim was made, but all such holdings were tenuous, and men were often pushed off their claims. Most failed to make their fortunes; some, like the Missourian John Strode Brasfield, saw that supplying miners was often more profitable than joining in digging. Others squatted on land belonging to Mexican ranchers and built homesteads when the owners were forced by American courts of law to compromise. Those who managed to keep their stock alive on the long journey made fortunes selling sheep or mules or oxen at great profit. Sheep purchased in New Mexico for fifty cents might sell for fifteen dollars.

Scurvy was a common affliction, as was dysentery. Inevitably, cholera made its appearance. Murder was routine, and thieves were thick; bandits and Mexican guerrillas roamed the roads. Indians made the occasional raid. An industrious digger with a decent claim might yield twenty or thirty dollars a day, sometimes more; sometimes much more, if a large nugget were found. Pancoast tells the story of a small boulder near his tent that he and his companions often used as a seat. A young miner came to visit one Sunday and asked if he might have the boulder, because he thought he could see a speck of gold on its surface. The miner sold the boulder to a storekeeper for two hundred dollars, and he in turn broke it up and sold the gold he found therein for three thousand dollars.

No reports of Perry's activities in the goldfields have come down to us, but everything that I have learned about the man suggests that he would have seen the more certain source of lucre in livestock and other supplies rather than dreary backbreaking speculations in the mud pits of Coloma or Hangtown. Family tradition holds that he made more than one trip to California, which suggests that he profited more from horse and mule flesh than from prospecting. Men who knew the trails and how to handle livestock could make good time, especially if they avoided the company of greenhorns and emigrant families. Perry made the journey by sea as well, according to family tradition, and it's likely he did so on his return trip.

The sea route would seem to be free from worry compared with the overland slog—no deserts, Indians, or snowy mountain passes and no livestock to husband. Passage on an ocean steamer was easily made, and a ticket from San Francisco to New York could be had for $150, not a small sum, but far less than the cost of an overland journey. Perry and his companions, probably his Adamson relatives, would have disembarked at San Juan del Sur, with perhaps a short stop in Acapulco. From the San Juan harbor it was twelve miles by mule from a rough beach landing to Virginia City, on Lake Nicaragua, where a small steamer ferried passengers across the lake to the San Juan del Norte River, where they could take a light river steamboat across the isthmus to the town of San Juan del Norte, or Greytown, and a northbound steamer for Havana, New Orleans, and points north. From New Orleans, young Perry would have made river passage to Missouri.

If he was traveling with his uncle Jacob, the sea voyage might not have gone so well. In about 1852, Jacob set sail from California with some two hundred men, headed for Nicaragua. A drunk captain and bad weather conspired to set the ship adrift for seventy-four days. After eating through their supplies, including mules, men began to speak of drawing lots to see who would be eaten first. The Adamson group made clear that they'd use their pistols before they submitted to such a lottery. A fresh breeze settled the issue, carrying them to port.

In 1854, the same year Charles Pancoast, his wanderings complete, arrived home in Philadelphia, Perry came back to Weston, presumably from California, but probably he had already been in Texas. His cousin Larkin Adamson was gone by then, exchanging his residency in Weston, Missouri, for that of Weston, Texas, in Collin County, part of the old Peters colony north of Dallas. Perry returned to Missouri to fetch his sweetheart, who was also his first cousin, Welmett Adamson.

They married and set off, no doubt in the company of other Texas travelers, down an old trail through Indian country known as the Texas Road.

Like most of the western trails supposedly blazed by pathfinders such as Lewis and Clark, John C. Frémont, and Kit Carson, the Texas Road was originally an Indian highway. When Europeans first penetrated the region, it was largely controlled by the Osage, and the well-traveled trail southwest from St. Louis, through what we now call Missouri, Kansas, and Oklahoma down to the Red River into the land of the Tejas, was known by the Chouteaus and other French traders as the Osage Trace.

The best descriptions of this route come from the writings of Washington Irving. By the time Irving left Cincinnati on September 3, 1832, bound for the western prairies, the Osage Trace was already busy with traffic bound for the Anglo colonies in Mexican Texas. There were eleven thousand Texan colonists in 1832. The first stirrings of rebellion—the brief, quixotic Republic of Fredonia—had been put down a few years before, and within a month fifty-five delegates would meet in San Felipe de Austin, at the Convention of 1832, to draft a petition to the Mexican government for a greater role in the government of their state.

Irving had spent the previous seventeen years living in Europe, tormented with dreams of his homeland. Upon his return, a chance meeting with Henry Ellsworth, appointed by President Andrew Jackson to administer the Indian Removal Act, led to an invitation to visit Fort Gibson in what is now eastern Oklahoma. He left Cincinnati late on a Monday afternoon, aboard a steamer called *Messenger*, and noted the weather (thundershowers, mist on the water) and the reflections of moonlight playing on the surface of the river. There was some drama on board that night when a passenger was slashed across the face. An old black steward in a white outfit and checkered apron, a handkerchief made of bright madras cotton covering his head, catered to Irving's various needs. In a journal, Irving sketched fragments of scenes, glimpses and images set off by copious dashes. Here is a passage from Kentucky:

> Little, well-dressed negro girl brings in salver of peaches—
> fat negro wenches drying apples and peach on board under
> trees—wild gorse, flowers, etc., about house. In neighboring

field negro boys exercising race-horses. Flower garden—iron gate on cotton-wood stanchions—flowers and fruits of various kinds.

A few days later, still on the Ohio River:

> Evening scene on Ohio—steam-boat aground with two flats each side of her—we take part of cargo on board—moonlight—light of fires—chant and chorus of negro boatmen—men strolling about docks with cigars—negroes dancing before furnaces—glassy surface of river—undulations made by boat—wavering light of moon and stars—silent, primeval forest sleeping in sun-shine—on each side still forest—forest—forest.

Like many Yankee travelers in the South, Irving was especially struck by the behavior and appearance of the slaves, whom he observed with ironic condescension, as when he describes an "old negro steward scolding young negro boys for lying—he aims at monopoly." He noticed casual injustices, such as the plight of a Negro woman who lived in a log hut by the river, cooking for men who supply boats with firewood. She was cheerful and contented, a good whistler, but when she was asked about her children, the tears welled up: "I am not allowed to live with them—they are up at the plantation." On the Mississippi he meets a Negro merchant off to New Orleans with forty dozen chickens he bought for a dollar each. He'll sell them for three and return with "nothing but money," which he buries. He pays his master at a rate of fifty dollars a year and next year will have enough saved to buy his freedom. He won't be able to afford to buy his wife or children, but he plans to see them when he can. Later, in Missouri, Irving praises the Negroes for their good cheer and merry laughter, remarking that they are fine gentlemen and the politest people he has met.

Irving's fellow passengers hailed from all over, each of them personifying a type. There was the merchant from New York, a "smug, dapper, calculating Yankee," a boastful and reckless Virginian, a Swiss count, and a young Kentucky dandy he calls Black Hawk. The dandy wears a short green merino coat and a low-crowned broad-brimmed hat and plays cards "with a kindred genius." Irving dubs one serene Quakeress "the Princess Hullaballoo." Onshore he meets other Quakers, a couple from Philadelphia, settlers for fifteen years who profess homesickness and disgust for the crude poachers they have for neighbors. They regret their removal from the City of Brotherly Love and pray for schools. He visits another log cabin inhabited by a pretty woman from Nashville and her handsome husband. They miss their church and will return to Tennessee soon. Irishmen and Frenchmen come aboard, all with a story or a scheme to get rich. One Frenchman, beguiled by a countryman, bought land sight unseen, expecting paradise in Kentucky, and emigrated with his wife, only to find their promised land was an uncleared wilderness. Having abandoned the fraudulent dream of easy living on the frontier, they were steaming toward New Orleans.

Nine days' travel brought the famous writer to St. Louis, where he met the great Indian trader Auguste Pierre Chouteau, son of Jean Pierre Chouteau of St. Louis, and Governor William Clark, military director for Captain Meriwether Lewis's celebrated western expedition. His short buggy drive to the governor's farm crossed a verdant prairie, fragrant with wildflowers. Arriving at the farm, Irving noted the productive orchards of walnut and peach trees, bending to the breaking point under their bounty, grapevines, beehives, happy Negroes (freed from bondage yet continuing in loyal service to the governor) whispering and preparing food on tables in a shady grove, golden sunshine and bright skies and pure breezes, all serenaded by the autumnal lamentations of the cricket. A pastoral wonderland now replaced by weedy fields in fallow, hog farms, and suburbs. On his way back to St. Louis, Irving passed by a circle of Indian burial mounds; a local potentate had built his house so as to use one of these noble sacred sites as a terrace. Irving notes the desecration without comment.

Setting off down the trace toward Independence, accompanied among others by Clark and Colonel Chouteau, as everyone called him, Irving collected Indian lore: Cherokees and Kickapoos, serial victims of American bad faith, had been thrown together as allies and neighbors in a new territory; formerly, they had always sworn to fight until all were dead, and even then, they claimed, their bones would continue the fight. The governor, in a remarkable comment, recommended that Indian horse thievery be understood, and perhaps forgiven, as the only remaining avenue for Indians to achieve honor and distinction.

Two days' journey from Independence, Irving's party came to the Grand River, where they encountered a pair of bee hunters, with a wagon drawn by four oxen, carrying large barrels for the honey they'd be harvesting in the vicinity. Most of the honey closer to Missouri had been hunted out. Indians, Irving notes, see the advance of the honeybee across the West as the harbinger of the white man, who brought the honeybee from Europe, and so the pleasure of suddenly finding formerly hollow moldering trunks in their woodlands filled with a sweet, exotic, and ambrosial delicacy must be tempered by the knowledge that their ancient hunting grounds would soon be overrun by pale hordes from the East.

Irving seemed to thoroughly enjoy his jaunt across the prairies toward the frontier, sleeping under the stars, dining on honey cakes and roast ducks, entertaining pretty pioneer wives with his stories, taking notes on Indian language and customs. The Osage, he learned, never ate breakfast early when traveling; the women led horses packed with skins for beds, corn, meat, puppy dogs, babies wrapped up in papooses. Young men walked. The Osage were tall and erect. The women, when they rode, carried umbrellas against the hot sun. Noble and austere, like ancient Romans, the Osage remained aloof from the whites.

The Creeks, in contrast, reminded Irving of Turks or Arabs, wearing bright fringed calicos of brilliant colors, embellished with twinkling beads and tassels, and gaudy bolts of cloth bound about their heads like turbans.

As a man of culture and refinement, Irving was particularly fascinated by the mechanics of hunting and killing. "Man is naturally an animal of prey; and, however changed by civilization, will readily relapse into his instinct for destruction," he wrote after a deer hunt. "I found my ravenous and sanguinary propensities daily growing stronger upon the prairies."

Irving's blood rose when a prairie wolf appeared within range and the expedition's half-breed scouts instantly pursued it. He jumped out of his wagon and mounted his pony to join in the chase, and though their tactics were sound, the beast escaped. Another quarry presented itself shortly, and again the company mounted its charge, along with a greyhound named Henry Clay. After the horsemen attempted to trample the wolf, someone managed to fire off one barrel, breaking the animal's leg. "We surround and kill him."

Sitting at camp next to a creek, Colonel Chouteau told the story of a young Indian man returning from St. Louis to his tribe, who had been camping at that very creek. When he arrived, the camp had been abandoned, except for one young girl, his beloved Flower of the Prairie, to whom he was betrothed. What was she doing there? "Waiting for you." So they set off together, she carrying his bundle of belongings in the Indian way, until she sat down below a tree and declared she would not enter the village with him, because it was not proper. He went on ahead and, when he arrived among his friends and family, asked his sister to go and fetch Flower of the Prairie. His family surrounded him, weeping, and told him that she had died several days earlier. He could not believe it, but when they all returned to the tree where he had left her, they found his bundle lying on the ground. The young man died of grief.

When they arrived at Fort Gibson, near the confluence of the Neosho, the Arkansas, and the Verdigris Rivers—known as the Three Forks—Irving met Sam Houston, who was living in a wigwam with a Cherokee wife on the west bank of the Neosho, and rode with him about thirty-five miles up the river to Chouteau's nearby home at La Grande Saline, a strong salt spring and geyser where Chouteau had one of his trading posts. After crossing the beautifully clear river, where a "group of Indian nymphs" lounged half-naked on the banks, Irving was greeted by an old slave, grinning "from ear to ear." Indians and half-breeds stood around a tree in the courtyard, Negro girls ran about giggling, dogs and cats and chickens wandered in and out, as did turkeys and geese. A large buffalo robe hung over a railing. They dined on venison steaks, roast beef, bread, coffee, and cakes, waited on by the sister of Chouteau's Indian concubine, as Irving called her. "In these establishments," Irving wrote in his journal, "the world is turned upside down—the slave the master, the master the slave." He was struck that the master was forced "to plan, scheme, guard, and economize" whereas the slave "thinks only of living, enjoying—cares nothing how it comes or how it goes."

Colonel Chouteau was a remarkable figure in the history of Indian relations, and as Irving obliquely suggests, his business and financial affairs were not always in good order. Chouteau was continuously in debt, in no small part because of his commitment to the Indians with whom he spent most of his life.

In 1804, after traveling with his father and fourteen Osage to meet President Thomas Jefferson, Meriwether Lewis secured a spot for him at West Point. Chouteau graduated and served as aide-de-camp for General James Wilkinson at Natchitoches but resigned after six months to become a fur trader. Although his rank was merely that of an ensign when he left the service, Chouteau was thereafter always known as "Colonel."

Like all Indian traders, Chouteau was a speculator, and his schemes often went awry, as when he was attacked by Pawnees while illegally trapping along the upper Arkansas and trading with the Kiowa, Arapaho, and Cheyenne. He was later arrested by Spanish authorities and imprisoned in Santa Fe for forty-eight days. He continued to trade with the Osage all his life and kept a large extended family among them. When the Creek, Cherokee, and Choctaw began moving in along the Verdigris, forced out of their lands east of the Mississippi, Chouteau acted as go-between and peacemaker. Treaties had promised the Creek $200,000 in annuities, as well as food and clothing, guns, ammunition, and traps. They were cheated and received nothing at all, but Chouteau extended credit, fed them and gave them clothing, and spent the rest of his life trying to collect those debts from the U.S. government. He never did.

Sam Houston seems not to have made a large impression on Washington Irving, for he left him out of the travel book, *A Tour on the Prairies*, that he subsequently published. From Fort Gibson, Irving and his companions—among them a comic French Creole he calls Tonish, a half Indian named Beatte, and the twenty-one-year-old Swiss count on his grand tour—caught up with a troop of rangers who were off to patrol the Pawnee hunting grounds. Over the next month, Irving wandered across what is now central Oklahoma, sleeping under the stars and shooting anything that moved. The rangers were a motley troop of young greenhorns, with a few old-timers mixed in, eager for adventure and Indian fighting, despite Commissioner Ellsworth's stated mandate to bring messages of peace and goodwill from the Great White Father in Washington. Beatte, who was serving Irving's company as a scout, looked upon the rangers with a mingling of contempt and indifference.

After gamboling across the prairies, punctuated by dreary interludes of bushwhacking through the post-oak and blackjack thickets of the Cross Timbers, with their innumerable ravines and rocky defiles, the company at last managed to capture some wild horses and slaughter a few dozen buffalo. They forded crumbling streams, got lost, suffered false alarms and panics over imagined Pawnee ambuscades, huddled together during prairie thunderstorms, and finally limped home in rags, their horses mostly lame and too exhausted even to graze.

By 1854, when Perry and Welmett set off, the Osage Trace had long been trampled and beaten down into an emigrant and military road. Jackson's Indian removal was complete, and the Trail of Tears was history. Sixty thousand Choctaw, Chickasaw, Creek, Cherokee, and Seminole Indians were uprooted from the southeastern United States, by means of force and fraud, and settled largely in eastern Oklahoma. It was the year of the Kansas-Nebraska Act, which reopened the question of slavery in the western territories. Immigration to Texas had increased steadily throughout the period of the republic, and much of that traffic passed down through the Indian Territory to the Red River along the Texas Road. A decade of Texas independence gave way to annexation by the United States and the Mexican War.

I said farewell to Patricia and Grant and set out from Prairie Village on a bright, sunny spring day, more or less the time of year when wagoneers would have hitched up their teams to cross the prairie. Timing was important, for fresh green forage would be wanted for the livestock; leave too early and there would be nothing to eat. Those who were California-bound would be anxious to cross the Rockies before snows set in. Perry and Welmett would have come out of Weston and crossed the Missouri on a ferry just west of Kansas City. Driving south, searching for signs of the Texas Road, I saw a life-sized replica of an "overland stage," labeled just so, sitting in front of a UMB Bank. A road sign welcomed me to the Santa Fe and Oregon Trails.

Overland travel had its share of hardships, I know, but at least they didn't have stoplights in 1854; as I descended a mellow rise, I saw before me a hideous procession of red lights diminishing into the hazy

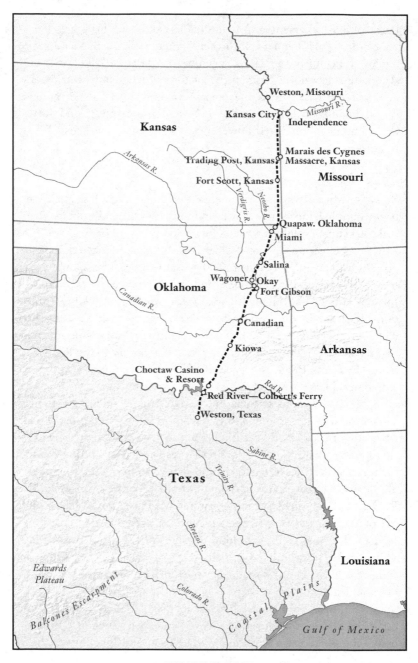

**THE TEXAS ROAD**

distance. Blocky stucco condominiums lined the thoroughfare, alternating with certified pre-owned-automobile dealers. The clouds above
were silvery and delicate, reflecting on the windshields of Dodges and
Jeeps lined up in ranks like white-topped wagons ready to conquer
the Great Plains, sunshine glancing off polished chromium bumpers to
burn ephemeral sunspots on my corneas. A phalanx of warring big box
stores arose before me, a Super Target vying for customers with the
Costco across the way, and then I spotted an actual human female on
foot: a jogger taking her chances out among the automobiles and Mar-
riotts, trying to forestall the slow onset of cardiovascular disease and
diabetes. Finally, I managed to push out beyond the stop-and-go exur-
ban landscape into a sixty-five-mile-per-hour zone, and casual groves
of hardwoods and planted evergreens began to dot the gaps between
parking lots.

Not far beyond the Overland Park Convention Center, I struck
U.S. Highway 69, the approximate route Perry and Welmett would
have traveled on the Texas Road. Trappers and traders had very sensibly taken the paths broken by uncountable generations of Indians. So
too did settlers, and when, as a matter of course, highways were laid
down, they traced more or less the same courses. From Weston and
Kansas City and Independence, and other trailheads, the various trails
eventually converged and became one. As a guide, I had with me *Down
the Texas Road: Historic Places Along Highway 69 Through Oklahoma*, a
booklet published in 1936 by Grant Foreman, the dean of Oklahoma
historians.

Farmland opened up before me, complete with silos and barns and
the occasional huge round bale of hay. I was abroad in Kansas, flying
down the macadam surrounded by a landscape that Washington Irving
would not have recognized as a prairie. After an hour a sign advertising
the Trail of Tears flashed by, and I passed a country road called 247th
Street, which seemed a surprisingly optimistic assessment of Kansas
City's future growth potential.

A massive coal plant appeared on the horizon as I entered Linn
County, Kansas, silver clouds of greenhouse gases steaming from its
candy-striped stacks. When I came abreast of the plant, I stopped at a
convenience store and learned from the counter clerk that a new stack
was under construction, which accounted for all the traffic. There

were two or three pickups outside. I spotted another truck driving up toward the plant. A farmer woman chatted with the clerk and wondered whether it might rain, discussing the lotion she liked best and whether or not she could afford to buy what she needs, the kind she likes. Pushing on, pushing south, I passed bait shops, cabin rentals, and signs for catfish, all you can eat, and suddenly I crossed the Marais des Cygnes River. That sounded familiar. When I saw a sign for the Marais des Cygnes massacre site, I swerved wildly for the exit and went in search of atrocities. Instead, I found a national wildlife refuge and much helpful information about the local flora.

What once had been tall-grass prairie, with two or three hundred different species of plants growing together in glorious equilibrium—home to scissor-tailed flycatchers, short-eared owls, and loggerhead shrikes—was plowed under, cultivated, and then abandoned to the invading Ozark forests of oak and hickory, spreading down from the uplands. Nonnative grasses such as fescue invaded or were deliberately seeded by well-meaning agricultural technicians as a range-improvement measure. But deer don't like to eat it, and even cattle turn up their noses. In fact, nothing eats it, and small birds that nest on the ground, such as bobwhite quail, die out or go elsewhere. Some varieties of fescue are even toxic to small mammals.

If the former grasslands are now monocultural deserts, at least the woodlands harbor some diversity. I learned that the forests are full of white oak, chinquapin, post oak, and shagbark hickory and that wild turkey, coyotes, and bobcats lurk in their shadows among the wild lilies, trillium, and Dutchman's-breeches.

I never did find the monument of the Marais des Cygnes massacre, one of the most notorious of the Bleeding Kansas incidents. Some well-meaning civic leaders apparently moved it. But what happened was this: In 1858 a band of bloodthirsty pro-slavery Missouri border ruffians, out to harass Free-Soilers, rode into the nearby town of Trading Post, so named for another of Colonel Chouteau's commercial establishments. They captured eleven men, marched them out of town, turned them in to a gully, and started shooting. Five men died, five were injured, one got clean away, and the best-selling Quaker poet and abolitionist John Greenleaf Whittier was moved to publish his immortal elegy "Le Marais du Cygne" in *The Atlantic Monthly*. Here are the first three stanzas and the last:

A blush as of roses
Where rose never grew!
Great drops on the bunch-grass,
But not of the dew!
A taint in the sweet air
For wild bees to shun!
A stain that shall never
Bleach out in the sun!


Back, steed of the prairies!
Sweet song-bird, fly back!
Wheel hither, bald vulture!
Gray wolf, call thy pack!
The foul human vultures
Have feasted and fled;
The wolves of the Border
Have crept from the dead.


From the hearths of their cabins,
The fields of their corn,
Unwarned and unweaponed,
The victims were torn,
The whirlwind of murder
Swooped up and swept on
To the low, reedy fen-lands,
The Marsh of the Swan.


On the lintels of Kansas
That blood shall not dry
Henceforth the Bad Angel
Shall harmless go by;
Henceforth to the sunset,
Unchecked on her way,
Shall Liberty follow
The march of the day.

This wasn't Whittier's only Kansas poem. He also eulogized John Brown, who in his zeal to avenge the wrongs of slavery murdered his share of innocent men.

Perish with him the folly that seeks through evil good!
Long live the generous purpose unstained with human blood!
Not the raid of midnight terror, but the thought which underlies;
Not the borderer's pride of daring, but the Christian's sacrifice.

I pulled in to the combined Trading Post museum and rest stop. There was a primrose path with interpretive panels, with ponds and pretty pink wildflowers. In the distance, near the highway, was a wooden cutout of a horse and rider, silhouettes in the misty light of that cool spring morning. I stood and gazed out at the bright green no-longer-prairie, intersected by the highway, invasive woodlands thriving on gently rolling hills in the far distance, an endless procession of Walmart tractor-trailer rigs speeding past.

When I arrived in Fort Scott, Kansas, I saw a sign that read EXPLORE FT. SCOTT: SIMPLE PLEASURES, HIDDEN TREASURES. In the distance little black dots of Angus cattle lolled about a stock pond in the middle of a bright green field. Trees grew along fences as windbreaks, like hedgerows. Old fields were infested with young weedy trees, some with signs of halfhearted attempts at brush removal, but evidently the reluctant farmer lost interest or died and simply left a few piles of brush in the field, adding to the clutter as the woods continued their patient invasion of the prairies. I decided I had to obey the sign and explore Fort Scott, boyhood home of Gordon Parks. I skipped the trolley tour and went straight for the old fort. A small troupe of young boys walked by with fishing poles over their shoulders.

The buildings in Fort Scott were beautifully reconstructed. Most impressive were the old barracks, stately white clapboard buildings with wide front porches buttressed with pillars of native stone. In 1855, I learned, just about the time Perry and Welmett would have been passing through, the U.S. government abandoned Fort Scott, and both the barracks and the officers' quarters were converted into hotels. On one side of the parade ground was the pro-slavery Western Hotel, and on the other side was the Free State Hotel. Fort Scott grew rapidly after

Trading Post, Kansas

the passage of the Kansas-Nebraska Act as pro-slave settlers poured
into Kansas from Missouri, South Carolina, Georgia, and elsewhere.
After the Marais des Cygnes massacre, a Campbellite minister named
James Montgomery, a notorious horse thief and marauding jayhawker,
raided Fort Scott in response to a rumor that the massacre had been
planned at the Western Hotel. He failed to burn it down, though he
tried mightily. In another raid Montgomery's gang did manage to kill
a former lawman named John Little, who had fired into the crowd of
Free-Soilers. Little took a bullet as he leaned out a window. Later, his
fiancée sent Montgomery a letter. "Oh, the anguish you have caused,"
she wrote. "Now the cry of 'the Osages are coming!' can awaken him
no more. He sleeps quietly in our little graveyard. But remember this.
I am a girl, but I can fire a pistol. And if ever the time comes, I will
send some of you to the place where there is 'weeping and gnashing of

teeth.' You, a minister of God? You mean a minister of the devil, and a very superior one too."

After half an hour of walking through the fort, I browsed the gift shop's fine collection of books on Bleeding Kansas, avoided talking to the five bored park rangers working the desk, and pressed on toward Pittsburg, home of the fighting Gorillas football team, and Oklahoma. Fort Scott was slightly sad and dilapidated, a town seemingly bereft of any reason for being, much like my hometown of Del Rio. More small dried-up towns awaited my gaze, with empty storefronts and lines of people waiting to sell their scrap metal. Dead armadillos, pioneers of climate change, littered the roads. Camptown Greyhound Park sat empty, shuttered. Even the dog track had gone out of business. A helpful local church had put up a sign: SMILE, YOUR MOM CHOSE LIFE. And another: ABORTION: GROWING, GROWING, GONE!

I just kept going. Kansas continues to bleed.


I was listening to the Flatlanders, with Jimmie Dale Gilmore crooning "Dallas." *Have you ever seen Oklahoma from Highway 69 at night?* I sang, twisting the lyrics. This stretch of country, like Dallas–Fort Worth, purports to be the place where East meets West, where the West begins, and I suppose that's always true, wherever you happen to be, but there's something about Oklahoma, especially along the eastern border, with its heritage of the Five Civilized Tribes and their southeastern legacy, that gives the claim a certain legitimacy. I was still following the Frontier Scenic Byway, trying to stick to Route 69, but I kept seeing signs for Route 66. Quapaw and Vinita and Miami rolled on by, amid the rolling prairie with trees clustered along the drainages. I had to stop at Quapaw, had to get out of my rented Ford, just to marvel at the emptiness. Not just shuttered downtown storefronts, lovely in their ruination, a common enough sight in so many little towns across rural America and beyond, but bare foundations, slab after concrete slab. The very buildings had been carried off. There's no mistaking tornado country.

I ignored the turnoff for the Will Rogers Turnpike, though the fact of it made me curious, and I saw another dead armadillo. Then another. Pretty soon I was counting them. Picturesque round hay bales punctuated green fields while backpackers pushing baby carriages strode down the shoulder of the highway. They were going somewhere.

My phone rang. It was John Stambaugh calling, a distant relative. Patricia had introduced me, and we had spoken on the phone a few weeks back. Another amateur genealogist, he had written several thick volumes tracing the Adamsons and the Wilsons. One was titled *Adamson and Related Families*. Patricia gave me a signed copy. John sent me a letter with directions to his home in Dallas, but I never received it. We spoke again when I was in Kansas City. Several times. He would call and ask me if I was going to be arriving today, whatever day today happened to be. He wondered aloud whether he had sent his letter to Del Rio. I told him again that I lived in Brooklyn. He gave me directions over the phone. His directions were fantastic, shapeless: *it's either three or seven blocks, but I think four, and then you take a right, or maybe it's a left.* John was having a hard time remembering the code one pushes at the gate of his apartment complex, so he took my number and said he would call me back about thirty minutes later. He walked outside to

Quapaw, Oklahoma

check, and by the time he called me back, he'd lost the paper he wrote the code on. He wanted to go back outside and check the code again, but I insisted that I'd be able to figure it out. A lovely, generous man, he had no short-term memory. John lived, perpetually confused, in the eternal present. He planned to show me around Collin County, and he said that he had a bed and a private bathroom waiting for me.

Thirty minutes later John called again. It was as if we had never spoken. What follows is a direct transcription of my side of the conversation. "Hello? Yes, John. How are you doing? Not too bad, I'm on the road, so, uh, yeah, I'll be there tomorrow. Yes, tomorrow. Yes, sir. You did. And we spoke yesterday. And I'll be there tomorrow. That's always been the plan. For Sunday. Yessir. Yessir. And I have your instructions, and I know which buttons to push when I get to your gate. That's right. Yes. That's right. Yes. That's right. Yes, sir. It'll be late in the afternoon, evening, certainly before dark. I'm not exactly sure when. Close to evening. In the evening. I think I'll be there before dark. Great, thank you so much. I can't wait to meet you. Okay. Bye-bye."

I was now briefly on the trail of the fascinating Auguste Pierre Chouteau. My plan was to visit what remained of La Grande Saline, where Chouteau built his trading post on the banks of the Neosho River. I avoided Rocklahoma, where life, liberty, and the pursuit of rock give meaning to lost souls, and pressed on through Pryor. According to Grant Foreman, I was only five or six miles west of the actual wagon track of the Texas Road, but if I just turned my nose east, I would cross the ancient trace, and if I were lucky and very observant, I'd see the persistent depression left by the wagons where they came down the ferry. Then, on the east bank of the Neosho, also confusingly known as the Grand River, I would find the site of Chouteau's old trading post.

I followed Grant Foreman's directions to the letter. But I came upon a lake. My edition of Foreman's book was published in 1954. Ten years later, in 1964, Lake Hudson was constructed by damming the Neosho, thus submerging the original site of La Saline, including, as far as I was able to determine, the salt spring that had been such an important resource for many generations of Indians and the pioneers who displaced them. Arriving in the township of Salina, I marveled briefly at the T-38 Talon training jet mounted on a concrete pedestal in the front yard of the American Legion Post 240. According to the Salina Chamber of Commerce, local veterans had wanted an anti-aircraft gun, but they couldn't find one. So they eventually settled on this T-38, located at Sheppard Air Force Base near Wichita Falls, Texas. As it happens, I spent much of my childhood watching T-38s flying through skies in Val Verde County. I probably saw this jet take off and land at Laughlin AFB, just outside Del Rio.

I wandered around Salina. The public library was closed. I asked some teenagers pushing a baby carriage down the highway shoulder if they knew where the Chouteau memorial might be. Or the old spring. They were befuddled by my questions. There was a little creek in the town park. Maybe that was it. Never before had I seen anyone pushing a baby carriage down a highway, but today I had seen it twice, though the first time it was backpackers and the carriage was filled with gear. I pulled in to a spot next to the library, got out of my car, and walked around. In the city park I found a springhouse apparently built in 1844 by Lewis Ross, the brother of a Cherokee chief who took control of the springs that year. I'm told it's one of the oldest buildings in Oklahoma. Presumably, it was relocated before the flood came and consumed the historic trading post and spring. Shaped like a pentagon, built of unmortared local stone, the little old structure stood in the middle of a weedy lawn, with a restored wood-shingled roof. There was garbage within and it smelled of urine.

Salina was a disappointment, so I decided to go in search of Sam Houston's Wigwam Neosho.

Sam Houston suffered a long run of bad luck before he emigrated to Texas and helped the renegade Mexican state break away from its motherland. He was just thirteen when his father died and his mother loaded up her belongings and her children and moved to East Tennessee, just south of Knoxville. Three years later, feeling frustrated and persecuted and working as a grocery boy, Houston ran away to live among the Cherokee, learned their language, and was adopted as a son by Chief Oolooteka, also known as John Jolly, who gave him his Cherokee name, the Raven. In 1813, Houston joined the U.S. Army and fought with Thomas Hart Benton and Andrew Jackson, suffering serious injuries while fighting renegade Creeks in the Battle of Horseshoe Bend, in Alabama. First he received an arrow in his groin, a terrible wound that troubled him for the rest of his life; then, after leading a foolish charge against the enemy's makeshift fortifications, he found himself alone and caught two musket balls in his right arm and shoulder. Amazingly, he survived.

Andrew Jackson took notice and soon assigned his new protégé to sort out some difficulties with the Cherokee, who were bound by a fraudulent treaty to move west of the Mississippi. Young Houston took his job as Indian subagent seriously and fought to ensure his Cherokee friends, already cheated by means of the treaty, were treated fairly. He failed of course, but the Cherokee loved him for trying. In 1817 he escorted a delegation of chiefs from Knoxville to Washington, where they met first with Secretary of War John C. Calhoun and then with President James Monroe. Houston made his appearance in Cherokee dress and received a severe rebuke from Calhoun. Before long, Houston was compelled to defend himself before the secretary against trumped-up charges of slave running. Although he was exonerated by the president, Houston resigned from the army in disgust, and Calhoun remained his bitter enemy forever after. Houston moved to Nashville, proved himself to be a talented politician, entered Congress, fought a celebrated duel, and was elected governor of Tennessee. His relationship with Andrew Jackson grew stronger day by day.

Everything went bad again when he fell in love with Eliza Allen of Gallatin, Tennessee, where, as it happens, some of my relatives owned a hotel at the time. The marriage was doomed before it was even celebrated, and years later Houston told a story of a raven falling dead in the road before him as he rode to the wedding. Eliza spurned him, it seems, and no one has ever advanced a fully satisfactory explanation why. Some say that Eliza was in love with another man; others that Sam was insanely jealous; the most plausible story seems to be that Eliza was disgusted by the oozing wound in Houston's groin. Late in life, Old Sam told intimates that she had in fact pledged herself to another man. Whatever happened in private with Eliza Allen, Houston resigned his office, abandoning his adopted state and his position as political heir to President Jackson. It was a national scandal.

Houston boarded the *Red Rover* and steamed down the Cumberland bound for Little Rock and the bosom of his good friends the Cherokee, whom he had unwillingly banished to the Indian territories. "The most unhappy man now living," as he described himself, Houston ended up in the cantonment of Fort Gibson, at the confluence of the Verdigris, Arkansas, and Neosho Rivers, running a little trading post he called the Wigwam Neosho, where he was welcomed by his adoptive father, Chief John Jolly. He found comfort in the arms of a Cherokee wife and spent the next several years engaged in furious bureaucratic warfare with the Indian and War Departments in Washington and allegedly plotting the conquest of Texas with Andrew Jackson.

In June 1829, Jackson wrote to his melancholy friend: "It has been communicated to me that you had the illegal enterprise in view of conquering Texas; that you declared that you would, in less than two years, be emperor of that country, by conquest. I must have really thought you deranged to have believed you had such a wild scheme in contemplation; and particularly, when it was communicated that the physical force to be employed was the Cherokee Indians. Indeed, my dear Sir, I cannot believe you have any such chimerical visionary scheme in view." Even so, Jackson asked the governor of Arkansas to keep an eye on his old protégé.

Of course, Jackson *did* want Texas for the United States, and in the end Houston was both the hero of the Texas Revolution and the new republic's first elected president.

Over the next few years Houston spent much of his time drunk or on the road. He seems not to have spent much time selling dry goods at his trading post. In December 1831, on his way to Washington on Cherokee business, he boarded a riverboat bound for New Orleans and happened to meet Alexis de Tocqueville, who first spied Houston high atop a riverbank, mounted on a magnificent white horse, like Napoleon. The story of Houston's rise and fall in Tennessee seemed to confirm Tocqueville's growing conviction, bolstered by a recent meeting with Davy Crockett, that in a democracy "it's singular how low and how far wrong the people can go."

Three months later, in Washington, D.C., a congressman named William Stanbery defamed Houston on the floor of the House, suggesting that he had sought a fraudulent contract for Indian rations. Houston sent him a note that Stanbery refused to accept. Ten days passed, and then Houston recognized Stanbery on Pennsylvania Avenue and gave him a thrashing with a hickory cane he'd cut at Andrew Jackson's Hermitage. At one point during the struggle, Stanbery got his pistol out and fired it point-blank at Houston's heart. It misfired and the beating continued, ending with Houston grabbing Stanbery by the ankles and delivering a dramatic kick to the groin. The House of Representatives itself convened a trial, charging Houston with violating the principle of congressional privilege, which protected speech uttered on the House floor. The trial became another national sensation; President Jackson loaned Houston money to buy a new suit, and Francis Scott Key was engaged as Houston's lawyer. Houston, with great dramatic flair, presented his own arguments on the floor. Young ladies called out to him from the galleries and actors offered him laurels. Houston lost in the House but won in the court of opinion; his national reputation was rising again, and his thoughts turned to Texas.

Houston needed a cover story, and his dear friend President Jackson provided one by appointing him as a presidential envoy to the Comanche and the Pawnee. In September, Houston returned to the Three Forks, where he met Washington Irving. By December, he had crossed the Red River into Texas.

By 1854, Houston had served two separate terms as president of Texas, gone to Washington as a U.S. senator, and made a serious bid for the White House. He spent much energy that year doing all in his power to prevent passage in the Senate of the Kansas-Nebraska Act, which he saw would not only set the nation on a course toward civil war but also represented yet another betrayal of the eastern Indians, in whose removal he had reluctantly participated. (He had failed to protect his brother Cherokees in Texas from the genocidal attentions of Mirabeau Buonaparte Lamar, Houston's successor as president of Texas.)

When his eloquence before the Senate failed to kill that bill, Houston confided to a friend that in the election of 1860 he feared that the Free-Soil Party would unite with the abolitionists to win the presidency. "Then will come the tocsin of war and the clamor for secession," he predicted. "What fields of blood, what scenes of horror, what mighty cities in smoke and ruins—it is brother murdering brother." He envisioned a military dictatorship over the vanquished South, "in a sea of blood and smoking ruin," and assassinations and anarchy in the North.

.    .    .

Driving south from Salina, I stopped at a restaurant called JL's Barbecue and, upon leaving, eavesdropped on a family's conversation as they
debated whether or not to go "do Walmart." A little boy, about nine or
ten years old, waited impatiently, while his elders weighed the pros and
cons. His floppy grown-out Mohawk had faded from red to brownish
pink. I began to see large signs every few miles advertising concealed
weapons certification courses. They were huge banners mounted in
fields between poles. At Flat Rock Creek a man wearing a bright yellow
T-shirt fished, while a friend or perhaps a complete stranger picked
wildflowers nearby. Cattle grazed happily in electric-green fields.

I pulled in to Wagoner, which became Indian Territory's first
incorporated town in 1896, and spotted an information center along
the roadside. A homemade sign on the grounds advertised tree work,
yard work, and seasoned firewood, we deliver. The info center was a
beige galvanized-metal building with a reddish metal roof. There were
some picnic tables out front under some shade trees. I stood next to a
table and wondered who might eat here, on a busy thoroughfare called
South Dewey Avenue, across from a Walgreens and a Pizza Hut. There
was some kind of mall visible on the far side of a large parking lot and a
McDonald's sign on the horizon. The woman inside was named Patty
Stewart, and she was just closing up. She handed me some brochures
and commenced a sales pitch about the glories of Fort Gibson Lake.

"We have more shoreline than Michigan, you know."

Is that right? I said. That's a lot of shoreline.

"That is a lot of shoreline," she repeated. She asked if I'd been to
Tulsa, and I told her I was planning to spend the night there, visiting
friends.

"Go see the aquarium," she said. I told her I would.

I asked about Chouteau, and she confirmed that the lake had inun-
dated the old trading post. "A lot of their burial grounds ran through
that—what was it, a kind of stream?—and kind of a swampy area," she
decided, "so they had to either move them or leave them. Their burial
grounds were kind of humped up." I realized she was talking about the
Indians and their burial mounds.

I told her I was following my family's route down the Texas Road, and she began to chatter about Native Americans, the cotton gin, "all kinds of military stuff."

"This was a great farming community," she said. "There are five marinas here."

Is that right? I said.

"Here's a map of the lake."

I asked about Sam Houston and his wigwam.

"Oh, we know it was near Okay," Patty said, and she gave me directions. "That takes you right to Okay. They have parts of the bridge still there, and they swear it was there, his general store. I think his wife is buried at Fort Gibson."

Patty said she needed to close the shop because she was off to get her hair done.

"Here are some coupons," she said. "Would you sign in, please? And here's some more coupons. And this is a gun from the Vietnam era, if you're interested in that."

I thanked her and made to leave.

"What's your name?" she asked.

I told her.

"Well, Roger, you come back."


I followed Patty's directions, taking a left on Fifteenth Street, passing the industrial park with its large Unarco sign, and John's Jewelry with its more than six thousand patterns, to Route 16. I saw the Clover Leaf Lodge, of the Independent Order of Odd Fellows, and more stock ponds. A longhorn cow with one horn sticking up at an odd angle chewed its cud next to a fence. Sweet little baby calves romped behind her in the field.

Okay, I learned, was the home of the Lady Mustangs, and a sign told me that "God is the only one in a position to look down on others." A worthy sentiment from the Okay Christian Fellowship Church. I saw no sign of Sam Houston, so I pulled in to an Easy Mart where I met a young woman in a tan clerk's uniform smoking outside. Her name was Jody, and she was on break. I told her I was looking for the place around here where they say Sam Houston had his cabin. I thought the word "wigwam" might be too obscure. I asked if she knew anything about that.

"No, I sure don't. I know the lake's down that way." The folks around here were sure proud of their lake. "Um," she asked, "who's Sam Houston?"

I told her that he was the first elected president of the Republic of Texas and that he lived here in the early 1830s with his Cherokee Indian wife.

"Wow," she said. "You might go back up here to Martin's fish restaurant. They're older and have been here for quite a while. They might know."

I turned around and did as she suggested. Martin's was just about half a mile back up the way I had come. It advertised itself as "Okay's Floppin' Little Fish House." I went inside and asked a gray-haired woman behind the counter if she knew anything about Sam Houston's wigwam. She told me I should ask Richard, because he was born and raised here. "I'm just his mother."

After a slight scramble out back in the kitchen a woman came up. She had dyed hair, very dark, with a wide gray stripe along her part. Her name was Susan Martin. I repeated my question.

"Uh-huh, just down the way, there's a big stone." She told me her husband's grandpa had lived up north, came down here and met his wife, went home, and then came back. "Ended up," she said, "he was the fish man. Right over there on the Verdigris River. Everybody came to him to buy their fish. And that's why we ended up here. His grandpa ended up purchasing most of this land. Now the land that is still in our family, you can still see the wagon tracks. You can see it. We do think there is a hanging tree in their front yard."

Really?

"Well, yeah, because we kind of like had a few ghost experiences. So we do think, it's not far behind that building, you can still see the wagon tracks." She continued, "Okay was actually the first settled place here in Oklahoma. Fort Gibson became a township first, so they got the glory of that. But a lot of famous people lived around here. My husband's sister lives over there where the tracks are."

I asked if I could go look at the tracks.

She told me to hang on a minute. "Where's Ben?" There followed another scramble. Ben was missing. Someone said that Adam was up mowing the ditch. He could show him. Somebody else said that Adam wouldn't know about the tracks. Susan gave me Ben's phone number, and then Richard's mother said Ben wasn't born and raised here, to which Susan responded, "But he knows about it, Momma."

A woman named Paula came up. She looked skeptical. She shook her head when Susan told her about the wagon tracks. "Where did you hear this? Ben said I knew where it was?"

"No, Ben does."

"Well, call Ben. He should be home." She was shaking her head at the boundlessness of human folly.

"I've been down in there and seen them, Paula," Susan said in a low earnest tone of voice. She sounded slightly hurt.

"Well, there are lots of tracks down in there, but that doesn't mean they're wagon tracks."

Susan got on the phone.

"Hey. Can you still see the old wagon tracks that went through there up in the field?" There was a pause. "You can't? Okay, okay, I'm a retard then." She looked at me and shrugged. A long pause. "Okay, then I'm not a retard. Okay. Well, you said I was a retard. Okay, thank you. Bye."

Susan put down the phone and reported that Ben had said, yes, a few years ago we could see them but you can't see them now. It's grown up too much.

Then Paula said, "That's tick heaven, back up in there."

I thanked Susan and Paula and Richard's mother for their trouble and made to leave. Susan stopped me and asked if I had a camera with me. She sent me out to the car to fetch it. When I returned, she took me into the dining room and showed me a fascinating map of the Three Forks, a "sketch map" by someone named Tom Meagher. The map, which appeared to have been engraved by hand, showed the confluence of the Arkansas, Grand (Neosho), and Verdigris Rivers and nearby landmarks, including Houston's wigwam, which was across the Neosho from Fort Gibson, the Osage Agency, and the Texas Road. Susan's mother-in-law had owned the original, and Susan donated it to the Three Rivers Museum in Muskogee. She gave me directions to the monument, put up by the Muskogee–Indian Territory Daughters of the American Revolution, that memorialized the Texas Road, and the Irving Trail, and other items of historical interest.

More interesting than the monument, which was simply a roadside

historical marker, was the Three Rivers road itself, which seemed to
follow more or less the exact route of the Texas Road through a broad
V-shaped bottomland, defined by the three rivers and narrowing to a
point, known as French Point, at the mouth of the Neosho.

The bottoms, according to Meagher's map (which I later acquired
and discovered was composed in collaboration with Grant Foreman,
the historian), were in the 1830s and thereabouts the site of a scattering of Indian villages. Today they are largely covered with beautiful
meadows filled with wildflowers or fields under cultivation and irrigation. Some of the fences I saw had irregular pieces of what looked
like firewood as fence posts. Trees flowered everywhere. There were
ruined falling-down shacks and fences grown over with blooming hon-
eysuckle, its thick scent heavy in the air. A hand-fashioned wooden
signboard depicted an American flag, with the word FREE where the
field of stars would normally be, a lone star in the upper portion of the
R. Below the flag, stenciled in black spray paint: KEEP AMERICA FREE OF
TERRORISM. Down the road a bit was a burned-out mobile home adjacent to a large field, waist-high with a yellow-topped grain crop, filled
with feasting crows.

I came to the banks of the Neosho, which was spanned by two
beautiful rusty metal bridges, one with rails, the other a single-lane
auto bridge. The rail bridge was supported by stone and concrete towers; the auto bridge by mere concrete. I turned in to the Ray Clinken-
beard Memorial River Park, got out of my Ford, and walked along
the bank. As near as I could figure, Houston's wigwam was located
right here. Or across the road in what was now an impassable thicket.
I stepped into an outhouse made of a single large sheet of corrugated
steel, rolled in on itself and set up on its edge. It was like entering a
tunnel of shit. I quickly exited. At the edge of the park, where I was
cautioned against illegal dumping, I saw a broken-down sign for the
Jean-Pierre Choteau (*sic*) National Recreation Trail, which had fallen
into a state of neglect and after about a hundred yards was completely
overgrown. Families stood along the bank, fishing for catfish. When I
returned to my car, it was covered in butterflies, their long curly pro-
boscises unfurled, drinking pollen through their tubular tongues from
the smooth, warm silvery metal surface.

At Fort Gibson, I met a group of men dressed up in mid-nineteenth-

Near the site of Sam Houston's Wigwam Neosho

century U.S. Cavalry uniforms. Most were late 1840s and 1850s, but some were Civil War. They worked for the Oklahoma Historical Society. I asked if they were reenacting something.

"Yeah," one replied. "Here in a few minutes we're going to reenact taking that flag down there."

We chatted about the Texas Road, and I listened to the friendly costumed historians compare uniforms and the heft of their swords. They were obsessed with the small details of garrison life. I admired their rigor as the flag descended to the elegiac bugles and drums of the evening colors.

I found Sam Houston's wife near the circle of honor at the Fort Gibson National Cemetery. The stone read

Talahina R.

WIFE OF GEN.

SAM HOUSTON

Her name was actually Diana Rogers. She was a Cherokee, and like many other Cherokees her name did not sound particularly Indian. The graves extended as far as I could see: John P. Decatur, Sutler, 1832; Charles O. Collins, Assistant Quartermaster; Unknown, no date; Billy Bow Legs, Captain, Indian Territory, no date. A large iron cross at the center of the circle of honor listed 2,123 interments. Known 156. Unknown 1,967.

In Tulsa, I had dinner with some writer friends at a fine restaurant and drank too much wine. A couple of women from Durant, Oklahoma, were eavesdropping on our conversation and told me that I should be sure to stop there on my way to Dallas and see the world's largest peanut. They said I'd be driving through the hometowns of Reba McEntire and Carrie Underwood and that I should be sure to stop at the big Choctaw casino.

Driving through Oklahoma, I noticed that even the rest stops had casinos, sad smoky little square rooms filled with slot machines. You take a break from driving and play some slots. They reminded me of the video arcades of my youth, where I played games like *Pac-Man*, *Galaga*, *Defender*, and *Stargate*. I visited one at the Choctaw Travel Plaza, in Atoka. There were old folks, young folks, people wearing trucker caps and jeans, faded dirty T-shirts. Overweight people with bad complexions and spreading bottoms sat in front of these weird digital slot machines in an atmosphere of stale cigarette smoke. Across the street was a shuttered store with a sign that said SHEFFIELD's and a defunct bank. Just down the street, past a long row of empty stores, was a Walmart with a parking lot jammed with cars. I drove on past, past a pretty old field with a green tractor and a red barn, then an odd architectural confection up on a hill that resembled a Swiss chalet, with stone paths winding down to a pond. Just off the highway was another dead armadillo amid a patch of pink wildflowers.

While listening to Ryan Seacrest, apparent heir to Casey Kasem, hosting America's Top 40 countdown, I saw the first patch of prickly pear cactus. Texas was near. A flying dinosaur with a mouthful of teeth perched atop a pole in front of a yard full of derelict dump trucks. A broken-down Stay Inn motel flashed by; it looked like a good candidate for freelance meth cooking.

Growing bored, I tuned in to a country music station. "Real life, real feelings, real music," said the announcer. Banal generic guitar rock belched from the speakers, sung with a vague southern drawl. Sweet-faced country people were getting up early to get to the Church of Christ, back in *our town;* small-town redneck boys sat around talking shit and picking fights, where it's all for one and one for all, with a seasonal refrain about those boys that rhymes with "appall," which I won't quote for fear of copyright persecution. One nostalgic kitsch crime followed another as city-dwelling entrepreneurs sought to entertain their largely urban audience with slick ballads about getting out of the concrete jungle, back past a couple of little shacks, where the crickets sing and you can hear somebody's mother's uncle plucking at a banjo, with a blonde who's hotter than a Georgia summer wearing Daisy Dukes and dancing barefoot on a tailgate near a pond. That's America, by God, love it or leave it, the Stars and Stripes are the best, but the rebel flag's okay too, small towns are beautiful, you ought to be able to pray in schools, and you better watch out for that tidal wave down on the border.

The happy, happy, sappy-slick country music was bringing me down, so I decided to listen to a radio preacher deliver a sincere sermon about empty pleasures and sour grapes while I watched a group of young people on the other side of the highway climbing up on big round hay bales and taking pictures. I looked for the giant peanut in Durant but couldn't find it, but I did come upon the giant Choctaw Casino Resort. The parking lot was enormous and almost completely full on a lazy Sunday afternoon. I noticed that Merle Haggard would be playing there soon; too bad I couldn't find his songs on the radio.

I found a parking space and got out. Inside the casino was a crazy din of competing bells, alarms, beeps, and jingles. A band played somewhere in the neon distance. It was just like the rest-stop casino only much, much bigger. I saw a woman playing two slots at once, her two casino cards slotted in with personalized lanyards hanging down; one machine was adorned with the smirking image of Harrison Ford as Indiana Jones and the other with Red Hot Ruby. The player just sat there on a stool, pressing both buttons at once, her face slack. When I first saw Red Hot Ruby, I thought she was the Little Mermaid but soon realized my mistake. Ruby was a devilish girl, with much larger breasts than the Disney character and red flames caressing (or perhaps emerging from) her backside. Red Hot Ruby was all over. Sometimes she appeared as Hot Red Ruby. I couldn't bring myself to play with that sexy, ravenous devil girl and her bottomless coin slot, so I retreated to the safety of the parking lot, which was patrolled by armed security guards on mountain bikes. Hall and Oates sang "I Can't Go for That (No Can Do)" as I drove south toward home.

When I came to Colbert, site of a famous ferry across the Red River, I inquired at the Texas Info Center and was told that the ferry was just about where the railroad bridge now spans the river, just east of the highway bridge. The nice woman there gave me directions, and I drove back across into Oklahoma. I found the River View RV park and made my way down to the bank.

In 1858, the Butterfield Stage first passed through this place. It was a speculative enterprise, a government contract secured by an old stage driver from New York named John Butterfield; he was friendly with President James Buchanan and a founder of the American Express Company, along with Henry Wells and William G. Fargo, who also founded Wells, Fargo & Company to bring mail and banking services to California. It was a big contract for the time, $600,000 a year to establish roads and stations and biweekly mail service between St. Louis and San Francisco. The first stage left Missouri on September 16, 1858, with a single through passenger named Waterman L. Ormsby, a newspaper reporter for *The New York Herald*. The stage arrived at Colbert's ferry on September 20, thirty-four hours ahead of schedule. Ormsby describes Benjamin Franklin Colbert as "a half-breed Indian of great sagacity and business tact," with a white wife and a large gang of slaves hard at work cutting down the banks of the river, pushing away the sand, and improving the approach to the ferry. The ferry itself was little more than a raft pushed across the shallows by stout slaves wielding poles. "He is nearly white, very jovial and pleasant, and, altogether, a very good specimen of the half-breed Indian."

Standing on the bank, looking across the shallow river at Texas, I could picture the scene. Both sides of the river were bound by red bluffs that dipped low near the river, and it was easy to imagine the wagons lined up on the north side, waiting to make their crossing from Indian Territory into the promised land beyond.

A family of campers wandered nearby, and a man named Santiago fished for catfish with a hand line, twirling his hook and sinker, baited with a worm, over his head like a lasso and tossing it into the channel. He was from Plano and drove about forty-five minutes to get here, not so far to travel for a good fishing hole. I told him I had come all the way from New York. He said that today the fishing was not good. Just then he got a bite. We both laughed when the fish got away.

I had John Stambaugh's address right, fortunately, so I found his apartment on Sandhurst Lane in Dallas, despite his bizarre directions, and I managed to locate the gate he was so concerned about. It was one of those low-rise garden-style apartment complexes with separate entrances for cars and pedestrians. I pressed the apartment number on the keypad and waited. Several minutes passed. I tried again. Through the steel bars of the gate I could see the grassy courtyard with its tasteful trees and orderly sidewalks linking redbrick dwellings. After about two minutes I heard a voice through the intercom. It was John. He said he'd be right out. Several minutes passed and I began to grow uncomfortable. Then, just as I was about to ring him again, I spied a small hunched man making his slow, painful way toward me. He was naked except for a pair of pale yellow shorts that hung low on his hips. As he approached, I could see that shaving cream covered much of his face. There were dribs and drabs of shaving cream on the parts of his face that he'd shaved and on his neck, ears, and shoulders.

John and I introduced ourselves, and he apologized for his appearance. I had caught him shaving. He said he hadn't known when to expect me, though I had spoken to him every day that week, and I had spoken to him earlier that morning. He seemed to be in some pain. His feet, which appeared to be flat, were puffy, turned out slightly, with long yellow toenails. He was bent over in the shape of a banana.

He said his feet were swollen and that it hurt to walk on the sidewalk. I offered my arm as a support, and we proceeded slowly through the grass toward his home. John winced with each step, especially when he had to cross the sidewalk. His back was densely freckled and his skinny bottom, exposed by his drooping shorts, was pale. A large mole protruded from his shoulder.

Inside his apartment, mail and papers were scattered over every visible surface, including card tables that were set up in the living room. A blue theme predominated. There was a blue floral couch and a painting of greenish-blue horses galloping over a featureless blue plain, pursued by a blue-gray storm cloud. Another painting was a blue fantasia of a blue lake, a dark island silhouetted against dark blue clouds, ringed by the misty blue-white clouds of memory. In the foreground was a clump of white lilies. Unread rolled-up newspapers in plastic sleeves littered the floor. In another room I saw a painting of a dirt road bounded by bluebonnet flowers; in the background was a metal ranch gate and a live oak tree.

I noticed a couple of old telephones in the living room and remembered that Patricia had told me John possessed a remarkable collection of antique phones. In a wood-paneled den, there were by my count twenty-eight ancient telephones mounted on the walls. The wall phones were wooden cabinets of various shapes with wooden ringer boxes mounted on them, metal receivers hanging on the hook and transmitters projecting near the top. No two were alike in design. There were Northern Electrics and Kelloggs and phones from Sears, Roebuck. Some had dialers, but most did not. At least thirty-five old metal candlestick telephones from the second and third decades of the twentieth century crowded the surfaces of a sideboard and the side tables adjacent to another blue couch, which was also covered with papers.

That's a lot of phones, I said, marveling at the collection. "They're beautiful."

"I think so," John replied. "Don't know if anybody else does. But then I don't really care."

I had come to see John because he was the most serious and accomplished genealogist in our family. He was descended, I knew, from Perry Wilson's sister Lydia. He had offered, through Patricia, to show me around Collin County and point out the ancestral Wilson and Adamson properties. Or so I thought.

We were driving through Dallas to a restaurant. Patricia had warned me not to let John drive, but he insisted. He wasn't doing a bad job, though he occasionally made a wrong turn. I asked him how he got interested in genealogy. Was it something he'd always been interested in?

"No," he said. "It wasn't. I really don't know. Just trying to think. I don't know."

Seems like you did a lot of work on it, though, I prompted.

"Yes, I did at first. But I just don't remember how I got interested in it."

It turned out that John not only didn't remember how he became interested in family genealogy but didn't remember what he had learned. He had written several books, but their contents had simply disappeared from his memory. He thought maybe Patricia had got him into it, but he wasn't sure. Come to think of it, he couldn't remember how or where he had met Pat either. He wondered if maybe she saw his name on something. I said she probably saw his name on one of his works of genealogy. Trying to stimulate his memory, I asked him if he was descended from Perry Wilson's sister.

"Ah." He paused. "I should know." Another long pause as the lights of the city played on the windows of his Buick. "Yes, that's right. Lydia Wilson, she was my great, my great-great-grandmother. Esther Wilson was her mother. Lydia was next. My ancestor was one of Lydia's daughters. I got really deep into that for a while, but it's been so long that I don't really remember a lot of it now."

A small selection of John Stambaugh's antique telephones, Dallas, Texas

We sat down at one of his regular haunts, a Mexican food place where he always sat at the same table and the waiters knew to bring him the Martinez plate to eat along with a bourbon and Sprite to drink. I ordered a large plate of guacamole.

John had spent his entire career working for telephone companies, first in Dallas and then in San Angelo, where he was district manager, and then in Dallas again. I asked how he got interested in telephones.

"My mother claims that when I was too little to walk even, she was carrying me in her arms, and at that time we had wall telephones with a crank on the side, and I reached out and cranked a telephone."

He told me this story several times over the next twenty-four hours.

When he got out of the army, in 1946, John went back to the University of Texas and majored in personnel management. He didn't care what he majored in, he said. He just wanted to get out. Then he went to Dallas to work for the telephone company. He was even hired over the telephone, he told me, after he called a fella named Wigley in Dallas about a job. Mr. Wigley, who knew one of his professors, said he could hire him today but maybe not tomorrow, because of budget cuts. So John got on a bus and started work that day. He spent the night at the Dallas Y. In 1957 he went out to San Angelo to work for GTE, which later became Verizon, because he had a problem with a new man who came in at the telephone company in Dallas. Nobody could please him. John was the manager of the San Angelo district, which included Comanche, Sonora, and Big Lake. But after a few years he took a pay cut and a lesser job at his old company, he said, so he could get back to the Dallas scene.

He noticed my ring and asked if I was engaged or married? I said I was married. "Oh, you are? To a guy or a girl," he asked, "not that it matters?" I began to understand why he might prefer Dallas to San Angelo.

We went back to his apartment, and John showed me his autobiographical novel, set in World War II. He had served in France and in Germany and wrote the novel about his experiences. His father had served at the same time, called up from the reserves and based in Muskogee, Oklahoma, as a range officer. One of his duties had been the relocation of Indian cemeteries in the Fort Gibson area.

Many of John's old telephones were connected to an antique switchboard from 1887, and he showed me how it worked. He could make phones ring all over the house. Telephone technology had remained stable enough that he was able to route his outside line through the switchboard.

Back when he was running the San Angelo district for GTE, John often met with his rural clients, who sometimes owned their own lines and poles. Many were on party lines. I asked how the party lines worked, and he explained that there were many different arrangements, depending on the telephone company. People had different rings, and it depended on whether the ringing was by frequency or not. Sometimes everyone heard all the rings but usually only those who had the same frequency. He told funny stories about party-line feuds involving families with names I knew, like Cauthorn, Whitehead, Wardlaw, and Wardlow, and he wondered about the similarity of the last two names. He told one story about a woman who called him up and wanted to know how much it would cost to get a private telephone line out to her ranch south of Sonora somewhere. She was sick and tired of being on a party line. He said that her neighbors owned their own line, and they owned the poles as well, so maybe she could run her line on their poles and save some money. She wasn't interested. She said that her neighbor was her sister and that son of a bitch is my brother-in-law. John laughed a long time at the memory.

The room with the switchboard contained dozens of black metal telephones from the 1930s and 1940s and one green plastic wall mount phone from the early 1960s that looked just like the phone we had in my first childhood home, a rental house on 219 Johnson Street, in Del Rio. They were all jumbled together on a set of wooden bookshelves on which were tacked six index cards listing the names, neatly typed, of telephone collectors who had visited the collection. They came from as far away as Edmonton, Alberta; Brea, California; and New Richland, Minnesota.

John showed me to a small bedroom and warned me that the toilet in the bathroom was broken. The faucet was leaking badly. The housework seemed to have gotten away from him. He mentioned a lady who used to clean for him, but she evidently hadn't been there for a long time. I put a musty set of sheets on my bed and pushed the soiled pillow to the floor with my shoe. I decided to sleep in my clothes.

The next day John took me to a Burger King for breakfast, and we set off for Collin County, where Larkin Adamson in 1850 named the town of Weston after his hometown in Missouri. He built a store there and became the community's first postmaster. We drove to a town called Celina and stopped at the visitor center and museum, formerly the home of the newspaper *The Celina Record*. John had donated an American flag, with forty-five stars on the blue field, that his mother, Lilian, had carried in a school play in 1895. The flag hung on the wall. We visited with Jane Huddleston, a very nice woman who helps run the museum, and looked at a book listing all the graves in the Cottage Hill Cemetery, where John's parents were buried. We looked for Larkin Adamson and found his son, Larkin H., who died in 1900. His obituary, which was reprinted from the McKinney *Democrat*, said that he had died of consumption, "that fell destroyer."

"Every spring time," the text read, "the lovely flowers will raise their blooming heads above his grave, but he will continue to sleep the long, sweet sleep."

As we left the museum, John spotted an old telephone in the window of an antiques store. I squinted and saw that a wooden wall phone was barely visible among the usual rocking chairs and armoires. John said he didn't need any more telephones.

Are you sure? I asked. "I thought I saw a spot on the wall in your bedroom." John just chuckled to himself.

I asked him if there were any good stories about the phones in his collection.

"No, not really."

He said he found most of them in flea markets. On our way to the cemetery, I drove and John told me where to turn. We passed lush fields filled with pink wildflowers. "I don't know where we are," John would say, "but turn left. Wait a second, let's go that way." More fields, often populated with old tumbled-down barns, and then, "I think maybe I told you wrong. I think we need to go back."

All of a sudden John said, "My grandfather's farm was right there." I stopped in the middle of the road, a narrow two-lane blacktop.

He was very serious and intent, staring hard at the weathered barn with a rusty roof in a green field.

"That was his barn at one time. That's where it was. That's where my dad was raised, but the farm they lived in when I was growing up was this way." He pointed.

I asked him if he used to play in that barn. A barn was a paradise for me when I was a child.

"Yeah," he said. "We did."

Eventually, we found ourselves in Weston, a pleasant little town without sidewalks or curbs. The sign out front of the First Baptist Church said OUR CHURCH IS PRAYER CONDITIONED.

Jane had told us to stop in and see Steve Goldstein, who sells eggs at the Weston store, but the store was closed. A sign advertised Texas honey. A scrap metal sculpture of a rooster stood guard out front of the charming redbrick building. Next door was the Weston Country Cafe, also closed. John said the café used to be the store. Down the street was a tiny little building with a sign that read OLD WESTON POST OFFICE, MARCH 15, 1900, POP. 316, RURAL FREE MAIL DELIVERY.

I got out and John waited in the car. The old post office was locked, but just up the street I noticed a weather-beaten wooden clapboard building with a metal roof. Pale strips of paint peeled from the walls,

Kenneth Cowan, Weston, Texas

and redbrick pillars supported a carport. A bright blue tractor was parked in front. Sitting in the carport, before a pair of swinging garage doors, surrounded by lawn mowers and engines, was Kenneth Cowan, proprietor of Cowan's Garage. A small sign with red letters bore a black silhouette of a Ford Model T.

Kenneth wore blue work clothes and blue suspenders and a black gimme cap that said TEXAS STAR BANK. His socks were white.

Kenneth said he was born in 1930 and had lived in Weston all his life. "Yeah, I been here about eighty-two years. Took time out and spent a couple of years in the army, but I hadn't got very far from home."

"Well, it's a nice place, I don't see any reason to get very far. I'm trying to figure out why my relatives left and ended up in West Texas."

"Somebody come by and told them to go west."

Kenneth told me that Mr. Adamson used to live right there in that house, right there. He pointed at a neat white house with blue trim across the street.

Larkin Adamson?

"Elby Adamson."

He must have been Larkin's son, or grandson, and thus a distant relative of mine. I asked about the post office, and he said it had been in quite a few different buildings and that it started out as a grocery store, as he recalled, right there where the little store is now. He gestured at the rooster.

Kenneth gave me clear, simple directions to the cemetery. On the way we passed a field with a ring of large pecan and oak trees. John said his father's farm was right there. "I used to love to go there," he said. "The house was right there. We used to swing on that big tree. The house was here, and a garden." Somebody named Chad Alexander was advertising the property for sale.

We found the cemetery and the old marble obelisk marking the grave of Larkin H. Adamson. The inscription read IN MY FATHER'S HOUSE ARE MANY MANSIONS. With the help of a detailed map of the cemetery that John compiled many years ago, we came to the graves of his parents: J. Lee and Lilian J. Stambaugh. He stood before his parents' graves for a long time. Then he suggested we get some lunch.

On the way to the restaurant he said if I wanted to, we could go back to the museum in Celina and look in the cemetery book to see where old Larkin was buried. I reminded him that we had already tried that.

I didn't care where Larkin was buried anyway. A few minutes later he suggested that we could look in the cemetery book in Celina to see where old Larkin was buried.

At Lucy's restaurant the waitress asked if we'd like to start off with some "fried green tomatoes, fried pickles, fried mushrooms, fried zucchini, fried jalapeños, or fried cheese." John ordered ranch-style chicken and two sides and then asked the waitress to remind him what he had ordered. I decided to stick with sides: fried green tomatoes, green beans, and some okra.

Mounted on the wall behind me was a stuffed bobcat wearing a hat and a bandanna.

John spent much of his childhood in the lower Rio Grande valley, in the town of San Juan. He knew a man who made his living as a ditch rider, riding his horse along the irrigation canals that crisscross the rich alluvial floodplain. The irrigation company used to have its own

John Stambaugh, Collin County, Texas

private telephone switchboard that connected the telephones of all the ditch riders.

Dr. John Brinkley, the famous border radio charlatan, had a hospital in San Juan in addition to his operation in Del Rio. John told me he thought Dr. Brinkley's son Johnny had committed suicide while talking on the telephone with his mother.

"Do you know about Dr. Brinkley?" John asked me. "He had been a politician in Kansas, but they ran him out. His thing was he put goat glands in people instead of testicles. It was supposed to make them more potent. I don't know what he did with the testicles."

Our food arrived and John explained that there were two antique telephone collectors' clubs. One of them, his club, organized a show every year in Abilene, Kansas, but the headquarters was in McPherson, Kansas, because that's where the secretary lived. The other one was headquartered in Pennsylvania, because one guy got his feelings hurt and formed his own club. John thought that was very funny.

As we left, I struck up a conversation with the flirty young waitress, who told me her name was Caitlin, but "people call me Red." She pronounced it "Ray-ed."

Caitlin had a pretty oval face and strawberry blond hair. She asked me where I was from and was curious about my travels. I told her I was headed to Clay County and asked if there were any local attractions that she could recommend, and she immediately replied I should *be sure* to go see the Wichita Falls haunted insane asylum.

"My mom bought me this book that's called *Haunted Texas*, and it's all the places all over Texas that are super haunted. Do you have to go to Sherman? There's either a black statue of Jesus in the Sherman cemetery or it's the Happy family that died all on the same day at the same time. I forget. It was the coolest book I've ever had. I've got to find it."

I asked her how I would know where to find the haunted insane asylum in Wichita Falls.

"Everybody knows it," she said. All I had to do was ask. For a moment I thought maybe this was a roadside attraction, but she assured me it was simply an abandoned insane asylum and that it was super haunted. But trespassing?

"Well," she said with a lilt, "we don't care about that in Texas!"

I suggested that in Texas trespassing was a good way to get shot.

"Yeah, it's a game," she said, all flirty and gay. "We just see who can run faster and who's a better shooter."

I was about to take my leave when she thought of another haunting I might enjoy.

"Did you ever go to the Anson Lights, in West Texas? I swear to God, this is so true. It's out by Abilene, you go down this dirt road, and you flick your lights three times—right, and it's really far, and I didn't believe it, I'm like this is so stupid, it's the dumbest thing I've ever done, I mean, why did you make me come here? So I was in college," her voice ascending, as if in questioning, "so we went down it, and it's in the middle of nowhere, ahright, and this, you'll see this lady come with a lantern, right, looking for her kids—you've heard that story a million times, right?—and when you go down there, there are two lights, one big light that you can see, have you seen like on a farm? how they have one big light, it's got one light kind of in front of you, but way down there and it's got a little bitty way over there?—anyways, I swear to you, I, Jesus Christ is my witness, ahright, and we went down there and we did it, and I mean, so stupid, and I swear to you, here comes the light and it's doing this, all the way—"

"Swinging back and forth," I offered, "like a pendulum?"

"Yes, I swear, like if somebody's holding, you know—oh my gosh, it scared me to death!"

"So you click on your headlights three times? And people down there would tell me where to go to do this?"

"Yes, near Anson, just down a dirt road in the middle of nowhere. It's terrifying. It scared me worse than anything. I was like, Ahhh! Get me the hell out of here! I haven't seen the Marfa Lights, but I'd really like to."

At this point John, who had been gamely trying to follow her narrative, piped in: "Have you seen the Marfa Lights?"

"I have not," said Caitlin.

"But she's seen the Anson Lights," I said, "and that sounds scarier."

I thanked Caitlin for all the good advice, and we turned toward the door.

"Thank *you*," she said. "Y'all be good!"

.   .   .

Driving back to Dallas, I asked John if he knew anything about La Réunion. He mentioned a stadium by that name, and I explained that I meant the old French colony, a failed experiment in Fourierist socialism on the Elm Fork of the Trinity River, across from the old village of Dallas. He didn't know anything about that, but he suggested I look in the history of Collin County that his parents wrote. I dropped him off and, after nosing around in his parents' book, set off to find the last vestiges of the New Jerusalem in Texas.

Texas in the late 1840s and the 1850s, for a certain type of European radical, must have looked like paradise. Americans were busy with their own feverish schemes. The conquest of northern Mexico had melted away the western border, opening vast new territories to the American imagination, into which poured the blood-and-soil agonies of slave power and the abolitionists as well as the laissez-faire frenzies of the California gold rush. European liberals and socialists, desperate for a new start after the failed revolutions of 1848 and gulled by shady offers of cheap land south of the Red River, came to see Texas as a good place to start over. Germans ended up in the Hill Country. The French were attracted to the tall-grass prairie country north of Dallas.

The first of these French colonies was the brainchild of Étienne Cabet, a socialist politician and newspaper agitator, who hatched a plan to found a utopia based on his 1840 novel *Voyage en Icarie*. Cabet made a deal with the Peters Company, which still controlled much of the land in North Texas between the Red and the Trinity Rivers, though titles were often far from clear. Cabet believed he had purchased a million acres and announced to the readers of *Le Populaire* that his followers would soon settle in a "new terrestrial paradise." In fact, Cabet had secured grants of less than ten thousand acres, much of it in tracts scattered across the prairie north of present-day Dallas.

The first sixty-nine Icarians—"soldiers of Fraternity" charged by Cabet with the "regeneration of the human race"—arrived in New Orleans on March 27, 1848, and soon steamed up the Mississippi and the Red River to Shreveport, where they were astonished to discover they were more than 250 miles from their new home, a practically roadless stretch of swamp and prairie dotted with the occasional Anglo settlement. The Icarians spoke little English and had no realistic prospect of transporting their piles of steamer trunks over such a distance.

They began a long march of suffering; dysentery, malaria, malnutrition, and exposure conspired against them. Many did not survive the summer. A second party of Icarians arrived, only to retreat to Shreveport and New Orleans. Cabet finally showed up in January 1849 and blamed the Texas disaster on its primary victims. He never set foot in Texas. Eventually, he took his last three hundred followers up the Mississippi to Nauvoo, Illinois, the former Mormon colony. After some years of prosperity under the dictatorial ministrations of Cabet, the colony fractured over the question of tobacco, with the pro-smoking "reds" arrayed against Cabet's anti-smoking "whites." The reds took control, and in November 1856 Cabet died of a stroke while planning yet another colonial venture.

Undeterred by the Icarian misadventure, another French socialist dreamer followed close on Cabet's heels. La Réunion was founded in 1854 with the establishment of the European Society for the Colonization of Texas, by Victor Considérant, a French socialist and republican revolutionary. Considérant had been an engineer in the French army but resigned his commission in the 1830s, after becoming radicalized by the corruption of the monarchy, and sallied forth into the hurly-burly of French politics as a socialist propagandist.

In time he became the primary exponent and popularizer of the decidedly peculiar political philosophy of François Marie Charles Fourier. Considérant authored many books and edited several different newspapers. His writings seem to have greatly influenced Marx (and Dostoyevsky, albeit negatively), and his *Principes du socialisme* of 1847 reads like an early draft of *The Communist Manifesto*.

Considérant's general critique of capitalism bears striking similarities to Marx's, though his conclusions are very different. For Considérant, violent revolution was a great evil, and its prospect was treated as a warning rather than a desirable end. Like Rousseau, Considérant believed that man was born free yet was everywhere enchained by the fetters of society, which had corrupted man's naturally virtuous passions and impulses. Although he espoused one of the least realistic political philosophies of modernity, during his period of political activity Considérant was far from being a starry-eyed utopian. Humanity as he found it was not prepared for Fourier's orgiastic phalanstery—communal living arrangements that involved the abolition of the family, free love, and other polyamorous schemes. Much work remained in the area of social evolution before anything like that could be viable in the nineteenth century. As a political revolutionary and socialist, Considérant worked to democratize the society that he lived in. He advocated the creation of social welfare programs, democratic and dispersed ownership of railroads, low-interest government loans, separation of church and state, freedom of expression, pacifism, and disarmament. In the midst of France's permanent revolution, Considérant was a relatively practical democratic socialist. Life on the Texas frontier proved a far greater challenge.

Convicted of treason in 1849, Considérant fled to Belgium. His follower Albert Brisbane, whose work inspired the Brook Farm utopian community in Massachusetts, had long encouraged him to found a community, or phalanx in the jargon of Fourier, in the United States. Considérant did not at first wish to found a commune, and for a long time he spurned Brisbane's entreaties. Like Marx, he thought that a socialist society must arise from an industrialized, fully modern society. But after Considérant was driven from France into an unhappy exile, Brisbane and other Fourierists persuaded him to attempt an experimental phalanx.

In 1852, Considérant came to America and visited a commune in New Jersey called the North American Phalanx. He saw little in that mismanaged community that he recognized as Fourierism. He met up with Brisbane near Cincinnati. Together with other Fourier disciples they steamed down the Ohio to the Mississippi and up the Arkansas River, passing through Little Rock and finally disembarking at Fort Smith. From there they rode horseback down the Texas Road through Indian Territory and crossed the Red River into Texas.

Considérant was enraptured by the countryside north of Dallas. His doubts about America were conquered, at least temporarily. "Nature has done all. All is prepared, all is arranged: we have only to raise those buildings which the eye is astonished at not finding; and nothing is appropriated nor separated by the selfish exclusiveness of civilized man; nothing is cramped. What fields of action! What a theatre of maneuvers for a great colonization operating in the combined and collective mode! What reserves for the cradle of Harmony, and how powerful and prompt would be its development, if the living and willing elements of the World of the Future were transported there! A horizon of new ideas, new sentiments and hopes, suddenly opened before me, and I felt myself baptized in an American faith."

After returning to Belgium, Considérant soon published two books—*Au Texas* and *The Great West: A New Social and Industrial Life in Its Fertile Regions*—announcing his great plan to colonize the future in Texas. The books contained detailed plans for the future colony, together with dire and, as it turned out, prophetic warnings of the difficulties that attend those who seek to win the future. "On our globe," he wrote, "America is at present the Country of Realizations. Its spirit is that of diversity, of movement and enterprise, the love of inventions, of experiments, of adventures. It is absolutely the opposite of our old Europe, timorous and enslaved to routine, even in its progressive aspects; despotic even in its aims of liberty. Oh my friends, how beautiful and powerful a thing is Liberty! . . .

"Friends, the Promised Land is a reality," Considérant declared, indulging, as often, in fanciful biblical metaphors. "I did not believe it, I did not go to seek it, I was led there step by step. We have seen it and traversed it for forty days, and I have now described it to you. The redeeming idea sleeps in the captivity of Egypt. Let it awaken! Believe, and the land of realization, the Promised Land is yours. One strong resolution, one act of collective faith and this country is conquered. I bring you news of salvation, I show you the way and I propose the inauguration. Let us only unite in purpose, and little as the outside world may dream of it, the new social era will be founded."

Considérant was an influential man, with followers all over the world. He soon raised more than a million francs, though far less than he had hoped, and colonists began making plans to become the workers of the future.

When Considérant arrived in New York in 1855, he discovered that the events on the ground in Texas had changed, as had the political climate. The rise of the Know-Nothing Party and the dramatic collapse of Icaria had generated a wave of newspaper-driven bigotry directed at the French colonists. The *Texas State Gazette* and *The Texas State Times* both denounced the colonists in advance, branding them "an armed band of seditious, lawless, foreign abolitionists" who "were seeking to sap the foundations of society."

"The socialist is an *abolitionist* everywhere," wrote another editor. "It is part of his creed." Considérant was alarmed, so he published a pamphlet titled *European Colonization in Texas*, addressed to the people of the United States, in which he put forth his case. Shocked that a nation founded and composed so recently of immigrants should give rise to a party based on hostility to foreigners and immigration, he sought understanding.

"Now, as the human never shows itself absolutely illogical, even in the greatest errors," he wrote, articulating one of the core principles of his political faith, "it is impossible, I said to myself, that in an enlightened country, in the midst of an intelligent population, a great party should be formed in absolute contradiction to the origin, the character, and the destiny of the country itself."

Considérant went on to reason away the existence of the Know-Nothing Party and its fundamental platform, explaining gently but firmly the errors of fact and logic leading to its mistaken impressions of his enterprise, as well as the clear reasons why Know-Nothings, if they truly existed, far from being alarmed by the coming of a colony of French utopians, should welcome it with open arms.

The Know-Nothings of Texas, if they noticed his pamphlet, were not convinced. But they were the least of La Réunion's problems. The lands Considérant had hoped to acquire from the State of Texas were occupied, and the homestead law he had counted on, which would have granted each settler 160 acres, with additional land available for fifty cents an acre, had been repealed. Land prices had inflated drastically. Charging ahead nevertheless, the colony was obliged to pay up to five dollars an acre for some poor land along the banks of the Trinity River.

In March 1854, thirty-three colonists—among them Swiss, Germans, Poles, and Alsatians—landed in Galveston with their luggage, trunks, and crates full of grape, peach, apple, pear, and other fruit tree cuttings that they imagined were unknown in Texas. Thirty-two days later, they arrived at La Réunion to find one building with four rooms in which they were obliged to continue their camping life, albeit under a wooden roof. They set to work, attempting to garden under the hot Texas sun. Nothing grew. More colonists arrived, including Considérant. As their numbers swelled, so too did the opportunity for discord. The colony began to fail almost immediately.

As with Brook Farm and so many other utopian experiments, practical people—farmers and mechanics—were in short supply, and the colony was composed mostly of intellectuals, musicians, writers, artists, scientists, and philosophers who were unprepared for the hardships they necessarily would face. Considérant's hopes that Americans would join his European colonists were in vain. By the end of the summer, major investors were already pulling out. Some arrived to extract their investment personally.

European idealists were not well suited to withstand the harsh extremes of Texas weather. Their poorly built homes were too cold in the winter, and the summer heat was unbearable. Both 1855 and 1856 were drought years in Texas, and the colony's spring dried up, requiring them to haul water.

One Polish colonist named Kalikst Wolski kept a diary and later published a book about his adventures in the New World. After a hard summer that ended with eight dead of fever, on September 1, 1855, Wolski was beginning to lose hope. "Here with us, want is beginning, and there is present already the prophesied lack of sugar and salt. For two days we have had no salt for our food, and had to drink our coffee and tea without sugar."

Wolski also dreaded the "unpleasant visits of snakes, always crawling in uncounted numbers everywhere in this region." Snakebites were apparently rather common, and the colonists made use of a folk remedy they had learned in Houston. "When the poisonous snake bites, it is necessary at once to suck the spot and so draw out the poison," he wrote. "Then you must spread the spot with the gunpowder and burn it, after this covering it with a handkerchief soaked in ammonia. Finally, drink as much as you can hold of the whiskey, a whole bottle of it if you can." For rattlesnake bites, the foregoing cure was useless, and death was almost certain, but for the smaller green snakes that were even more common, it worked splendidly, especially because they were not, in fact, poisonous.

On the other hand, Wolski very much enjoyed the literary salons hosted by Madame Julie Considérant, in which the colonists reclined in hammocks, listening to the pleasant harmonies of songbirds. "Often these gatherings lasted to a late hour, even until one or two in the morning, in the salon of that cedar grove where extraordinarily captivating and often highly erudite conversations went on, though more often the talk was of a light and witty nature, with anecdotes exchanged back and forth."

How lovely! A pity they weren't able to get any real work done, and too bad as well that Considérant and his Brook Farm wise men had chosen such poor land for the settlement. Apparently, they had thought it resembled wine country, but as it turned out, the soil was unsuitable for farming anything they might eat, such as corn or wheat or vegetables.

As with Icaria, the colony split into factions. Considérant grew depressed, medicating himself with whiskey and morphine, but somehow managed to purchase about sixty thousand acres near present-day Utopia, north of Uvalde. He considered suicide but instead wrote a book, titled *Du Texas: Premier rapport à mes amis*. The colony collapsed, leaving a tangle of lawsuits for the society's board of directors. Con-

La Réunion Cemetery, Dallas, Texas

sidérant moved with his wife and mother-in-law to San Antonio and eventually returned to Paris, where he settled in the Latin Quarter. The colonists fared much better. Many became leading citizens of Dallas. A number fought for the Confederacy. The former colonist Émile Remond bought some land near the colony and in the 1880s began making bricks and cement from deposits of chalk, limestone, and shale he found on the property. In 1900, a group of investors founded the Texas Portland Cement & Lime Company there; by 1908, the town of Cement City came into being to house workers for the plant. In 1935, Lone Star Cement bought the plant and expanded its operations, eventually consuming all the lands of the old French colony and demolishing the last of its buildings. Only the cemetery survived.

By 1970, the limestone was mined out and the plant shut down. In 1973, Rondel V. Davidson, America's leading scholar of Considérant, described the old neighborhood around La Réunion in grim terms: "This territory now harbors an industrial park with all its pollution and a black ghetto complete with a de facto–segregated high school and a government housing project."

I found the cemetery without much difficulty. It was surrounded by a chain-link fence, with locked gates, in the midst of a pleasant if nondescript and slightly shabby park. It was hard to imagine people actually doing anything in the park, but the same can be said for almost every park I've ever seen in Texas. Texans, for the most part, just don't go to the park. Nearby was a tidy middle-class black neighborhood of brick ranch houses with white shutters and garage doors. Cedar fences enclosed backyards. I was reminded of my maternal grandparents' almost identical neighborhood in Lubbock. Or my aunt and uncle's street in Cleburne. Or someplace in east El Paso, if you subtract the grass. There was a high school nearby, and the kids were just getting out of school for the day. It was all rather peaceful.

I sat there for a long time. I could hear birds singing in the trees, and I thought of Kalikst Wolski and Julie Considérant, lounging in their hammocks, entertaining each other with witty stories and dreaming of a different future.

# CHAPTER 4

# BEYOND HERE LIES NOTHING

T exas has never been known for utopian projects, but they have always abounded here. Icaria and La Réunion are unmistakably utopian, but no less impractical and dreamy were the schemes of Sam Houston and the other founders of the Texas Republic. Today the utopian impulse can be seen in the capitalist fantasies of Governor Greg Abbott and Senator Ted Cruz and in the attempt to "secure" the Mexican border.

One day in early 2011, my grandmother, who was then in her ninetieth year, told me she had seen a drone flying above El Indio, a little hamlet south of Eagle Pass, during an outing with some of her friends. The newspapers that summer were filled with stories about the Predator drones that would soon be patrolling the skies above the Rio Grande, but the date of deployment was not yet at hand, and a Predator ordinarily flies far too high to be seen from the ground, so I decided to take the afternoon and investigate the mysterious white object my grandmother had spied that day.

As a lone male in a rented minivan bearing New Mexico plates driving down a remote stretch of Highway 1021, which tracks the South Texas borderline for one hundred desolate miles, I most definitely fit the profile. My first encounter with the Border Patrol came when I pulled off the road to study with my binoculars the white speck I could see high in the cloudless sky. It was not a Predator; it was a blimp. I put down my binoculars just as the Border Patrol pickup pulled up along-side. We both lowered our windows, and I asked, in my best Texan, what in the heck was floating up there in the sky.

"It's a weather balloon," he said with a smile.

Well, how about that, I said. I thanked the kind officer, and we both waved as I drove off, still headed south. When I got to El Indio, a village comprising a small white country store and a post office, I stopped to buy a Dr Pepper. I asked the little old lady behind the counter, in my poor Spanish, whether she knew anything about *esa cosa blanca en el cielo*, that white thing up in the sky. She declined to look me in the face and pretended that she couldn't understand my primitive attempt to speak her language. I paid for my soft drink and thanked her.

I decided to inquire at the post office, but the window was closed. Just then, another minivan pulled up. I asked the lady driving the vehicle if she knew what that white thing was up in the sky.

"It's a satellite for the drugs," she said. "My brother-in-law works for it."

Her son, or someone I took to be her son, chimed in from the backseat that if I kept driving south, I'd see "the building that controls it." I thanked the nice family and continued on my way. As I drove, Border Patrol vehicles continued to pass me coming and going as before. They were as thick as flies. As I neared the base of what I could now see was a tethered blimp, a Border Patrol truck had come up right behind me and showed no sign of passing. Although I was doing nothing illegal, I began to sweat. Soon I passed a couple of midsized white buildings. In front was a sign on which I read the following: UNITED STATES AIR FORCE AEROSTAT RADAR FACILITY. Well, that settled the question. It was a radar blimp, and the nice family in El Indio was no doubt correct in their description of its mission. Having attained my goal of identifying the mysterious white object my grandmother and her friends had mistakenly thought was a Predator drone, I was now confronted with a dilemma: What was I to do about the Border Patrol vehicle that was so determinedly following me? I had never driven this highway before, and I feared I might drive for hours before reaching another human settlement. I spotted a place to pull over and decided to turn around. That's when the flashing lights went on behind me.

Tethered radar blimps were deployed decades ago when drug

Surveillance blimp, south of El Indio, Texas

smugglers were having a grand time flying over the border with their cargo. Some mild controversy exists about whether such assets are worth the investment, because the harsh Texas weather is said to keep them grounded much of the time. Many times I've driven past an almost identical aerostat in West Texas, near Marfa. Apparently, one of the blimps once got loose in a high wind and was blown almost to Oklahoma.

Meanwhile, on that bright summer day south of El Indio, I found myself surrounded by Border Patrol agents. Several trucks had pulled up, and men in green uniforms were peering through all the windows of my minivan.

"What seems to be the trouble, Officer?" I asked.

"You turned around," came the reply.

The lead agent was friendly enough, but he was insistent. He wanted to know what I was doing out there in the middle of nowhere on a remote stretch of highway not far from Mexico. My explanation, that I had driven south from Del Rio because I was curious about the security infrastructure that had materialized in recent years along the border, struck him as implausible and weird. I told the assembly of agents that I was curious about that blimp up there in the sky, the aerostat. They looked at me as if I were a space alien rather than the sort of undocumented immigrant to which they were accustomed. I fought the urge to become indignant, to protest my rights as an American citizen to go where I pleased on a public highway. I knew they were just doing their jobs, and I was inarguably a suspicious character. Fortunately, being a suspicious character is not yet a crime in the United States, and I was permitted, after a time, to continue on my way, at liberty.

Driving north back to my grandmother's house, as I passed one Dollar Store after another, road signs ordering me to obey the road signs, and the curiously discontinuous segments of the new border fence, I thought about Richard Latham and the changes that had come over the border country since he was murdered in 1984.

Richard's death took place at a time when security along the border, especially at crossings, was taken for granted. Much had changed since then, but it wasn't clear to me that the omnipresence of law enforcement had done much to prevent random killings or to stop determined criminals from entering the United States. Billions had been spent since then on border security, but what did it really mean to secure a 1,954-mile border—of river valleys and canyons, mountains, deserts, and vibrant communities that straddle both sides of the line—that people have crossed more or less freely for hundreds of years? Is it akin to building a dam, like the one at Amistad Reservoir, to stop the unwanted flow of people and goods? And if a secure border is something like a dam, what happens if the pressure behind it grows too great?

I didn't have the answers to these questions, so I decided to do some reporting on the subject, to find out what the Border Patrol and its institutional masters in the Department of Homeland Security thought it was accomplishing along the Mexican border. I resolved to re-create, in a rough and highly approximate manner, the journey of the first illegal immigrant to enter Texas, Álvar Núñez Cabeza de Vaca. Instead of the Mariame or the Patarabueye, however, my journey across Texas would be in the company of the Border Patrol.

.  .  .

I arrived in Brownsville, Texas, shortly after the murder of Jaime Zapata, the Immigration and Customs Enforcement agent who was shot dead at a roadblock on the highway between Mexico City and Monterrey, in the state of San Luis Potosí, by members of the Mexican drug cartel known as Los Zetas. Zapata, a former Border Patrol agent, was a Brownsville native, and his funeral was held two days after I pulled in to town. A procession passed through the community as residents lined the streets waving American flags. Some of the Border Patrol agents I spent time with in the Rio Grande valley attributed the relative quiet along the line that week to the Zapata killing; the cartels seemed to be watching and waiting to see what the American response would be. The Gulf Cartel, which had been fighting a war with its former enforcers the Zetas for control of the smuggling markets, or "plazas," along the South Texas border, resulting in more than a thousand deaths over the previous year, denounced Zapata's killing and called for justice. "It's clear that the federal government should act without delay against these assassins," the cartel said in a statement. "Because the spilling of blood in the country is now drowning society."

I did not attend the Zapata funeral, but several weeks later, sitting in an office in the Ronald Reagan office building in Washington, D.C., I watched high-definition video footage that was taken of the Zapata funeral from a U.S. Customs and Border Protection helicopter. The video was shot from about three miles out; the mourners at the funeral were probably not even aware that a helicopter was in the area. I watched playback of that video feed on the web portal of a system called the Big Pipe, a surveillance "asset" that I first learned of in Brownsville, which is where I met Kenneth Knight, deputy executive director of national air security operations for the Office of Air and Marine. Ken Knight is the man who built the Big Pipe.

Knight is a man with a persuasive personality, authoritative white hair, a strong jaw defining a ruddy complexion, and a disarming West Virginia accent. Both times we met, he was dressed in the khaki jumpsuit that all OAM pilots wear, and it turned out that he was a helicopter pilot himself. When we met in Brownsville, I had no idea who he was, but he already knew about me. "I need to talk to you," he said, with conviction, deftly hijacking my tour of the sector headquarters. Knight was in town to coordinate air support for the Zapata funeral, and he didn't have much time for me just then, but he gave me a quick demo and briefing on the Big Pipe and then invited me to Washington, where he promised to give a full bells-and-whistles demonstration of his baby.

What was the Big Pipe? The answer wasn't obvious to me at first, but Knight tossed out terms like "total domain awareness" and strongly suggested that he possessed the means of attaining that state. From the quick briefing I received in Brownsville, the Big Pipe sounded as if it might be the framework for the elusive "common operating picture" that would integrate and rationalize the increasingly unwieldy data streams generated by the high-definition surveillance technologies policing the endless flow of commodities, both licit and illicit, that pour across our international boundaries. The dream of an integrated system fusing these rivers of data into a comprehensive and intuitively manageable real-time graphical interface had been one of the primary aims of the Secure Border Initiative Network, or SBInet, the doomed mega-contract with Boeing to build a "virtual fence" along the nation's borders. It was a reasonable ambition; the military has deployed similar command and control systems for a decade. But the international boundary between Mexico and the United States is not, certain appearances notwithstanding, Afghanistan, and there remain certain niceties, such as the U.S. Constitution, that complicate the ambitions of our paramilitary border guards.

In January 2011, after years of effort and more than $1.5 billion had yielded just a few dozen miles of partially operative tactical infrastructure in southern Arizona, the DHS secretary, Janet Napolitano, had canceled SBInet. The demise of the Boeing program immediately inspired a flood of punditry, both from advocates of high-tech solutions to border management and from critics. Yet here was something that was potentially even more ambitious, which had somehow escaped notice. Could the Big Pipe succeed where SBInet had failed? Would a more comprehensive and sophisticated common operating picture enable us to secure the border? I suspected it would not, but I was curious to know more.

The path to total domain awareness is not straight. Down by the river, clear lines of sight can be difficult. Weedy, fast-growing brush often chokes the banks of the Rio Grande as well as the no-man's-land between the river and the border fence. Carrizo river cane, an invasive species that aids and abets the passage of other such species, grows everywhere. Single-track trails snake through the tall grass. A dirt road runs alongside the border fence. The road is heavily trafficked and well maintained; dust lies thick on the ground and offers up a rich testimony to a tracker who knows the art of sign cutting. The Brownsville and Matamoros bridge, the oldest crossing in Brownsville, rises up behind us as we walk along the river. Broken shards of glass twinkle in the dense ground cover. Thick vegetation does a good job of hiding the ubiquitous debris of human civilization: cast-off plastic water and soft-drink bottles and small articles of clothing—socks, T-shirts, a sneaker. Torn black plastic trash bags rustle in the light breeze, especially along the landing spots worn slick from the passage of bodies who slip out of the oily black nighttime river, briefly pause, quickly pull dry clothing and supplies from trash bags, then dress themselves and furtively crawl, scramble, or run toward the black steel pickets. They could try for one of the many gaps in the fencing, but that would be too risky. Some do it anyway and get a quick ride back across. The fence can be climbed, and so they climb.

It was just before dusk on a warm February afternoon, during the magic hour when the low angle of the sun lengthens all shadows and bathes the landscape in a golden glow. Agents D. Milian, R. Caballero, and C. Croy took me down to the river. We were in the middle of town, right next to a port of entry, where you'd think people would not dare to cross, but you would be wrong. The river is perhaps ten yards across, maybe fifteen, the railroad bridge of the port not more than fifty yards away. Even here, they cross. The Carrizo and the brush offer a million opportunities for concealment, and acres of empty land lie between the river and the nearest paved road; once reached, the beckoning neighborhoods of Brownsville will provide the safety of a stash house or a waiting vehicle.

As we walked, I asked questions, and a German shepherd named Crazy, from the local K-9 unit, demonstrated her skills. "I'll take a dog over a piece of electronic equipment any day," Croy said. Caballero agreed, as did Milian, who had just hidden himself, for my benefit, amid a tangle of weeds, vines, and thorny bushes so that Crazy could sniff him out. K-9 dogs all work for their own special toy; Crazy loved her well-chewed and nasty segment of black PVC pipe. Such dogs are trained to detect dope, firearms, cash, humans. They smell fear, yes, but more important they have the uncanny ability to smell conceal- ment. In tests, dogs can smell the difference between a person they can't see and a person they can't see who is hiding. They can smell the difference between twenty dollars and twenty thousand dollars.

We walked down a trail looking for fresh signs of traffic, and I noticed how much thicker the brush is on the other side. The people on that side have no incentive to clear it and many incentives to let it grow. We observe no signs of human activity. An eerie quiet reigned. Such appearances are deceptive, however, because Matamoros is right there; people live and work and perform their daily routines just a few hundred yards away. Down here, the cartels often employ spotters to watch the river. Sometimes they fish, but often they just sit and watch from the bank, staring with impunity and insolence or maybe just bore- dom. Attempting to counter the smugglers' natural advantages, a Bor- der Patrol camera tower looks almost pretty against the evening sky as it peers up and down this broad bend in the river from a height of sixty feet. The spotters, I was told repeatedly, study the cameras and try to ascertain the pattern in their movements. The spotters watch the agents in their vehicles, and they watch the agents on foot. They were no doubt watching us right then as three men in their olive-green uniforms, a writer with his notebook, and a dog with her toy all picked their way along the riverbank.

Border Patrol agents can't be everywhere, all the time, and the cameras have blind spots. The cartels choose when and where to cross; they control the other side, the "Mike side." And nowadays the cartels—by which I mean the infamous Mexican drug-trafficking organizations, also known as transnational criminal organizations, who scatter dismembered body parts along commercial streets, fill mass graves with the bodies of economic refugees, kidnap gringo tourists who venture into border towns, and hang decapitated bodies adorned with political messages from highway bridges—own the monopoly on human traffic just as they do the traffic in dope. No one freelances any- more. No one crosses without paying the ferryman.

A seismic sensor buried alongside an active trail detects foot traf-

Camera tower, Rio Grande valley

fic and transmits its radio signal to a high-tech command and control center at the Border Patrol station in Olmito, just outside Brownsville. Such unmanned ground sensors have been used for decades, and the technology keeps improving, reducing the size and increasing the sensitivity of the devices, which greatly enhances the ease of deployment for sensor technicians. Border Patrol agents constantly shift some eleven thousand sensors along the southwest border, depending on traffic patterns on the infinite forking paths that radiate outward from the line like capillaries. They must identify a promising trail, one that shows signs of recent traffic, and haul the equipment in. Once a suitable spot has been found, they must dig a hole, deploy the sensor, conceal it with dirt and vegetation, and then test it to make sure the transmitter has a good connection to the nearest radio tower. If not, the sensor must be dug out and moved to another spot. And, again, it must pass the test. It is difficult, frustrating, highly physical work.

Twenty large screens lined the front wall of the control room; a television in the middle of the wall had been tuned to Fox News. Glenn Beck appeared to be delivering one of his curious history lessons, but the sound was off and everyone ignored him. Four agents sat at desks, scanning the monitors and occasionally speaking on the radio with agents in the field. Behind us were three sector enforcement specialists, whose duties include the coordination of radio communication for the sector. Radio communication among agents in the field is constant and vital to their mission. My attention returned to the screens and the bird's-eye point of view they provide of the border zone.

The Brownsville sector employs dozens of remote video surveillance systems, or RVSS, most of which are on fixed towers. Others are attached to preexisting infrastructure such as water tanks, cellphone towers, bridges, or buildings. Each RVSS is composed of four cameras, two for daytime and two infrared cameras for night duty. The agents who are assigned to camera duty in the control room zoom and pan the cameras as needed; at night they can manipulate the contrast of the infrared video, shifting from "black hot" to "white hot," rewinding and forwarding through the digital file as needed to identify what is often merely a fleeting glimpse of an unidentified animal, possibly human. The big screens constantly flicker from one river camera to another. Sources of thermal energy abound. Rocks, concrete blocks, even the plants, radiate heat, but warm-blooded animals stand out most vividly, and they move. I have been here before, during daylight hours. There's more action at night.

Agent José Mancillas received the signal from the ground sensor, glanced left to a small screen displaying the current locations of his "bugs," then quickly typed a few keystrokes. One of three large flatscreen monitors at his desk instantly displayed a river camera's infrared image. Using a joystick controller that would be familiar to almost any American child, the agent panned the camera and zoomed in. Eight ghostly white bodies sprang out of the Carrizo and sprinted in an awkward hunkered-down posture toward the eighteen-foot black steel pickets of the border fence. They had activated the sensor about fifty yards south of the levee; the river at this point was three miles away, so the group has probably been lying up in some dense brush, waiting for the right moment to hit the fence. Sometimes it seems that the groups all come at once, Mancillas told me, as if they were timing their incursions. As soon as he confirmed that he had traffic on the move, Mancillas was on the radio, alerting a unit he knew was standing by just around the bend. "I've got eight bodies going over the levee," he said, giving a shorthand code for their location along the fence. Several of the bodies were up on the fence; apparently, the lead man got down on all fours, and the rest stepped on his back for a boost. The agents then came into view and the aliens retreated; one man leaped from the top of the fence and hit the ground hard. We all winced. Eighteen feet is a long drop. But he got up and ran south toward Mexico with the rest of his group.

Suddenly all motion stopped; then the file ran backward as Mancillas worked the controls. I glanced up at Glenn Beck, who gestured at his own camera with great sincerity. We watched the footage again— Mancillas explained that the group had made it back south to try again another day—and then he showed me more footage of recent traffic. Often you just get a flash of white, and it takes an experienced eye to determine whether to respond. The cameras are a good tool, but they can't see everything, and the harsh South Texas weather degrades their performance. In January, during a severe cold snap, the cameras simply froze in place. Some won't focus properly even in mild weather and really should be replaced.

Another location, another incursion—four luminescent human bodies loped directly toward the RVSS, apparently assuming the cameras won't pan straight down. What the guide didn't know was that he and his little group had already tripped a bug. The eyes of Texas were upon them. Four demure Spanish goats glowed ghostly white on the screen before wandering off to nibble elsewhere, in private. Line agents, in one of those white and green patrol vehicles that are ubiquitous in the border country, were already on the move, driving fast along a dirt road that curved down through the cane and mesquite to run parallel to the border security fence. We gazed at the screen as the truck pulled up fast. The four bodies were already over the fence. The lead man was probably the guide, and he ran swiftly in the direction of a nearby neighborhood, juking and zigzagging before he finally disappeared offscreen, eluding the pursuing agent. The others just gave up and waited; once they've lost their guide, they usually have no idea where to go. Later that evening a call came in from a citizen advising of

an agent in need of assistance; it turned out that the agent was in a scuffle with the very guide we had watched escape, a juvenile well known to
the Brownsville agents. Such minors are valuable assets for smugglers,
because authorities in the United States typically don't prosecute them
for repeated offenses, even when they're caught with narcotics.

The river cameras are a relatively new weapon in the arsenal of
the Border Patrol, part of the huge post-9/11 buildup of manpower
and technological assets that has resulted from a 100 percent increase
in the amount of money directed toward border surveillance and control, most of which has flowed toward the Mexican border. This large
but finite stream of federal money has been directed to the southwest
border with the aim of stopping the infinite river of illegal drugs and
bodies that pours across a permeable international boundary. Other
virtual rivers, both licit and illicit, converge on the border as well—
steady streams of illegal money and guns heading south, and an enormous, scarcely quantifiable flow of legal imports going north by rail

Border surveillance camera, Roma, Texas

and truck. All this traffic must be scrutinized, questioned, examined, searched, and if necessary interdicted, apprehended, seized, or arrested. And then there is the flow of data—electronic manifests, lists of travelers' names, dates of entry, and the like, but also untold terabytes of video footage—all of which must be analyzed, quantified, archived, and stored so that it is available to forensic investigators when something goes wrong, such as when a gun bought near Dallas is found near the body of an ICE agent in San Luis Potosí.

Vehicles pass through the land ports with drugs stashed in a hidden compartment, or strapped to bodies, or secreted in some fleshy cavity. Speedboats drop bails of pot on the Gulf Coast, on South Padre Island, or on the beaches near Boca Chica, where the Rio Grande meets the sea. They do likewise along the beaches near San Diego. Ultralight personal aircraft make short flights across the border into New Mexico and drop their cargo. And hundreds of thousands of Mexicans and people "other than Mexicans" enter the United States illegally, either out in the remote scrublands or at the ports of entry, traveling with false documents. Many are caught, and some who enter have no intention of staying. Dedicated "mules" swim across the Rio Grande, sprint to a drop-off point, often wearing nothing but swim trunks, and then run back across. Agents know them by the bare footprints they leave behind. Larger groups trek through remote desert landscapes with fifty-pound loads on their backs; on their way home they burglarize ranch houses and other remote habitations.

In 2006, Congress mandated the construction of new "secure" fencing along the southwest border, and the result has been the subject of much heartburn in the border zone and beyond. Since then, just under seven hundred miles of fencing has been constructed, at an average cost of $2.8 million per mile. Depending on whom you're talking to, the fence is either a monumental boondoggle or a highly effective tool that should have been built long ago. Farmers, environmentalists, and cynical bystanders in the border communities all hate it. Farmers who are cut off from their fields resent the inconvenience. The people whose homes are on the wrong side of the fence feel sacrificed and abandoned. Ocelots and other wild creatures are said to be experiencing disruptions of their migratory wanderings. It's easy to laugh at fencing that abruptly ends in a tangle of brush; surely, people say, the

Border fence, Rio Grande valley

Mexicans can figure out how to use a ladder or simply walk around. In Sonora, comically, smugglers have used a catapult to hurl drugs into Arizona as well as a portable ramp that permits vehicles to drive right over the fence.

From the perspective of the Border Patrol, however, the fence is not so easily dismissed. Agents like Milian and others I spoke with in the Brownsville area appreciate the border fence because it increases an agent's minimum response time, which in urban stretches of the Rio Grande valley must be measured in seconds. Immigrants, led by experienced guides, disrobe on the Mike side; place their belongings in plastic garbage bags; swim, raft, or wade across; quickly dress; and then make a mad hundred- or two-hundred-yard dash for the nearby neighborhood. Once that nearby haven has been reached, they will either blend in instantly, perhaps slipping into a giant H-E-B supermarket, or duck into a stash house or waiting vehicle. Whatever the plan, if the agents do not catch them during those first crucial seconds, they're long gone. The border fence adds perhaps a minute to the equation, and that's often more than enough. The fence, Milian told me, channels the flow of aliens toward the gaps. We're watching those gaps, he said. They might not see us, but we're there. The cameras are watching, too. The idea is to push the border crossers away from the populated areas, out into the brush, where the response time is measured in hours and days.

Upriver from Brownsville lies McAllen, a more affluent community where local pressure, in the form of height restrictions, coupled with natural obstructions such as the particularly heavy brush growing along the river, has prevented the deployment of remote video surveillance towers. Here the Border Patrol employs mobile surveillance systems that can be moved to hot spots as needed. Agent Jaime Medina joined us in McAllen and led an excursion into the broad fields that run alongside the levees that crisscross the broad fertile floodplain along the Rio Grande. Because the river meanders broadly through its valley, there are often bubble-like intrusions of Mexican territory into the United States, and vice versa, which are bounded on three sides by the opposite state. These broad bends in the river make a line agent's mission extraordinarily difficult; lines of sight from any point near the river are severely compromised, and high ground is often distant. A riverbed is an ephemeral geologic structure; over time the river changes course as the meanders slowly drift downstream through the landscape, occasionally forming oxbow lakes, thus ceding territory from one country to another by riverine fiat. The levees are a vain attempt to stop that inexorable flow. Oxbow lakes testify to their failure.

Border Patrol vehicles prowl these areas day and night and use scope trucks, a mobile surveillance system, which are basically pickups equipped with retractable camera towers, to enhance their surveillance capabilities. As with the tower-mounted remote video surveillance systems, the scope trucks typically possess both conventional video cameras and thermal cameras. Scope trucks also have the ability to use a laser targeting system; the camera operator can guide agents wearing night vision goggles to a group by fixing them with a laser beam that is invisible to the naked eye but brightly apparent to anyone wearing the proper eyewear.

Driving along a levee at night is a disconcerting experience. The land drops away sharply into an abyss of chirping crickets, singing frogs, and other loud gregarious creatures of the subtropical night. I drove with Agent Milian through a night in which all fields were black and strained my eyes to find some landmark to ease my disorientation. I tried to imagine what it was like patrolling these fields and levees with nothing but flashlights and a good sense of direction. We finally came to a scope truck parked on a kind of promontory or juncture in the levee; in daylight we no doubt would have been treated to a spectacular view of South Texas's agricultural production. Historically, most of these wide fields have been worked by Mexican migrant workers, many of them undocumented. Earlier that day I had asked Agent Milian whether the Border Patrol conducts raids of the local farms. He responded that such raids were not permitted, apparently for political reasons, and that anyway such matters fell within the jurisdiction of ICE.

After an impressive demonstration of the scope truck's thermal camera, I was able to examine the individual night vision equipment used by the agents out on the field, such as the Recon Lite, a thermal binocular that is often mounted on a tripod and has a range of four miles, and the TAM-14, a thermal monocular with a two-mile range, as well as the standard night vision goggles that most agents carry. Such portable night vision equipment, which was in short supply in previous years, has now become standard issue. As Agent Mancillas told me in the Brownsville control room, "It makes a huge difference when you can see in the dark."

From the relatively lofty viewpoint of a McAllen levee, we descended to a riverside boat launch at a lonely spot called Chimney Park. A small fleet of riverboats patrols the navigable portions of the Rio Grande; the boats are "owned" by the Office of Air and Marine but manned by Border Patrol agents. The shift was ending, and the agents prepared to haul the boats out of the water. I was supposed to go out on patrol in one of these so-called safe boats, but the Zapata murder had made the sector officials nervous, so I was obliged to content myself with a sky box, a somewhat more cumbersome mobile sur-

Falfurrias checkpoint

veillance unit than the scope truck, and learned about its uses, both as a surveillance instrument and as a deterrent. Unlike the scope truck, which possesses its own means of locomotion, the sky box is basically a surveillance tower mounted on a trailer; a hydraulic lift raises and lowers an enclosed platform on which are mounted the standard combination of conventional and thermal cameras. Downriver, at a popular restaurant called Pepe's, traffic had been pretty hot, so they deployed a sky box and the traffic moved elsewhere. Last summer's big floods threatened to wash the sky box away, so they pulled it out. Inevitably, the traffic resumed, and so the sky box returned to Pepe's; it wouldn't do to have the restaurant's patrons watching the immigrants run by as they sat eating their carne asada and listening to the nighttime song of the Rio Grande chirping frog.

Come daylight, after consuming plates of breakfast tacos, Agent Milian and I traveled to the Falfurrias checkpoint, which consistently maintains the highest seizure rate of any checkpoint in the country.

Every agent carried a personal radiation detector, a small pager-like device on his belt. An agent demonstrated a device that identifies the particular radioactive isotope detected; almost invariably, a radiation alert turns out to have been the result of a medical procedure. Another agent showed me how to use a "buster," a small handheld device that detects anomalous variations in the density of, say, a car door or a tire. I watched as a rented red Hyundai driven by a group of young people got worked over in "secondary." The color of the men's skin and their manner of dress suggested that they were not from the Rio Grande valley, where few African Americans live. But it was not their skin color that triggered the extra attention; something had alerted a K-9 search dog when the car passed through "primary," the quick and simple interview conducted by an agent with every one of the drivers who pass through this busy checkpoint every year. The buster detected nothing along the perimeter of the vehicle or in the tires. Neither did a camera scope detect anything in the gas tank. I peered down that long, narrow passage and saw the intact wire mesh marking the aperture of the fuel tank. A new dog passed through the vehicle without incident. Perhaps the driver or one of the passengers had smoked a joint that morning, and the dog could smell the residue on his fingers. Nothing turned up; the red Hyundai went on its way.

I was shown into a locked container in which the walls were lined with neat stacks of dope, small bales of pot, mostly, awaiting pickup by the DEA. Some baggies of smaller quantities were hanging on the wall. One bag contained a quarter ounce seized from a young man who was planning to celebrate his eighteenth birthday that day but made the mistake of driving through a checkpoint while he was holding.

Meanwhile, I was attracted to the sight of a white pickup equipped with what appeared to be an extremely bulky camper driving very slowly by a large refrigerated truck that had been pulled over into secondary. It was a Z Backscatter Van, a mobile backscatter X-ray scanner similar in concept to those used for full-body scans at airports. Backscatter technology works by exploiting the fact that low-density organic materials, such as explosives, drugs, or human bodies, contain elements with low atomic numbers, which cause X-rays to scatter, whereas high-density, high-atomic-number elements such as metals are more likely to absorb them. By interpreting the ways in which

X-rays, fired in a narrow beam that rapidly scans the target, respond to the materials under examination, and plotting the position of the beam relative to the target, backscatter scanners produce remarkably clear, photo-like images of organic materials that conventional X-ray techniques are unable to capture. Dense, metallic materials are grayed out and resemble conventional X-ray films. Agent E. Manzanares allowed me to sit in his cab as he slowly scanned a load of frozen broccoli.

As with the infrared cameras I'd already seen, Manzanares can manipulate the contrast of his scans, shifting from white hot to black hot, but his video display software has the added capability of applying different color scales. All of which permits the scanning technician to determine whether a given load is free of suspicious voids. Cube-shaped spaces in the middle of a pallet of cilantro might not necessarily be packages of dope, but the odds are good. The bad guys are often stupid, and sometimes they are just greedy, such as when they attempt to cram just one or two more packages into a well-concealed cavity in a vehicle, and those extra packages that don't quite fit in the compartment are often the ones the scanner picks up. The smugglers are frequently ingenious, however, such as when they hid a load of narcotics under a large tank of used oil, which is organic and thus shows up as one big undifferentiated mass. These smugglers were perfectly aware of the limits of the scanning technology. What they were unable to defeat was the power of a dog's nose, which every field agent I spoke with credited as the single most valuable asset in their arsenal. Dogs, at checkpoints like Falfurrias, have found people hidden in the engines of vehicles, sewn sitting upright into the backseat of a car, and wedged into a modified console so that when the hatch between the front seats was opened by a customs officer, there was a man's face staring up. Because the dogs are such reliable detectors of concealed bodies, most smugglers will drop their human cargo before reaching the checkpoint and send them out into the brush to make the long walk to a pickup location. Once a group of immigrants has made it that far, past the gauntlet of high-tech surveillance cameras and scanners, the last line of defense is the art of sign cutting, the foundational discipline of all Border Patrol agents.

Perhaps you have witnessed the curious sight of a green-and-white pickup dragging a load of tires alongside a highway. It is a common

Sign cutting at the border

spectacle in the borderlands. The object of that behavior is a clean slate, so that any foot traffic can be located in time and pursued in space. Sometimes, instead of dragging, agents will put down tire tracks and then check back periodically to see if any footprints have appeared. This was the technique used in Laredo, in an industrial park right on the edge of a bluff overlooking the river. There are no border fences in Laredo, and no RVSS towers, so sign cutting and old-fashioned stake-outs remain the essential techniques of the art of "hunting humans."

Footprints, to one who knows how to cut sign, are eloquent testimony of the nature of the man, woman, or group of humans moving through the countryside. The tracker can tell you whether the body in question is fat or thin, fit or exhausted, his approximate age and height, how fast he is moving, whether he is carrying a load, and how heavy that load is likely to be. I've been told that at least one agent based in Laredo can cut sign from horseback at a gallop. Sometimes a group will walk in a guide's footsteps in the vain hope of disguising its number; fatigue and carelessness invariably lead to self-betrayal. Drug mules will attach carpet to the bottoms of their shoes, and guides will lay down carpets when a group crosses a drag to hide their path, yet broken twigs, upturned pebbles, and ranch fences, the wire pushed down by the weight of bodies, bear silent witness to their passage.

Agents working a group will leapfrog one another, with sign cutters positioning themselves at different points along a probable route, communicating constantly by radio, describing the sign at one point as another agent a few miles farther along attempts to pick up the trail. Sometimes air support will be called in, and a helicopter or an airplane will try to locate the group from the air. The landscape is vast and filled with good cover; detecting a group led by an experienced guide is far from easy. On the very day when drug traffickers in Del Rio were being arrested as part of Operation Fallen Hero, organized in retaliation for Jaime Zapata's murder, I was attempting to keep my lunch down in a Eurocopter AS 350 B3/2B1 helicopter as we watched agents on the ground work a group near Sycamore Creek, on land that my family ranches. The group was out there in brush somewhere, in an endless expanse of live oak, mesquite, and other brush; no visual contact had been made and might not be made for hours.

Our helicopter was equipped with a Star Safire HD camera that was capable of zooming in on a target from miles away. As with the camera that took the video footage of the Zapata funeral, the Star Safire can carry out surveillance from so far out that the subject would never know he was being watched. The software that drives this camera is responsive and feature rich; point a laser at a house, and the monitor instantly gives you the address, the latitude and longitude, and a moving map that toggles from road-map view to topography to aeronautical chart. If you're following a moving car, the camera will lock onto the vehicle and hold it in view. By fusing low-light video with infrared, which cannot penetrate glass, the camera can look right through the window of a suspicious car parked in the shadows of that undeveloped cul-de-sac down by the lake.

But when you're looking for a group of people who know they're being pursued, all that high-definition wizardry, supremely useful in surveilling a drug transaction, does little good, especially in the daytime. At night, on the other hand, these airborne FLIR cameras can pick up the thermal signature of the bodies, even if they're hiding in brush. They are sensitive enough to pick up the ghost image of a body that was lying up in some high grass, long after it has moved on. The Star Safire comes equipped with a laser targeting system and a powerful infrared spotlight that can be slaved to the camera, thus either pointing the way to NVG-equipped agents on the ground or bathing a group of fugitives in light they cannot see.

The acquisition of some perspectival advantage is the core goal of most technologies of surveillance and control. The cartels have the advantage of surprise and secrecy, as well as a ruthless indifference to human life. The night I arrived in Laredo, two bodies were fished out of the river. They were tied up with barbed wire; one was missing a head. The cartels also have an enormous funding advantage, the leisure to develop new strategies and tactics, and freedom from the sometimes inconvenient oversight that a constitutional system of government imposes on its law-enforcement agencies. The pursuit of superior viewpoints has thus led to the deployment of ever more sophisticated surveillance and control technologies at our ports of entry as well as in the immense territories that lie between them.

In Laredo, home to the busiest commercial land port in the United States, the World Trade Bridge processes more than a million north-bound trucks a year and almost that many going south. Each vehicle passes through a layered enforcement procedure. The first layer is the mandated submission of an electronic manifest, as well as other pre-arrival information, that must be received at least one hour in advance of the truck's arrival at the port. A team of analysts, using software known as ACE, short for "Automated Commercial Environment," then scores the shipment using a variety of criteria, including the carrier's prior record and the importer's history of compliance with U.S. laws and regulations. Every vehicle passes through a radiation portal, large yellow towers that have been modified to accommodate the largest eighteen-wheeled tractor-trailer rigs. Shippers who participate in the Customs-Trade Partnership Against Terrorism or the Free and Secure Trade program get priority service, because their vehicles and drivers have submitted to a special vetting process. Such vehicles are still scanned, but they get to cut in line.

All the trucks pass through primary processing lanes, where drivers are interviewed by a customs officer. All vehicles then pass through what's called secondary express, where K-9 units are heavily deployed, and then, depending on their cargo, the trucks are directed to different stations within the port. Almost everything undergoes some kind of scanning procedure, either X-ray, gamma ray, or high-energy X-ray. Certain high-risk commodities such as pottery and wooden furniture, and most agricultural products, are off-loaded and inspected by hand—the first because they are so often the bearers of contraband, and the second because the pests and diseases that the ag specialists are looking for can only be seen at close range.

When I visited the World Trade Bridge, the facility was nearing the end of an expansion project that would double the number of primary processing lanes. Acting Port Director Jose Uribe gave me an overview of the port's operation as he drove his official car across and against oncoming truck traffic, dodging and weaving like a veteran player of *Grand Theft Auto.* To my inexpert eye, the scene was a chaotic riot of monstrous trucks and looming scanners, huge barnlike structures, and long lines. As the tour progressed, however, structure and pattern began to emerge in the apparent chaos, and I could see that the operation here was a miracle of logistics. Each vehicle, as it passed through the layered enforcement process, was tracked from station to station, and at any point a customs officer can create an "issue," tagging the shipment for more intensive scrutiny, which could mean anything from a higher-resolution X-ray scan to off-loading the complete contents of a shipment.

Five thousand trucks a day on average, laden with every conceivable commodity, from consumer goods to auto parts destined for just-in-time delivery to a factory in Tennessee, pass through this facility. "I've been in Laredo for thirty-four years," Uribe told me. "I can remember back in the late '70s, we had mostly curios, some heavy steel." Then came NAFTA. "Now you name it and we see it. Everything from laptops to three-piece suits. Mexico produces just about everything nowadays."

I was curious to know more about the scanning technologies, about the differences between gamma ray scanners and backscatter, between low- and high-energy X-rays. The technicians were only too happy to explain everything, especially about the underlying technology, but my public affairs handler, a former reporter named Richard Pauza, was more circumspect about the criteria governing their use. The arms race with the cartels is unceasing, and CBP field officers are loath to give away their tricks of the trade. What was clear, however, is that the density and structure of a target is the primary determinant of which scanning technology is best suited for it. I was especially impressed with the high-energy X-rays used to scan the most challenging commodities. The resulting scans are marvelous, almost gallery-quality works of visualization. Strong-edge enhancement of a large tractor-trailer rig permits one to see its structure with hallucinatory clarity: everything inside was made visible, clean, and clear—the gears inside a transmission, the pushrods in the engine. I saw scans of a steamroller, the kind used to compress hot asphalt on a newly paved street, and inside the large dense roller wheel were packages of narcotics; a load of gypsum board Sheetrock was laden with marijuana, the voids inside the pallets revealed by the scan. Another scan, of a southbound truck carrying rolls of fabric, revealed suspicious areas of density; using software enhancement tools, the scanning technician was able to see that it was a large quantity of cash: as it turned out, $1.2 million, a small fraction of the estimated $18 to $39 billion that the cartels smuggle south every year. I was told about someone who showed up without a manifest, in itself a tip-off, with a load of refrigerators. A dog alerted, and the load was brought in for additional scanning. Close inspection revealed contraband inside the compressors of each unit, cocaine and crystal meth. Another scan I was shown, of a truck brought in for scanning by ICE, showed packages of cocaine stamped with the logo of the Gulf Cartel.

At the Laredo port and at ports serving the public, like the much smaller but extremely modern crossing in Del Rio, security measures are directed not only at the endless stream of commodities that pass through these facilities but at the bodies of the individuals presenting themselves for entry, their facial expressions, postures, affects, clothing, and emotional dispositions. Sharon Ansick, a tactical logistics officer who went to high school with my sister, gave me the grand tour of the Del Rio facility. Video cameras were everywhere, 150 in all. Doors and windows were secured, and passage in and out of facilities, as well as from one area to another within a compound or a building, was tightly

Border fence, Del Rio, Texas

controlled, though this was not always necessarily evident, especially
to routine travelers. This was termed "passive security." All who enter
this facility, whether they know it or not, have entered a panopticon
in which their every move is registered, recorded, observed, and controlled. No one leaves without being cleared. Border runners are met
with road spikes that jut up from the pavement at the push of a distress
button. Only the unlucky criminals ever realize the degree to which
their liberty has been constrained.

All incoming and outgoing license plates are photographed, as are
the drivers. All recently issued passports, green cards, and day-entry
cards contain radio-frequency ID chips that broadcast the identity of a
traveler at the primary checkpoint, and the Del Rio port was the first
to deploy a special RFID lane to speed processing. When I was there,
traffic was slow and lines were short, but there was a sense of high
alertness throughout the facility. ICE agents armed with M4 tactical
rifles loitered near the secondary station. Supervisory agents, in a glass-

encased control room overlooking the traffic lanes, kept watch over the whole proceedings, monitored the video feeds, and maintained radio contact with personnel all over the port, making certain that what happened in 1984 to Richard Latham, in this very port, never happens again.

Unlike the shipments that pass through the import lot, the port's noncommercial traffic, which amounts to about two million vehicular travelers and about fifty thousand pedestrians annually, is not routinely scanned. CBP officers interview drivers in a primary lane and use special angled mirrors to inspect the underside of all vehicles, and if a K-9 alerts or the driver or one of the passengers seems nervous, or if something about the car seems unusual, or perhaps simply because the vehicle originates in an area of interest such as San Luis Potosí, the state where Jaime Zapata was murdered, the officer pulls the vehicle over for a secondary inspection. At that point, dogs, density meters, mirrors, X-ray scanners, and the whole repertoire of what CBP terms nonintrusive inspection techniques comes into play. Nowadays few cars are dismantled or drilled without evidence derived from one of these methods. One recent seizure came about because an officer manning the primary lane noticed that a vehicle, driven by a lone male, was uncommonly clean. Not only was the body of the car clean, but so were the wheels and the inside of the wheel wells. A trip to the VACIS X-ray scanner revealed a suspicious space behind the firewall of one of the wheel wells, whereupon agents started probing and chipping away at some relatively fresh Bondo, thus revealing a compartment containing twenty-eight and a half kilos of heroin, plus two and a half kilos of meth. Over the previous five years, this port had seized thirty thousand pounds of marijuana, thirty-five hundred pounds of cocaine, ninety-five pounds of heroin, and thirty-seven thousand units of steroids and other restricted drugs.

Meanwhile, the routine business of inspection and seizure continues all around us. Officer Ansick points out that CBP enforces the regulations and laws of forty-four different governmental agencies, including the FDA, the EPA, and the USDA. Cars are turned inside out after dogs signal they have found something of interest. Inspectors go through agricultural loads by hand, searching for tiny insects, egg casings under leaves, and other stowaways on legitimate imports.

Palo Verde wood borers show up in stacks of firewood. Cattle must be examined for Rocky Mountain spotted fever ticks. People arrive with juicy, stinky fermenting cheeses, deer heads, oranges, cowboy boots made from endangered species like sea turtles. The guy with the sea-turtle boots was a recent case, a native of San Luis Potosí, and the officer interviewing him just happened to notice the boots; the poor man, who naively admitted what they were, left in his socks, and the boots went into a freezer. An agricultural specialist named Tara Elliott, a vigorous young woman with neatly penciled eyebrows, showed me a horned toad that had been salted and dried, with a rattlesnake rattle clattering in its open belly; it was a good-luck charm. Herbal teas for Lenten intestinal cleansing were an object of particular scrutiny at that time of year. The next day a load of big horned sheep was scheduled to come through, headed back home to New Mexico; they had been sent south to help repopulate an area where the species had been wiped out by poaching. Nowadays cattle get scanned by an X-ray machine; in the old days, all cattle were off-loaded and counted at Darrell Hargrove's commercial pens, where at age twelve I broke my pelvis working my first summer job.

Eggs, potatoes, and chorizo are strictly forbidden entry, as are all birds, because of diseases such as exotic Newcastle disease and avian influenza. Indeed, the port has a special room where seized birds are kept before they're gassed. One notable bird seizure involved some very rare and valuable African gray parrots. A woman bought the birds in Mexico and wanted to smuggle them into the United States, so she went to a vet and asked him to anesthetize the birds so they'd be asleep and quiet, instead of talking and squawking, when she passed through the port. As it happened, a CBP officer was at the veterinary office with his dog, and he witnessed the whole exchange and saw the woman take the sleeping birds to her car. So he called the port and gave the woman's license plate number. Sure enough, she showed up not long after, the parrots hidden in little sleeves, and was arrested and prosecuted in federal court for smuggling the rare birds. Those parrots were not euthanized, however, because they were so valuable, but were donated to a zoo. Ansick also told a story regarding an educational video about agricultural import regulations that includes a photograph of some birds that had been seized. "They're real pretty little blue parakeets, but they're dead, because they forgot to take the picture before they euthanized them. So they propped them up in each corner of the little cage, you know, like they're trying to get out. It's hilarious!"


Everywhere I traveled along the Rio Grande, I asked about the striking emphasis, in all the security arrangements I had seen and in the public relations literature I had read, on terrorism. Had there ever been a significant terrorist apprehended along the Mexican border? Nobody could think of one. What about the politicians who thump their podiums and list all the people from terrorist countries who are crossing our borders? Yes, many people from countries like Iran and Syria have been apprehended trying to enter the United States, along with people from more than seventy other countries, including Chinese, Indians, Pakistanis, and Russians. They were all normal undocumented immigrants, economic and political refugees, trying to get to the promised land. Crossing the great Chihuahuan and Sonoran Deserts is far from easy, and for a potential terrorist it's probably much more efficient to just get a standard tourist or educational visa and enter the country legally, like Mohamed Atta, though admittedly that procedure has become more vexing for everyone in recent years, including both tourists and terrorists. Radiation detectors are ubiquitous, and every vehicle that enters the United States passes through one. Had there ever been a case in which a dirty bomb or some other dangerous radioactive substance was detected along the Mexican border? Nobody could think of one. It would probably be easier and cheaper to acquire radioactive materials for a weapon inside the United States; it's certainly easier to purchase a gun over here. Conventional explosives are another matter. Mexico has a large mining industry, and explosives are not well controlled. But whether or not the threat of terrorists crossing over our purportedly wide-open borders is credible, as politicians and agitators of various political stripes like to claim, there can be no doubt that the various departments of U.S. Customs and Border Protection are working very hard to make sure that they don't make it across the line.

The other question I put to my various guides and companions among the Border Patrol, the Office of Air and Marine, and the Office of Field Operations had to do with unmanned aerial vehicles, the Pred-

Patrolling the no-man's-land along the Rio Grande, El Paso, Texas

ator drones that have been the subject of so much media coverage. Yes, the OAM does operate a Predator drone out of Corpus Christi, Texas, as well as others in Arizona and elsewhere, but agents in Brownsville and Del Rio were not aware of a drone being used as air support in their areas. In Laredo, on the other hand, Agent Narcizo Ramos said that a drone had been used in his area, at least occasionally. When I asked Mark Borkowski, assistant commissioner for the Office of Technology Innovation and Acquisition, about drones as we sat in his office in Washington, D.C., he laughed. "I knew you were going to ask me about that."

As Borkowski explained it, the UAVs have a very limited role in border surveillance. "With something like SBInet," he said, or the RVS systems and unattended ground sensors in the Rio Grande valley, "I want to watch a big area, with just a few people sitting at monitors, rather than having an agent every one hundred yards. I want to watch a big area all the time. Now, a UAV can get somewhere fast, and can stay there, but it looks through a soda straw. Different purpose. Different mission." There's just too much territory to watch for the drone to be an effective instrument on routine patrols. If, however, you have intelligence that tells you something is going to happen in a particular area, especially a remote or rugged area where deploying a ground system isn't practical, the nice thing about a drone is that you can send it out there and have it loiter, at high altitude, for twenty hours, far longer than a manned airplane or a helicopter.

The week before I spoke with him, Borkowski had testified before Congress on the demise of SBInet and its replacement, the Alternative (Southwest) Technology Initiative, which sounds an awful lot like the systems that are already in place in South Texas, with the addition of ground radar. I asked him what had gone wrong with the Boeing project, because many of the field agents I spoke with in Texas, some of whom had spent time in Arizona, thought it had been effective. "Well, they liked it after we fixed it," he said. The problem with SBInet, Borkowski explained, was that the project was ill-conceived and poorly executed, and there was plenty of blame to go around, for both DHS and Boeing. Borkowski's candor about the failings of SBInet was remarkable, and it was clear that he had no illusions about the ability of technology, by itself, to solve problems with deep political and economic roots.

As Borkowski tells the story, SBInet was destined to fail. When the contract went out, DHS was a new agency, inexperienced with managing major government contractors, and the problems initially flowed from that source. He also pointed to a pervasive naïveté—among the general public, the media, and the government—about the ability of technology to solve a vexing political problem. In the years after 9/11, the border suddenly began to be viewed with a new sense of urgency. There was a strong sense that something had to be done to secure it and that technology, which everyone agreed was a good thing, was the answer. Unfortunately, no one had a clear theory of what exactly technology was supposed to accomplish. But instead of figuring out what needed to be done and then deciding the best way to go about achieving those goals, DHS decided to let industry tell us what needed to be done. And that led to the attempt by Boeing to build a comprehensive system of surveillance that not only would include radar towers, camera towers, unattended ground sensors, and satellite communications but would integrate drones and hooks for everything else that might come into play. "Boeing had charts talking about the calculus of border security" and all kinds of very impressive claims about its security networks, said Borkowski, "and it really wasn't a bad concept," but the execution lacked discipline. SBInet tried to do everything from the beginning. "Everything was going to plug in to this common operating picture," he said, "and you remember how technology is good—well, a common operating picture is really good."

The problem was that Boeing did not yet have a functional system. "If you go off and say I want to build something that can do everything, you'll never build anything." The prototype went up in Arizona, Project 28, and the results were not good. The work was sloppy; the cameras were out of focus; the satellite system had too much latency delay; the towers were not structurally sound; the radar had too much clutter. The Border Patrol hated it. "We never tested it. We just put it up, turned it on. Didn't work!" Borkowski says. At that point, the "clue light comes on."

Borkowski had come to DHS from the air force, where he had long experience dealing with military contractors. When he arrived and began to see what had been going on with SBInet, he realized he had a big mess on his hands. "I thought, Oh my God, this program is doomed." Before long, however, Borkowski found himself trying to salvage what he could from the wreckage. Changes were made, and ambitions were scaled back. Then, after a yearlong cost-benefit analysis and reassessment, Secretary Janet Napolitano decided to kill the project.

Although he freely admitted that a great deal of time and money was wasted, Borkowski argued that CBP and DHS had made progress. "SBInet, for a whole lot of reasons," Borkowski said, "does not make sense" as a universal solution to the border security problem. But the integrated tower systems that were built do have some utility, in the right terrain. The hard part in general is to find solutions that fit the particular challenges of different stretches of the border. Borkowski advocates targeting technological solutions toward specific problems, with clearly defined objectives, using equipment that has been field-tested and is ready to go. Not every sector needs every kind of technology. Not every mile of the border requires a fence. Not every bend of the river requires a surveillance tower. Ground radar simply doesn't work in some areas, and drones are not a silver bullet. Nor, he made clear, will every border security problem be solved by the application of new technologies. The trick will be to get the border situation managed to the point that other resources, such as policy, such as comprehensive immigration reform, can pick up the difference. "That would cut off a lot of the traffic between the points of entry; in fact, at a certain point, you would only have the really bad people left, the drug smugglers and the terrorists." Of course, there aren't many terrorists wandering around in northern Mexico, and Borkowski made no mention of comprehensive drug policy reform.

After mounting a fairly persuasive critique of the idea that technology is the key to securing the border, as I was leaving his office Borkowski nonetheless remarked that CBP was beginning to realize that as an agency it needs to get all of its technological assets connected in one place, and that place would seem to be the Big Pipe.

Not many of the agents and officers I spoke with in South Texas knew anything about the Big Pipe; others had heard about it but weren't able to offer any specifics. At GovSec, the big government security trade show in Washington, D.C., none of the vendors I spoke with had heard of the Big Pipe, not even the people who were selling IP surveillance cameras to state, local, and federal agencies. It was completely under the radar.

At its most basic level, the Big Pipe is a video distribution hub, a web portal that integrates video feeds from a variety of assets and makes them available via the DHS secure network and the Internet. When Kenneth Knight was in Brownsville coordinating air support for the Zapata funeral, one of his prime objectives, aside from providing air support to the security operation, was setting up the helicopter video feed, which was transmitted via direct downlink from the helicopter to a microwave antenna, which he had installed on the roof of the Border Patrol station for just this mission. From there, the signal feeds into an encoder, which then pushes the video back through the DHS1 secure network to the National Data Center in Washington and outward into the Internet cloud. When we sat together in Brownsville, Knight pulled up the Big Pipe portal on a Border Patrol PC and logged in, and within a few mouse clicks we had the helicopter's video feed on the screen. In this case, the whole point was to make a God's-eye perspective available to whoever might need it—operational supervisors in a situation room or people in other locations who were unable to attend the funeral.

Several weeks later, in Washington, we went back over the architecture of the system. The core, as with any web application, was the server, which hosts mission feeds originating in assets such as the Predator—or a Guardian, the maritime version of that drone. Predators, unlike traditional metal-framed aircraft, have a composite skin, so one can put a parabolic dish inside the aircraft, which permits the transmission of extremely high definition video over a Ku satellite system to the National Data Center, from which point the data can be pushed out through the Big Pipe to wherever it needs to be. Other sensors, such as the helicopter-mounted camera I saw in Del Rio, or the camera in a scope truck, transmit their feeds via microwave downlink. Still others might be hooked directly into a router, such as an IP video surveillance camera in the Atlanta airport or on the side of a building in Washington, D.C.

One example that Knight gave me was a Guardian mission in the Bahamas in which the drone encounters an unidentified watercraft. All the individuals, no matter where they might be, who have an interest in this mission can be logged in to the Big Pipe, each one watching the same video feed in real time. Using a split screen, everyone can also be viewing a moving map, a maritime chart that shows the drone's position, in real time, relative to the target and anything else that happens to be in nearby waters. In addition to watching the video simultaneously, they would all be communicating by means of a chat log. The drone operator might not be able to identify the particular ship that's being "rigged," but a Coast Guard analyst who is also online could pipe in and identify the craft without having to wait for the pilot to verbalize what he thinks he's seeing down there on the water. Perhaps it's a shrimper, or a type of vessel known to be used by drug traffickers. The Coast Guard might even have intelligence on that very craft. Whatever happens, all the video, the chat logs, the geo-spatial coordinates, the flight path, flight points, the line of sight, sensor points, marine surface radar pictures, and all the other metadata associated with the mission are recorded and fused, synced to the video, and bundled in a mission package that typically includes a geo-spatial page containing a graphical representation of the flight path, with video that can be rapidly cued by clicking at any point on the path. Click at a given point in the flight path, and you see what the camera was looking at right then, and you have access to the audio, the flight log, altitude, directional orientation, air speed—everything. After the mission is complete, the OAM generates this mission package and hands it off to the agency customer, perhaps JIATF South, the Joint Interagency Task Force South, which monitors suspect aircraft and marine vessels in the Caribbean and nearby waters.

Knight spoke quickly, running through examples and illustrations, development strategies, and plans for the future. Far from being merely a Homeland Security video server, it was clear, the Big Pipe aimed to be a comprehensive mission data distribution system, whatever that data might be, though surveillance video was often the most crucial component of the operational picture.

"We're doing some really cool shit," Knight told me when we first met. "The military does some of the same stuff, but they can't do what we do. They work in the classified world; we actually cross domains." The distinction was a crucial one. A military version of the Big Pipe would never be made available via the Internet to civilian law enforcement or to FEMA during a natural disaster or to some other partner outside the military domain. "We're literally paving the way. The cool thing is that a lot of the stuff you're seeing with the Border Patrol, like the RVSS towers, the mobile surveillance systems, all that gets integrated with this. So now we have worldwide distribution capability for situational awareness and exploitation purposes."

Given that the system was created from within the OAM, it was perhaps natural that Knight focused initially on getting the sensor data off the aircraft and into the network. That also happened to be the hardest piece of the puzzle. The infrastructure for the unmanned aerial systems was relatively easy, however, because Predators can use the government's Ku satellite network. Microwave downlink from other aircraft has been more difficult. "Wireless just doesn't work very well for us," Knight told me, "because the bandwidth isn't there." Consequently, BMS microwave antennas are going up. "We're putting these things in strategic locations around the country. They reach out about seventy-five miles," Knight said. "We're closing the gaps." The next stage was IP video, which can capture the feed from any IP-enabled camera that is made available to the system: CBP surveillance video at ports of entry, at shipping ports, checkpoints, airports, train stations, on the sides of buildings, anywhere. At that point, sitting in his office in Washington or at any registered computer anywhere in the world, Knight could click from a TSA surveillance camera pointed at the security line at the Atlanta airport to a feed originating from an aircraft such as a P3, a helicopter, or a Predator monitoring the Red River flood. Click, scroll, click; just like that. Getting more coverage would seem to be a matter of logistics as much as anything, making contact with other agencies, making sure that systems talk to one another, ensuring that laws and regulations are respected, programming firewalls, and such.

Supporting disaster response to something like the spring floods in the Midwest would be an ideal mission for a drone and the Big Pipe. The Predator, because it can remain airborne for so long, can use its synthetic aperture radar, or SAR, to map the flood zone of an entire state in one flight. Prior to that year's flood season, a Predator had been doing just that, and with the SAR providing change detection based on previous pictures, actually highlighting the differences as the situation on the ground evolves. This capability can give response teams on the ground crucial intelligence about flood patterns or ice breakage in real time. And, as it happens, the Big Pipe was born during a national disaster, in Corpus Christi, Texas, when the OAM was working to provide air support to the phalanx of agencies responding to Hurricane Katrina. When Knight started, he only had five feeds, but it was working, and extending the capacity of the system was mostly a matter of building the right systems architecture. That was no small task. "I built this thing, and then I just looked at it and said, Oh, my God, what did I just do? I've created a monster."

From that original do-it-yourself server in Corpus Christi, the evolution of the Big Pipe has been rapid. It is now supported by CBP's Office of Information and Technology and has dedicated developers who work to ensure that it will function on every conceivable platform, from old x86 PCs in a sheriff's office somewhere using a slow Internet connection to a PDA or smartphone on a 3G mobile network. A custom content management system allows Knight to control access with whatever granularity he desires, giving the customer only what he has a need to see.

Although it is part of Customs and Border Protection, the OAM plays a support role for an array of other agencies—other Homeland Security agencies such as ICE, the TSA, the Secret Service, and FEMA, as well as the DEA, the FBI, NASA, NOAA, the Coast Guard, JIATF South, NORAD, and the U.S. Geological Survey. Knight told me he had at least one hundred DoD partners, though he cautioned that in accordance with the Posse Comitatus Act the military receives only limited access to the Big Pipe, on a temporary basis, in operations such as disaster response. He said he worked with the National Guard, state-level authorities such as the Texas Department of Public Safety, local police, and sheriff's departments. Then there was the Air and Marine Operations Center, in Riverside, California, which integrates the Big Pipe into its core mission of monitoring and securing the entire national airspace, as well as the marine environment extending one hundred nautical miles offshore.

In the business of border security, the potential for the Big Pipe to provide the architecture of a common operating picture for a supervising agent, sitting in a control room like the one I saw in Brownsville, was pretty clear. Rather than just staring at a flickering sequence of video feeds from RVSS cameras, one begins to imagine a geo-spatial interface on a large screen showing every RVSS tower in a sector, along with every ground sensor and the ports of entry, with their hundreds of cameras. The radios used by the Border Patrol are all GPS enabled, so it's no great leap to integrate them as well, so that anytime an agent cues the radio it shows up as a blip on the screen. Add the mobile surveillance systems like the scope trucks, the aircraft, and the riverboats, and you would have all your fixed infrastructure and all your mobile assets captured and represented graphically on a digital map, in real time, with the ability to click in and see what's happening from any point in the system. The supervising agent in charge would know where all his agents are, and where the aircraft are, and he could see at a glance where they were in relation to one another.

Such a system would approximate the command and control software used in war zones around the world. But Knight wasn't just talking about a specific operational zone like the Rio Grande valley sector;

he was aiming at a much larger domain, fusing the national air radar picture with the coastal marine surface radar picture, and adding in all the CBP feeds along the border, and the video surveillance cameras in the ports, along with airborne video sources, as well as surveillance assets in metropolitan areas, so that the scope of operations expanded to the widest possible extent. This broad spectrum of surveillance is really what Knight seemed to have in mind when he spoke about total domain awareness—an operating picture that encompassed pretty much the entire United States. At that point, the potential for real-time persistent surveillance of a target comes into view. Total domain awareness means the ability to apply these tools anywhere in the United States.

Knight came back to his example of the Guardian drone following a target at sea. As that target vessel approaches Miami, the Guardian, which as an unmanned vehicle is not permitted to fly into the airspace of a major metropolitan area, hands off the target to a P3 aircraft. Then, as the vessel enters the port, it gets handed off to fixed video cameras, whereupon ground personnel can also play a role. One platform can't do it all; the air assets can't stay airborne forever, the still cameras can't move, "but if you start putting all these camera systems together, you've functionally closed the gap." Over time, Knight said, "we might be able to provide persistent surveillance coverage of a target, moving from outdoors to indoors in a major metropolitan area, from the airport to downtown city streets." All through the Big Pipe. Knight laughed. "It's a lot like what you see in some of these—what was that show called, *24*? It's the same principle behind it. But we've been working on it since before that show came out. At least I have been."

As I listened to Knight talk about his vision for the Big Pipe, Borkowski's skepticism about the functional payoff of a common operating picture continued to resonate with me. It wasn't clear, for example, that a fully robust Big Pipe could have prevented the gun that killed Jaime Zapata from ending up in the Zetas' arsenal. But judging from the logistical expertise that I saw demonstrated by Customs and Border Protection at the World Trade Bridge in Laredo, and by the surveillance infrastructure CBP is building along the southwest border, I had little doubt that Knight's ambitions were not only technically possible but almost logically inevitable.

Yet what was most striking to me, as I reflected on the full scope of the Big Pipe and the ambitions of its creators, was the extent to which the border has become a laboratory, a controlled environment in which new security techniques can be perfected and where military tactics can be adapted for domestic application. The mission of securing our national borders has become indistinguishable from a new and still emerging understanding of what constitutes homeland security. It was hard to avoid the conclusion that the border itself was slowly expanding to fill the entire continent. Before long, we all may find ourselves inside the Big Pipe.

West from Del Rio the border grows wide as the Rio Grande recedes behind private ranchland. There are a few points of approach, although there is at least one place where you can cross the international boundary with impunity, Amistad Reservoir. Not long after I said farewell to my guides in the Border Patrol, my sons and I spent a pleasant morning reeling in black bass under the expert eye of a fishing guide by the name of Ray Hanselman. I had no idea we were in Mexico until Ray mentioned that the spot we were fishing was called Lobo Canyon. Lobo Canyon? I asked.

That's right, said Ray.

In Mexico? I asked.

Yep.

I just stared straight ahead, blinking. There wasn't much I could do about it at that point, but I couldn't help but think about that couple on Jet Skis who came under fire from pirates on Falcon Lake, in Zapata County, just a few hours south. The epidemic of kidnapping was no joke.

Don't worry, said Ray. I have all the permits we need.

Farther west, past Comstock, the highway swings within sight of the border at the mouth of the Pecos and a few miles later at Langtry, where in 1896 Judge Roy Bean staged a world heavyweight boxing championship on a sandbar in the Rio Grande.

That was a time of optimism and expansion. The Indian wars were over, and the western reaches of the state were opening up. What's left now is largely ruin—crumbling towns, rotting remnants like Cedar Station, Pumpville, Dryden. People come out here to hunt, the rail-

Lobo Canyon

road still runs through it, and there are still a few working ranches, like the one my family has operated since the 1970s, despite the drug traffickers who sometimes threaten to turn our long perilous road down to the river into a smugglers' superhighway.

And it was in this remote corner of Texas that Cormac McCarthy set his great neglected novel *No Country for Old Men*. The title comes from a line by William Butler Yeats, in his poem "Sailing to Byzantium."

The evocation of Byzantium amid the vast wastes of the Chihuahuan Desert might seem jarring at first, but McCarthy's novels are messages from lost worlds, artifacts of vanished histories. His characters are solitaries, dying animals, fugitives from the present who go forth into the rotten holdings of the vanquished in search of something they cannot name. They know not what they are. McCarthy, at his best, gives voice to a strange traveler from a distant land who has taken it upon himself, as in Yeats's poem, to keep a drowsy emperor awake by singing of what is past, passing, or to come.

*Who is that traveler and what does he want? The horseman approaches but dear friend do not attempt to call out his name, for to do so is to ask him in. Rest content with the telling. Read the news of civilizations old and new. Read those records of blood and violence, conjugations of joy and sorrow. As it was then, is now and ever shall be. Curious the small and lesser fates that lead a man to his end, the small enigmas of time and space and death. What do you believe? He said he believed the last and the first suffer equally. That a curtain is falling on the western world.*

*No Country for Old Men,* McCarthy's ninth novel, unfolds right along this stretch of the Texas-Mexico border, in the 1980s, when the drug war was just beginning to change the character of all the communities along the Rio Grande and beyond. The book can be seen as a coda to the enormously ambitious and successful Border Trilogy (which comprises *All the Pretty Horses, The Crossing,* and *Cities of the Plain*). Like many of McCarthy's novels, it plays with the conventions of genre, but unlike the last four the genre in question is not the western but the thriller. Critics made much of this formal shift when the book appeared in 2005. James Wood, writing in *The New Yorker,* declared the book "an unimportant, stripped-down thriller" that "gestures not toward any recognizable reality but merely toward the narrative codes already established by pulp thrillers and action films." Joyce Carol Oates, writing in *The New York Review of Books,* dismissed the novel as being little better than a "meretricious thriller." It was, she said, "increasingly confused" and "ineffectual" and yet somehow perfectly suited to the movie screen.

Perhaps it is not so unusual for major writers to receive bad reviews for good books, but there was something about the rough treatment this novel suffered that struck me as being symptomatic of the shallowness and haste that characterizes so much of our literary culture. It was hard to miss the malice creeping into the reviews but not so easy to explain it. William Deresiewicz, who wrote an intemperate review in *The Nation,* and Joyce Carol Oates both objected to the novel's alleged politics; Deresiewicz went so far as to claim that McCarthy had enlisted his fiction in the culture wars and was "rubbing our tender little modern liberal noses in death's horror by making us watch it in slow motion." Wood, one of the finest literary critics writing in English and the author of a novel called *The Book Against God*, admitted that McCarthy was good, but not that good, and insinuated that there was something morally suspect, offensive even, about his books. "McCarthy stifles the question of theodicy before it can really speak. His myth of eternal violence . . . asserts, in effect, that rebellion is pointless because this is how it will always be." The thriller, Wood concluded, "is the perfect vehicle for McCarthy's deterministic mythmaking, matching his metaphysical cheapness with a slickness unto death all its own."

How interesting, I thought, that Cormac McCarthy should fail so spectacularly at writing a theodicy—which is to say, a James Wood novel. But it might be even more interesting, at least when confronted with an author of McCarthy's undeniable skill, to figure out what he was trying to do and to evaluate the book on its own terms instead of trying to plug it into an arbitrary category like "theodicy." Wood's claim that the events and characters and landscape of *No Country for Old Men* correspond to no recognizable reality, it seemed to me, confused the limits of reality with those of suburban domesticity. To anyone born and raised in the border country, which McCarthy since 1985 has taken as his primary setting, McCarthy's novels just feel like home. They may be the products of a world that in large part is already extinct, but they are not figments of a merely literary imagination. McCarthy's novels are the works of an artist who has excavated the tailings of that dying world.

In the years between 1965 and 1979, McCarthy published four Appalachian novels. His method, so far as one can tell, was as rigorous as it was unusual. He lived among the people about whom he wrote. Like them, he worked in almost complete obscurity and in absolute poverty. McCarthy's second ex-wife, Annie DeLisle, reports that she and her husband lived for almost eight years in an old dairy barn and used a nearby lake for baths. McCarthy spent much of his time with old woodsmen and moonshiners. His work was beginning to attract the attention of professors, but he firmly rejected the seductions of the lecture and workshop circuit. "Someone would call up and offer him $2,000 to come speak at a university about his books," DeLisle

Amistad Reservoir, west of Del Rio

told a reporter, "and he would tell them that everything he had to say was there on the page." Throughout these years, as he published *The Orchard Keeper, Outer Dark,* and *Child of God,* McCarthy was husbanding his experiences, working on *Suttree,* his great comic novel of Knoxville in the 1950s, and that book did not appear until five years after he moved to Texas in 1974. McCarthy's habit of holding on to his manuscripts (*Cities of the Plain* apparently existed as a screenplay for more than ten years prior to the publication of *All the Pretty Horses*) beggars attempts to divide his career into distinct periods. In 1985, McCarthy published his first Texas novel, *Blood Meridian,* and the Border Trilogy began to appear in 1992. Critics tend to draw a line between the Appalachian and the southwestern novels, but *Suttree* and *Blood Meridian* resemble each other more than they do the other books whose landscapes they share.

McCarthy's singular vision was already fully formed in his first novel. His insistence on time, on the rhythm of the seasons, the phases of the moon, and most of all the evening redness in the West, manifests itself in almost the first image of *The Orchard Keeper*, and in the last, and rises to its most extreme pitch in *Blood Meridian*. In *Suttree*, McCarthy exchanges solar time with animal metabolism, and his temporal markers become urination, defecation, and vomiting. His Tennessee River is a slow-moving septic mass, a colossal intestinal tract, beside which the damned and forgotten give themselves over to drink and debauchery, their "lives running out like something foul, nightsoil from a cesspipe, a measured dripping in the dark."

By whatever means McCarthy measures before and after, the shape of the story so defined is always tragic. In *The Orchard Keeper*, the motions of the drama are as old as Antigone: a father killed; the son befriended by the killer, who becomes a surrogate father; an old man hounded out of his home by the law, because he follows an older law.

In the interplay of such primeval oppositions, McCarthy obsessively explores the borderline between the human and the animal, especially in those instinctual rites by which some humans maintain their ancient allegiance to the predator. Wolves and coyotes, panthers and house cats, hawks, owls, minks, and other varmints populate his novels, as do those human hunters, trappers, and fishermen who are animal in their innocence and love of blood. They hunt because they live, and they feel the blood rise with the moon and must run their bluetick hounds or set their traps. (A reference work, *Trapping North American Furbearers*, a rare written testament of a dying craft, is cited both in *The Orchard Keeper* and in *The Crossing*.) Other men, damaged by violence or some nameless perversion, lose the pure sense of the hunt and descend into a subhuman realm of murder and treachery. True hunters smell the murder on the skins of such men and recoil from them instantly.

But these perverted hunters are not the worst of the killers in McCarthy's fiction. His true villains arrive at murder as if it were a higher calling and consciousness, the purest and most scientific expression of civilization. They are rationalists, technicians of amorality. We first glimpse such a killer in *Outer Dark*, a smiling, bearded, and black-suited highwayman who travels with two brutal companions and builds his fires high, because you never know who might be passing by. "We ain't hard to find. Oncet you've found us." He gives no name because "some things is best not named," though he admits that "they's lots would like to know that." A dark rider bound, he declares, "by nothin," this figure will follow the western road to Texas.

McCarthy's plots are austere tragedies interwoven with absurdly comic set pieces. Gene Harrogate fucking watermelons or chasing pigs or poisoning bats in *Suttree*; the stampede scene in *Outer Dark*, which turns into a near lynching after a band of pig herders attempts, with the help of a compliant preacher, to blame Culla Holme for the death of their fellow herder, who was swept off a cliff by the panicked hogs. And everywhere the magnificent imagery of onrushing doom. Small gray nameless birds struggle and cry out, having been blown by the wind of a desert cloudburst onto the sharp daggers of a cholla cactus; drinkers on a saloon's back porch, poised over a hollow, fall into the abyss when the old boards and nails give way; a ferry breaks free and shoots down a swollen river as a crazed horse rushes back and forth on the deck until it finally goes over the rail; a hawk so intent on its prey that it fails to notice an approaching automobile.

McCarthy's youths all set out to recapture something lost and elusive. One, the nameless kid of *Blood Meridian* (born in '33, like his author, though in a different century), is so ignorant and damaged that he knows not for what he searches or even that he searches at all. He simply drifts and in drifting finds his vocation as a hunter of men, an Indian killer, and a trader in scalps. Even as he participates in the slaughter of men and women and children, both Indian and Mexican, he seems somehow other than his compatriots and especially other than Judge Holden, one of the most vivid and demonic characters in American literature. The judge accuses the kid of a tacit treachery, an unwillingness to give himself over completely to the task of war, war not only on the Indian but against all autonomous life. The freedom of the birds is an insult to man, says the judge, who would have them all in zoos.

Driven by a merciless causality, McCarthy's characters wander through nightmare landscapes, horse-borne witnesses to a tree adorned with the pale larva-like corpses of dead babies, a shallow desert pond surrounded by the bones of a thousand sheep, a mummified Apache hanging from a wooden cross. A lone tree burning at night in the midst of an empty plain. A prairie covered with the gleaming white skeletons of a million buffalo. Men hung upside down, scalped, strange menstrual wounds between their legs and genitals protruding from their mouths. Horsemen rope wild dogs atop a mesa and drag them to death. A boy on horseback with a muzzled she wolf in tow crosses the low border scrublands toward Mexico. Gypsies carry a tattered airplane through the desert and tell enchanting lies about its provenance. And everywhere are the ruins of those ancient and not so ancient peoples who were slaughtered in those places and whose lives left no articulate testament to bear witness to the joys and hopes and dreams and sorrows that they shared before pale riders the color of dust swooped down and spilled their blood onto the thirsty ground.

The voices of hermits, anchorites, priests and ex-priests, herdsmen and gypsies and trappers, old men on their deathbeds and old women educated in Europe and horse traders and young peasant girls cry out their prophecies in these bloodlands of the West. *These things are known to all the world. The world is construed out of blood and nothing else but blood. Death is the condition of existence and life is but an emanation thereof. What is constant in history is greed and foolishness and a love of blood. Before man was, war waited for him. The idea that man can be understood is an illusion. All horses possess one soul. What the wolf knows man cannot know.*

The course of history for McCarthy is one of never-ending destruction. He will give no solace to those who dream of an end to suffering, and yet offers some of the most delicate and sensitive representations of sorrow that I know. The sorrow of an old woman who lost five children and fills her days with milking and churning and cursing her sorry husband: "Sorry laid the hearth here. Sorry ways and sorry people and heavensent grief and heartache to make you pine for your death." The sorrow of Rinthy Holme, in *Outer Dark*, her incestuous offspring stolen from her at birth, wandering barefoot and ragged, her rotten cotton dress soiled with two tear-shaped milk stains, searching for a tinker she has never met, hoping to retrieve a baby she has never seen. A stonemason's sorrow for his grandfather, his father, his sister, and the life they all once shared. The stoic mourning of John Grady Cole, Lacey Rawlins, and Billy Parham, young cowboys born into a world that has no use for them or the high lonesome morality of honor and work that defines their way of life.

What sweeps away these characters and all that they love is war—and not only the kind of war that announces itself as such. War is also the name for what civilization does to wildness, to autonomous life, whether it be human or not. The freedom of the birds is an insult. There is room on the stage for one beast and one alone. The American West, for McCarthy, is a place where the truth of history declares itself with unambiguous and ferocious candor. Men kill men for gold and glory. Women and children will be killed if there's money to be made or good sport to be had. And yet, within the broad current of such slaughter, fragile eddies of safety form and sustain themselves briefly, before the floodwaters, touched here and there with pink foam, rise again and wash them downstream.

Just as McCarthy's change of landscape from Appalachia to West Texas and beyond reflects the historical path of American continental expansion, so does the trajectory of his Texas novels follow that of history. *Blood Meridian* depicts the savagery of conquest and genocide, and out of that southwestern holocaust emerged a society that began to disappear almost as soon as it was formed. Scarcely two generations enjoyed its prime. Horsemen and cattlemen and sheepherders, imperfect and often crude, dismissive of the Mexicans, with whom they had so much in common, became in the end tragic creatures of the West, more like the Indians than unlike. The Border Trilogy traces the arc of that ranching society's decline, with old Mexico standing as witness.

The broad sweep of the interlocking stories that make up *All the Pretty Horses*, *The Crossing*, and *Cities of the Plain* is historical, but the phantasmagoria of *Blood Meridian* has been replaced with an economy of scale more proper to a love story. The nostalgia for the Wild West that sends John Grady Cole and Billy Parham into Mexico, a nostalgia that superficial readers might be tempted to attribute to McCarthy himself, should be understood as one among the many forces that drive these characters to their unhappy fates. In their headlong pursuit of a way of life that in the larger temporal scale of this landscape can hardly be said to have existed at all, Cole and Parham, whose separate stories in the first two books of the Border Trilogy become one in the third, manage to destroy much more than their own lives. Parham makes a decision that ultimately leads to the death of both his parents and his little brother. Cole's doomed love for a Mexican whore leads inexorably to lifeless bodies, drained of blood, staring at the blue vault of the sky. These individual stories, love affairs and knife fights, the loss of siblings and parents and friends and ranches, all take place within a matrix of converging histories, the encroachment of military bases, overseas wars, and national economic policies that render family-scale agriculture virtually impossible.

With *No Country for Old Men*, the sun has set decisively upon the dream of the West, and the eternal law of McCarthy's bloodthirsty landscape has reasserted itself absolutely. But with a difference, it seems. This novel is spare, shorn of the high rhetoric and gorgeous descriptive passages that McCarthy's readers have come to expect. The absence is painful, and therein lies a clue to the writer's intentions. All the enchantment seems to have gone out of the world. Or nearly all. Here is a passage that comes just after Ed Tom Bell, the sheriff of Terrell County (not, as Joyce Carol Oates would have it, the sheriff of Comanche County, which is more than three hundred miles to the northeast, an error that explains the otherwise inexplicable title of her *New York Review* essay, "The Treasure of Comanche County"), has moved a dead red-tailed hawk from the blacktop, where, "lost in the concentration of the hunter," it closed in on its prey, oblivious to fate hurtling toward it at seventy-five miles per hour: "He stood there looking out across the desert. So quiet. Low hum of wind in the wires. High bloodweeds along the road. Wiregrass and sacahuista. Beyond in the stone arroyos the tracks of dragons. The raw rock mountains shadowed in the late sun and to the east the shimmering abscissa of the desert plains under a sky where raincurtains hung dark as soot all along the quadrant. That god lives in silence who has scoured the following land with salt and ash. He walked back to the cruiser and got in and pulled away."

Perhaps it is no accident that this small glimpse of McCarthy's grander eloquence appears in the vicinity of a noble predator whose life has been snuffed out by our civilization's bane and glory. Sheriff Bell, a contemporary of John Grady Cole and Billy Parham now grown old, can barely imagine the world that came before his own. He knows something of that country's history but not enough. He knows that a change has come over the land, though he cannot fathom its depths. "Somewhere out there is a true and living prophet of destruction and I dont want to confront him. I know he's real. I have seen his work." *Blood Meridian*'s scalpers have returned to the borderlands, and Judge Holden has been reincarnated as Anton Chigurh, a cartel assassin whose philosophical disquisitions on the subject of murder are as chilling as anything in McCarthy's body of work.

Near the beginning of the book, Llewelyn Moss, poaching antelope on the land of someone McCarthy calls Harkle, just west of Lozier Canyon, in Terrell County, Texas, happens upon the remains of a shoot-out among drug smugglers. Moss finds a suitcase full of money and takes it, and from this decision all else in the novel follows. Anton Chigurh searches for the money, leaving a trail of bodies—sheriff's deputies, random drivers, hotel clerks—in his wake. The chase takes us west to Sanderson, then east to Del Rio and Ciudad Acuña, south to Eagle Pass and Piedras Negras. McCarthy's stark descriptions are often limited to the mere motion of these characters as they move through space and time, a narrative behaviorism that corresponds well to the

Cedar Station

flattened perspective of a world in which the only significant scale of meaning and value is monetary. Whereas in McCarthy's previous works blood was the measure of all things, in *No Country for Old Men* the yardstick of all thought and action, both physical and metaphysical, is an abstraction that his characters can scarcely comprehend.

"We're bein bought with our own money," Sheriff Bell worries late in the novel, shortly after he asks a county prosecutor if he knows who Mammon is: "And it aint just the drugs. There is fortunes bein accumulated there that they dont nobody even know about. What do we think is goin to come of that money? Money that can buy whole countries. It done has. . . . The other thing is the old people, and I keep comin back to them. They look at me it's always a question. Years back I dont remember that. I dont remember it when I was sheriff back in the fifties. You see em and they don't even look confused. They just look crazy."

It is not only the old people in this novel who have lost their way. Moss takes the money he finds in the desert with the full knowledge that in doing so he will forfeit all that he loves. And yet he cannot leave it. Leaving it would be unthinkable; the world in which he finds himself has foreclosed that possibility. That world, of course, is precisely the world of the thriller, and it could very well be that the impoverished world of the thriller is the one in which we find ourselves as well.

In places where life is harsh and cruel, in barren lands where human habitation finds only precarious purchase, McCarthy follows a causality strict and inevitable. As Guy Davenport wrote in a 1968 essay, every sentence in McCarthy's fiction conveys swift and significant action: "He does not waste a single word on his character's thoughts." Such austerity may offend the self-appointed guardians of bourgeois consciousness, but book reviews leave little trace in the strata of literary history. What lasts are those monuments, like the pictographs and painted pebbles of the Pecos River people, like the stone water trough whose image closes *No Country for Old Men*, that are made to last ten thousand years:

> You could see the chisel marks in the stone. It was hewed out
> of solid rock and it was about six foot long and maybe a foot
> and a half wide and about that deep. Just chiseled out of the

rock. And I got to thinkin about the man that done that. That country had not had a time of peace much of any length at all that I knew of. I've read a little of the history of it since and I aint sure it ever had one. But this man had set down with a hammer and chisel and carved out a stone water trough to last ten thousand years. Why was that? What was it that he had faith in? It wasnt that nothin would change. Which is what you might think, I suppose. He had to know bettern that. . . . And I have to say that the only thing I can think is that there was some sort of promise in his heart. And I dont have no intentions of carvin a stone water trough. But I would like to be able to make that kind of promise.

Cormac McCarthy takes the long view, and any reading of his work that fails to understand that, any reading that suggests that this most disciplined and rigorous novelist had any object in mind other than making a novel that will outlast our cities of the plains, has failed to reckon with his art.

Not all art will comfort us as we age, and McCarthy's least of all. His fiction, like so much of our oldest literature, is tragic, and as such is held together by the very warp of the world. Sometimes his subject is the tragedy of history, in which two laws equally just and true come into unavoidable and violent conflict. Sometimes it is that of transgression, as when a brother and sister come together in the darkness and out of that furtive grappling are undone. Most often it is the simple natural drama of predator and prey, of hawks and wolves, trappers and hunters and snake catchers and those who run dogs under the moon; the drama of muskrats and field mice and catfish, wild house cats aloft in the claws of owls, all of which fall prey to man, who hunts all things. In *No Country for Old Men*, we witness the drama of householders and peaceful folk who wish only to be left alone but who are drawn in to inevitable strife with the world's hidden powers. At its root, McCarthy's fiction arises from the tragedy of all wild creatures, of whatever is begotten, born, and dies, the tragedy of autonomous life in a world increasingly circumscribed by a rage for order and captivity. More than merely human, it is the tragedy of warm blood itself, of blood and time.

.   .   .

Lozier Canyon lies about twenty miles west of Langtry, along a lonely stretch of road that McCarthy's readers have encountered more than once in the Border Trilogy. And just west of Lozier Canyon lies my family's eastern fence. McCarthy presumably took the name Harkle, whose land he says this is, from Harkell Canyon, which lies some miles to the northeast and opens onto the Pecos River. Shortly after reading *No Country for Old Men* for the first time, I got my father on the telephone. McCarthy several times refers to Harkle's cattle guard, and as far as I remembered, the only cattle guard along the highway anywhere near Lozier was ours. My father agreed that based on the landmarks mentioned in the text, it did appear that Bell and his deputies, Moss, Chigurh, and several anonymous corpses were all trespassing on our Cinco de Mayo ranch.

I thought I should see for myself, and so I flew from New York to San Antonio and then drove 150 miles to Del Rio, where I spent the night with my grandmother. The next day, my father, my stepmother,

Cattle guard

and I drove out to the Cinco, tracing in reverse Moss's path across Amistad Reservoir and through the town of Comstock. The road to Pandale, where in *All the Pretty Horses* Jimmy Blevins first picks up the trail of John Grady Cole and Lacey Rawlins, forks off to the right. Low hills spread out in all directions, covered in purple cenizo blossoms. Mesquite and black brush thrive in this landscape, as does the creosote bush, an aggressive competitor for water that can live more than ten thousand years. Vicious, thorny plants such as dog cactus, prickly pear, ocotillo, catclaw, lechuguilla, and Spanish dagger lie in wait for unprotected limbs.

We crossed the high bridge over the Pecos River, green and salty in its deep canyon, big black crows perched on dead trees near its confluence with the Rio Grande. We passed by Langtry, the legendary home of Judge Roy Bean, and Eagle Nest Canyon, across from a massive nest on the Mexican side that has remained in a cross-shaped cliff hollow for more than a hundred years. After we passed through Lozier, we began to slow down. When we reached the cattle guard, we pulled off the highway. In *No Country for Old Men*, Anton Chigurh did the same, then "he drove across the bars of the cattleguard and got out and closed the gate again and stood there listening. Then he got in and drove down the rutted track." We too drove down that primitive road, heading south toward Mexico.

McCarthy imagines pickups crisscrossing this jagged canyon country, off road, all the way down to the Rio Grande. He describes volcanic gravel, lava scree, the caldera of some long-extinct volcano. He populates it with antelope. All of these details are false. The geology here is upper and lower Cretaceous limestone, Del Rio clay, the Devils River and Buda and Eagle Ford formations. Volcanoes lie far to the west, near Marfa and Alpine, or down in the Big Bend. This is canyon country, the geologic record of water's inexorable erosion of the western reaches of the Edwards Plateau as it seeks the Rio Grande. Although from the highway it might seem that a sturdy pickup could make its way over what looks to be a gently rolling greasewood flat, countless ravines, arroyos, draws, and canyons cut through the land, carving bluffs that appear without warning, and eventually one approaches the great cliffs of Palma draw and Lozier Canyon. (Anyone hoping to build a wall through this country would soon come to grief.) Passage to the river is extraordinarily difficult, and the cliffs along the Rio Grande, which here makes a broad horseshoe-shaped arc, are three hundred feet in places. Mule and white-tailed deer, not antelope, populate the area.

But McCarthy's liberties with landscape, it seems to me, can be excused. His factual sins are committed in the service of story. He prefers the volcanic subtext because it is violent, and its violence gives his story a geologic narrative to go with its historical one. Why, then, did he not set his novel farther south and west, in the Big Bend, where volcanism and mountain building produced the most graphically violent landscape in the state? Perhaps because the area near Langtry remained wilder longer than any other part of the state. Because it was, and is, a place of outlaws and smugglers and rustlers. It is also the site of a lost culture whose traces are still visible in the ancient rock shelters along its canyon walls.

In *No Country for Old Men*, as in every other novel he has written, McCarthy insists on the relics of ancient, vanished peoples in his landscapes. And he makes no secret of his view that those whose lives he describes are no less ephemeral. Indeed, what the landscape of West Texas suggests is that the ranchers who have peopled the last four novels are a good deal more likely to vanish without a trace than were the Indians, whose art, exposed to the elements for thousands of years, still bears witness to their lifeways. The metal implements used by the ranchers to make horseshoes and axes and elaborate irrigation systems have rusted and are crumbling into dust, together with concrete water troughs and cedar picket stock pens. Some of these artifacts may survive to be puzzled over by future generations, though perhaps it will be the opium tins and pipes and iron woks of the Chinese workers who populated railroad camps for a year or two along the Rio Grande in the 1880s. Or other nameless implements that were used to chisel passages and tunnels for the railroad. Or the clever wire swivels used by Mexican goatherds to stake kids under rock lean-tos in kidding camps. This landscape, which appears almost empty today, is a palimpsest of cultures. All of them lost, undone.

The Pecos Canyon had made passage through this land difficult and dangerous, and stagecoaches, mail riders, emigrants, and cattle drives had to cross the river far to the north. It was still Indian country long

Handprints left by the Pecos River people

after most of the state had been settled. In historic times, the Lipan Apaches and the Jumanos were known to hunt the area; the Comanches and the Kiowas traveled all the way from the Llano Estacado to gather peyote. So far as we can tell, humans first passed through the Pecos region about fourteen thousand years ago, when piñon pine forests covered the hills and prehistoric horses, camels, bison, and mammoths ranged through it. Small bands of nomadic hunter-gatherers made homes in the shallow rock shelters and caves; when the climate changed and the desert advanced, some remained, made do with what the landscape provided, and eventually began to record their experiences in vivid colors along the limestone walls of their dwellings. By the time Cabeza de Vaca journeyed through the Trans-Pecos in 1535, the people who inhabited these canyons for so many thousands of years, painting their stories in their shelters, had vanished.

On a warm October afternoon, Jack Skiles, a local historian and author of *Judge Roy Bean Country*, took us into an ancient Indian shelter, in Eagle Nest Canyon, not far from his home along the edge of the caprock. From the mouth of the east-facing shelter we could see Highway 90 as it crossed the gorge, providing drivers with a brief glimpse of the steep limestone cliffs. A nearby spring explained the Indians' choice of this spot, and on the far rim of the canyon the remains of a windmill built by Guy Skiles, Jack's father, testified to more recent attempts to exploit that precious resource.

A talus slope of burned rocks spilling down from Eagle Cave immediately announced that humans once made their dwelling here. We saw a deep metate ground into the limestone bedrock by generations of hands. Scrambling up the talus, we entered the shelter, and Jack explained that humans lived here almost continuously for ten thousand years. We were standing on a midden composed of more than ten feet of ash and garbage and burned stone. Bits of sotol cud, a fibrous plant chewed for its high sugar content, lay here and there all over the floor, as did grindstones and bits of chipped and worked rock, a charred jawbone of some small critter, thousands upon thousands of empty snail shells. Excavation and archaeological analysis have revealed countless grasshopper mandibles, minnow bones, dart and arrow points, a dead child.

Four-thousand-year-old pictographs in the Pecos River style adorned the walls: a faded shaman, circles and beasts and hunting symbols in what appears to be a ritual narrative. Jack told us that the shelter had been used near the turn of the century as a shearing barn, which explained all the sheep dung that littered the floor. As a consequence, many of the pictographs were lost, rubbed off by the sheep as they milled about in their timeless, mindless anxiety.

Not far up the canyon was Bonfire Shelter, a kill site where fourteen thousand years ago pre-Clovis hunters drove herds of animals off a cliff.

In a small building adjacent to his home in Langtry, Jack was kind enough to show us his private collection of local artifacts. First among them was a twelve-hundred-year-old mummy that his father dug up in a cave along the Pecos. The man died a horrible death: his bowels, which look like huge, petrified cow patties, were compacted as a result of Chagas' disease, an infection carried by the bloodsucking conenose bug. He lay wrapped in a finely woven mat made from sotol; around his midsection, presumably to help support his painfully swollen gut, were long strips of deer hide, tanned and dyed red with local ocher. The leather, a piece of which I held in my hand, was still soft and supple. Binding this burial package together was a hundred-foot length of rope, made of human hair.

All along the walls of Jack's museum was further evidence of the ingenuity of the Pecos River people: delicate drawstring bags, and sandals woven from lechuguilla and embellished with rabbit fur; fire sticks and stone tools for grinding meal and baskets so finely woven they were used to carry water; other baskets used for cooking; a variety of arrow points, and atlatls used to propel them; painted pebbles, some dating back six thousand years, in enigmatic patterns.

And there was another sort of evidence as well. In a glass case, carefully displayed, were two heads: a mother and child. Lithified brains, now released from their containers, lay side by side. Just below the skulls was the mother's hip bone, an arrow still protruding from it. Both skulls had been crushed.

I was wandering through downtown El Paso, not far from the old neighborhood of Chihuahuita, when I saw the white van. It was parked

El Paso, Texas

in the shade, under a tree, and spray painted across the side was the word YAHWEH. I parked and walked over. Two people were sitting inside, a black man and a white woman. Their son was asleep in the back. I asked about the words on their van. They told me to read the other side, so I walked around that way. YAHWEH SAID: GIVE ME YOUR HANDS!! EXO CHAP 20. The handles of the van's doors formed exclamation points.

They were travelers, coming from California and heading back toward Ohio. We talked about God for a little while, and I had a hard time following what the man was saying. I asked them what they thought about the whole border situation. The man looked at me and said he didn't want to go all Nazi or anything, but it wasn't anything a few machine guns couldn't take care of. He wasn't talking about the drug smugglers.

*And God said, Make an altar of earth for me and sacrifice on it your burnt offerings and fellowship offerings, your sheep and goats and your cattle. Wherever I cause my name to be honored, I will come to you and bless you. If you make an altar of stones for me, do not build it with dressed stones, for you will defile it if you use a tool on it. And do not go up to my altar on steps, or your private parts may be exposed.*

Later that day I met Rudy Garcia for the first time. He gave me a tour of his mountain shrine, a very high altar indeed. I came back a few months later, on the last Saturday in October 2011, the day before the annual pilgrimage of Cristo Rey, a mountain straddling the Mexican border just west of El Paso, crowned with a forty-two-foot-high statue of Jesus standing before his cross. Up to thirty thousand pilgrims were expected on Sunday, and preparations were under way. Garcia, a longtime member of the Mount Cristo Rey Restoration Committee, had invited me to spend the night on the summit with him to guard against the depredations of what he called "the Satanics from Juárez." No barrier other than the mountain itself would protect us from the most dangerous city on earth.

I arrived shortly before 10:00 a.m. after driving west through El Paso alongside the Rio Grande on Paisano Drive, a stretch of road that only a decade before had been subject to cross-border bandit attacks, past a weedy, dilapidated park commemorating the spot where in 1598 Don Juan de Oñate forded the river with his colonists and his army and his priests to give El Paso its name, past the remaining buildings of Old Fort Bliss, now converted into seedy apartment buildings. An enormous smokestack displaying the word "ASARCO" dominated the view, not quite rivaled by the novelty of the fifteen-foot-high Homeland Security border fence looming over the roadway. Eventually, after crossing the Rio Grande into the state of New Mexico, I turned off the macadam onto a gravel road that led through the bleak and blasted landscape of a defunct silica mine where paleontologists study lithified dinosaur remains. The winding road led me across the tracks of the Union Pacific Railroad and up to the base of my destination, the jagged Cristo Rey pluton, an igneous intrusion exposed by eons of erosion, jutting upward from its ancient cradle in the sediment of shallow seas. I left my rental car along the edge of an expanse of an empty parking area and walked up toward a rock, cement, and galvanized-steel shelter surrounded by human figures. It was already getting hot. Jeeps and pickups drove this way and that, fine powdery dust billowed and hung in the air. Several ranks of blue portable toilets stood off to the side, and the doors of storage sheds and containers swung open, disgorging their contents. A dozen or more men and women busied themselves in obscure tasks, laughing and calling out to one another in Spanish and English. Walkie-talkies crackled, and power tools whined. The music was loud.

I gazed up at the cross on the summit, the ragged boulders and cliffs and lesser peaks, the creosote bushes that alone seemed to thrive in this arid landscape, then spotted Rudy kneeling as if in prayer. He was helping two other men rebuild kneelers to be placed before small shrines lining the alarmingly narrow two-and-a-half-mile hanging road that snakes its way up the mountain in broad switchbacks alternating with hairpin turns. Such building and rebuilding never ceases at Cristo Rey, and not only of kneelers but of altars and grottoes, roads and walls and culverts, even the large statue of Jesus Christ that stands atop the peak, 4,675 feet above sea level. Rudy spotted me lurking nearby and delivered an enthusiastic greeting. Within minutes I was helping him load two blue portable toilets into the back of a small, well-used Mazda pickup. Rudy showed me how to lean my back against the heavy plastic

Mount Cristo Rey

sanitary receptacle as he and another helper tilted it way back so that they had only to lift a few inches before I was commanded to push and the load slid easily into the pickup's bed. I could hear the antiseptic chemicals sloshing noisily inside. I dreaded leakage. We repeated the exercise, tied a rope around the two toilets, and climbed into our vehicle.

Rudy Garcia was born in 1937 in a village called Smeltertown, on the banks of the Rio Grande, where the river, flowing south through its rift valley in New Mexico, bends east through the Paso del Norte and fuses with the U.S.-Mexico border. Smeltertown, a community of Mexican immigrants employed by the Guggenheim family's American Smelting and Refining Company, or ASARCO, no longer exists; nor does the smelter, though the company name lives on as a division of the Grupo México conglomerate. In the 1970s, Smeltertown was dismantled and its residents dispersed after medical tests revealed that a high proportion of the population there was contaminated with lead. Residents fought to keep their homes; some were unwilling to accept that they had been poisoned by the smelter. Rudy told me he thought the lead contamination had come from Mexican pottery. The ASARCO smelter was shut down in 1999, after 112 years of operation, amid lawsuits over the toxic by-products belched out by its stacks, the highest of which, at 828 feet, had been a local landmark since 1967. In 2009, ASARCO settled the largest environmental bankruptcy in U.S. history, agreeing to pay $1.79 billion in fines to clean up sites in twenty states. In 2011, residents of El Paso were arguing about whether the two remaining stacks should be demolished or restored as historic landmarks. Eventually, the demolition contingent won the argument, but Mount Cristo Rey endures as a monument to Smeltertown and its diaspora. Here, more than any other place I have traveled in the borderlands, I could feel the full weight of the region's history.

In 1933, Father Lourdes F. Costa looked out the window of his rectory at San Jose del Rio Grande, the parish church once located more or less on the spot where the ASARCO smokestack was built thirty-four years later, and envisioned a huge cross on the mountain then known as Cerro de Muleros, Mule Drivers' Mountain. He spoke to the members of his congregation, among whom were Rudy's parents, and eventually to the bishop of El Paso. Inquiries were made, and a search for the owners commenced, resulting in the purchase of two hundred acres. In March 1934, members of the congregation planted a simple twelve-foot wooden cross on the summit. Later, vocational students from ASARCO built a larger cross out of angle iron. Father Costa commissioned an old friend from his home in Catalonia, a sculptor named Urbici Soler, to build the permanent monument, which was dedicated in 1940 as an offering of thanksgiving to Christ the King and "a fortress against Communism."

Rudy put the pickup into gear, and we started up the narrow hanging road. The previous May, when I first met Rudy, his brother Art, and some of the other members of the committee, we drove up in a Jeep. It was one of the most terrifying experiences of my life. Today was even worse, because at least the Jeep held the promise of leaping to safety if Rudy miscalculated by a few inches. The pickup would be a misfortunate mausoleum. As he drove, Rudy kept up a steady patter of stories about the mountain, the history of the committee, his family, and mild tensions with a local Catholic church in Sunland Park, New Mexico, that had recently asserted control of the shrine. I sat still, my body tense, my foot pressed hard against the floor of the pickup as I silently willed the vehicle leftward toward the sheer rock wall and away from the jumble of sharp-edged scree that dropped precipitously down the talus slope just below my right elbow. I wondered aloud in what I hoped was a brave voice whether we were taking this load all the way to the top. "Sure!" said Rudy, who almost always speaks in exclamations. At one point he told a story about a visitor who panicked on the upper road. "We got to where the monsignor is," a memorial to Mount Cristo's founder, "and he said, Drop me off here, Rudy. I said, Why? and he said, I'm afraid of heights." Rudy laughed loud and long at the memory. "Well, I'm going to make you a man!" and he kept driving, heedless of his passenger's protests. Rudy has made that drive thousands of times, in daylight and in darkness. Only once has he gone over the edge.

Soon we were standing about thirty feet below the peak, on the

Hanging road, Mount Cristo Rey

first of three terraces linked by a steep rock and concrete ramp that rises to the great cross. Like the road we had driven, the ramp is just wide enough for a Jeep or mini pickup. Unlike the road, the ramp now has guardrails, both for the Jeep and for the often elderly pilgrims who face that sharp incline at the end of a difficult climb. We had just unloaded two toilets and shifted them into place. Using a shovel and a rake, we made sure they stood on a level platform; it wouldn't do to have one tip over with someone inside.

I was looking down over the south face of the mountain toward Colonia Anapra, one of the most dangerous neighborhoods in Juárez. Tiny cinder-block houses crowded right up to the base of the mountain, within a few yards of the borderline, which was marked by nothing more imposing than a handful of white boundary markers spaced within eyesight of one another. Last time I was here, one of the markers had been stolen, leaving a gap in the imaginary line. Today, the small white pyramid was back in place.

Trails leading up the mountain from Anapra were clearly visible. Off to the west the international boundary runs through a shallow dusty basin that drains toward the Rio Grande. An aging silvery chain-link border fence, its terminus at the foot of Cristo Rey, bisects the basin and meets up with the new, much taller border fence at the base of a sandy outcropping known to local geologists as the La Mesa formation. On the upper edge of La Mesa, on the Mexican side of the fence, I could see the top of Monument 3, one of 256 such white pyramids established by the International Boundary and Water Commission, stretching from Monument 1 at Madero Plaza, between the Rio Grande and the eastern base of the mountain, across the Sonoran Desert to the Pacific Ocean. Rudy could not understand why Homeland Security chose not to build a fence through this little stretch of the border, which local Border Patrol agents call no-man's-land, or why the decades-old wire fence, about six feet high, was left standing, especially given the long history of robberies and assaults at Mount Cristo Rey.

Rudy had told me stories of hikers and pilgrims being mugged and worse along the road to the summit, tales of women running naked and screaming down the trail, families held up at gunpoint, a bandit who sprang out of an arroyo and put a gun to a child's head, demanding money and valuables from his family. Several members of the committee, including Rudy, have been made deputies by the local sheriff, and they all carried guns. Rudy wore a .38 Special strapped to his hip and often kept a high-powered rifle in his vehicle. Gunplay with the *cholos* from Anapra was once commonplace, and occasionally the rival gangs of the three nearby *colonias*, as the poorest neighborhoods are called—Anapra, Asarco, and Chihuahuita—would stage shoot-outs in the foothills along the border south of the mountain. Thieves from Anapra would steal anything that was not bolted, welded, or cemented down. The water, soft drinks, PA system, lights, and toilets we'd spend the day hauling up the mountain would vanish by tomorrow if someone didn't stand guard all through the cold desert night.

Twenty years ago, Rudy was maneuvering a Jeep on this terrace, pulling a trailer loaded with a large water tank, when his brakes failed. He remembers the sound of water sloshing in the tank and the edge rushing nearer. "I couldn't stop, and I couldn't stop, and I saw myself going over the side, and that's all I remember." The trailer came loose and caught on the edge of the drop-off. The Jeep rolled down the mountain toward Juárez. Looking down a rocky incline that I would not have hazarded on foot, I had difficulty imagining how he had survived. I wondered aloud if the Jeep had bounced over him. "No, no, no," said Rudy. "I must have jumped! I'm here!" he said, laughing. "But see, if I'm going to jump, how did I land on this side?" He showed me where he was lying when he came to, his feet dangling over the edge of a rock wall that dropped straight down into the tangle of boulders and scree. "The guardian angel took me and flipped me over here," he said. "The guardian angel pulled me out!" Rudy's radio did not survive the accident, so he had no choice but to start walking. Two hours later, when Rudy, Art, and some other members came back up the mountain to see about the wreckage, thieves had already climbed the mountain. "We got up here," Art told me, "and the sons of bitches had already taken all the tires, the battery, and all that. And Rudy was so angry he took out his little Betsy and started shooting at them. He emptied that gun." During the 1950s another member went over the edge, on the east side, about halfway up, near the memorial to Father Costa. He was backing up a Jeep and misjudged the distance. He survived but was paralyzed for the rest of his life. The guardian angel was off duty that day.

On the edge of the third terrace, one level below the cross, there stands a permanent white altar, on two pillars of stone, used to celebrate Mass during the pilgrimage and on occasions such as Good Friday. "One day I came up here," Rudy told me, "and St. Pius Church was coming up, and I got up here early." Rudy gestured, his weathered and calloused hands spreading across the white surface of the altar, which was marred by some crude black graffiti scribblings. "It was beautifully painted." He paused. "Two naked angels making love, on the altar. Honest to God." Rudy turned and pointed up toward the cross, ringed by a concrete crown 126 feet in circumference. "Then inside: big dicks, big balls, about like that," he held up his hands to show the size, "painted inside the crown." Rudy quickly painted everything over before the visitors arrived. Mount Cristo Rey's role as a fortress against communism may be history, but the struggle against vandalism never ceases. We walked up the ramp to the cross. Inside the crown, where

Rudy Garcia

the offending illustrations had been painted, were twelve plaques, each engraved with the name of an apostle as well as eleven donors. Around the base of the cross were commemorative tiles, purchased by supporters, now chipped and broken by vandals who threw rocks and smashed glass candles against them. Someone had tried very hard to destroy the tile of Franklin D. Roosevelt, which occupies a position of honor near the center of the battered mosaic. Rudy wasn't sure whether the president had ever visited the mountain, but he had seen photographs of military escorts bringing dignitaries, clad in evening wear and silk top hats, to the summit in motorcycle sidecars.

Urbici Soler's limestone Jesus is the risen Christ, in white robes, standing before the site of execution, arms spread before the instrument of his torture in a triumphant gesture of resurrection. He is a figure of hope, meant to inspire a small community that has suffered many trials.

Like the community of Smeltertown, the statue has endured many trials since it was carried up the mountain in pieces, on the backs of mules. Vandals paint vulgar slogans and scratch their initials into the stone. Someone named Lupe, or perhaps her boyfriend, has testified, in deep scratches, that a person by that name once walked this earth. Jesus's feet have suffered the indignity of blue spray paint, and his toes, now broken, have been repaired more than once. During one assault on the graffiti with sandpaper, a well-meaning helper erased Soler's signature. "History! History!" Rudy cried out, remembering the horror of that day. Lightning struck the statue and cracked it, letting water penetrate the stone, which cracked it further and caused the internal rebar to rust. In 1990 a strong wind knocked pieces loose, and Rudy had to shoot them off with his rifle. Engineers from ASARCO and the University of Texas at El Paso were consulted about a restoration; they declared that it was hopeless. The committee persevered. God would show them how. "The quarry is still in operation, near Austin, Texas," Rudy recounted, "and we ordered the stone, and we put scaffolding up to the top, and we put beams on top, with chain blocks and come-alongs, and then we put foam and straps to protect the stone, and then we anchored everything with three-quarter-inch stainless steel rebar." A special paste was devised, using epoxy, and whitewash was applied, and slowly the statue resumed its familiar shape.

"Now Jesus, as you know, we cannot paint this, 'cause if we do it will break. It's got to breathe. What we do, we get that beige color, real nice, we go to bars in El Paso, and over here in New Mexico, and we ask them to save the cigarette butts. We soak them, and then we take sponges and dab it like when you stain wood. From down there," he said, pointing toward downtown El Paso, "on a nice moonlit night, you can see it shine. Like there's a light inside. Honest to God."

As the afternoon progressed, we carried load after load of blue plastic toilets to strategic points along the pilgrimage route and down to the old silica mine, in the overflow parking area near the dinosaur footprints. Rudy said that the museum was planning to charge for parking on its property next year. As we made our rounds, we passed pilgrims who were already walking the way of Christ, some of them without shoes. "There go the barefooted ladies," Rudy said. "I need to do that." Barefooted? "Yes. I remember one time the road was messed up. It was rough! Right there before I got to Saint Anthony, I started bleeding. But I made it all the way to the top. I attempted to come down. Made it to the Virgin of Guadalupe," about a third of the way. "I couldn't go further. The pain was terrible." I asked Rudy to explain the significance of such a sacrifice. "It's just something in return for favors granted. I ask God or the Virgin, or a saint for that matter. A lot of people pray to the saints. I pray to God and the Virgin, also the saints. When I ask favors and they're granted, and even if not, I still do it. I promise to come up here, walk it barefoot, and light two candles on top."

Down below, I met other members of the committee: Tore, a master mechanic with spiky gray hair and a face like a stone Aztec deity; Debbie, who from what I could tell was largely responsible for the smooth functioning of the base camp; George and Ruben, both dressed in tight Wrangler jeans, cowboy boots, wide-brimmed cowboy hats, and bandannas. When Ruben saw that I had gone up the mountain with Rudy in the Mazda, he asked me whether I'd checked my shorts. He wasn't kidding. All the while Rudy told me stories about his friends on the mountain, many of whom had passed away; about his wife, Alicia, who suffers from Alzheimer's disease; about his nine children and sixteen grandkids and eight great-grandkids ("The flower of the plant is still giving!"). We were sitting in the pickup, near a shrine to Our Lady of Fatima, so that Rudy could rest his left leg, which was atrophied from an old accident and tired from working the clutch. We were on our way down, and I was happy we were well past the more perilous turns. Rudy pointed out a biodiesel plant off in the distance where he had worked as a young man, when it was a cottonseed oil mill.

"We used to fill the railroad cars with oil, and I would go and draw it up there on top and drop this thing down in there and draw out a sample. And then close the lid, and those lids screwed on like so, and they had a four-piece cross made out of pipe. And you would stick a pipe in there to tighten it. As I was tightening it, that thing came out—I guess I didn't put it in far enough, and I went down, but I pushed myself so I wouldn't go on my head. I landed on my butt, on the railroad tracks, and I broke my back. At the time I had three little kids." It was a desperate situation, but at least he had insurance, so he didn't lose his house. "I had some hunting rifles, a British .303 rifle. Oh, I loved that big gun. I sold it so I could buy food for the kids." It was eleven days before he woke up, and he was in the hospital for about two weeks. When he was finally released, his family had planned to move him to his parents' house, but Rudy insisted on going home. "Roger, I'm not lying. We went home and I got me a piece of ass that night!"

No one would ever cast doubt on Rudy's virility or his devotion to his wife. He had planned on staying up at the summit all night, but eventually he admitted that he needed to go home, because he was taking his wife to church in the morning. He put me in the care of his brother Art, known since childhood as Tata. Rudy wanted me to take his pistol, his little Betsy, which he was waving around as he spoke to his friends at the base in rapid Spanish phrases. Ruben kept telling him to put the gun down, to which Rudy replied, "Don't worry! The safety is on!" I was tempted by Rudy's offer of the gun until he said something about a friend who somehow managed to jam two shells into the chamber, so in the end I chose to rely on Tata for protection.

Five of us would be spending the night on the summit. My companions, in addition to Art, with his bushy white mustache, were Chuy Gonzalez, a retired Linotype machinist for the El Paso newspaper; Danny Rodriguez, a burly young biker with a remarkably bushy goatee; and Danny's younger brother, Larry, who had never before ascended Mount Cristo Rey. We loaded up our trailer with firewood, tools, ice chests, jackets, blankets, tarps, and lights to illuminate the cross as a reminder for the faithful down below in El Paso del Norte, the Pass of the North, of which Mount Cristo is one pole, that tomorrow was their day of devotion. The drive up the mountain, my fifth or sixth trip in as many hours, was now routine, though Larry, on his first such voyage, kept up a nervous bilingual commentary. The other men explained, mostly in Spanish, the stations of the cross along the roadside and told stories about bandits and shoot-outs and the dead man who'd been found in a ravine near the Via Matris, a series of small shrines depicting the most difficult moments in the Virgin's life. We passed a small stone ruin where Urbici Soler had lived while he worked on the cross and a large berm or earthen dam to protect the road from erosion. The berm concealed a D7 bulldozer that broke and was too expensive to fix, so they just buried it.

Shadows were beginning to lengthen when we arrived at the summit, and the Franklin Mountains, illuminated on the other side of El Paso's river valley, were more lovely than I had ever thought possible. I've been coming to this dusty border city for two decades, ever since my mother followed her railroader husband here in the 1990s. Until tonight I had never understood why anyone would live here if not compelled to do so. There are few trees and virtually no grass, and the eye falls on little that is not brown or tan. The wind blows continuously, and the landscape has been brutalized by industry and real estate developers. Pawnshops and paycheck loan usurers infest every strip mall. Little remains of the charming oasis of fruit trees and vineyards described by travelers such as Julius Froebel in the 1850s. Yet here I was, roughly fifteen hundred diagonal feet from a virtually undefended border adjacent to one of the worst little slums in the Western Hemisphere, if not the planet, and I felt strangely serene. Perhaps I was inspired by the odd fellowship I had fallen into with these devoted guardians of a faith that was both intensely familiar and curiously alien.

Such thoughts continued to run through my mind as I was roused by the need to set up floodlights. Chuy and I carried the lights up the steep metal staircase that runs along the steeper stone ramp to the summit, then Art showed me where to run extension cords from a generator housed in a heavily armored bunker on the lowest terrace. Danny worked to get the generator running. Once that crucial task was accomplished and the lights were working, we began to make our

Urbici Soler's Jesus

camp. Art had driven the Jeep up the stone ramp to the second terrace; we unhooked the trailer, rolling it out of the way, and Art pulled the Jeep around to the west side of our platform so that it could act as a windbreak. A Border Patrol helicopter flew by, and a fire pit, cut from a steel drum, was retrieved from the trailer. Ventilation holes had been cut to resemble a face, and someone had added a white mustache in chalk. It looked just like Art. As the sun began to set and the evening redness began to spread across the western horizon, I saw a bloody waxing crescent moon poised to set behind the mountains of Juárez.

While the fire kindled and darkness dropped all around us, the lights of the valleys on either side of the mountain popped into being and Juárez revealed its true size: with 1.3 million inhabitants, it was more than twice as large as El Paso. Looking south at the small out-cropping of the mesa on the other side of Anapra, I remembered what Rudy had told me about it, that dozens of young women had been found up there, raped, murdered, left to blacken in the sun. Hundreds of women were murdered here in Juárez over the decades, many of them drawn to the border to labor in foreign-owned factories known as maquiladoras, and for a while those killings made headlines. More recently, that story had been eclipsed by President Felipe Calderón's quixotic war on the cartels. Since 2006, some forty-seven thousand Mexicans had died in drug-related violence, and more than thirty-seven hundred people had been murdered in Juárez the previous year. Chuy wondered aloud whether we'd hear any AK-47 shots down there. "At night," he said, "the sound travels." Danny pointed out the local police station and said that last year they heard shots down in Anapra, then watched a police car leave the station and drive a few blocks before turning off and taking a meandering path back around to its home base. "It was like, nahh, never mind, they're okay." Everyone laughed. A big new divided highway, entirely devoid of traffic, stretched off along the borderline toward Santa Teresa, a small port of entry that was lighting up the western horizon. The road was built by Foxconn, the Taiwanese manufacturer, which had recently opened a new maquiladora near Santa Teresa to assemble computers for Dell. The previous summer, a Foxconn executive gave a *New York Times* reporter a tour of the squalid *colonias* near his plant and told him that Anapra, because it was the poorest area of Juárez, is "the easiest place to pull labor."

Loud music blared from some obscure but nearby location in Mexico, and Larry speculated that a well-lit building on the far side of the *colonia* was a meth plant. Suddenly the music stopped. "We had the DJ down there," said Larry, "but somebody shot him." I asked Larry and Danny if they had grown up in El Paso and what they thought about all the violence in Mexico. Larry launched into a story about how he was almost abducted off a street corner in Juárez when he was three or four.

"Yeah, my brothers were up on the hill," Larry said, drawing out the vowels in his pleasantly musical Mexican accent, with its characteristic emphasis on penultimate syllables and the last two words of a sentence. "They were sliding down, playing, on cardboard. My parents were in church. I was looking at my brothers—ah, cool, ahaha—all of sudden *Poom!* I get inside a car! Kind of remember some lady grasped me, and the driver took off. But there was an intersection where you have to go left or right, and then, right at that time, my mom saw me crying, and said, Hey! Then all of a sudden the patrol was right there—perfect timing! My mom went hysterical. My kid! My kid! There was congestion in the intersection. And they got me back. I would have been gone! Like for body parts, 'cause that's what most people do, you know, they kidnap kids for either their body parts, or to sell, or I don't know, that couple must've been in need of—a child."

"Ransom," said Danny. "Or something," finished Larry. The brothers often completed each other's sentences. That was roughly twenty-eight years ago, back before the current troubles. Danny and Larry grew up going in Juárez, where their grandparents had built a church. They would go across every weekend and on Tuesdays and Thursdays for Mass. Even after the kidnapping attempt they still went to Juárez. "We actually stopped going to that hill," said Danny. "That's what happened. Ever since then, we said, you know what, we're here for church."

"Let's just stay together and go to church, and go to dinner, like a family thing," Larry said. "Stay wise, open-eyed."

Neither of them go to church much anymore, but their father still goes across occasionally. "I know it hurts him, 'cause of what's going on," Larry said. "But he still goes once in a while. But it's not the same." Tata's radio was dialed into the local college football game. Every hour on the half hour he'd check in with the base on his walkie-talkie. There was some confusion with the communication system, because the base had the wrong kind of radio, and then somebody broke down on the first horseshoe, one of the broad switchbacks along the road. We watched headlights slowly ascending through space. I wouldn't want to be in a Jeep on that road at night. The FM radio announcers' voices faded in and out of my awareness. I heard the radio say, ". . . left, out of the gun, snap is back . . ." American football makes no sense to me, even though I grew up in Texas and played the game for one bewildering season. When Tata learned that I followed Spanish soccer, that my team was Barcelona, he stared at me as if I were a space alien.

Danny was talking about the cartels and the government. He said that he saw no hope for the future in Mexico. I asked him if he thought life over there would settle down if one of the cartels succeeded in exterminating the others. "I don't think it will. Just going to be that way," he said. "The government's already paid off. Everybody's paid off." Juárez, he said, was dying. The streets were empty; stores were boarded up. "Five years ago I was in Juárez, and it wasn't that bad.

But the last time, maybe about a month ago, I was looking everywhere where I would cruise around, you know, and it was just a ghost town."

Larry shook his head. "You can't win, then join them. That's what's happening. Pay me off! Nobody gets caught. Nobody gets tried. Even before this was going on, the women murdered. The bus drivers. The rapists, and then—ah, get this sucker, wrap 'em up. It's paid off. You can't win, so just join it."

We ate tamales and fried chicken and roasted jalapeño peppers on the fire. Larry and Danny drank beer after beer but showed no sign of fatigue or intoxication. Danny sat with his back against the Jeep, his stomach round and full; he looked like a Mexican American Buddha. Larry straddled a long, thin piece of lumber, holding two other pieces in his hands like ski poles. The temperature dropped as the wind picked up, and I quickly exhausted my stash of warm clothing. Tata gave me a large parka he had brought along. Eventually, I also squeezed myself into a pair of coveralls that were not quite tall enough. I must have looked a sight, as my grandmother would say. Larry used to work as a forklift operator in an ice cream warehouse, where the temperature was thirty degrees below zero. They worked half-hour shifts, wearing insulated boots and jumpsuits. During breaks they would defrost the forklifts and drink coffee and cocoa. The cold tonight didn't seem to bother him at all.

The football game had been over for a long time, and we had long since shifted to a country music station, and we listened to generic rock songs belted out in an ersatz southern accent. The songs were all intolerably optimistic. At one point someone dialed up a "soft rock" station playing "Little Red Corvette." Poor Prince, he probably never expected to be a golden oldie.

The cold desert wind was now so brutal that Art wrapped a blue plastic tarp around the windward side of the Jeep. I crawled into the backseat and curled up, in a space far too small for my body, wearing several layers of wool, a wool cap, fleece gloves, a heavy insulated canvas jacket, a borrowed bright orange parka, and an undersized pair of coveralls, shivering. I dozed and then awoke in a confused panic, clambered out of the Jeep, stripped off my coveralls, and stood by the fire, listening to Larry and Danny and Chuy and Art tell stories. One year three drunk guys from Anapra showed up. They had been drinking all night and saw the fire on the mountain, so by God they decided to climb up there. Art and Rudy, well armed and resolute, persuaded them to leave. They went right off the edge where Rudy's Jeep had gone over—they call it Rudy's Sleep—and lit cactuses on fire all the way back to Mexico. In years past, hundreds of Sunday school kids from Juárez would climb the mountain for the pilgrimage, but after 9/11 the Feds put a stop to that.

At 3:15 a.m. the Border Patrol finally showed up. First to arrive was a figure striding very quickly, wearing a large backpack and a balaclava: a female agent, it turned out, who had hiked all the way up in the dark, surely wearing night vision goggles because we did not see any lights along the path. She didn't say a word, just marched right up the ramp to the cross. Ten minutes later a male agent named Rocky walked up and exchanged greetings with Art and Chuy. Soon thereafter we noticed a fire down below near the boundary marker. More Border Patrol. Our two agents set up a tripod and started scanning the valley with a large thermal binocular called a Recon Lite. They could see

Pilgrims

for miles. On the American side, cars began to make their way up the gravel road to the base. Flashlights appeared, bobbing up the looping switchbacks; the pilgrims would soon be here, so we started breaking camp. Water was poured into the fire pit, and the extinguished ashes then went down the side of the mountain. Floodlights were lit along the ramp. All our supplies disappeared into the trailer and the Jeep. By the time the first pilgrim arrived at 4:28 a.m., there was a steady line of cars backed up almost to the Rio Grande. Hundreds of lights bounced and pendulated in the hands of devoted Christians. After reaching their destination, some immediately turned around and headed back down, as if eager to avoid the inevitable crush of bodies and traffic. Others lingered at the peak, took their turn bowing down on the newly repaired kneelers, or paid penance on the hard whitewashed concrete, lighting candles, staring up at the Son of God, whose luminous presence in that dawning light was the result of so much care and effort on the part of a devoted band of men and women for whom work itself was prayer.

I had been waiting to see the *matachines*, the Indian dancers Rudy and Art had told me would be dancing for the Virgin. Now they were here. They wore tunics called *naguillas*, sewn with red, green, and silvery sequins and beads and spangles in a diamond-shaped motif, from which depended short lengths of Carrizo river cane or bamboo or some plastic imitation that swung and clattered and rattled with every step. *Matachines* drifted up and back from the cross, settling in a group on a rocky slope off the first terrace. I saw a figure wearing a hideous demonic mask, and another that was less sinister, though still grotesque. They were Danza Guadalupana, from El Paso, and they told me they were soldiers who danced to honor the Virgin of Guadalupe. As the first glimmers of light appeared on the horizon, the drummers stepped forward and the dance began. *Matachine* has its origins in Moorish dances imported by the Spanish, but it enacts the primordial drama of Mexico's founding. The main characters are La Malinche, the Aztec mistress of Hernán Cortés; the Monarca, or Montezuma; and, in this version of the tradition, a sinister figure called *el viejo*, the old man. The *matachines* I spoke with told me that *el viejo* was evil, yet he also was clearly the leader of the troupe. He carried a double-headed plastic battle ax and wore brown coveralls. Before the dance, he walked through the crowd terrorizing small children, who squealed and laughed and hid behind their parents. He did his best to scare me as well. *El viejo* was clearly a trickster figure of ambiguous virtue, in contrast to La Malinche, the lead dancer, a symbol of purity and grace, performed by a lovely teenage girl. *El viejo* and La Malinche faced each other and played out the ancient drama of conquest, love, betrayal, and conversion. I searched in vain for Cortés the killer. The whole spectacle was confusing and wonderful, with dancers spinning and stomping and crying out loudly in the billowing clouds of dust. Most of the dancers carried small stylized bows and arrows. The Monarca held a sword. People sat and watched for a while, resting before making their final push to the top or the long descent to the base. Behind us Christ the King appeared to glow as dawn broke in the east.

When the *matachines* finished their performance, Art signaled that it was time to go. We gathered all the floodlights, stepping delicately among the worshippers and the rapidly growing array of candles in glass jars, bunches of flowers, desperate prayers written on slips of paper. An American flag waved proudly, reiterating the patriotism of the Smeltertown diaspora. I took one last look down at the ASARCO plant and

*Matachines*

its monumental smokestack, and the little plaza with Monument 1 and the adobe house where Francisco Madero met with Pancho Villa and established a provisional government during the Mexican Revolution. I was dubious about our ability to make our descent along that narrow Jeep track crowded with pedestrians, but other volunteers were there to help; they had made their way up the mountain and were busy selling water and soft drinks. Ruben Gallegos helped block human traffic as the Jeep lumbered down the narrow ramp toward the first terrace, then, after a pause to collect all our passengers, we set out past Rudy's Sleep and toward the first hairpin turn. The most harrowing moments came when we began to round a blind turn. Art would press on the Jeep's horn, which was not at all loud, and slowly release the clutch, whereupon the Jeep would lurch forward and we would suddenly see the astonished faces of a family who would dart back out of view and press themselves against the sheer rock wall as we passed.

By mid-morning the path up the mountain was mobbed with people ascending and descending. Several other troops of *matachines* made their way up, and others danced at the base next to a large tent set up by the local church. The *matachines* here at the bottom wore far more elaborate costumes. Some wore huge brightly colored feathered headdresses. Others wore elaborate headgear made of feathers and fur. The leaders were young men and women in their twenties; some dancers were children; others could have been grandmothers. One drummer sported impressive face piercings. They all stomped and rattled and performed their footwork while shaking their musical gourds in ecstatic concentration. They all told me the same thing: they dance to honor God, to show him that they appreciate everything he has given them. I spoke to pilgrims on their way back to their cars. One woman said that she had walked because her mother had just been diagnosed with cancer again, after enjoying a remission of seventeen years. She said that next year she would come again, and every year thereafter. "I'm going to do it for all the sick people, not just my mom. It's a sacrifice we have to make."

Then I saw a beautiful young girl walking slowly down the path, leaning slightly on her mother's arm. Her name was Ashley Chavez, and her feet were bare. She had short dark hair and wore blue nylon basketball shorts. Her wide feet were dusty but showed no signs of injury. I asked about her pilgrimage. It was good, she said. I asked her if she felt pain. "Yeah, it hurts a lot. It was a challenge, but I made it through." I asked why she had walked without shoes. She hesitated and glanced at her mom; her pretty face was wide open and innocent, and she smiled a sweet, shy smile. Behind her the morning sun reflected off the giant figure of Christ on his mountain. "I needed a favor," she said. "A really big favor."

Pilgrims sat in the shade of the tent eating tacos and *menudo*. Nuns had set up tables and were selling trinkets and rosaries and crucifixes, small icons of saints and pamphlets proclaiming that the cult of Santa Muerte, a figure of veneration among the gangs and the desperately poor inhabitants of the *colonias*, is not a true Catholic cult. The bishops of El Paso and Las Cruces gathered their processions under colorful standards and set out to walk the Vía Crucis, the Way of the Cross. Everyone prayed and sang *en el nombre del Padre, y del Hijo, y del Espíritu Santo*, lingering at the shrine of Saint Anthony of Padua, and slowly proceeded through the stations, past the Vía Matris and Our Lady of Fatima, reverently reversing the course of my earlier descent, in a formal peripatetic Mass, ending finally at the high altar of Cristo Rey, where two profane angels make eternal love under six coats of white paint.

The day after I came down from the high altar at Mount Cristo Rey, I met up with Agent Jake Nuñez for a tour of the Border Patrol's El Paso sector. Nuñez took me to Monument 3, on the mesa looking down at Colonia Anapra, just across from Mount Cristo Rey. As we drove, he told me about the sector, with its twenty-seven hundred agents monitoring 125,500 square miles. I asked about surveillance systems, and he told me that RVSS cameras were used only in the urban areas. Field agents also carried handheld and tripod-mounted night vision equipment, more or less the same kit I'd encountered in the Rio Grande valley. We talked about response times and how agents reacted to incursions. Responses in the city were measured in seconds and minutes. Border runners could scale the fences in about a minute using ladders or screwdrivers and hurry toward shops and crowds, hoping to quickly blend in. Out in the rural areas, and in the remote portions of the sector, the agents relied on ground sensors to alert them to incursions. Smugglers or migrants could walk for hours or days, in extreme temperatures, before they reached their destinations, and sometimes they got into trouble, from exposure or accidents, such as falling down a mine shaft. Nuñez described the Border Patrol Search, Trauma, and Rescue teams and how they operate. He spoke of ultralight aircraft that fly across the border and drop two-hundred- to three-hundred-pound bundles of drugs. It's so dark out there, he said, sometimes you just hear a buzz and know it's an ultralight. We talked about mobile surveillance systems, the most advanced scope trucks, with their ground radar, and the radar-equipped aerostats that try to detect low-flying aircraft so that agents in the field can intercept the trucks that hurry to pick up the contraband they drop.

We stood next to the new border fence, and Nuñez pointed out that not too many years ago the only barrier here had been two strands of barbed wire strung along crooked fence posts. For more than a hundred years that was all we really needed. Remnants of the old wire rusted in the thick powdery dust. Monument 3, covered with graffiti, was just out of reach, on the other side of the fence. We drove back to Monument 1, in Madero Plaza. Rudy Garcia had brought me here once before, and I had stepped briefly across the international boundary. This time, accompanied by a Border Patrol agent, I stayed firmly on the U.S. side. We talked about ASARCO and Smeltertown, and Nuñez told me his great-grandfather had worked at the smelter and lived in Smeltertown. Two of his grandparents were buried in the Smeltertown cemetery.

Later we drove along the river and the irrigation canals that radiate out from it, and Nuñez pointed out the sites of gun battles between the cartels and Mexican forces and told of stray bullets striking buildings at the university and El Paso's city hall. We walked through a processing center, and young men in cells stared blankly at me as I walked past. They were migrants, not smugglers, and had been apprehended within the last few hours, trying to escape from the war zone that had been created by decades of blinkered drug war policies in the United States and the rivers of cash that flowed south to the cartels. At that time, the Sinaloa Cartel had not yet won the war with its rival cartels, and Juárez still felt like a ghost town. Nuñez spoke about the small businesses

Former border fence, near Monument 3, Sunland Park, New Mexico

that had closed because the owners couldn't afford to pay protection money. He said that in the last year Juárez had recorded thirty-one hundred murders.

We stopped in a small control room and watched as a sector enforcement specialist named Willie Acosta monitored cameras and sensors covering about fourteen miles of the border. Two large screens dominated the wall, and a bank of lights represented the status of a host of ground sensors. Most of them showed activity. Every hit was a "definite possible maybe." Acosta said that 99.9 percent of the hits were false alarms, set off by birds, wind, weather, seemingly nothing at all. Each active sensor had to be cleared. He maintained constant contact with field agents who called in to report the disposition of their sensors. I could feel the stress in the room as Acosta barked into his mic, acknowledging clearances from agents, impatiently explaining to them they might have thought they'd transmitted but they hadn't, saying to me that the agents get upset but it's not personal. "It might be personal for them, but it's not for me." He complained that some people just weren't trained right, and talked about the spotters, the kids on bikes or the guys just standing around, who work for the cartels and keep them informed. He told me that the cartels know if a camera goes down long before we do, because they watch them 24/7. We have so many blind spots, and they have none of this expensive technology, but they know far better what's happening along every segment of the line. Your technology is only as good as your people. It gets difficult in here, he said. There should be more than one person on these monitors. He laughed and said he'd been known to say his piece.

I asked how long he'd been on the job. "I was an agent for twenty-four years," he said, "then I had a little accident. In 1985, I got shot in the chest with a machine gun. I did therapy and came back. In '06, I had to retire, so I made them give me a new job. This is where I've been since '06."

# CHAPTER 5

# TEN GUNS, TEN HORSES, TEN WIVES

The Wilson brothers and the other Texans who pushed west into the grasslands of the Red River valley and beyond had little conception of where they were trespassing. They weren't the first to make that mistake. Most of what we now call Central and West Texas was Comanche territory, and Perry Wilson spent much of his life on the borderlands of what we now recognize as the Comanche empire. Two hundred miles to the southeast, on May 19, 1836, in year one of the Republic of Texas and less than a month after a ragged army of Texans defeated Mexico at the Battle of San Jacinto, a large group of mounted Indians rode up to the gate of Parker's Fort, near present-day Mexia, east of Waco. The Parker clan had arrived on the extremities of the Texas frontier three years before with thirty oxcarts of belongings and a religious zeal that was anything but missionary. By 1835, six of the Parker families, three of whom had received grants of forty-six hundred acres, built a heavily fortified cedar stockade that covered an acre of land; it contained six log cabins and four blockhouses and was riddled with gun ports. The Parkers had fought Indians in Illinois, Tennessee, and Georgia, and they obviously expected to fight them in Texas as well. These land-hungry Anglos probably did not realize that their grant from the Mexican government had placed them deep in Comanchería, or that their presence had been intended by policy makers in Mexico City to create a human shield between the Comanches and their traditional raiding grounds farther south, but it is unlikely they would have passed up the free land in any case. The Parkers were devout and aggressive hard-shell Baptists who believed that God had empowered them to make the barbarian deserts bloom. "The elect are a wrathful people," according to Elder Daniel Parker, "because they are the natural enemies of the non-elect."

When the Indians arrived, ten of the Parker men were working their fields about a mile away. Six men, including James and Silas Parker, both Texas Rangers, remained at the fort, along with eight women and nine children. The heavily armored gate was open. The Comanches (along with some Kiowa allies and probably Shoshones) were apparently taking advantage of the disorder caused by the Texas Revolution to carry out raids among settlements that had penetrated too deeply into their hunting grounds. Estimates of their number range from one to five hundred. Their horses painted for war, the Indians approached the fort with a white flag. Benjamin Parker walked out of the open gate and spoke with the warriors, who asked for a cow; Parker refused, though he offered other supplies, and thus abandoned whatever hope he and his family had of surviving the encounter.

Comanches were accustomed to accepting tribute from Euro-Americans, and gift giving was integral to Comanche political culture, so the frequent refusal of Texans "to share" was considered insulting and hostile. The Spanish had learned that lesson early in the previous century. While Benjamin spoke to the Indians, other members of the Parker family were fleeing out the fort's back door. Rachel Parker Plummer, who survived twenty-one months of Indian captivity (probably among the Shoshones in southwestern Wyoming, rather than the Comanches, as she believed), watched as the "work of death" commenced and her uncle Benjamin was surrounded by the warriors, clubbed, impaled with lances, shot with arrows, then scalped. Rachel took her little boy James and ran, but, as she wrote years later, "a large sulky looking Indian picked up a hoe and knocked me down." Silas Parker went for his bag of shot and soon died, as did the other men who remained in the fort, attempting to protect the women and children. Some of those who fled were caught, mutilated, and killed. Granny Parker was raped and stabbed but survived. Taken captive, along with Rachel, were Elizabeth Kellogg and Silas Parker's children John and

Cynthia Ann. John grew up to be a Comanche warrior, perhaps ending his life as a rancher in Mexico; Elizabeth was ransomed; Cynthia Ann became the wife of the war leader Peta Nocona and the mother of Quanah Parker, often called the last chief of the Comanches. It might be more accurate to call him the first chief, but that would diminish the mythological attraction.

Such attractions are undeniable, as the long bibliography of works on the Comanches attests, though Quanah's prominence among popular Comanche narratives probably owes as much to his condition as the half-breed child of a captive white woman as to his prowess as a war leader. The romance of unvanquished and defiant noble savages was not so popular as long as the Indian wars still raged. For much of the last 175 years it was Cynthia Ann who received the literary attention. The story of her abduction and the slaughter at Parker's Fort was told and retold in newspapers, magazines, and romantic novels that imagined love among the prairie flowers between a lovely pale white squaw and a darkly handsome young buck—all with the encouragement of her uncle James Parker, whose determined quest to retrieve his captured relatives was eventually given cinematic treatment in *The Searchers*, with John Wayne as James and Natalie Wood as his missing niece. Cynthia Ann's son Quanah was largely unknown, except to the soldiers and rangers who pursued him along the cliffs and plains of the Llano Estacado. It was not until Quanah finally surrendered in 1875 and presented himself to his former opponent Colonel Ranald S. Mackenzie at Fort Sill, Oklahoma, that his parentage became known and the slow work of fashioning his legend began.

Since then, dozens of books have been written about Quanah and the tragic life of his mother, whose Comanche name, Naudah, means "someone found." No other story of frontier hardship can quite compare. Cynthia Ann was abducted twice, once by Noconi Comanches and once by Texas Rangers. Twice she lost everything she knew and loved; twice she lost her family. Whether or not Sul Ross killed Naudah's husband, Peta Nocona, at the Battle of Pease River (Quanah always claimed his father died years later), she never saw him or her sons again. She did everything she could to escape from her white family before she died in 1870. When Coho Smith, himself a former captive, visited Naudah in East Texas and spoke to her in Comanche, she screamed and threw herself at his feet, begging to be taken home. When Smith refused, she told him that her heart was always crying out for her boys, that she knew where they could steal some first-rate horses, and that she would reward him with "ten guns, ten horses, ten wives."

The Comanches entered written history in 1706, when residents of the Taos pueblo complained to their Spanish governor about attacks from Utes and a previously unknown tribe of "very barbarous" Indians. They called themselves Numunu, the People. Spanish officials, who had been preoccupied with Apache raiders, knew nothing about this new tribe of mounted Indians, whose given name probably derived from the Ute word *kumantsi*, which historians have generally interpreted as meaning "anyone who wants to fight me all the time," or simply "enemy." A recent reinterpretation, however, endorsed by Pekka Hämäläinen in his magisterial *The Comanche Empire*, suggests that the word actually meant something closer to "newcomer" and carried the further meaning of "a people who were considered related but different," which accords with the current scholarly consensus that the Utes and Comanches were both Numic peoples, speaking variants of Uto-Aztecan, who took different migratory routes out of the Sierra Nevada. One group, in the first wave of the Numic expansion, traveled south and founded the Aztec Empire; another was the Shoshones, the parent group of the Comanches, some of whom migrated into the Great Plains by the sixteenth century. The Plains Shoshones employed sophisticated communal hunting techniques and used dogs to haul their hide teepees and other belongings on travois; the archaeological record, including hundreds of bison jumps found throughout their former territories, suggests that they enjoyed a flourishing economy and a relatively prosperous existence. At some point in the late seventeenth century, the Shoshones broke into two groups. One of them became the Comanches, who went south in search of game and Spanish ponies.

The early alliance with the Utes was highly profitable for both groups; the Utes, who had inhabited the Spanish borderlands for some time, introduced the Comanches to European goods, including guns and metal tools. More important, the Utes shared their knowledge of horses. The Comanches in turn assisted the Ute in their wars with the pueblo Indians, the Navajo, and the Apaches. Together they terrorized the more settled inhabitants of New Mexico. It was as if the Comanches had been waiting for the arrival of the horse. Within a generation, they had revolutionized their culture; within two generations, they were fully mounted. Life on the plains would never be the same, especially for the Spaniards' old enemy the Apaches, against whom the Comanches waged a brutal campaign. The Apaches were horsemen, but they were also farmers, thus vulnerable to raiding, and they had not mastered the arts of mounted warfare. Like the Europeans, they typically fought on foot and thus were no match for the Comanches, who all observers agreed formed the finest light cavalry in history.

The Comanche invasion of the southern plains was not simply a matter of military conquest. The horse enabled the Comanches to raid widely among the Spanish pueblos and ranches of New Mexico, but it also greatly expanded their economic opportunities. By the mid-1720s, the Comanches had established control of the Arkansas valley, which had long been a center of trade among the peoples of the plains. Soon a process of reverse colonization began to take place as the Comanches entered into complex and lucrative trade relations all across the Spanish borderlands, stealing horses along the lower Rio Grande and trading them in New Mexico, or with the Comanchero traders who passed unmolested into the Comanche *rancherías*, or with French, British, and American traders in the east. The mid-eighteenth century saw a lucrative trade alliance develop with the French and the Taovaya in the eastern Arkansas valley. The Comanches tanned buffalo hides and prepared bear grease and traded these goods—as well as slaves they captured in raids—for guns, ammunition, metal tools and other implements (often refashioned into arrow points), swords (which became the points of lances), textiles, pottery, iron cookware, blankets, candles, maize, flour, bread, tobacco, vegetables, beads, and clothing. The Comanches demanded, and received, political gifts from those who wished to trade with them, and access to such highly desirable objects (uniforms, medals, flags, colored capes, and other trinkets) was an important component of their political economy.

Comanche chiefs were men who through a combination of kinship ties, patronage, courage in battle, and personal charisma were able to persuade other men to do as they suggested. War leaders were frequently young men who had little control over civic affairs, such as hunting, trade, or the frequent need to move a *ranchería*, or local residential band, to find new pastures for the horses. Comanche politics was radically democratic, if also radically constrained by custom, and all important decisions were made in council. Women, who performed most of the community's manual work (tanning hides, drying meat, preparing meals, breaking down or setting up camp), were not consulted, though they did have considerable influence over the economy of honor and martial prestige; the esteem or contempt of women was a potent political force. Chiefs, or *paraibos*, were only leaders so long as they had followers, which made relations with European colonial empires somewhat fraught, because the men who signed treaties often had little means of enforcing their provisions. But when the Spanish, French, Mexicans, Texans, or Americans provided resources to leading men, leaders were generally able to justify peaceful relations. When trading opportunities became scarce and tribute payments were not forthcoming, ambitious young men soon commenced raiding and pillaging, which often led to a cycle of revenge and warfare.

Historians who wrote in the first half of the twentieth century tended toward the view that the Comanches lacked any politics, properly speaking, that their social organization never rose above the level of the hunting party or war band. More recently, however, scholars such as Thomas W. Kavanagh and Pekka Hämäläinen have marshaled considerable evidence of a sophisticated if highly decentralized politics. Unlike the rigid hierarchies familiar to Europeans, Comanche political organizations were typically fluid and consensual. They were composed of alliances of local groups, based on kinship, trade, and mutual interests, and were centered on the exploitation of nutritional and economic resources. Despite their fundamental anarchism, the Comanches were clearly capable of coming to general points of consensus in matters of warfare, foreign policy, and trade. Treaties with the Comanches were not exactly worthless, and were often followed by long periods of relative calm, and alliances with other peoples such as the Utes, the Taovayas, the Kiowas, and the Pawnees took shape, prevailed for years, and then broke down as collective interests changed. Likewise, general policies of war, especially against the Apaches and the Osage, were broadly recognized. Huge multidivisional gatherings were recorded, especially by the Spanish, and war leaders such as Cuerno Verde appeared from time to time who quite obviously exercised broad civic authority.

The first period of Comanche expansion began in the 1720s, when they pushed east into the plains and took control of the Arkansas valley. In the 1750s, several bands of Kotsoteka Comanches pushed south from the Red River and established their dominion over the Texas plains. Comanchería by that time stretched from eastern New Mexico to the Arkansas valley, from the Red River in the north to the Balcones Escarpment in the southeast, a domain of a quarter million square miles. They raided along the lower Rio Grande and deep into the northeastern provinces farther south. New Mexico was increasingly dependent on trade with the Comanches yet continued to suffer depredations. Governor Tomás Vélez Cachupín attempted to solve the Comanche problem by seeking peace through trade. He also perceived that close ties with the Comanches might discourage the French from infiltrating Spanish territory. A treaty was signed in 1752, the first of many, though the Comanches never stopped raiding entirely, and that peace did not last long. Meanwhile, the Ute-Comanche alliance collapsed, and war returned to the southern plains. Another treaty followed in 1762, followed by more warfare.

After Cachupín retired in 1767, his successor failed to understand the importance of Comanche diplomacy, and as a result his colony was nearly destroyed by almost unceasing raids. Spanish authorities in New Mexico recorded 106 attacks by Comanches between 1767 and 1777; nearly two hundred New Mexicans were killed in 1777 and 1778 alone. Officials in Santa Fe complained that the Comanches would raid one day and then appear a few weeks later eager to trade. Largely ignored by Mexico City and Madrid, the New Mexicans had little choice but to submit. "The alternate actions of this nation at the same time, now peace, now war, demonstrate their accustomed faithlessness," wrote Governor Pedro Fermín de Mendinueta in 1771. "Since it is impossible to . . . limit their freedom so that they do not do as they fancy, I have adopted the policy of admitting them to peace whenever they ask for it and come with their trade goods and of waging war whenever they assault our frontiers and commit plunder. From war alone, all that results is loss of life and property, but from the alternate this poor citizenry gains some good."

Authorities in Spanish Texas made attempts at peace but were somewhat less successful. During the years after the American Revolution, Texas was overrun by Comanche raiders, and its population dropped from 3,103 to 2,828. The Comanche population during this period might have reached 40,000. Meanwhile, the Comanches began supplying horses to northern plains peoples such as the Pawnee, Cheyenne, and Kiowa, who traveled to the Comanche bazaars along the Arkansas. The French and British supplied guns, agricultural tribes to the east supplied carbohydrates, and in return the Comanches supplied horses, slaves, and buffalo hides, which were of unsurpassed quality.

Other treaties were signed in 1785 and 1786, following the Bourbon reforms, which revitalized the Spanish Empire's administration of its northern frontier. New Mexico's new governor, Juan Bautista de Anza, pursued the Comanches into the plains and killed the great chief Cuerno Verde, then made a peace that lasted, more or less unbroken, until the Mexican Revolution of 1821. Spain thought it was pursuing a policy of "peace through deceit," hoping to bind the Comanches to the empire through relations of dependency and cultural assimilation, and the Numunu played along, keeping the raiding to a minimum and assisting the Spanish militarily in their Apache extermination policy. The Spanish saw the Comanches and other friendly Indians as a buffer against the territorial ambitions of the Americans, yet trade with the Americans, contrary to Spain's wishes, merely intensified. With the collapse of the Spanish Empire, trade ceased to be so lucrative along the southwestern margins of Comanchería; in Mexico City, the government was preoccupied with internal matters, and the Comanches were still expanding their reach.

The early nineteenth century was the acme of the Comanche empire's power; disease and environmental pressures soon began to undermine its foundations. Eastern Indians were being driven west, and that created both opportunities and conflicts. Trade with the Americans was flourishing, and the Comanches looked to Mexico for plunder. The commercial heart of the Southwest was no longer Santa Fe but Comanchería itself, because most trading now took place in the *rancherías* along the Arkansas, Red, and Brazos Rivers. In desperation, the Mexican government permitted *empresarios* such as Stephen F. Austin to bring American settlers into Texas, hoping to use the Anglos as a buffer against the Comanches. It didn't work; in fact, the policy had the opposite of its intended effect. Raiding south of the Rio Grande only intensified; the zone of Comanche depredations, dotted with desolate smoking ruins, at times extended nearly to Mexico City. Nor was Texas spared. In 1832, five hundred Comanches rode right into San Antonio and had their way with the citizens of the provincial capital without apparent concern for a local garrison of Mexican troops, who did nothing to interfere. Lacking funds for gifts thereafter, San Antonio suffered raids for the next two years until the flow of tribute resumed. Purchasing peace in this way disgusted Anglo Texans such as Mirabeau Buonaparte Lamar, who when he succeeded Sam Houston as president of the Texas Republic pursued a policy of extermination toward all Indians.

For more than one hundred years, the Comanches presided over a vast indigenous empire of the southern plains. They largely dictated the terms of their relations, both military and commercial, with New Spain, England, France, Mexico, Texas, and the United States, not to mention the many Native peoples who dwelled in their orbit. New Mexico for much of its history was nothing less than a Comanche colony. If trading in Taos, Pecos, Santa Fe, or Bexar became difficult or unprofitable, they turned to the Wichita or the Pawnee, the French or the Americans, who were always willing to trade guns, powder, flour, or tobacco for Comanche horses, whether or not they carried brands.

The Comanches were buffalo hunters, but they were very far from being primitive hunter-gatherers simply following the herds and making raids in the spring and summer. The same adaptability that led them to adopt the horse so enthusiastically enabled them to create a hybrid market-based culture, combining their original nomadism with pastoralism as they bred enormous herds of horses and mules, both of which produced substantial surpluses for trade. In a way, the Comanches were hunter-capitalists whose enormous wealth was accumulated above all in the form of horses.

Nor did their society cease to develop once they were mounted. Between the 1730s and the 1830s, as their wealth, population, and power grew, Comanche society became more hierarchical, with greater material disparities between those who were horse-rich and those who were horse-poor. Their rising wealth did not come without costs; the growing herds of Comanche horses competed with the buffalo for food, and in sharp contrast to the romantic image of the ecologically virtuous natives who took only what they needed, the Comanches killed far more buffalo than they required for subsistence. Long before the railroad brought the white hunters with their Sharps rifles to the plains, the Comanches in the middle decades of the nineteenth century were already causing the bison population to crash. They themselves were slaughtering far too many of the animals for hides, which they had traded for Spanish goods and groceries since the early eighteenth century.

When drought came in 1845, the Comanche empire began to crumble along with the dead grass; economic collapse swiftly followed the ecological crisis. By the 1850s, Indian agents were discovering large groups of Comanches near starvation, and raids became more desperate.

Although the Civil War gave them a brief respite, the Comanches' power was in terminal decline by the time Quanah came of age as a war leader in 1869. He would be on the reservation within six years.

Some writers have seen the Comanche decline in terms of cultural contamination. The Comanches, according to this line of reasoning, grew weak and decadent from their promiscuous adoption of the white man's ways—his whiskey, his iron pots—and abandoned their austere, stripped-down hunting culture. But the Comanches were never "pure" in any sense. Their extraordinary rise was predicated on a European import, the horse, and they were intimately exposed to European crafts and manufactured goods from the early eighteenth century onward. Syncretism in religion and dress—their adoption of elaborate war-bonnets and the Kiowa Sun Dance—was the rule among Comanches rather than a decadent affectation. The emergence of the Kwahada band is revealing. The Kwahadas coalesced as a political group very late in Comanche history, probably the 1860s, after the resources on which their society was based had been lost. They first enter the writ-

Quanah, Texas

ten record in 1872. The Kwahadas' primary economic resource was stolen Texas cattle, hardly the basis of a traditional Numunu lifestyle.

Thomas Kavanagh's exhaustive sifting of the documentary record pertaining to Comanche political organization provides overwhelming evidence that the various Comanche bands or divisions—such as Kotsoteka (Buffalo Eaters), Penateka (Honey Eaters), Kwahada (Antelope Eaters), Yamparika (Yap Eaters), Jupe (People of Timber), Tenewa, Hois, and Noconi—were contingent political organizations, rather than static tribal entities, that shifted and evolved with the vagaries of geography, natural resources, and political alliances. The Comanche people were highly mobile both within their territory and among themselves. Individuals and families frequently moved from one to another social or political grouping. Major divisions appeared and disappeared over time as groups dispersed or emerged from one another. Quanah, for example, was born among the Noconi but spent much of his adulthood with Kotsotekas and Kwahadas.

As the larger material basis of the Comanche economy collapsed and most Comanches submitted to demographic and military inevitability, the bellicose Kwahadas seem to have formed as a kind of end-times movement, complete with a charismatic cult leader named Isatai (Wolf's Vulva) who convinced his followers that his *puha*, or medicine power, was so powerful that it would protect them from the American soldiers' bullets. It was Isatai who was most influential in the ill-fated decision of Quanah's Kwahadas to attack the Adobe Walls trading outpost in 1874, and it was Isatai who initially made the decision in 1875 that it was time to surrender to Colonel Mackenzie at Fort Sill. Quanah's concurrence came the following day. Once the Kwahadas arrived at the reservation and Quanah announced that he was the son of Cynthia Ann Parker, his transformation into Quanah Parker, the first principal chief of the Comanches, was rapid. Not everyone among the Numunu was ready to accept Quanah's ascendancy, but the Americans, perhaps because he was half-white, made their preferences clear. On most accounts, however, Chief Quanah was a just and decent leader who did his best to protect his people from the white man's perpetually forked tongue.

The Comanches have long been seen as a buffer to American settlement, and of course they were in a superficial sense. But by lashing the Spanish and Mexican frontiers with raids for more than a century, the Comanches unintentionally prepared the way for the American conquest of northern Mexico. By destabilizing the borderlands, which their empire of fear had made as broad and porous as possible, the Comanches fostered the conditions that led to the Texas Revolution and the Mexican War and the collapsed horizons of a thin brown borderline along the Rio Grande. Moreover, the Comanches' highly lucrative trade in buffalo hides helped create the market that impelled the American buffalo hunters westward, resulting in the permanent collapse of that most important resource. The lesson to be learned from the rise and fall of the Numunu is not so different from that of the British or the Romans: the Comanche empire, like most expansionist and aggressive powers, contained within itself the logic of its own undoing.

# CHAPTER 6

# OVERLAND

During the first few years after Perry and Welmett came to Texas, Perry was running cattle along the Red River, in what soon became Clay County, along the western frontier with the Comanches. I followed them out there, sticking as close to the Red River as I could.

The road to Clay County was typical North Texas farmland, big round bales in the fields that were under cultivation, herds of cattle nosing along the lush pastures, broken occasionally by red banks of thick sediment. Dusk set in as I drove along the monotonous highway, and Henrietta, the county seat, appeared dreary and dull. I stayed the night at a Best Western, and the pretty young clerk told me to keep an eye out for the hotel ghost, but it made no appearance.

I had an appointment around noon at the local history museum, so I set out to explore the countryside. I had a vague idea, based on land records, of where the Wilson ranch might have been. By this time, Perry's brother Levi was in Texas, or maybe he had set out with them from Missouri in the beginning, I really don't know, but I do know they were running cattle together along the Red River by the middle 1850s. Clay County turned out to be beautiful, excellent cattle country, a rolling prairie dotted with the occasional stands of hardwoods. Red and purple and white wildflowers were scattered abundantly, lovely under a blue sky and puffy white clouds. Darla, pulling morning duty at the hotel, had directed me to the old cemetery, which I found with little difficulty, though the maze of all-weather caliche roads spidering across the prairie was slightly confusing. I pulled off at a rusty metal gate, as instructed. I could see about a mile distant what appeared to be a fenced-in graveyard, but I feared that my rental might get stuck out in the field, because I could see a shallow rain-fed pond nearby. I drove a short distance, parked, and walked along the narrow track. A tall metal sign over the gate to the cemetery confirmed that I was in the right place, as did a discreet metal plaque erected by the state historical commission: Cambridge Cemetery, established circa 1852. Inside were a variety of stones in various states of decay. One stone simply said "sister." Others were eroded beyond recognition. Sometimes they were simply stones placed around the outline of a notional grave. I saw no one I recognized. It was a beautiful spot to spend eternity.

I walked back to my car and drove to meet with Lucille Glasgow, who had kindly agreed to open the town's museum, situated in an old jail from the 1890s, and show me around. Most of the artifacts were from the second period of settlement in Clay County, after the Civil War, but I was interested in the 1850s. I found a display titled "Clay County's Beginnings," listing the Indian tribes that wandered across this prairie—Wichita and Comanche among them—and then the Spanish explorers who passed through in 1759 (Diego Ortiz Parrilla) and 1789 (Pedro Vial), and the Anglo explorers Dr. Henry Connelly in 1840, on his surprisingly uneventful expedition from St. Louis to Chihuahua via La Junta in the Big Bend; the Santa Fe expedition of 1841; the Snively expedition of 1843; Randolph Marcy in 1849; also mentioned was Major Enoch Steen, in 1855, and General Albert Sidney Johnston in 1855. All these people were just passing through, hoping to keep scalps on their heads.

Under the heading "Early Ranchers" was a list of people who had lived, it said, in Montague County and grazed their herds in Clay County but suffered heavy losses to Comanche depredations. Among them were Perry and Levi Wilson.

In 1858, Perry and Welmett loaded up their wagons and set out again. Perhaps they were discouraged by the Comanche raids. Why else would they abandon these fertile and gorgeous prairies, cattle country without equal, for a trail filled with certain peril? Maybe they had other hopes and dreams. Perry, like many other Texas cattlemen, could have been lured by the promise of high prices in California for cattle, horses, and mules. He had been down such roads before, but now he had two children. Thomas was the older, born in 1856, and William, called Bud, was born a year later. By 1859 his family would be one less; by 1863 they were down to two.

The destination was California, and they took the southern route through West Texas, New Mexico, and Arizona. Perry and Welmett probably had livestock with them on this new California expedition. He might have had partners, possibly including Levi, though I've found no evidence that Levi joined him on this journey. They might have simply joined up with other emigrant families or a cattle drive. It's unthinkable that Perry would make such a trip alone with his young wife and two baby sons.

John Butterfield's Overland Mail Company went into service the same year, 1858, and that celebrated stagecoach, from its point of departure in Tipton, Missouri, took a relatively direct route across the western extremes of Texas, skirting and then passing over the dreaded Llano Estacado, through unsettled and perilous Indian country, from the crossing at Colbert's Ferry on the Red River to stations at intervals of thirty to more than a hundred miles. The longest stretch in Texas was between the Pecos River and Pope's Camp, 113 miles. Paying passengers were welcome; the ride was swift but not comfortable. Indian attacks were always a danger; during the roughly two and a half years that Butterfield's contract was active, the company lost more than fifty men to the Indians, though the stage itself was never attacked. Emigrant trains and cattle drives did attempt to cross the Llano Estacado, but this was country firmly under the dominion of the Comanches, and the white men didn't know where to find water.

Waterman L. Ormsby, the first Butterfield through passenger, at first did not believe he had entered a desert when they made the ascent up the great caliche caprock that marks the high plains, because so many living things were present to his view: high grass, Spanish daggers, cactus, prairie dogs in their labyrinthine subterranean cities. The breeze, he said, was delightful. But the evidence, to his eye, was soon unmistakable, though perhaps slightly exaggerated in the telling, because "far as the eye could reach along the plain—decayed and decaying animals, the bones of cattle and sometimes of men (the hide

Wind farming on the Llano Estacado

drying on the skin in the arid atmosphere), all told a fearful story of anguish and terrific death from the pangs of thirst. For miles and miles these bones strew the plain—the silent witnesses of the eternal laws of nature, which, in the hope of gain, man hesitates not to brave. They are silent but speaking monuments of undeviating fate."

Butterfield wasn't the first mail carrier, and there were other routes that were popular with westering emigrants and argonauts. Henry Skillman held the first contract to carry mail from San Antonio to El Paso and San Diego, from 1851 to 1854. Known as the Jackass Mail, for Skillman's use of donkeys, this route went directly west from San Antonio to Fort Inge and the Devils River along a military track that like most of the other western wagon roads was an Indian highway of great antiquity. There was also the upper road, from Fredericksburg, that was forty miles shorter, but it was used somewhat less frequently in those early years because water was scarce.

The road up the Devils River was pioneered by the Hays-Highsmith expedition in 1848. John Coffee Hays, the celebrated Texas Ranger, and Samuel Highsmith led a group of thirty-five rangers west from San Antonio. It was a speculative affair; merchants and traders in San Antonio were eager for a new route to Chihuahua, and important San Antonio citizens were investors, including Samuel Maverick, the prominent Texas personage whose name has entered the English language as a type. Maverick went along for the ride and kept a daily journal. The expedition, celebrated in all the local newspapers, was not a complete success.

After getting some directions from friendly Indians at Las Moras Creek, the rangers found their way to a trail up the river that Spaniards had named Río San Pedro. Castaño de Sosa called it the River of Rocks. According to Hays, he was so irritated by the meandering course of the river, which they were compelled to cross again and again, not to mention the beastly canyon at its mouth that opened into the Rio Grande, that he named it the Devils River. Hard as the Devils country was, it was better than what lay ahead in the Trans-Pecos. Soon provisions ran low. Horses and mules were eaten, as was a mountain lion. By the time the expedition staggered into the adobe compound at Fort Leaton in the Big Bend, Hays and his men had been without food for twelve days. Some had attempted to eat bear grass.

After their difficult passage, this band of hardy Texas Rangers was just too worn-out to continue up the old easygoing Camino Real from La Junta to El Paso, so they rested at Fort Leaton for ten days and then went back to San Antonio, defeated. They followed a different route home.

It wasn't long before the U.S. Army sent other, more competent expeditions west from San Antonio to El Paso, including one led by Lieutenant William H. C. Whiting. On his return, Whiting descended the Devils River, noting "a still and beautiful lagoon of clear blue water," probably Beaver Lake, with remnants of Indian lodges around it. Whiting avoided the deeper canyons at the confluence of the Rio Grande and rediscovered a ford, already known to Spaniards and Mexicans, that came to be known as First Crossing. Nearby was Painted Cave, a rock shelter filled with ancient pictographs. Both First Crossing and Painted Cave are under the waters of Amistad Reservoir today. Whiting also skirted the canyons and high mountains of the Big Bend, striking a more direct path from the Pecos to El Paso. Despite the constant danger of Indian attack, the road up the Devils River provided ample water and forage for animals, so it came into common use. Two years later, Skillman's Jackass Mail began using the Devils River road, and so did countless emigrant trains and cattle drives. Fort Clark was established at Las Moras Creek, and Camp Hudson on the Devils. A mail station was built near Beaver Lake. Given Perry's and Thomas's later movements along the Devils River, it seems most likely that the young family passed through those narrow canyons on their way out west.

The lower road stretched 673 miles, more than 500 miles without a settlement. There were ephemeral military camps, exposed, with insufficient supplies and ammunition, soldiers sometimes barefoot, clad in rags. "Scarcely a mile of it," wrote one soldier, "but has its story of Indian murder and plunder; in fact, from El Paso to San Antonio is but one long battleground."

Frederick Law Olmsted traveled a segment of the lower road in 1856–57 with his brother, on assignment for the *New-York Daily Times*. Olmsted was not yet the great landscape architect he would become; he was a restless young man who had been given the gift of an assignment to write about the South. Dispatches from his first trip were collected and published in a fascinating if slightly tedious book, *A Journey in the Seaboard Slave States*. Texas required a separate trip, one that resulted in a masterpiece of travel writing and cultural polemic, *A Journey Through Texas; or, A Saddle-Trip on the Southwestern Frontier*. His descriptions of traveling through Texas in the mid-1850s are unrivaled, and he is by far the most eloquent of Perry's and Welmett's historical fellow travelers. Through his eyes we can see not only Texas as it then existed but also the Texas that would come to be after its passage through the horrors of civil war.

Olmsted entered Texas from the east, by river, after a long and picturesque journey by train and steamer from his home on Staten Island, filled with marvelous observations about southerners and the Great West: a Virginia gentleman's effortless ability to spit across a train compartment and out a narrow window; a white baby suckling a black nursemaid; "black and yellow boys, shy of baggage, but on the alert for any bit of a lark with one another; the buxom, saucy, slipshod girls within, bursting with fat and fun from their dresses, unable to contain themselves"; the "unstudied equality of black and white" that reigned within the open kitchen; "loafing nobles of poor whites, hanging about in search of enjoyment or a stray glass of whisky or an emotion."

From his vantage on the deck of a steamship, Olmsted's pitiless eye roved the landscape, constantly assessing the view and grading it accordingly. The forest primeval soon grows boring: "rocks, forests, and streams, alone, for hours, meet the eye. The only stoppages are for wood and water, and the only way-passengers, laborers upon the road. The conquered solitude becomes monotonous. It is a pleasure to get through and see again the old monotony of cultivation." Towns along the Ohio are "repulsively ugly and out of keeping with the tone of mind inspired by the river. Each has had its hopes, not yet quite abandoned, of becoming the great mart of the valley, and has built in accordant style its one or two tall brick city blocks, standing shabby-sided alone on the mud-slope to the bank, supported by a tavern, an old storehouse, and a few shanties. These mushroom cities mark only a night's camping-place of civilization." We pass the great forgotten vineyards of Ohio, which grow along the river above Cincinnati "as on the Rhine," and he offers a prayer that "honest wine and oil shall take the place of our barbarous whisky and hog-fat." Alas, it was not to be, and Olmsted would soon grow to hate the taste of hog even more. When he reaches Kentucky, the corn bread and bacon begin. Unused to such fare, he enjoys the novelty at first, having no idea that he will eat little else for six months.

Here, in Kentucky, Olmsted makes the first of many penetrating observations of the slaveholding class, planters addicted to hunting who see any form of physical labor as a degradation. All such work must be performed by black muscle. The details and character sketches pick up a theme elaborated in a lengthy prolegomenon, sensibly printed at the back of modern editions, titled "A Letter to a Southern Friend." There Olmsted presents the argument directly, bolstered with statistics, that Texas will never develop civilized amenities or an advanced economy so long as slavery endures. Slavery prolongs and even perpetuates the evils of the frontier, where no one would reasonably expect to find a gristmill or a baker, a printing office or a bookseller. A settler in Texas, needing to improve his land, takes his profits and invests in slaves, sending his capital to Houston or New Orleans. Now he has nothing left over, and the slaves add little or nothing to the local economy. When he does come in to a windfall, he buys more land and more slaves, and so the cycle continues. Now a *planter*, as opposed to a *dirt farmer*, the Texas pioneer gets by without wheat bread or sweet butter or even glass windows. Such luxuries—Olmsted hears this refrain a dozen times if he hears it once—are "not worth the trouble." Cattle require little care, and hogs run wild in the thickets. Slaves tend to the corn. The planter occupies himself with hunting, and when he wants fresh meat and has no venison, he simply saddles up, takes his dogs, and runs down a hog. By contrast, a settler in a free territory such as frontier Iowa needing extra help simply places an advertisement for skilled workers, who gladly travel west to earn better wages than they might earn at home back east. They offer their labor as a loan and receive a good return, which they invest locally with merchants and farmers, bakers and butchers and shopkeepers. Over time, other "small capitalists of labor" appear on the scene to provide for the growing population of paid workers. And so the local economy flourishes, the frontier retreats, and civilization with all its commodious benefits takes hold.

Even more pernicious than the direct economic effects of slavery on a community are the moral effects, the manner in which slavery cultivates the "natural lust of authority," which renders obnoxious the idea of employing servants and workers who may refuse the demands of their employer. The man raised and educated under such a system will thus prefer smaller profits and endure greater inconveniences rather than submit to the degrading and undignified influence of free labor. Slavery, among such people, transcends economics. It is a matter of identity and status, self-respect. A social by-product of the slave system, of course, is the "miserable intermediate" class of what Olmsted calls "mean whites," who hold no slaves and are forced by necessity to demean themselves with manual labor. Perversely, it is this class that would be aroused most violently in the great conflagration that was coming, that insisted with missionary fervor that civil war was better than free soil, and that for decades defended the shadows of slave power by fraud and violence.

Olmsted's arguments were far from academic, of course. The

annexation of Texas had upset the old compromises and, together with the Kansas-Nebraska Act, passed in the year Perry and Welmett left Missouri for Texas, set the nation on an inevitable course.

What's fascinating about Olmsted's observations about the southern character, for a reader today, is the extent to which they retain their cogency as an explanation for a particular set of personality traits that anyone who has spent time in Texas and the rest of the South can recognize instantly. It has not been so very long, in historical terms, since slavery was abolished. The cultural patterns it engendered have found new avenues of expression, as the 2016 presidential election so forcefully demonstrated.

(And yet even Olmsted himself, principled abolitionist that he was, cannot avoid the stain of slavery and racism, as in a passage in which he makes fun of three mulattoes, "exceedingly white," whose conversation, when overheard, is "ludicrously black." Or when he reveals sentiments such as this: "The general impression, from the Negroes we saw in both city and country, is one of a painfully clumsy, slovenly, almost hopeless race. Intercourse with them, and dependence on them, as compulsory as is that of a master, would be, to a man of northern habits, a despair.")

Olmsted left New Orleans on a steamer bound for the Red River and Natchitoches, arriving in mid-December, where he and his party acquired horses, mules, rifles, Colt revolvers, and other supplies, then proceeded along a road that was not a road so much as "a way where people had passed along before." A track then, loosely followed, through the piney woods, each man or horse or cow taking the path that spoke to his animal spirits, trying as far as possible to avoid sinking in the mud. Along the way they overtook emigrant trains, many of them, every day; several families traveling together, on some long road from a place that not so long ago was a frontier—Alabama, perhaps, or Georgia. The trains were heard long before they were seen, the cries of drovers urging on their jaded livestock. Dogs, stragglers, "fainting negroes, ragged and spiritless," make their appearance, then old people holding hands with sickly children, "too old to ride and too young to keep up." Wagons, wearing white covers, bounced and jerked, followed by more slaves, and slave children—"pickininnies," he calls them—and the young white mothers and the babies. The master, "frequently ill-humored," rides a horse or walks with his rifle. "As a scout ahead is a brother, or an intelligent slave, with the best gun, on the look-out for a deer or a turkey."

The trains carry food, and they camp near water or else dip into their barrels. They are self-sufficient. Vagabond journalists and solitary travelers must depend on the hospitality of homesteaders, who are used to the imposition. Everyone thereabouts plays innkeeper, from the lowliest homesteader to the planter who makes six thousand dollars a year on his cotton. The womenfolk serve corn and bacon, and the boys, or the slaves, might see to the horses, giving them some corn if there is any corn to be had. Often the travelers were compelled to care for their own horses. Then, at bedtime, they will get a corner of an open cabin, sometimes in the same room with the host, or a guest bed if very fortunate. Sometimes they will sleep in a barn or in a lean-to. Breakfast will be the same as dinner: pork, corn bread, sweet potatoes. The host will charge a dollar and a quarter.

In towns such as St. Augustine and Nacogdoches, Olmsted looked in vain for refined sugar or wheat flour.

Frequently, the company would set up their tents out of doors, and immediately the camp would be invaded by hogs. Once a hog carried off a roasting chicken. Often the most determined hogs would resist "even a clubbing, eating and squealing on through the blows." The acquisition of a good dog became necessary.

Hoecakes were purchased from a family slave, a man who had been away all night visiting his wife on another farm. He arrived home at 4:00 a.m. to grind the corn for breakfast, because the white woman did no housework. "Life there was certainly cheap," Olmsted observes. "This one negro, supposing them to be squatters, was the only investment, except a few days' work once in a lifetime, in cutting and piling together the logs that composed their residence. A little corn and bacon, sold now and then to travelers, furnished the necessary coffee and tobacco; nature and the negro did all the rest."

At one plantation in East Texas, where two little slave girls spent all day hauling water for the family from a creek about a quarter mile away, Olmsted witnessed an eight-year-old boy, already addicted to chewing tobacco, whipping his puppy. "I've got an account to settle with you," he swore as he beat his pet. "I've let you go about long enough; I'll teach you who's your master."

. . .

East Texas is boggy and the roads, to Olmsted's despair, were often "pretty wet." Once, near Beaumont, trying to traverse the Neches bottoms, the companions and their horses were put off a ferryboat on a slip of mud about ten feet wide and given directions to look for a big tree and bear right. Muddy water, as far as they could see, extended over a broad flat, with trees and rotten logs protruding intermittently. Spurring their horses forward, they descended into the soft, sucking mire, horses plunging and wild, struggling against roots and loose poles. A mule bogged down, a mare panicked, everyone was wet, muddy, frantic. "Fanny," the mare, "delirious, believes all her legs broken and strewn about her, and falls, with a whining snort, upon her side. With incessant struggles she makes herself a mud bath, in which, with blood-shot eyes, she furiously rotates, striking, now and then, some stump, against which she rises only to fall upon the other side, or upon her back, until her powers are exhausted, and her head sinks beneath the surface." Thinking of all their notebooks, money, and other belongings, and feeling "uppermost sympathy" with the drowning horse, which has served so well, they plunge in and haul her nose above the surface. They tie a rope around her neck and cut her saddle free and, in the end, succeed in dragging the poor horse out of the horrid porridge of quicksand. After a ridiculous struggle back to the muddy "bank," the ferryman receives their payment for a second time "with a dry nod."

Life improves as Olmsted moves westward out of the piney woods, and so do the vistas. The descriptions match the scenery. One day, after he forded a stream and crested a hill, it was "as if a curtain had risen, upon a broad prairie, reaching, in swells like the ocean after a great storm, to the horizon before us; a thick screen of wood edging it in the distance on the left, and an open grove of low, branching oaks breaking irregularly upon it, with spurs and scattered single trees, to the right." Olmsted and his companions ride along the broken edge of the woods, "crossing capes and islands of the grove, and bays of the prairie." They observe deer and gray horses and red cattle as the "waving surface" of the prairie rises and subsides "like the swell of the ocean after the subsidence of a gale which has blown long from the same direction. Very grand in vastness and simplicity were these waves." Here and there, in the evening gloaming, he marked the red glow of distant fires.

Amid this rolling oceanic prairie, during a blue norther, Olmsted encounters a grazier, a cattleman of old Texas stock, whose father settled in during the long decade of Mexican rule and managed to weather the "trouble times" of the revolution. The patriarch came with nothing but horses and a wagon but was now a cotton planter, raising some fifty bales of cotton ("equivalent to informing us that he owned twenty or thirty negroes, and his income was from two to three thousand dollars a year"). The son described himself as a "regular Texan." He had no interest in tending a plantation and slaving himself "looking after niggers." Any honest Texan, he said, "could live as well as he wanted to, without working more than one month in the year." During that month, in the spring, he worked his cattle hard, marking calves. All his neighbors helped one another during the gathering. He raised some corn. He had little need of money. If he wanted to buy something, he could always sell some cattle. "It did not take much to supply them with all they wanted."

That was evidently true, Olmsted observes rather mordantly. The cattleman lived in a rude one-room cabin, seven by seven feet, with his family. There were three doors and no window. A bed filled a large part of the room. Some wooden boxes served as storage. Everyone sat and ate with winter clothes on, hat and coat on. The wind blew right through the walls. "As I sat in the chimney-corner I could put both my hands out, one laid on the other, between the stones of the fire-place and the logs of the wall."

Common topics of conversation among Texans were the ridiculous doings of Senator Sam Houston and complaints "about niggers."

Austin was a pleasant town, if somewhat exposed on the thinly settled western frontier, "at a point the speculative, rather than the actual, centre of the state." Olmsted was surprised to see how many drinking and gambling shops there were, "but not one book-store." As usual, the cuisine consisted of the "eternal fry, pone and coffee." Wheat flour was rare, "too much trouble," and the butter usually rancid, though Austin did have a German baker.

As Olmsted moves westward, the character of the prairies changes as well: "Live oaks, standing alone or in picturesque groups near and far upon the clean sward which rolled in long waves that took, on their various slopes, bright light or half shadows from the afternoon sun, contributed mainly to an effect which was very new and striking, though still natural, like a happy new melody." So pleased were they that they stopped and sketched the vista, unaware that the scene would repeat itself a thousand times, for they had entered a vast terrain that covers what Olmsted naturally called West Texas, it being the westernmost settled area, but that we would term Central Texas. Here, too, the plantations and ranches he encountered began to change. They were well-ordered and neat. At one, the house stood near a spring, "tastefully grottoed with heavy limestone rocks," now covered in moss under the impetuous stream that gushed forth into a delightful gurgling current. He felt as if he were in Virginia, or Italy. Other travelers were staying at this plantation, and over a meal that included wheat bread the conversation turned to the Germans, whom the Texans called "Dutch." They were suspicious about the Germans, and accusations of "agrarianism" were cast. An odd aspersion, Olmsted thought, in an overwhelmingly agrarian state, which could only mean the Germans were abolitionists and free laborites.

Meeting German merchants in the towns was to be expected, but Olmsted had not thought he would find such a large number of German settlers along the western frontier. In Bastrop he found a copy of the *San Antonio–Zeitung*, which he thought far better than any other Texas newspaper. Olmsted was delighted; he loved the Germans. They were free-minded and "thought it better that all men should be free." They sang arias from *Don Giovanni* to one another in the evenings. There were seven wagon factories in the German settlement of Neu-Braunfels. There he stayed at a delightful inn that could easily have been found on the Rhine. Everyone was cultivated, educated; they read books! Cheerful little troops of children carrying knapsacks of books marched off to school in the morning. People made butter and delicious wheat bread. Here, at last, he had found civilization in Texas.

Many of the German immigrants were poor, but their condition was rising. Every year they improved their holdings. Some were refugees from the failed revolutions of 1848, liberals who lost everything when the reaction set in. Near Sisterdale, set in a lovely valley adjacent to the Guadalupe River, he met a judge who had been an intimate of Humboldt's, an acquaintance of Bettina von Arnim's and Goethe's. Sisterdale, also known as the Latin Settlement, had been founded as a

A spring, Central Texas

kind of communist utopia, more intellectual and spiritual than revolutionary, and Marx's brother-in-law Edgar von Westphalen was an early immigrant. One evening, after a dinner party, the gathered neighbors danced and sang, accompanied by a piano. "I think, if one or two of the German tyrants I could mention, could look in upon us now, they would display some chagrin at our enjoyment," one of the immigrants confided to Olmsted, "for there is hardly a gentleman in this company whom they have not condemned to death, or to imprisonment for life."

Delighted by the picturesque jumble of buildings, races, languages, and costumes of San Antonio, Olmsted could only compare it to New Orleans. He admired the ease and freedom of the city's Mexican culture, as well as the evident comfort of the young women with their bodies, whose loose dresses "seemed lazily reluctant to cover their plump persons," with necklines extending "as low as possible, sometimes even

lower." Unsurprisingly, he learns that Texans tended to treat the Tejanos with contempt, as if they were not fellow citizens but a conquered
people, without civil rights, their land and property seized unjustly,
their participation in the revolution conveniently forgotten. Lynchings
were not uncommon, and whole Mexican communities were driven
out of Austin in 1853 and Seguin in 1854. "Even at San Antonio, there
had been talk of such a razzia," and the sheriff attempted to organize a
posse to drive all the Mexicans out of the neighborhood, but the Germans refused to participate, and so the mob failed to coalesce.

Discovering that a mule train to El Paso and Chihuahua was about
to leave San Antonio, Olmsted considered joining the excursion.
He rode to where the train was camped, just outside the town, and
was pleased to discover it was under the command of Julius Froebel,
the great Swiss republican leader, a scientist and former member of
the Frankfurt Parliament who narrowly escaped a death sentence in
Vienna. Froebel traveled all over North and South America, frequented
Sisterdale, and wrote for the *New-York Tribune*. Froebel advised against
joining the train (which consisted of twenty-six wagons, 260 mules,
and professional hunters and drivers), discouraging his fellow journal-
ist with stories of the tedium of such travel. Likewise, George Wilkins
Kendall, founder of the *Picayune* newspaper, celebrated war correspondent, author of the best-selling *Narrative of the Texan Santa Fé Expedition*, and progressive sheep rancher, advised against travel in Mexico,
telling Olmsted that "the scenery was composed of desert plains and
cactus, and once a day, perhaps, of a stone wall, in addition. We should
wear out about one horse a week, and would be robbed each day of
something we had, until we should reach Mexico without a sou in our
pockets, and without one rag with which we started."

Olmsted chose to disregard Kendall's advice. Although there was
some danger of encountering Comanches, Olmsted and his company
rode out west of San Antonio, bound for Fort Duncan on the Rio
Grande, by way of the most extreme settlements. As they rode, they
passed trains for California. One was a cattle train, with four hundred
head of oxen and twenty-five men to drive them. Some of these men
were seasoned drovers, who knew the road and the waterings and had
experience dealing with the Indians. Others were young men, emigrants, who signed on for passage, working without wages, hoping to

find their fortunes in the promised land beyond the deserts and the mountains. They all rode mules and carried a short rifle and a Colt revolver. Two wagons followed as well as a cart all loaded with supplies, ammunition, cooking utensils. A family of French immigrants had joined up to travel under the protection of the train. Then out they went, beyond Castroville, a settlement of Alsatians, French-speaking Germans, to D'Hanis, Eagle Pass, and beyond.

D'Hanis was a village that puzzled me, growing up, because of its odd name. I had never bothered to look up its story. Olmsted was puzzled by it as well, but for different reasons: It struck him as singularly odd to see what appeared in all respects to be a tiny little European peasant hamlet—with twenty-odd hovels, made of poles and logs placed together vertically, chinked with clay, windowless, thatched, with beaten earth floors—out here on the border, at the mercy of Comanches. Populated by rigid Catholics, its children educated by a priest, D'Hanis was pleasant enough, if terribly poor.

Passing beyond a scattering of homesteads along the Frio River, Olmsted marvels at the landscape, the great chaparral desert before him stretching to the Rio Grande valley, live oaks giving way to mesquite, and at the kind of person willing to live out here, unprotected, exposed to the depredations of Indians, who were always showing up when least expected. He stops to inquire at one of these homes and has a conversation with a young black boy, about ten years old, who could only say that no one else was home. He hadn't been with these people long, and he didn't know his father. He was sold long, long ago. "As I left the house the child ran after me and called out, 'Massa, does you know how long it be to Kis'mas?'—'Oh, a long time yet. What do you want to know for?'—'Coss I'se on'y hired to Kis'mas; I'll get away den, go back whar I belong.'"

Onward then, beyond the Cañon de Uvalde, misnamed for a Spanish commander named Ugalde, down which Indians were known to come raiding off the high plains and where Victor Considérant had tried to establish a colony after the failure of La Réunion. The Rio Grande was several days' ride west, but Olmsted was in no great hurry. Stopping for a time at Fort Inge, at present-day Uvalde, Olmsted visited a nearby Indian camp, populated with Tonkawa, Mescaleros, and Lipans. He found nothing there but "the most miserable squalor, foul obscenity, and disgusting brutishness, if there be excepted the occasional evidence of a sly and impish keenness. We could not find even one man of dignity; the universal expression towards us was either a silly leer or a stupid indifference."

Olmsted's guide in these western districts was an old hand with the Indians named John Woodland, who understood their languages. "Why do people who write books," he inquired of Olmsted, "always make Indians talking that highfalutin way they do? Indians don't talk so, and when folks talk that way to them they don't understand it. They don't like it neither. I went up with Lieutenant ———, when he tried to make a treaty with the Northern Apaches. He had been talking up in the clouds, all nonsense, for half an hour, and I was trying to translate it just as foolish as he said it. An old Indian jumped up and stopped me— 'What does your chief talk to us in this way for? We ain't babies, we are fighting men; if he has got anything to tell us we will hear it, but we didn't come here to be amused, we came to be made drunk, and to get some blankets and tobacco.'"

Olmsted's attitude toward the Indians was by no means simplistic. "Nothing can be more lamentable than the condition of the wandering tribes," he writes. "They are permanently on the verge of starvation. Having been forced back step-by-step from the hunting grounds in the fertile soil of Lower Texas to the bare and arid plains, it is no wonder they are driven to violence and angry depredations." Of course, this was not true of either the Comanches or the Apaches, tribes whose whole economy depended on raiding and always had. "The borderers' idea, which looks upon them as blood-thirsty vermin, to be exterminated without choice of means, was imperatively uppermost in our minds while in their presence. A look into their treacherous eyes was enough to set the teeth grinding and rouse the self-preservative tiger herd of the animal man, latent since we ran naked like the rest in the jungles. If my wife were in a frontier settlement, I can conceive how I should hunt an Indian and shoot him down with all the eagerness and ten times the malice with which I should follow the panther. Yet the power of even a little education on these chaotic, malicious idiots and lunatics can hardly be overestimated."

Riding back to the fort, which was really more a camp where miserable soldiers huddled together in rude shanties and did their best to prevent Indians from stealing their horses, mules, and supplies, Olmsted found himself in the company of some "red brothers." The leader of the group turned out to be a Lipan Apache chief named Castro who was on his way to San Antonio. Castro rode a mule and wore a buckskin shirt covered in beadwork, a wreath of oak leaves upon his bare head, heavy brass rings hung from his ears, and a vermilion streak of pigment blazed across his face, including the eyelids. His eyelashes and eyebrows had been plucked. The Indians eyed their animals and their saddles, and Olmsted struck up a conversation with Castro in which they discussed "the various merits of whiskey, corn, horses, and Germans." Castro said he was on his way to San Antonio to meet with the Indian agent. He planned to propose that the Lipans make a series of raids into Mexico to steal horses and mules that they would then sell to the Americans.

That night, Olmsted later learned, a group of Indians killed a Mexican shepherd boy and captured a second, the third getting away. An Anglo settler named Forrester was shot in the back as he went inside his cabin to fetch food for his demanding guests. His wife ran out the back door and looking over her shoulder saw two of her children murdered, with hatchets. In San Antonio, when Castro heard the news, he offered to help track the villains, who he said must have been Comanches, but all signs ended up pointing toward his Lipans.

Shortly afterward, war broke out between the Lipans and the Texans. "Frontier murders became the order of the day, and for more than two years, hardly a week elapsed without a visit to some exposed settlement from a gang of Indians, who left their arrows sticking in cows and sheep, drove off cattle and horses, shot down whoever appeared least likely to resist, and carried sleepless excitement and terror before them."

Riding out toward Eagle Pass and Fort Duncan, Olmsted observed many deer, rabbits, jackrabbits (which he calls mule-rabbits), quail, a herd of antelope, and a wolf, which was probably a coyote. He marveled at a bird that he describes as about the size of a robin with a forked tail, "like a pair of paper shears half opened," that was often running along the side of the road. His guide called it a bird of paradise—we'd call it a roadrunner—and Olmsted thought that was amusing and ironic because he had never seen such a dreary country. The landscape was rolling like a prairie but with poor soil—arid, rocky, sterile—and blanketed with a "dwarf forest of prickly shrubs." All in all, a perfect description of South Texas.

Over the course of sixty miles they encountered only two men. "Seen any niggers?" the men asked. "Nigger-hunting," they said, "poor business." The proximity of the border was apparently a strong source of temptation for Texas slaves and frustration for slaveholders. Fort Duncan was a small collection of thatched sheds, cabins, and military storehouses. The village of Eagle Pass comprised about six "tottering shanties," mere confused piles of poles with hides hung over irregular openings to serve as doors. Piles of rubbish lay everywhere, broken wagon parts, wheels, scraps of leather; chickens roosted willynilly among the loose thatch. Hogs rooted about in holes in the shade. A single, dusty "woman's garment" fluttered on a clothesline.

The town appeared to be deserted, but after some loud hollers a friendly man appeared. All the rest of the town had gone to bury a man who had died the previous night. "What killed him?—Whiskey.—Well, I reckon that was it."

"See any niggers?" the man asked. He said two had crossed into Mexico the previous night. He offered his bed to the travelers, saying he preferred to sleep out here on the ground. "I don't like the bed, 'count of the fleas."

Twenty-five white folks lived in Eagle Pass. Nobody bothered to count the Mexicans. There were nine groceries and five gambling saloons. They all lived off the soldiers' station there at Fort Duncan, and the Mexicans from Piedras Negras, just across the river.

After a dinner of roast kid goat and eggs and vegetables, cooked by a mulatto from Louisiana, Olmsted crossed the river into Mexico, ferried across the swift Rio Grande by a Mexican with a skiff. A Mexican corporal wearing a sombrero reclined in stereotypical fashion in the shade on a blanket smoking a *cigarrito*, keeping watch.

While in Mexico, Olmsted met a runaway slave, born in Virginia and brought south to Texas. He had escaped four or five years before. He was fluent in Spanish and made a good living as a mechanic. He had worked as a servant and as a muleteer and had traveled all over Mexico. He said that slaves were constantly arriving here and that the Mexican women quite fancied them. It was easy to make a living over here in

Mexico, and colored folks could make money faster than the Mexicans themselves, he said, *because they had more sense.* The government here was very just, he thought, and colored people had full civil rights. Many former slaves had become wealthy, marrying into old Spanish families. They were set up as well as the best white people in Virginia. A colored man could do better than a white man over here, he said, because the Mexicans like them better. "These Texas folks were too rough to suit them."

Westward then, Perry and Welmett, with babies Thomas and Bud, out past Castroville and D'Hanis into that forbidding land, camping along the Medina and the Hondo Rivers, on the Frio and the Nueces, past Fort Inge to Las Moras Springs and Fort Clark. Perhaps, like other westbound migrants and cowboys, they bought vegetables there— cucumbers, beets, parsnips, lettuce, parsley—and haggled with the begging Lipans over trinkets. There was no settlement at Del Rio as yet, but they might have camped at Mud Creek, Sycamore Creek, San Felipe Springs, or along the banks of the Rio Grande. Onward then to First Crossing on the Devils River. Perhaps they admired the rock art in the Painted Cave and wondered about the people who left those markings.

Phocion R. Way, riding the Jackass Mail in 1858, inscribed his name and the date of his visit in Painted Cave. The Devils River, he wrote, was a "favorite resort of the Indians, and some bloody scenes have been enacted there, but we passed through unmolested." An engraver from Cincinnati, Way was employed by the Santa Rita Mining Company and was on his way to Arizona. En route to Fort Clark, he observed that "everyone that leaves San Antonio for the West goes well armed, and they do not conceal their arms but carry them in open view." His fellow passengers had large Colt revolvers on their belts, and rifles at their sides. The driver was well armed, and so were the escorts, astride mules. He was a greenhorn and enthusiastic. "All this was new to me and looked a little strange—it looked like we were indeed going through a country of savages and ruffians. However, to be in the fashion, I buckled on my armor also. I have a Colt's large Navy revolver, a very large Bowie knife, and a Colt's six-shooting rifle. I feel like I would almost as leave have a little fight as not, just to try my hand."

James G. Bell, twenty-two years old, like Perry born in Tennessee in the vicinity of Knoxville, traveled the lower road with a cattle drive in 1854. Another eyewitness of sights that would have been familiar to my ancestors, he followed the trails. Bell's family came to Texas down the Tennessee and Mississippi Rivers, by ship from New Orleans to Indianola. The father, Samuel Bell, was a jeweler, possibly the first in the state of Texas. Bell, one of 150 men working for John James, among them an old Comanche Indian, together with the cattle, left San Antonio on June 3 and made it as far as Castroville. Ten or fifteen miles a day wasn't bad at all. That evening, some of the cowboys swam in the beautiful clear waters of the Hondo; Bell predicted to his diary that they'd often look back wistfully on that happy afternoon. A few days later Bell bought a rattlesnake skin from a Mexican and stretched it over his saddle, believing it would protect his posterior from saddle sores. He swam in Las Moras, a fine cold spring, then camped in mud along creeks.

Three days later they were on the Devils River. The water there runs fast but not deep, coursing over limestone bedrock, eroding channels through which great fish thrash and spawn. At First Crossing, he climbed the slick stone banks of the river up to Painted Cave, describing the paintings within, which reminded him of decorations on a buffalo robe. "Probably," he noted, "this was a place of revelry." Over the next ten days they will cross the Devils River fourteen times, stepping over piles of stones under which lie the bones of men. Indian alarums will be frequent and almost always false. Grapes, plums, and pecans will be there to be eaten. Bell calls them walnuts. Then, as now, the Devils River runs fitfully. Some of the crossings were dry. Come rain and the river will rise; after a big rain, the river will roar, a mile wide, stretching across canyons and valleys. Greens will be picked, fair to eat, gelatinous like okra, but he knows not what to call them.

(In the spring of 1853, Julius Froebel, passing with a caravan up the old Chihuahua trail, came to what he called the "notorious Devil's River." He described this long, sinuous canyon as the most interesting locality he had seen so far in America, describing with a scientist's precision the structure of the geology, insofar as he could see it, and the character of the country. Heaped-up masses of stone were signs of the terrible power of the floodwaters that created this long defile in the Edwards Plateau. "I saw driftwood remaining high up the trees between forked branches, showing to what an incredible height the valley was sometimes filled with water." The course was dry where he entered it, but soon the riverbed was filled with a powerful clear stream varying with broad still lakes. He saw camping places of the Indians and piles of stones memorializing the murders of travelers. At one such place he saw "the half decomposed body thrown out, the head set up on a pole." Wagon boards, a makeshift coffin, were mysteriously arranged on the trail in some obscure insult. He observed the thousands of flowering spikes of sotol, though he used its Latin name. The area around Painted Cave he thought gloomy and painful, a dismal valley descending through a narrow cleft between grotesque rocks among peaks and pinnacles. Farther down the valley, Froebel hears a tale of desperation and cannibalism, escaped slaves, the remains of a human being roasted.)

A cattle drive carries its food on the hoof. A beef slaughtered, butchered, and roasted on spits for steaks, the remainder dried in strips for jerky, the old Comanche who traveled with them eager for the blood. Time moves along, like the river, in streams interrupted: The number of days will be lost. Debates break out. Was it Sunday or Monday? Upon reaching a post at Beaver Lake, they find it Monday. A pair of buffalo fish, bought from soldiers at the military camp, uncommonly fat, fifteen-pounders, twenty-five cents each.

Lingering at Beaver Lake for two days, Bell and company prepared for a forty-mile stretch with no water, resting their cattle and other livestock. They set out, crossing what a few decades later would be my family's land, and made twelve miles before a dry camp, no water to be found. At a prairie dog town they found ten barrels' worth of water, scattered in pockets and depressions, remnants of the recent rain. Lucky they were, and the cattle got a mouth wash. After twenty hours atop a mule, Bell made it with half the train to Howards Well, a spring that in later years will be found at the bottom of a hole, dug by hand, twelve feet deep, stone steps leading down, with a bucket.

Another thirty miles without water, passing a large prairie dog town, four miles in circumference. Some were shot, roasted, and eaten like rabbits. They made camp at Live Oak Creek on the Pecos River. The water was cool and clear, tumbling down a six-foot fall into the

Devils River

brackish, muddy, treacherous Pecos. There Bell found a pile of stones, oblong, and on its head the inscription "Amanda Lewis, 1852." Another young man cried out in disbelief, for he had known her in Mississippi as the mother of a large family. "How desolate must have been the husband and children when they performed the last sad rights over their loved mother,—when with mournful feelings thay turned away knowing that *then*, thay beheld the last of her whom thay had ever looked up to with love and veneration."

Night was coming on, and the men were compelled to go about the business of camp, posting guard, keeping watch through the long dark against molestations of Indians. Bell stared out into the bleak dusk, but he did not feel afraid. There, by that uncommon and fruitful spring, he felt strangely consoled "in this vast expanse of hill and plane when by mere chance I came upon this grave—a feeling of desolation and insignificance came over me, and I felt content in my ignorance of the wondrous creation of earth—the spot where this woman is burried, pobably could not be found in one year's search, for in 1852 this portion of Texas was outside of all civilization." The weather, he thought, had been unusually fine that day, and nature had smiled "in all her beautous colors."

Upon rising they find the air clear and cool, and the sun feels fine on their skin for a brief moment before it begins to burn. Two miles along the high banks, too high for cattle to cross, too high for wagons, the stream turbulent, rapid, pink with mud and minerals, alkaline and briny, searching for the crossing. Wild plums, ripe and sweet, green ones preserved. Some cattle, as always, do not survive the Pecos.

Lancaster Crossing, Pontoon Crossing, Spanish Dam Crossing, Horsehead Crossing, Emigrant Crossing, Pope's Crossing—none were easy, all were dangerous. Cattle, horses, mules, donkeys, and sheep crazed with thirst, diving off steep crumbling bluffs into the swift brackish water or, where the banks were lower, drinking until they were dead, or trampled to death. Indian ambushes, especially at Horsehead, directly in the path of the great Comanche war trail, were a danger. On the long waterless march to Horsehead, failing men were known to shoot down dying cattle and drink the hot thick blood.

Ten miles along the west bank before camp. Another beef slaughtered and devoured quickly along with several rabbits, for even cowboys grow tired of bacon. Nights spent guarding the ambulance, filled with supplies—mesquite for dinner, chewing on the pods, not the hard inedible bean. After a third night camping along the bank of the Pecos, no one is sorry to leave it behind. Ten miles to Escondido Springs; then on to Comanche Springs, where the bones of a man, a known horse thief, were recognized from his clothing. Although he'd been dead three years, there remained scraps of dried muscle, a kneecap, a foot mummified in the dry air.

The bottomless water hole at Leone Springs, beautifully blue water, brackish, with surrounding mud "lightly frosted with salt." Another spring, unnamed, preparing for a hundred miles without water. A trial. They sleep in the open air, saddle and horse blanket for a pillow, atop an Indian rubber coat, with a blanket over all. Usually with boots on, in case of alarm. "When it rains I roll up into a ball like a porcupine, and spread the gum coat over me." Horseback, with a coat tied behind him,

Fort Lancaster, near the Lancaster Crossing of the Pecos River

pants tucked in his boots, check shirt open at the neck, chest brown with sun, nose, ears, and neck scaling like a snake. A rope, canteen, tin cup, and iron spoon, a dead rabbit hanging by the neck for evening roasting or a slab of jerked beef flapping against the mule.

A plain covered with pyrites of iron. A large dog town. A miniature forest of cholla cactus. Into the Guadalupe Mountains, which loom solid black over them as they ride along precipices. Another cattle drive up ahead fights off a band of Indians, kills six. Cooking mescal, or perhaps sotol or lechuguilla, they do not much like it. "An epicure might call it delicious." They eat steaks that have been improved by salt and age.

Through Wild Rose Pass, said to be the most dangerous along the route, thorny with wild rosebushes, blessed with good water and grass; watching the moon rise as the sun sets, clear skies over the prairie, a barren waste appearing deceptively smooth and verdant from on high, listening to the yips of prairie dogs by the thousands below, popping out from their underground houses and singing to their neighbors, the young James Bell feels music in his soul and wishes he were a painter or poet so that he might possess the power to copy what he sees.

And then from Eagle Springs or Van Horn Wells, the long march without water. Water found on the first night, at the head of a canyon, mere puddles and tedious to water the stock, but water is water. Onward through long days under a relentless sun, waterless camping, then driving the cattle through the night, though they are almost perishing. "Thay are compelled to go forward or die." Seventy-five head of cattle lost.

Finally, they come to the Rio Grande del Norte, eighty miles from El Paso, running fast, fifty yards across, with collapsing banks. Exhausted cattle stumble to the river, some die with water in their bellies. A government station, goods for sale. Here they can eat corn bread and drink coffee or even good brandy. The drovers recover themselves, sleep without worry, take turns riding for lost cattle. Then up the Rio Grande. Mexicans, wearing loose cotton trousers and long tunics, cross the river to sell onions, eggs, mescal. Apples grow on trees in San Elizario, pears and good green corn in the fields. Thence to Franklin, the American settlement across the river from El Paso, now known as Juárez. The cattle graze in the open valley; a splendid rain falls. A week passes quickly, and then emigrants and cattle drives must move on again, past Camp Fillmore, past Las Cruces, Doña Ana, harassed by mosquitoes, herding cattle under a bright, clear full moon, up the east bank of the Rio Grande to the crossing at Mesilla. Fields of watermelons, onions, corn—too tempting for those who have been in the desert for months.

On then, all emigrants and cattle drives and mail stages and mule trains, across a desert of forking paths, past the City of Rocks, strange outcroppings surrounded now by barrenness, to the copper mines of Santa Rita. Travelers described this prairie in the 1850s as the most beautiful they had seen, especially in comparison with what they had passed through on the way to El Paso, thick ripe mesquite grass resembling oats ready for the harvest, so calm, so quiet, but water was too far along to stop and let livestock graze.

How different is this landscape now.

.  .  .

Emigrant trains, often six or eight wagons—four or five families, four women and fifteen men, fifteen children might be a typical grouping. The unmarried men travel as hired hands or work for passage and protection. Men are needed as drovers, herders, shooters. The women cook and care for children and worry about the men. The children sit in the wagons, walking through mud or over the steep hills when the wagons must be lighter—when ropes must be used to navigate sheer bluffs, or boulder fields, or quicksand-laden streams. See their wide wondering eyes, pale drawn faces, their confusion about what they are experiencing and why. Reading the diaries of the womenfolk is always different from the chronicles of the men. Here we find a record of suffering that is almost unbearable.

Graves line the roads west. The graves begin early, for Texans, often before they have left their home counties. These are the strangers. Later will come the companions, the husbands and wives and friends and children, graves receding in the distance, along a horizon stained with dust.

In the women's diaries we read the details of provisions, the daily accountings of cooking, washing, tending to the sick. A husband buys six hundred pounds of flour, and we learn how much it costs, four dollars for the hundred. Every ferry charges a different fee, ranging from fifty cents to cross some minor swollen creek to forty-two dollars to cross the Colorado below Fort Yuma. Oxen and horses sicken and die. At night the cattle stray, and in the morning the men must go in search of them, over and over again. Sometimes they lose days of travel while the menfolk search for the livestock. Women grade camps according to grass and water, yes, but also was there wood for cooking? Did the wind make starting the cook fires difficult? Sometimes they had nothing to cook with but weeds and dried grass. During off days the women would cook bread and boil hams and mend garments.

"June 19: We started early and it being cool and pleasant we got along fine. We pass the grave of a lady, Mrs. Rachel Drain, who died May 19, age forty years. It makes me feel so sad to see a lone grave here in this doleful looking country and kneel at the head to read the name. I can't keep from crying, thinking how I would hate to be left on this road."

So wrote Ruth Shackelford in 1865. She made the trip across the plains not once but twice. First on the northern route, the Oregon Trail, where she lost children and friends. Those who followed the Oregon trails suffered greatly from fevers, though settlements were more common and the desolation was perhaps not so great. The mountain passes, of course, presented special challenges, as the Donner Party learned. Three years in California was enough. Back they went, through the desert this time, the southern route, passing train after train of Texans headed to California, "going to the land of gold, they think." The desert was doleful, she wrote. Again and again, she writes that this country is the worst she has ever seen, the most ghastly and gloomy and dreary and forsaken. The wind blows so hard she can barely stand.

Thirteen-inch hail, missiles thrown by some malevolent genie, knock men onto the ground and wound horses. The trains pass burned-out settlements, abandoned ranches, unmarked graves, slaughtered and half-eaten horses surrounded by moccasin tracks. At the end of the day, after long hours of bouncing over roads that can be identified only by the scrapings of wagons on enormous stones, long hours comforting the crying children, the first thing Ruth Shackelford does is milk the cow.

The men go hunting, and the women cook bacon, beans, and rolls or maybe a big molasses cake. More graves. Days spent in difficult rocky climbs and descents, trudging through sand hills, wading rivers, mending broken axles and broken wagon tongues; a child follows her pet crow under the oxen and receives a kick in the head and a two-inch gash. Another falls from the wagon and cuts his leg to the bone. The roads are bad, the water is bad, sulfurous or alkaline or muddy from the hooves of oxen or rank with death.

At Horsehead Crossing, the whole countryside is burned up with alkali. Dead cattle lie thick on the banks. The children cry because the sun burns them and they cannot get away from it while the adults make preparations for the crossing. Some of the men take horses miles to find grass. A herd of cattle, two thousand strong, mills about on the other side of the river, waiting to cross. Mosquitoes swarm at night as the emigrants huddle around the fire, hoping smoke will keep them away, keep the insects from eating out their eyes; horses, covered in sores, have no escape. Finally, they cross as men swim back and forth with wagons used as ferries, barrels lashed to the sides, children and women huddled together, quaking with fear. "We reloaded our wagons and filled our water barrels with nasty, dirty water. We can see dead cattle floating down while we are dipping up the water and see them lying on the banks all over. This is all we will have to drink for eighty-seven miles. There is a man in now telling us there were three thousand dead cattle in the canyon we have to go through this evening."

Husbands, wives, and children die of fever on the road. Men die of hunting accidents. A young man, almost a boy, shoots himself in the chest, twirling his Colt pistol like a fool. Another grave. Women scald their feet when pots overturn on a campfire; dresses catch fire, skin blisters. A little girl, sick, finally gets up out of the wagon, catches a chill, and dies that night. "She suffered very much for two hours after her chill. She had but little fever and in about an hour before she died she rested easy but never spoke so they could understand her, only she called my name three times like she was going to sleep." Another little girl: "cold and clear. Little Annie died this morning just before daylight. She died very hard. She was teething and had diarrhea." Along the road, in the howling waste, there was no medicine for that baby. Another grave.

"They say this is a God-forsaken country. We are camped tonight in a nasty, dusty place and the dust is four inches deep. The wind blew the dust in our faces all evening and it is half soda. When we wash our hands they feel like we are washing them in soda water. They have to dip water out of the spring with buckets to water two hundred and forty head of cattle and it is three miles to grass."

As they approached Apache Pass, the alkali was so deep on the ground it looked like snow. They could see Indian campfires all up in the hills.


As I follow the westering trail of Perry and Welmett, on Paisano Drive in El Paso, the Rio Grande on my left, obscured by the rusty hulking mass of the newfangled border fence, the Franklin Mountains loom up to my right, Mount Cristo Rey with its tall white cross at the summit points the way west. The great smokestacks of ASARCO, demolished over the last year, no longer stand as a landmark, a reminder that a place called Smeltertown used to exist.

Decorative concrete barriers (terra-cotta and teal blue, vague line work signifying the outline of distant mountains) flew by the car window, as camera towers maintained their eternal surveillance. I delayed my overland journey and exited the elevated highway and wandered through the strange landscape of a postindustrial borderland, winding in and among security barriers that are less successful than the highway itself in severing the connection between the old Spanish town of El Paso del Norte, now a killing ground for Mexican cartels, and the former village of Franklin, Texas, now known as El Paso. I passed the decommissioned barracks of old Fort Bliss. Just yards from the river, no longer historical landmarks, they have been converted into shabby apartments. In the old neighborhood of Chihuahuita, tiny stucco homes resembling adobe and painted in festive colors—sky blue, pink, yellow—nestle up right against the border fence along with the community center and a playground. Signs in Spanish for used clothing proliferate, in front of homes and on the sides of old warehouses.

Driving along a lonely road lined with garbage and empty water bottles and rusting chain-link fences, cut off from the rest of El Paso by an elevated highway, I glimpsed a sign for Oñate's Crossing and

Site of the historic crossing of Don Juan de Oñate, 1598

pulled over. I got out and walked into a weedy windblown historic site, where four markers, erected at different times, fabricated from different materials, commemorate significant doings in this place: the crossing of Don Juan de Oñate in 1598; the existence of El Camino Real, which linked the kingdom of New Mexico with the kingdom of Mexico, two great dominions of New Spain, by way of Chihuahua. The life and death of Major Simeon Hart, a pioneering El Pasoan, flour merchant, and ardent Confederate, was memorialized by means of an almost unreadable pink marble slab. A banal chain-link fence with three strands of barbed wire across the top separates the sad little park from the riverbank and a road used by Border Patrol vehicles. Surveillance cameras, high atop towers, keep watch. Pink gravel, clumps of dead grass, a few ancient dead mesquite trees, and a healthy stand of river cane competed for my eyes' attention with small piles of rubbish. Later I read that Simeon Hart and his wife, Jesusita, lie buried in an unmarked grave somewhere nearby; the mausoleum their son built in the 1870s was demolished for the construction of the freeway overpass that looms above this historic place.

I returned to my vehicle and drove out through the pass. The road took me into New Mexico. The old roads followed the water; the new roads just go. The old fields along the river, formerly filled with fruits and vegetables, melons and corn, have been converted into tract houses, a few irrigated fields of grain, the refinery where Rudy Garcia broke his back. Silica mines, for the paving of paradise, owned by Cemex. The Gila Mountains rose before me. A sign told me that God is on my side. I passed Camping World, catering to RVs, the new argonauts, and a defunct amusement park called Wet and Wild Water World. Official warning signs reminded me that DUST STORMS MAY EXIST. It seems the New Mexico Department of Transportation employs philosophers in its signage department. I passed historic old Mesilla, the old crossing of the Rio Grande, where a man once made a fortune selling water to emigrants at ten cents a drink, and continued on to Las Cruces. My plan was to stop at the old mining village of Santa Rita, now consumed by the enormity of the Chino copper mine. More RV parks, pecan orchards in the midst of a barren waste devoid of all grass, supporting little more than creosote.

In Deming, I saw a sign for Pancho Villa State Park, commemorating the Mexican revolutionary's brief bloody sacking of Columbus, New Mexico, in 1916, and I took a quick left turn.

Feeling betrayed by his former patron President Woodrow Wilson, Pancho Villa decided to kill some Americans, so he led fifteen hundred Mexican revolutionaries across the border and burned Columbus, taking nineteen lives. General John "Black Jack" Pershing countered with a punitive expedition. For two years Pershing chased Pancho Villa around northern Mexico. The expedition was a failure, and Pershing never even engaged Villa, but it was the United States' first military use of aircraft. The First Aero Squadron flew 540 missions, covering twenty thousand miles. I spent a pleasant hour wandering around the museum and talking with the staff. The old airplanes were beautiful, constructed mostly of wood, smoothly polished and gleaming as they hung from the ceiling. The border country has long been a laboratory for military applications.

Dust devil, New Mexico

.    .    .

I resumed my former course, heading to the old mines at Santa Rita del Cobre, where James Kirker began his career as a scalper. Small ephemeral homesteads dot the landscape. The desert has been given over to the mobility of senior citizens; a vast parking lot devoted to the restless twilight years of the American middle class. I wondered what they do out there, with their RVs circled like covered wagons, baking day after day in the sun, no golf courses or swimming pools nearby. Perhaps they simply watch television or browse the Internet, adding their opinions to the comment sections of The Huffington Post and Breitbart News.

As I approached the dry meanders of the Mimbres River, the character of the landscape changed from a sandy wasteland to an arid short-grass prairie. A small resort huddled around some geothermal therapeutic springs. I pulled in to City of Rocks State Park and chatted with a volunteer about the rock formations, which poke up from the desert floor like mushrooms. The rocks are the eroded and exposed outcroppings of the Kneeling Nun Tuff, formed from volcanic ash deposited here thirty million years ago. They are cousins of the hoodoos along the Rio Grande. The volunteer told me she tried to volunteer at the Big Bend but the park did not have a space up at the Chisos headquarters that would accommodate her forty-foot trailer. The Mimbres people lived here for fifteen hundred years, before the Apaches came. I asked about pictographs. She smiled and replied that they do not really tell people about those unless they ask, hoping to avoid vandalism, it seems. They were petroglyphs, carved, not painted, and she gave me a handout and a map showing me where to find them. I found one and photographed it, high up on an outcropping, a dark figure with zigzaggy legs playing what looked like a flute.

I rejoined the endless stream of RVs on the highway and made my way to Hurley, a small town perched on the edge of the Chino copper mine, an enormous open pit owned by Freeport-McMoRan. Signs warned that I was entering a blowing-dust area, and then I could see why. A few years before, I flew over the mine with the artist J Henry Fair, who makes gorgeous abstract aerial photographs of environmental crimes. It was like flying over the Grand Canyon. Deep in the bottom of the terraced pit, gigantic earthmovers and dump trucks the size of three-story houses scooped up the copper-laden ore. They looked like toys inside the yawning depths of the mine. They lay the ore out in broad pads, called stockpiles, monstrous artificial mesas of pale pink rubble. Sulfuric acid dribbles through the ore, leaching out the copper, collecting in huge ponds that reflect psychedelic colors, especially from the air. It was dust blowing from these gigantic acid-laced pads that I was now driving through.

The old Santa Rita copper mine, where the War of Apache Scalps was treacherously inaugurated by John James Johnson's hidden blunderbuss, was long ago consumed by Chino. I wondered if I would be able to somehow feel the ghost of James Santiago Kirker in a landscape that had itself been scalped. I guessed there would be some kind of museum in town and soon discovered that a festival was going on, with old restored cars, vintage hot rods, amplified music. It was a cel-

Chino Mine, Hurley, New Mexico

ebration of Hurley pride. I parked and walked through the gray-haired crowd of civic-minded residents, wounded-warrior devotees, and mine workers enjoying a day off. The Democrats of Hurley were holding a voter-registration drive. A person with a microphone urged parents to get their children fingerprinted. "Why? Because they're criminals? No, not necessarily. To keep them safe and secure if they happen to wind up missing. It's a pretty good idea." I had a hard time following the logic. I suppose fingerprints would help identify the bodies.

On Cortez Avenue, I found the Old Hurley Store and Art Gallery. I spoke with a woman named Karin about James Kirker. She showed me a couple of books about him, but they were not for sale. They were from her private library. She told me that a descendant of Kirker's lived nearby, over in Bayard. Kirker was a "horrendous man," she said. "Got to be just about anything that had black hair he'd scalp." Her voice was deep and smoky. She showed me a sheet of raw copper she had picked up off the ground and a painting her husband had made, a detail of the rusty side of a ship in San Diego harbor. It was a good painting. They retired here to Hurley so that her husband could have his own art gallery. I walked outside. I could hear the sound of the machinery in the mine just out of sight.

I drove to Bayard, where the giant ore pads of Chino, hundreds of feet high, loomed over the town. In Silver City, I parked next to a Jaguar and ate lunch in a restaurant called the Curious Kumquat, then drove west through the bottomland along the Mimbres River. As I crested hills, I could see more copper mines in the distance, and then I suddenly came upon the Tyrone Mine, a crazy pink-terraced devastation. I had to pull over, had to soak in the enormity of what I was seeing. How nice, I thought: there was a scenic overlook and welcome center, but the chain-link fence was locked. I climbed over. A plaque explained that environmental protection is just a part of modern mining and that the monstrous stockpiles of mined rock before me, millions of tons of waste, were the result of a twenty-million-dollar reclamation project. "Seeding," I read on the weathered and faded sign, "will occur in the future." Not a single living thing grew on the site.

A few hours later, as I descended from the Continental Divide (6,355 feet), I could see dozens of dust tornadoes passing across the plain.

In 1858, the emigrants crossing this stretch of modern New Mexico, part of the Gadsden Purchase that finally established the western portion of the border with Mexico in 1853, faced a series of relatively straightforward marches from watering to watering, thirty or thirty-five miles between springs: Cooke's Spring, the Mimbres River, Stevens Creek. The danger was not so much the desert here as it was the Apaches. Whether or not attacks came was simply a matter of luck and timing. Sometimes soldiers saved the day; most of the time they did not. Mail and stagecoach stations came under regular assault, stock was stolen, emigrants were harassed. In later years forts were established. Ruth Shackelford, in her diary, describes horses being stolen by Indians in the night, deserted and abandoned ranches. Cooking with weeds and dried grass at Soldiers Farewell, Cow Springs, Barney's Station. Each day seemed to bring another grave.

In Bowie, Arizona, I drove through a huge pistachio plantation to follow a winding road to Apache Pass. The road threads its way between the Dos Cabezas and the Chiricahua Mountains. Spits of rain splattered on my windshield and clouds hung low over the mountains, but as I ascended the pass, trying to imagine what the road would have been like in 1858, the year Butterfield established a mail station near Apache Spring, the sun broke through. Perry and Welmett probably came this way. Not much daylight remained when I parked and hiked down the trail toward the ruins of the Butterfield station. The Chiricahua Apaches, led by Cochise, were mostly friendly in those years, and they remained so until the Bascom Affair of 1861, when an inexperienced U.S. Army lieutenant named George Bascom led a punitive expedition into Apache Pass, believing wrongly that Cochise and his warriors had attacked the ranch of John Ward, stealing livestock and kidnapping a child. A series of violent exchanges resulted in both sides killing hostages, and the Apaches captured a wagon train, tying several people upside down on wagon wheels and building fires under their heads, boiling their brains until their skulls popped. The ensuing war lasted until 1872.

Apache Pass reminded me of Juno and the country along the Devils River, though here I was in the presence of mountains, not canyons. I walked along a narrow trail, through gullies and clumps of mesquite. I have rarely felt so isolated and alone. Not a sound of industrial civilization could be heard: no jets overhead, no rumbling eighteen-wheelers along the highway. Cedar dotted the grassy slopes above me, and live oaks clustered along the dry creek bed. A pair of scruffy-looking mule deer, does, stepped out of the brush and eyed me without fear. Red and black crossbred cattle lounged nearby, chewing their cud, as I walked up to the ruins of the Butterfield station. Remnants of low stone walls, about a foot high or less, traced the outlines of two or three buildings. Sunbeams poured through a break in the clouds, as if some choir of angels were about to burst out singing.

Many travelers described the beauty of these mountains and the divide between them. Descending on the other side of the pass, often along hanging roads, I was grateful I was not at the mercy of a team of exhausted horses or mules.

When Ruth Shackelford came through here with her family, she described seeing Indian campfires in the hills all around them. It was

Butterfield station, Apache Pass, Arizona

not an easy passage, and there were many graves of soldiers and emigrants, victims of Bascom's folly. Phocion Way describes Apache Pass in 1858 as "deep" and "wild looking": "The mountains rise on either side from six hundred to a thousand feet above our heads, and in many places it presented a perpendicular wall of rock for a great height, with only just space enough for one wagon to pass between. Near the end of this pass is the Apache Spring. This is a bad place for the Indians." Way and his companions also saw Indian fires on the mountains all around them, but they were not molested. It reminded him of Bonaparte crossing the Alps.

Many of the great cattle trains were brought through Guadalupe Pass, farther to the south, near the present border with Mexico. But for an emigrant train in 1858, Apache Pass would have been the most direct route: from there to Dragoon Springs, the San Pedro River, and up toward the village of Tucson, by way of the ancient missions of San José de Tumacácori and San Xavier del Bac.

My own route took me down from Apache Pass along a well-graded road, all-weather caliche, through a beautiful basin with short grass the color of straw stretching out in a level plain toward the horizon, where more mountains rose, classic basin and range topography. The road was lined with a barbed-wire fence, five strands, supported often by irregular stumps of wood. Bored Hereford cattle watched me as I photographed the landscape and drove on. A sign told me to SLOW DOWN, SAVE A COW. In the little town of Willcox, Arizona, there was the Cowboy Hall of Fame, and an attraction called the Cochise Stronghold, and a couple of vineyards. The Desert Inn had burned to the ground, and in the middle of a field I saw a boot the size of a car next to a fiberglass teepee.

I made my way back up to the interstate, the sun setting, throwing a magical light over the Chiricahua Mountains; it was a Georgia O'Keeffe painting come to life—eroded mountain faces, mottled with shadows, dun brown to dark gray chiaroscuro, blue-purple accents, shifting in the distance, one mountain blending into another, range upon range upon range as I passed through infinite basins, linked basins, through staggered parallel ranges, flying in my air-conditioned rocket ship over thousands of feet of sediment, the leavings of shallow seas.

Chiricahua Mountains, Arizona

I passed what looked to be a copper mine, some kind of strange leachate seeping down the piles of slag of the mountaintop removal mine, a miniature Chino. Through Texas Canyon and into the Dragoon Mountains, surrounded by jumbled pink granite boulders in strange fractured shapes. The stage passed through here in 1858, and not far away Cochise made his last stand. Down into the San Pedro basin, I drove through Benson, an ugly town nestled in what appears to be volcanic tuff, much like Terlingua, and crossed the San Pedro River. South of here Philip St. George Cooke and his Mormon Battalion fought the Battle of the Bulls.

The whole country around me was dotted with little homesteads, shack-like houses off in the distance, maybe a trailer house, some kind of RV parked under a corrugated ramada; retirees or hippies going off the grid, moving out into the desert to get away from it all. It's a dog-patch subdivided wasteland of desert mystics and witches and meth cookers. Or perhaps it's really just a nice, nontraditional community and I have no idea what I am talking about, which is most likely. As I approached Tucson, the country became rougher, with multiple draws, gullies, dry streams. Somehow the mail and emigrant road passed through here. Now we have a different kind of migrant, and I guess they are not welcome in this state.

In the 1850s, Tucson was a little village, largely Mexican and Indian, a small walled fort for the garrison. South of there, the more significant landmark was the mission of San Xavier. It was founded in 1692 by a remarkable Jesuit priest named Father Eusebio Kino, who walked all over Arizona, converting Indians to Christianity and blazing trails to California before his order was expelled from New Spain. The mission is extraordinary, especially the interior, a baroque extravagance of statuary, wall paintings, icons, shrines, and relics. I sat in a pew and stared, trying to make sense of the riot of color and figuration. Devout pilgrims filed in and touched the life-sized head of Saint Francis stretched out in a white robe. They all reached down and lifted his head three times, then knelt and prayed, touching his forehead. San Xavier was in ruins by the 1850s, open to the birds and small furry mammals. Travelers from los Estados Unidos passed through, sometimes riding their horses into the sanctuary and wondering that such a building could exist in that wilderness.

Driving through this landscape, now, 155 years later, I fell victim to a similar wonderment, that so many millions of air-conditioned, dairy-fed, white-sneaker-clad, well-fertilized, and well-irrigated Americans have come to live against all climatic sense amid the northern reaches of the great Sonoran Desert. I decided to take a detour. Nogales, a community that has loomed so large in discussions of border enforcement over the last several years, was not so far away, so I drove south from San Xavier del Bac.

On my way to Nogales, I stopped at the mission of San José de Tumacácori, where in *Blood Meridian* the scalpers stop and shoot a mad hermit out of the rafters. The mission was closed, so I drove on, through a beautiful countryside in the late afternoon.

At Nogales, I stayed at a bed and breakfast called Frida's Inn. It had a Frida Kahlo theme. I slept in Frida's room, next door to Diego's room. There were some guests from the Mexican consulate who were cooking a carne asada outside.

In the morning I wandered around Nogales. The new border fence runs right through town, and both Nogales, Arizona, and Nogales, Sonora, nestle right up against it. The new fence, which was in the picket style but with flat solid panels across the top to discourage climbers, reminded me vaguely of a Richard Serra sculpture, and I decided it was far more attractive than the fence it replaced. The camera towers struck me as being more obnoxious.

I drove north, back toward Tucson, then west through millions of saguaro cactuses and cut down toward Ajo, just wandering now, avoiding the dullness of life on the interstate. I passed through the Tohono O'odham Nation, where I saw a bicyclist in a bright crumpled heap on the side of the road, a policeman and a border patrolman looking down at him, just standing there doing nothing. The man lay there, his body twisted together with his bike, staring up at the blue vault of a cloudless sky.

I passed a community college, miles from nowhere, surrounded by cholla cactus and mesquite. The brush grew right up against the

Border fence and camera tower in Nogales, Arizona

road. There was no right-of-way, and I worried about wildlife darting in front of my vehicle, but I saw no animals. I passed a small concrete box, in the middle of the desert, miles from any settlement, covered with graffiti. I hadn't seen a car in hours. Town names slipped by: Quijotoa, San Simon, Why. Then an ambulance, probably going to pick up that dead bicyclist. I could understand why they call this stretch of Arizona the Devil's Highway.

The slag pile for the Ajo copper mine was monstrous. Pink slag to my left, white slag to my right—I felt as if I were driving inside the mine. When I arrived in Ajo, I pulled over and filled up with gas. The man at the counter used to work at the mine, which shut down in 1984. It was owned by Phelps Dodge.

By that point I was longing for the interstate, and I drove north through Barry M. Goldwater Air Force Range, a horrible, hideous, godforsaken wasteland.

During a favorable season the road from Tucson to Yuma might not have been so terrible. During a dry spell it was brutal, and I fear that was the case for Perry and Welmett and young T.A. and Bud. The trail led north to meet the Gila River, then west. There might be grass for the animals or not. After a rain the country was covered with what cattlemen called the Gila Lagoons, broad muddy puddles, trod in and soiled by cattle. Livestock fared well enough, but humans often sickened from drinking that water. The villages of the Pima Indians extended for miles along the Gila. Travelers often commented on the beauty of the Pima women, their well-formed figures, their modesty, their sweet laughter.

Once travelers reached the Gila, the water situation improved, for a time. But then came the great bend of the Gila and a *jornada* of some forty miles without water. The Butterfield more or less followed this route, and there was a mail station near a pictograph site known as the Painted Rock. This was a hard stretch of desert in the 1850s, though some fortunate travelers, such as John Russell Bartlett, the hapless boundary commissioner, reported good forage. Today it is still a barren, desolate wasteland, without doubt the worst country I have passed through yet.

Driving along Interstate 8, I marveled at how sorry the country was, when all of a sudden I was surrounded by lush green fields of what looked like alfalfa, thousands of acres of green, and what I soon recognized as a dairy in the distance. Legions of Holstein cattle, gorging themselves on grain and hay, in the middle of an artificial oasis. The dairy and its fields stretch for miles, maybe ten miles on one side, and when I exited the highway for Painted Rock Road, I saw that right next to the dairy extends a huge solar power plant, at least ten square miles of solar arrays.

I drove along a dirt road for several miles, the Painted Rock Dairy to my right, solar arrays to my left, and then I passed once more into the desert, approaching an outcropping of what appeared to be a mound of boulders. The thermometer in my car told me the weather was cool for this place, about a hundred degrees Fahrenheit. Faded information panels informed me that these petroglyphs, some of them, date back twelve thousand years. The oldest are in the Western Archaic style; others are in the Gila style. I see clusters of circles, grids, shapes that look like rakes or tridents, ladders and mazes and atlatls. I have seen similar shapes along the Lower Pecos and the Devils River. The Gila River–style images, five or six hundred years old, are anthropomorphic and zoomorphic—humans, snakes, scorpions, lizards, deer. Archaeologists think some of the round shapes might represent planets or stars. Thousands of figures cover the rocks, scratched (not painted) into the desert varnish covering this basaltic volcanic intrusion. Naturally, there are also more recent markings, including at least one from 1967, the summer of love and the year of my birth.

I was the sole visitor at this lonely place, radioactive green fields not far away, perhaps along the banks of the Gila.

On my way back to the interstate I stopped at the gate of the solar plant. A large sign identified it as the Solana Generating Station. A security guard stood near her vehicle, under a fabric sunshade. I approached and asked whether she thought there was something strange about having a dairy out in the middle of the desert. She said she didn't think it was strange, because the dairies have to move out here because of the HOAs. I didn't understand at first, but as she spoke I got it: homeowner associations. As housing developments expand outward from suburban Phoenix, homeowner associations begin to complain about the dairies. Because it smells bad? I asked.

"It's not just that; it's the flies. I don't know if you noticed them, but when you get in your car again it's going to be full of flies."

I looked back at my car, the door wide open. It was 103 degrees as I drove down the interstate toward Yuma, my windows down, eighty miles an hour, trying to evict my hundreds and hundreds of stowaways.

Wandering around the city of Yuma, Arizona, I found myself unable to make historical sense of the city. It has been divided by highways that pass directly through the old historic areas of town. I stopped at the Yuma Quartermaster Depot State Historic Park and looked at some old photographs and maps in the displays, trying to figure it out. Fort Yuma was across the Colorado River, in California, on a hill. I walked outside, got in my car, and drove back around, up on the elevated freeway known as the Ocean-to-Ocean Highway. Now I could see the hill where Fort Yuma used to be, and then I noticed the Yuma Territorial Prison State Historic Park, on a hill overlooking the Colorado, on the Arizona side. I pulled in to the parking lot and walked over to a kind of gazebo with an elevated perspective over the surrounding areas. A Border Patrol vehicle passed, reminding me that Yuma is a border town. From this point of view, I could see what looked like it ought to be the mouth of the Gila River, but I knew that the Gila, dammed and drained to transform the Sonoran Desert into dairies and such, no longer flows to this point, entering the Colorado as a narrow muddy stream several miles upriver. The Colorado itself, also diverted and dammed and exploited, no longer flows to the sea. Some kind of wetlands restoration has been attempted in the old Gila mouth, along with questionable municipal landscaping.

Down below the old Ocean-to-Ocean Highway Bridge, the Yuma ferry used to carry emigrants and argonauts and soldiers across that river, under the puzzled gazes of the local Indian population.

Eventually, I saw how to access the riverside park and left my car in an empty lot. It was not particularly appealing, consisting of expanses of dirt, rare clumps of grass, random clusters of dried-up hay bales. Riprap sloped down from the prison museum parking lot. A long list of prohibitions greets the visitor: no four-wheel-drive vehicles, no ATVs, no hunting, no unauthorized vehicles, no camping, no fires, no barbecuing, no glass beverage containers, no alcohol. I saw a few solitary men lurking about on the dusty trails through the low brush, perhaps waiting for furtive sexual encounters.

The park was just sad. A little adobe-looking bathroom, some desert landscaping, a building that looks suspiciously like a refreshment

Yuma Crossing, Colorado River, Yuma, Arizona

stand, were put in by the Pecan Grove Garden Club in 2012. They were all so hopeful, with the pink gravel paths; they really thought people would use this place. A few scraps of cast-off clothing hung from thorny trees. I wandered through the park and read a full-color informational panel on hobos, which helpfully explained the difference between a hobo, a tramp, and a bum. A tramp, according to the park's authorities, works only when he needs to; a bum does not work at all; a hobo is a "worker who wanders." There were photographs of a hobo named Lucky, who was camping down by the river when the restoration of the Yuma East Wetlands began. Lucky the Hobo says he didn't mind giving up his camp at the old train jump, because it was about time someone cleaned up this place. The placard says Lucky helped plant more than five thousand trees.

I never did find any signage commemorating the old ferry.

.    .    .

In 1850, a scalper and outlaw named John Joel Glanton came into possession of the Yuma ferry across the Colorado River. Glanton, a former Texas Ranger and veteran of the Mexican War, led a gang of scalpers who, like James Kirker, received a contract from the governor of Chihuahua for a bounty on the scalps of Apaches. The historical sources are not by any means unanimous or reliable, but we do know that the Glanton Gang went on a meandering rampage through northern Mexico and the Big Bend. It wasn't long before Glanton developed a deserved reputation for scalping anyone with black hair and fell out of favor in Chihuahua. Having exhausted one market for scalps, the gang went next door to the state of Sonora and exhausted that one as well. The gang was on its way to California, when a scheme concerning the ferry suggested itself.

According to Horace Bell, author of a compendium of tales titled *Reminiscences of a Ranger*, John Glanton was a young prodigy of a Texas Ranger, instructed "in all the mysteries of Indian fighting, hunting, trailing, lassoing mustangs, and scalping an occasional Mexican." By age sixteen he was the captain of a ranger company, and as such he served in the Mexican War. Somehow this young desperado in training managed to marry "a most estimable and highly cultured lady" from one of the best families of San Antonio, but he left her behind. Arriving in Chihuahua at the head of an expedition of "desperate adventurers," and discovering that the governor of that Mexican state had offered a bounty on Apache scalps, Glanton proposed a campaign, and a carnival of blood followed. Soon the Glanton Gang marched into Chihuahua under triumphal arches, delivered their gory prizes, and received two doubloons for each. After a monthlong orgy of fandangos and debauchery, the gang went out on a second campaign, which was concluded even more rapidly and productively.

To Chihuahuans it appeared at first that the long-sought extermination of the Apaches was at hand. But then the whispers began that Mexican villagers and rancheros had contributed more than a few scalps to the bounty harvested by the barbarians from the north. It was whispered that these Texans hated Mexicans more than they hated Apaches. Glanton and his scalpers cunningly slipped out of town, pursued, too late, by soldiers.

After committing outrages on various towns in northern Sonora, the scalpers appeared at Tucson, just then under siege by the Apache chief Mangas Colorado. Glanton held a parley with Mangas, who was surprised to find Americans willing to fight on behalf of Mexicans. The Apache chief agreed to settle the disagreement with a feast, if the Mexicans agreed to slaughter seven bullocks. Mangas and Glanton drank mescal in the plaza, Horace Bell tells us, and the Apache confided that he has always discouraged his men from killing Mexicans, because "if we kill off the Mexicans, who will raise cattle and horses for us?"

When the scalpers arrived at Yuma, they found the ferry under the command of a solitary American, whom they killed. The ferryman had been friends with the Yuma Indians, who were present in great numbers. The next morning, to avenge the death of their friend, the Indians attacked and slaughtered all but two of the party. Bell says he got the story from Dave and Charley Brown, two survivors, who had gone down to the river to fetch water when the Indians attacked, and so escaped detection, walking across the desert to San Diego and arriving "little better than walking skeletons." Dave, Bell writes, was hanged in Los Angeles in 1854 by a mob of Mexicans, Dave's personal friends, who wished only to prove that Mexicans could lynch a man just as well as gringos. Charley supposedly died in Nicaragua, attempting to vindicate the principle of manifest destiny.

John Russell Bartlett tells a hearsay version of the Yuma story in which a party of Americans led by a Dr. Langdon of Louisiana appropriated a ferry operated by the Yuma Indians in 1849. Langdon hired a man named Gallatin—obviously, from the details, Glanton—who abused the Indians and the passing emigrants, charging four dollars a head for the crossing. Langdon tried and failed to rid himself of Gallatin. After a trip to San Diego, Gallatin returned, amply supplied with liquor, in which he then indulged. The Yumas rushed upon Gallatin and his men when they were helpless from drink and massacred them with war clubs.

The most famous version of John Glanton's legend appears in a novel, Cormac McCarthy's *Blood Meridian*. Untroubled by the discipline of fact, McCarthy renders his scalpers as avatars of the southwestern holocaust, fiends from some borderland hellscape who rape, pillage, and philosophize along the way.

In McCarthy's version of Glanton's demise, he and his scalpers arrive at the Colorado to find a camp full of emigrants, survivors of cholera who had eaten all their horses and mules, and a number of Yuma Indians, tattooed of face, with beautiful naked women scarred by syphilis. An old man with a long beard tells Glanton that the ferryman, a New York doctor named Lincoln, charges a dollar for the crossing. Glanton and his men concoct a scheme to seize the ferry. He convinces the Yumas that they should be operating the ferry and profiting therefrom. He, Glanton, will arrange it all if only they will attack and take control. Meanwhile, he tells Dr. Lincoln that no sane white man would trust an Indian, and seeing as how there happens to be a howitzer lying about at the partially fortified hill above the ferry, would it not be prudent to shore up those fortifications and get that blunderbuss in good working order? Lincoln reluctantly accepts. When the Yumas attack, Glanton and his men naturally turn the howitzer on them in betrayal. A great slaughter ensues, and the scalpers take control of the ferry, immediately raise the fare to four dollars, and then begin charging whatever the market will bear. "Horses were taken and women violated and bodies began to drift past the Yuma camp downriver."

It's not exactly clear from McCarthy's version of the story why Glanton felt the need to enlist and then betray the Yuma, unless he simply wanted to enjoy the sport of killing them. McCarthy takes details from various sources, from Bell, from borderland historians such as Ralph Smith, and from contemporary newspapers, which reported on the massacre with varying degrees of embellishment and accuracy, but his primary source is one of the most singular documents in American history, an illuminated manuscript, illustrated with vibrant watercolors, gouaches, and drawings, titled *My Confession: Recollections of a Rogue*, by an adventurer from Boston named Samuel Chamberlain. McCarthy had access to a bowdlerized version, published in 1956. Forty years later, the historian William H. Goetzmann published a beautiful new edition, with the complete text, a scholarly apparatus, and color plates of Chamberlain's paintings, though unfortunately it is out of print and very expensive.

Born November 28, 1829, in New Hampshire and raised in one of the better neighborhoods of Boston, Sam Chamberlain grew up singing in a church choir and boxing in a gymnasium. He describes himself as a "muscular Christian." He had long blond hair. He learned to paint and to dance and once beat up the church choirmaster. After his father died, in 1844, he went west to Illinois. Two years later, with the outbreak of the Mexican War, he joined a volunteer regiment and went south to San Antonio. Along the way he enjoyed multiple affairs of the heart.

Arriving in San Antonio, Sam found himself mustered out, so he began a career as a gambler. Here he claims he first met John Glanton in a saloon known as the Bexar Exchange. He describes a barroom filled with a variety of Texians: volunteers, regulars, Texas Rangers, Delaware Indians, and Mexicans. The rangers, he writes, armed with revolvers and bowie knives, "wore buckskin shirts black with grease and blood, some wore red shirts, their trousers thrust in to their high boots." They were uncouth, swaggering, with beards and brawny forms and fierce wild eyes. He noticed one peculiar character playing poker in an oddly mild manner, strangely at odds with his appearance: "short, thick set, face bronzed by exposure to the hue of an Indian with eyes deeply sunken and bloodshot, coarse black hair hanging in snake-like locks down his back, his costume was that of the Mexican herdsman, made of leather, with a Mexican blanket thrown over his shoulder." His opponent was a good-looking young ranger, tall and reckless. A dispute broke out, and the short dark character threw a glass of whiskey in the face of the taller man, who jumped to his feet, drew his gun, and pointed it at the breast of his adversary, demanding an apology. The dark-haired man did not move, but responded "shoot and be d——d, but if you miss, John Glanton won't miss you."

A look of horror passed across the tall ranger's face. He pulled the trigger and the gun misfired. "Glanton sprang up, a huge Bowie Knife flashed in the candlelight, and the tall powerful young Ranger fell with a sickening thud to the floor a corpse! His neck cut half through. Glanton, with eyes glaring like a wild beast, jumped over the table and placing one foot on his victim said, 'Strangers! do you wish to take up this fight? If so step out, if not we'll drink.'"

Chamberlain's painting of the scene shows Glanton standing over his victim, eyes wild, his finger pointing in warning at the motley assemblage standing near the bar. In his other hand he holds his bloody bowie knife. The caption reads, "John Glanton settles a controversy," above a death's-head framed by two bowie knives, extending outward like antlers.

All present simply turned back to the bar, some even touching glasses with the murderer; sawdust was sprinkled over the bloody floor. The lesson Chamberlain took from this encounter was simple: he immediately acquired a bowie knife. After an unfortunate altercation involving that knife with his erstwhile gambling partner, Chamberlain found himself in jail among "a very select society of Negroes, Indians and Texans, Horse thieves, murderers and the vilest characters of the lawless frontiersmen." The accommodations were not pleasant. After his release and a period of convalescence in the care of an amorous young German girl and her family, he reenlisted, this time in the First U.S. Dragoons under General John E. Wool. His enlistment records exist, and Captain Enoch Steen describes him as fair-haired, six feet two inches tall. Chamberlain describes the Battle of Monterrey and paints vivid, realistic depictions from the campaign, though his most recent editor, William Goetzmann, points out that according to army records he was in San Antonio at the time. Chamberlain did fight in the Battle of Buena Vista, which he also describes. He also describes in great detail his affairs with a variety of Mexican women. In 1849, Chamberlain marched with the army across Mexico into Arizona. Somewhere between Tucson and Los Angeles, disgusted with his drunken and abusive commander, he deserted. In *My Confession*, Chamberlain does so after meeting "Crying Tom" Hitchcock, who takes him to the camp of John Glanton.

Their first meeting is violent. Glanton reaches out to shake hands upon meeting Chamberlain and gives his nose a painful twist. Chamberlain strikes him in the face and attempts to flee before being lassoed and pulled to the ground. Glanton places a revolver to Sam's head, thinks for a moment, and then welcomes him to the company. "Real grit stranger!" he says. "Ya strike like the kick of a burro." The next day Glanton and ten other men leave to collect their scalp bounties. Chamberlain remains behind, along with Glanton's second-in-command,

> a man of gigantic size who rejoiced in the name of Holden, called Judge Holden of Texas. Who or what he was, no one knew, but a more cool blooded villain never went unhung. He stood six foot six in his moccasins, had a large fleshy frame, a dull-tallow colored face destitute of hair and all expression. Always cool and collected, but when a quarrel took place and

blood shed, his hoglike eyes would gleam with sullen ferocity worthy of the countenance of the fiend. His desires was blood and women, and terrible stories were circulated in camp of horrid crimes committed by him when bearing another name in the Cherokee nation and Texas. And before we left Fronteras a little girl of ten years was found in the chaparral, foully violated and murdered, the mark of a huge hand on her little throat pointed out him as the ravisher as no other man had such a hand, but though all suspected, no one charged him with the crime.

Holden, Chamberlain writes, was the most educated man in all of northern Mexico, speaking with everyone in their own language, whatever it happened to be, including "several Indian lingos." He would play the harp or the guitar at fandangos and charm everyone with his dancing and was "acquainted with the nature of all the strange plants and their botanical names, great in Geology and Mineralogy."

Glanton's men, together with Chamberlain, soon go on a rampage through northern Sonora, pretending to be Apaches, killing and raping and scalping. "Our life was indeed a merry one," Chamberlain writes. "And there is real enjoyment in a lawless, vagabond life on the Frontier. I liked it." At one point they come to the rim of a great canyon filled with magnificent sandstone formations, whereupon Judge Holden mounts a large rock for a rostrum and delivers a scientific lecture on geology. "His lecture no doubt was very learned, but hardly true, for one statement he made was 'that *millions* of years had witnessed the operation producing the result around us,' which Glanton, with recollections of the Bible teachings his young mind had undergone, said 'was a d——d lie.'"

After a fight with a large band of Apaches, four of the scalpers are so wounded they cannot travel. The men draw lots from a quiver of arrows to determine who will put the wounded out of their misery. Chamberlain was relieved to be spared that grim task. A similar scene occurs in *Blood Meridian*, and the nameless kid of that novel, based loosely on Chamberlain, draws one of the unlucky arrows.

Finally, they come to the Gila and follow the river to its confluence with the Colorado. In Chamberlain's telling, it was the Yumas who were operating the ferry. The scalpers seize control of the operation, along with nine of the prettiest Indian girls. There follow days of "hellish orgies," scenes of "shameful licentiousness and outrages on the defenseless maids." As in other accounts, Chamberlain has Glanton leave for San Diego and return with a keg of whiskey and several pounds of biscuit. After another night of orgies, four of the men decide they have had enough and plot their escape to the goldfields of California. The next morning, while putting their plan into action, at some distance from the fort, they look back to see Indians swarming across it. When they later encounter Holden in the desert, he tells them that Glanton had been drunk out of his mind, "tied hand and foot, as usual when on a spree to prevent him from doing mischief," when the Indians attacked.

The most objective account of the events at Yuma can be found in two depositions that were given at Los Angeles in 1850 before the first alcalde, Don Abel Stearns. A man who swore his name was William Carr said that he, Marcus L. Webster, and Joseph A. Anderson were gathering wood at the junction of the Colorado and the Gila on April 23, about three hundred yards from the encampment above the ferry, on the California side, when fifteen or twenty Yuma Indians showed up saying that John Glanton had sent them out to cut poles. The Americans grew suspicious, and a pistol was drawn, whereupon the Indians ran away. The three men were returning to their camp when they came under fire from at least forty guns. The description of the fight is hard to follow, but the results are easy to state: the Indians killed almost everyone. Carr claimed to have seen Glanton's dead body and that a Mexican woman told him Glanton and Dr. A. L. Lincoln were asleep when the attack came. She was sewing in Lincoln's tent, and the Yuma chief came in "and hit the doctor on the head with a stone, whereupon he sprang to his feet, but was immediately killed with a club." Glanton was killed in a similar fashion. Another Mexican woman saw it. The witnesses told Carr that the bodies of all the dead men were burned, along with their dogs, who were burned alive.

Carr testified that the ferry company at the time of the massacre was in possession of fifty thousand dollars in silver and perhaps thirty thousand dollars in gold, the proceeds of less than two months of business. He denied that Glanton or any of the other members of the company had robbed or mistreated anyone at the ferry. He justified the high charges of ferriage, claiming that expenses were high and the site was remote. He admitted that an Irishman named Callahan who had worked with the Indians on their ferry had been found shot dead, floating in the river near Glanton's ferry, but he said he believed the Indians had done it. He could not account for the Indians' hostility, saying that they had always been friendly with the company and had been treated with great kindness. He warned that the Indians were a danger to American emigrants, including women and children, and recommended that the public authorities do something about it.

Two weeks later, a man named Jeremiah Hill gave sworn testimony for the same court that he was a member of a party that crossed the Colorado after the massacre. Hill and his companions were several days away from the Colorado when they received word from one of their companions, who had been traveling ahead, that a massacre might have occurred at the Yuma ferry. As a result they approached the river with caution. They approached within six hundred yards of Glanton's ferry and could see that it had been abandoned. There was no sign of a boat. They went about six miles farther to where the Indians were maintaining their ferry and made camp nearby. There they sent for the chief of the Yumas, saying they wished to give him some presents and have a talk. The chief came and received gifts of "shirts, handkerchiefs, jewelry, pinole, etc." They asked about the massacre of Glanton, and the chief told them what had happened.

The chief said that he had received a boat from an American general named Anderson, who as it happens was the same commander of whom Chamberlain complains in his *Confession*. A large number of Mexicans had crossed using the Indian ferry but no Americans. One day Glanton's men came down from their ferry and destroyed the Indians' boat, killing an American who had been working there. They threw his body into the river. The chief went to see Glanton and offered to split the traffic across the river to their mutual advantage, but Glanton beat him over the head with a stick and drove him away. So the chief held a council, and it was decided that all the Americans should be killed. Glanton meanwhile went to San Diego, so the Indians waited until he came back. The chief went to the Americans' ferry and found that Glanton and his men were all drunk. They waited until the Americans were asleep and then killed them all, except for three who escaped by floating down the river. Most of the Americans, the chief said, were killed with clubs, except for Glanton, "who was killed with a hatchet."

The introduction to these depositions, which were printed in the annual publication of the Historical Society of Southern California in 1903, gives a little background. It seems that Dr. A. L. Lincoln was a relative of President Abraham Lincoln and established the ferry on the Colorado in January 1850, after visiting the mines in California. Glanton and his gang showed up in mid-February. After reports of the massacre arrived in Los Angeles, the governor sent a punitive expedition against the Indians, who fled. The force of Indian fighters camped on the banks of the river and "vigorously attacked their rations." After three months of this campaign, during which time no Indians were punished, the Gila Expedition, also known as the Glanton War, was concluded at a cost of $120,000 to the young state of California. Depredations by the Yumas continued for several years.

In *Blood Meridian*, when the Indians attack the ferry, they swarm up the hill, faces blackened and their hair caked with clay. First they enter the chambers of Dr. Lincoln, from which they emerge carrying his dripping head by the hair, dragging his dog along behind. The chief splits Glanton's head with an ax. Inside Judge Holden's quarters they find a cowering twelve-year-old girl and an idiot, both naked. The judge stands naked "holding leveled at them the bronze barrel of the howitzer," a lit cigar poised over the touchhole. The Indians, in a slapstick moment, fall over themselves in retreat. In McCarthy's imaginings, as in Chamberlain's, Judge Holden emerges triumphant.

Although Chamberlain might have embellished or made up large portions of *My Confession*, his portrait of life and death among John Glanton's scalpers remains a neglected masterpiece of America's frontier literature. His *Confession* is the sole historical source for the character of Judge Holden, who seems to have emerged from hell fully formed, playing a fiddle and dancing on small nimble feet. He will never die.

.  .  .

According to our family tradition, my great-great-great-grandmother Welmett Adamson Wilson perished somewhere along the wagon trail near Yuma. Did she make it to Yuma, or did she die in that last terrible stretch of desert across Gila Bend? There's no telling.

I got back in my car and drove across the Ocean-to-Ocean Bridge into California to wander around in the suburban fringes of the great and terrifying Colorado Desert. Even worse than the desert, and in some ways more fearsome, was the corporate landscape through which I passed. Every national chain was here: McDonald's, Denny's, Circle K, Wingate, Best Western, Marriott, KFC, Holiday Inn Express, Chevron, and Home Depot, as well as the Yuma Palms mall. Generic Americana, plus RV World. That Montana model is pretty sweet.

Was I driving over Welmett's final resting place, even now, or was she back there on Gila Ridge, that broad mesa overlooking the bottom where the Gila River once flowed? Or were her remains out there in the fields, irrigated with captured water, a desert transformed into a patchwork of light and dark green fields, a low range of banal mountains in the distance, a few peaks sticking up here and there, dust hanging on the horizon.

I was driving in circles. I found myself at the site of old Fort Yuma, established after the Glanton War to protect emigrants from the depredations of Yuma Indians, now part of the Fort Yuma Indian Reservation. The oldest buildings have been converted for tribal usage. There is a police station there. Down below, I saw a casino. I supposed that's what all the hotels are for.

I pushed out into the desert, heading toward San Diego, though I knew I would not make it that far. In fact I did not make it very far at all. I saw a sign for Felicity, California, and took the exit. Apparently, some of the inhabitants of this place believe it is the center of the world. There is a shrine in Felicity to that effect, a museum, and a small chapel on a hill. If you have a mobile home, you can stay at the Pilot Knob RV Resort just across the highway. They have palm trees there.

I could not believe the desolation of the landscape. Nothing grew, not even any creosote, really. The ground was hard and bare, almost paved. I could see old weather-beaten trailers out in the desert. The Mexican border was very near, but I could not imagine anyone trying

Close to the Mexican border, near Felicity, California

to make a crossing here. I suspect the Border Patrol agrees, because there was no sign of them anywhere. In the distance I could see sand dunes.

I went down a road that turned out to be a spur. The pavement just ended; beyond here lies nothing, nothing but sand. Sand and one other thing: a yellow road sign that said END. I took the sign as a sign and turned around. On my way back to Yuma, I wondered about Welmett's last moments. Did she suffer? Did she die hard? She was only sixteen when Perry went back to Missouri and married her. Four years later she was dead.

I went back to the old Yuma territorial prison, because it had the best vantage in town. I parked and watched a man in a Vietnamese hat scrubbing the sidewalk. How futile, I thought. Didn't he know that dust storms may exist? I got out of my car and walked up a nearby rise, and then I noticed the prison cemetery on the south side of the hill. Just then a Border Patrol vehicle passed by, and I heard a train whistle as it crossed the Colorado, heading north and then, presumably, west. Inside the cemetery were dozens of unmarked graves, mounds of stone dating from the late nineteenth century. A bronze plaque there memorializes these men in the odd grammar of some nameless and forgotten functionary. "In memory of the inmates who lost their life while serving their sentence at the Arizona Territorial Prison at Yuma. Of the 3,069 convicts, 111 met their death. Disease, accident, murder, suicide, and escape attempts were the causes of their demise. The remains of 104 unfortunate souls are interred in the cemetery." There followed a list of names, the known dead. Included was a man named Henry Wilson. Known dead and unknown dead. Another collection of graves.

In 1858, Perry buried his sweetheart, the mother of his sons, covering her grave with rocks, and continued to San Diego with two babies. He was never able to find her again in later years. For other emigrants, cattlemen, voyagers across the southern route to California, her small

Cemetery near the Yuma Territorial Prison State Historic Park

rough tomb, a mere pile of rocks, was simply another bad omen, if they saw it, a warning, a mute testament of suffering. I thought of Ruth Shackelford, kneeling before the remains of Rachel Drain, feeling so sad, and crying over the death of a stranger. It was not a lovely place to spend eternity. It was just another grave.

# CHAPTER 7

# MOTION OF LIMBS

Perry came back to Texas with his boys after spending two years in California, engaged in the mining business, or so says T.A. in a brief autobiographical narrative that has come down to us. Perry married again, to a woman named Nancy Hodge Rowland, who eventually bore him twelve children. He resumed his cattle business in partnership with his brother Levi. One history of the West Texas frontier locates the brothers' ranch in Clay County at the mouth of the east fork of the little Wichita River, though the range was not yet fenced in those days, and cattle would have drifted. Some sources suggest that Perry and Levi made their homes and kept their families back in Montague, about thirty miles east, which was presumably less exposed to Indian raids. T.A.'s little brother, William, who made it all the way to California and back, was buried in Montague in 1863.

One local historian writes that Perry was among the first to build a home in Henrietta, where in 1860 an election was held to name county officials. Those rolls list Perry Wilson as tax assessor and collector. He was doing his part for the community. That year the U.S. Census found that the population of Clay County was 107 whites and 2 free Negroes.

In 1861, Texas seceded from the Union. Because Clay County was so small, and the danger of Indian attack was ever present, no election was held, or at least there is no record of one. The county's records all burned in the 1870s. But it is safe to assume that Clay would have voted for the Union. In neighboring Cooke County, the vote was 221 against secession to 137 for. Jack County counted only 14 votes in favor of secession, 76 against. Montague cast 50 votes for secession compared with 86 for the Union. Statewide, sentiment was obviously quite different: 46,129 voted for secession versus 14,697 for union.

Most ranchers and farmers along the western border owned no slaves, and there were a number of free blacks living in these counties. Many of the settlers originally came from states that did not secede, and they probably calculated that the withdrawal of Union forces from Texas would leave them exposed to Indian attack. If so, they were correct. During the Civil War, the western frontier fell back almost one hundred miles, and Clay County was completely abandoned.

In tracking Perry's movements through Texas, I came across a number of puzzling references to his service in the Civil War, so I went to the Texas archives in Austin. I found a brief and enigmatic scrap of information, two scraps, really: the muster records of both Perry and Levi Wilson. Subsequent research cleared things up a bit. They both served as rangers in the First Frontier District, of the Frontier Organization, which was created by the State of Texas to defend the western settlements along the Indian frontier, which stretched for five hundred miles from the Red River to the Rio Grande at Eagle Pass. They were listed in Captain Sevier Shannon's B Company, under the command of Major William Quayle. They both served one tour, twenty-two days, and drew two dollars a day in payment. Perry was thirty-six; Levi was thirty-four.

The Frontier Organization was created by the Texas legislature in 1862 to provide some relief to the western settlements, exposed as they were to constant raiding from the Comanches and the Kiowas. So many of the able-bodied young men were fighting and dying in the East. The men who remained had organized ad hoc companies of minutemen and rangers to protect the western counties. The idea of the Frontier Organization was to provide some discipline and structure to the citizen militia. The Confederacy objected, General Kirby Smith most of all, because the generals wanted all the cannon fodder they could get their hands on. And so Texas engaged in a three-year political fight with the Confederate States of America over a question of states' rights. The historical ironies are endless. Texas refused to send its border rangers to fight the Union. They were needed at home, to fight Comanches.

Raids came in waves, and the rangers could do little to prevent them. Mostly they chased the Indians after the fact and tried to recover captives and take revenge. In December 1863, three hundred Comanches crossed the Red River into Montague County, where Perry and his family were living and where Perry, as an able-bodied man, was no doubt serving as a volunteer ranger. The Comanches attacked three settlements, killing a man, two women, and one child. Homes were burned, and the raiders rode back across the river. The next day the Indians attacked again. Ten homes were plundered and burned, twelve settlers were killed, a large number of livestock driven away. Citizen fighters confronted them and soldiers pursued, but the raiders easily outmaneuvered them.

In the Texas archives I read through dozens of reports, all written in a beautifully ornamental script, almost all of them detailed accounts of, and demands for, supplies. I much preferred the scouting reports, such as the diary of a certain William R. Peveler, who filed a long accounting of his patrols from March through December 1863. Amid the charming mundanities of entries such as:

> June 4th Thursday started Early struck the divide between the Brasos & Big Wichita followed it on down until we came in site of the upper Round timber when we came to Bull creek & camped for dinner after Resting a Bout two hours packed up & traveled on down By the upper Round timber & on to the head of Buffalow Byou creek & camped for the Night having traveled 20 miles this day

and the dreary monotony of:

> June 5th Friday traveled a Bout 15 miles & camped for the Night upon Browns creak
> June 6th traveled a Bout 16 miles and arrived at Belknap

suddenly this:

Trying a tune to tell you that I am in love with you but heart
has failed me in every attemt that I have made but I to come
to the point and would like to know if you think

The text breaks off. On the next page, after a list of "Rifles in good
repare" and shotguns likewise functional, another flight of broken
poetry:

N Wood Remember the that I will wherever thou may be for
I the Go ask the birds and flowers if they love sweat refresh-
ing showers

In late September 1864, William R. Peveler and several of his men
were unmounted, their horses tied, when they were surrounded by
fifty Indians. One of the men was shot through the body. He ran and
jumped on his horse but forgot to untie him. The horse ran to the end
of the rope and broke its neck, sending the rider flying, to be killed by
Indians. William was wounded in the arm but managed to get on his
horse. He was cut off from his other men and started down a ravine
when an Indian caught him by the neck; William, his brother Francis
later wrote, "shot back over his shoulder, hit him in the neck and broke
his neck." When he made it to Flag Springs, "he had nineteen wounds
and lived twenty-one days."

A few weeks later, on October 13, came the Elm Creek raid, in
Young County, one of the largest and most destructive Indian attacks
since the early days of the Texas Republic. Captain J. T. Rowland and
his men saw the smoke rising miles before they came upon the man-
gled bodies. Eleven settlements were burned; eleven settlers and five
soldiers were killed, and seven women and children were captured. At
the Fitzpatrick ranch, a young woman was scalped alive while an Indian
forced her mother to watch; a seven-year-old boy was shot down; later,
a thirteen-year-old captive was burned alive. Again, the mother, the
same mother, was forced to watch. Witnesses put the size of the raiding
party between three hundred and one thousand. The wife and children
of a free black man known as Negro Britt Johnson were taken. Over
the next three years, an estimated 163 settlers were killed by Indian
raiders; another 43 were abducted.

Johnson spent years trying to get his family back. On his third or fourth trip into the Indian Territory, depending on the source, Johnson succeeded in recovering his wife and two children, as well as other captives. In 1871, Britt Johnson was killed in another raid on Young County.

In 1867, Perry and his family moved south, keeping close to the Balcones fault line, to Hondo Canyon, near Bandera. Three years later the Wilsons were among the founders of Tehuacana, down near the Frio River. By 1880, the Wilsons were listed by the U.S. Census among the residents of Frio County.

In 1938, an old cowboy named Sam Houston Blalock told Mrs. Florence Angermiller, who was working for the Federal Writers' Project of the Works Progress Administration, that in 1876 he was working in Frio County for a man named Sam Hutchison, when some Indians came through and took a black man who was working with them. They found him dead, swelled up as large as a horse. "He had two bullet holes in him and his left hand was pinned to his breast with an arrow." These same Indians, he said, went down and stole all of Old Man Perry Wilson's horses. "He had a horse pasture fenced entirely with brush—every bit of it." One of the horses was a big gray, and they killed and ate him. "They left a great big chunk of that horse meat sticking on a stick where they had broiled it."

In 1879, Blalock moved back to Frio County to work for Old Man Perry Wilson. Blalock soon married one of Perry's daughters, Alice. She was a good ranch hand, though she was small, about 105 pounds. Sam said she was dark, with dark eyes. Perry moved his cattle to the Devils River in 1886. Sam and Alice went along and stayed three years. They all lived in tents. When they were driving the cattle to the Devils, there was an awful stampede. There were about twelve hundred head. "We lost them all. We were two days gathering them. We got nearly all of them—maybe twelve head short." Sam was on herd when the stampede started, and he never did figure out what scared them. "It was a moonshine night and bright as it could be. And we never could stop them cattle—just had to let 'em go. They run right through camp and this fellow, Swindler, was in bed. A little old yearling run right over him. That tickled me worse than anything that happened. Golly, he sure squalled."

The Devils River had some of the biggest catfish Sam had ever seen. "One boy caught one that weighed 140 pounds," Sam said. "Once, Tom Wilson caught a catfish out of there that weighed sixty-five pounds. He had a sheep camp on the river there and caught this fish and he had it tied to the horn of his saddle and the tail drug the ground."

After three years, Perry and Blalock sold their cattle. Sam and Alice went back to the old Wilson ranch in Frio County. Old Man Perry went west, no doubt for his health. The man was always looking for fresh air, a better climate, so he packed up his family, including his eight unmarried children, drove a herd of horses and mules, along with several wagons, a piano, and a schoolteacher, and took the lower road once again. Brother Levi and son Thomas Austin stayed behind with their families.

In 1891, after little Tommy, their baby boy, died in an accident,

The grave of little Tommy Wilson

T.A. and Bettie Wilson loaded up their family and went back to the ranchman's paradise on the Devils River. He was thinking about sheep and goats. I found little Tommy's grave in the old Tehuacana Cemetery. The town is long gone now; the smallpox came, and those who survived moved away. No one cares much about Tehuacana's dead nowadays or even remembers the town at all. Everyone down there has been too busy making money on the big oil and gas play. Fracking trucks speed up and down the highways thereabouts, hauling water to the oil and gas wells, drilling in the Eagle Ford shale. Weeds had grown up in the cemetery, and I had a hard time finding the grave. But I knew what to look for: a little marble Rambouillet lamb, curled up, and the inscription OUR DARLING BOY, GONE SO SOON.

Sam Houston Blalock told his WPA interviewer that Old Man Perry went to lower California. In fact, he was headed for some land he acquired in northern Mexico, near Yuma. He never made it that far. Perry's son Walter remembered traveling west by wagon and being stuck for three weeks on the banks of the flooding Pecos River. Perry and his boys turned one of their wagons into a ferry and set up business, carrying emigrants and their livestock across the river, before traveling on.

By 1888, Old Man Perry Wilson was one of the leading citizens of Phoenix, Arizona. He gave up the cattle business and started farming. Seems he specialized in strawberries. By the time he died, in 1899, he was known as Strawberry Wilson.

The summer of rains was followed the next year by drought and fire, as if in retribution for the rare and unreasonable gift of moisture. Fueled by unusual quantities of vegetation (tall grass, abundant weeds, thriving brush), wildfires burned all across the state, even threatening towns like Marfa, filled with Donald Judd's primordial geometry, and Fort Davis, with its astronomical observatory. One such fire started on the Massie West place, just northwest of our country, and burned 190,000 acres, including half the Juno ranch. The Deaton Cole fire, as it was called, burned for a month and drew firefighters from across the United States. The fire turned sixty-year-old fence posts, across which my father had stretched wire when he was a child, into charcoal in a matter of minutes and destroyed many miles of water lines, the black PVC pipe strung from one end of the ranch to the other, moving water according to the imperatives of topography and gravity from windmills and their reservoirs to water troughs many miles away. Both livestock and wildlife depend upon such human ingenuity.

In the early 1980s another fire came down from the northwest off the Mayfield ranch, where one of Jake Mayfield's men for some reason decided to burn a dead sheep and walked off and left the blaze unattended. That wildfire was comparatively small but still burned thousands of acres. Jake was a grand old man—half outlaw, people used to say.

When I was young, I spent many evening hours sitting in front of Jake's late-life folly, the Mayfield Country Store, which he opened in the late 1970s, listening to his stories. Unlike my grandmother, when we owned the old Juno store, Jake had no problem with the idea of selling liquor to grown men and women at his Devils River Liquor Store, yet even with a liquor license the business wasn't viable in the end. The country thereabouts was steadily losing its inhabitants, and there just weren't enough travelers meandering through the back roads between Ozona, Sonora, and Comstock. Before long, oilmen from Houston and environmentalists would begin buying up ranches for their own obscure purposes, including the Mayfield place, now owned by the Nature Conservancy.

The absence of livestock on our neighbors' ranches meant there was plenty of fuel that spring, and the fire traveled quickly up and down canyons, creating its own weather; winds swirled and changed direction without warning. At one point, as the front line of the fire was advancing into the wind, it seemed we might lose the whole ranch. The fire had jumped the firebreaks and crossed Highway 163. There seemed no way to prevent it from taking everything.

Then the weather turned, and a light mist settled in. The moisture was hardly even measurable, far less than an inch, but it was enough to permit the firefighters to contain the blaze. In the end, no one died, and none of our buildings were destroyed. We managed to drive our livestock out of the fire's path using helicopters.

Three months later I drove through charred pastures with my father, my stepmother, and my nine-year-old son, who had spent the last week hunting varmints and, more ambitiously, trying to shoot a big axis buck, one of the exotic species of deer that now roam the Texas countryside. We drove through thousands of acres of countryside, my father pointing out landmarks to his grandson, a special canyon that his father had always loved to hunt, places where he'd called up a fox, a spot where his grandfather had first shot a particular rifle. We saw no living creatures. Even the turkey vultures had forsaken the land.

Fire is a primordial element of this landscape, and we know that it once helped regulate periods of growth and regeneration. Lightning was often the spark that set the high plains and their eroded foothills ablaze, and the Indians were known to do so as well, often in pursuit of the buffalo, hoping to drive them off a cliff. Although we suffered a great loss of infrastructure to Deaton Cole, we did at least entertain the consolation that the wildfire might kill the mesquite and cedar that have come to choke our pastures. Grass would grow again in time. Yet in the months since the fire was contained, there had been no rain, and so in hours of driving we saw not one blade of grass growing in the thousands of acres that burned; just charred clumps surrounded by hard black soil, swept clean and smooth by the burning winds.

Mesquite trees, evil and thorny, bare of leaves, thrust their black trunks and branches upward. The cedar like the grass appeared quite dead, but mesquite possesses a deep root system that penetrates the broken limestone and shale to find the abundant groundwater down below. The only signs of green life in that vast burnscape were the delicate pale green shoots at the base of black mesquite silhouettes. Mesquite would thrive even in hell.

As the day settled into evening, we drove up an unpaved county road from Juno toward Pandale to see some of the West ranch where the fire had originated. We'd heard a rumor that the Deaton Cole fire was ignited by a burning automobile along a high-voltage power line that a company called EC was building through that country. A manmade fire, then, perhaps a result of negligence, but there was no hard evidence. EC was building something big, preparing the way for a new, capital-intensive westward energy play: necessary modern infrastructure for wind farmers.

In fading daylight we passed the headquarters of the old Mayfield ranch, surrounded by bulldozed firebreaks that succeeded in saving the

Mesquite, Juno ranch

old Mayfield house. The place had deteriorated badly since the Nature Conservancy took it over, and water gaps in the fences, designed to break free during floods, were still down along the highway from last year's rains. My father noticed that the grand old pecan trees in Jake's yard appeared to be dying from the drought. At least they survived the fire. Not spared was the Mayfield cemetery, which I had not seen in more than twenty years. Now cleansed by fire of the underbrush that seems to have infested it since this strange monument to an old outlaw was constructed in 1984, the cemetery and its gravestones appeared almost to glow in the dusky golden light. I was moved by its weird majesty. At the center of the graveyard was a small, flat-topped pyramid, constructed in Jake's honor, of large gravel stones turned round and smooth over the centuries by the undependable waters of the Devils River. Steps ascended the burial mound, and the name MAYFIELD was carved upon a slab of granite. I walked through the cemetery and paid my respects, trying and failing to recall some of old Jake's tales of his misspent youth along the Rio Grande.

Wrought-iron crosses, already going to rust, adorned the fence and the gate, which was swinging open. As I walked back to the pickup, I pulled it shut, closed the latch. In the world in which such men lived, there was something sinful about an open gate.


At the end of the last Ice Age, when the high glacial cliffs began to shrink back across a scarified continent, woodlands more typical of northern latitudes covered parts of what we now call Texas. Tall-grass prairies flourished, with pine and aspen growing along streams and rivers. On the Llano Estacado, where today giant windmills sprout from endless cotton fields, there might have been substantial forests, or short-grass prairie, or desert, or perhaps an open forest steppe, a grassy parkland with clumps of deciduous trees. Large Pleistocene mammals, such as mastodons, mammoths, giant bison, camels, and horses, grazed and wandered through seas of grass, among oak savanna, avoiding wildfires, hunted by dire wolves and saber-toothed cats. Then they died out about thirteen thousand years ago, victims of climate change or perhaps hunted into extinction. The coast, hundreds of feet lower and miles beyond the present shoreline, would have been much drier, perhaps with wide dune structures, sand laid down by cold glacial winds blowing over a bare midwestern tundra. The Trans-Pecos, now part of the vast Chihuahuan Desert, was temperate, with tall grasses and extensive open woodlands composed of piñon pine, juniper, and oak. As the glaciers withdrew and the oceans rose, the climate remained cool for a long time but grew progressively wetter, until it flipped and turned hot and dry, a trend that has continued, with some brief moist intervals, and dramatically colder episodes, for the last ten thousand years.

Life in West Texas has never been easy, and the idea that people might choose to live in such hard country has always seemed improbable. In the sixteenth century, when the Spanish first passed through the area defined by the confluence of the Devils River, the Pecos, and the Rio Grande, they encountered hunter-gatherers living in small groups and saw no profit in the land. When the Americans came through, three centuries later, they saw this canyon country as just another dangerous obstacle on the way to California, a desolate march between Fort Clark and Fort Lancaster best left to outsized characters like Jack Hays and Bigfoot Wallace. Military maps all noted the presence of Indian paintings, ghostly reminders of those who had been here before and were no more.

Westering migrants and settlers in the 1850s often entertained the pretty pseudoscientific fiction that human activity would somehow stimulate the rains. They believed that civilizing moisture would follow their wagons and herds as they pushed into what was then known to cartographers as the Great American Desert. When Texas cattlemen, among them Perry Wilson, drove their livestock into the open rangeland along the Devils River, they found what many called a stockman's paradise. Cliffs along the Rio Grande and the Pecos made access to water difficult for livestock, but the Devils was more approachable. Before long, the high grasses in its ambit began to fail as drifting cattle damaged the thin mantle of fragile soil. Herds of sheep soon followed, grazing the native short grasses, and when the hard desert thunderstorms came, little by little, the soil washed away. Perry and his cattle stayed on the Devils for three years and then moved on. T.A. returned with his wife, Bettie, and their young children. Some of us are there still, but the rural society and economy that nurtured generations of my family is mostly gone, swept away by the abstract forces of globalized economics, the vagaries of the commodities markets, and the brutalities of a desert climate. By the time I was wandering on horseback along the Devils River, the glory days of the sheep and goat industry were behind us. Grasslands had given way to the invasive mesquite and cedar, and drought was just a way of life.

The passage of the ranching world was swift. Not so the world of those who came before us. Humans first left enigmatic evidence of their presence there at sites like Bonfire Shelter, the oldest and southernmost example in North America of a bison jump, where pre-Clovis hunters drove their prey off a cliff, and Cueva Quebrada, another shelter where the butchered bones of Pleistocene mammals were found in deposits dating to some fourteen thousand years ago. As the rainfall gradually diminished over the millennia, and the big game disappeared, people either adapted and endured or moved on. Those who stayed developed an ingenious hunter-gatherer economy based on desert plants and small animals and the occasional deer. Eventually, they died out or moved on as well. Some left paintings as a record of what they had learned about life in this place.

Growing up here, I had little awareness of those ancient people, though signs of their presence, their flint-knapping sites and earth ovens and wickiup rings, were all around me. I heard about Indian paintings, but as a child I never paid them much attention. I had no idea that a complex of rock shelters just miles from my family's ranch contained one of the most significant bodies of rock art in existence. Still less could I have suspected that those paintings, created for mysterious reasons some four thousand years ago, might speak to us today.

I arrived at Seminole Canyon on a cool, windy morning in late March. The plan was to meet up with a group from the Shumla school, an archaeology and educational center near Comstock, and spend a

Seminole Canyon

week studying the rock art of the Lower Pecos. I hoped to learn more about the deep history of the landscape in which I was raised, about the ways humans had tried, successfully and not, to live in it. Rain had been falling all across the state, and there was some hopeful speculation that the drought might be drawing to an end. I was doubtful; the last year had been so dry that even the cedar was dying. I asked Elton Prewitt, a Shumla archaeologist, if he thought the drought was over. Paleoclimatology, it seemed, had some hard lessons to teach us. "What people don't understand," Elton said, "is that from around eighty-five hundred to about forty-five hundred years ago we had two back-to-back two-thousand-year droughts out here that were much more severe than anything we have experienced in historic times." These droughts were separated by a moist interval of perhaps a hundred years. "That's the way it goes out here. You get a brief cool moist period and you get hot and dry, with flashy spring-summer rains, which of course creates erosion and floods." We talked about the big 1954 flood, a "one-in-over-ten-thousand-year event in this country," which scoured many of the local canyons but didn't reach any of the major pictograph sites. The Pecos River people were no strangers to heavy weather.

Once our group of professional archaeologists and amateur rock art enthusiasts had gathered, greetings and introductions behind us, we hiked down into Seminole Canyon, which feeds into the Rio Grande gorge a few miles to the south. Scarlet ocotillo blossoms stood out in pleasant contrast against gray skies and gray limestone. Clumps of green thorny shrubs, black brush and catclaw, prickly pear and sotol, dotted rocky hillsides almost devoid of grass or anything resembling soil. Looking up and down the steep canyon, I saw two great cavities in massive limestone cliffs, where water, cutting its meandering way through the sedimentary bedrock, exploiting joints and weaknesses thereunder, had over time carved out spaces where humans and other animals might find shelter from the sun and wind. Early settlers and ranchers used such shelters as well, both as dwellings and as ready-made barns for livestock.

Pictographs came into view as we approached Fate Bell Shelter, reached by a narrow trail along a jumble of boulders and small trees, Gregg ash and persimmon among them. Spilling out of the shelter was a talus slope of burned rock, untold centuries of household garbage.

The largest pictographs were massive—one is about twenty-eight feet tall—and when these paintings were in full, vibrant color, about four thousand years ago, they would have been visible from across the canyon. Most of them had faded over the centuries, and dust from excavations and looting still clung to their surface, but many remained vivid and distinct. These were mostly Pecos River–style pictographs, which appear in a dizzying variety of shapes and sizes. Figures of deer, a mountain lion spitting blood or speech, a winged anthropomorph sprouting antlers from his head, and strange ghostlike creatures covered the wall in what at first appeared to be a chaotic jumble, with images running into and over one another. Carolyn Boyd, Shumla's executive director, pointed out the careful lines and the challenges that faced the ancient artists. Slowly, I began to glimpse the planning and skill that must have gone into these paintings.

Interpreting ancient rock art requires hard physical evidence as well as an openness to the possibilities of visual communication. The paint itself provides clues. Using pigments derived from local minerals such as manganese, limonite, hematite, and ocher, the artists needed something to act as a binder, like egg white or blood. The most likely candidate, Boyd believes, was animal fat, specifically deer marrow, mixed with a soapy liquid extracted from yucca root. That combination not only works, she said, it makes a gorgeous paint. From the archaeology of these dry rock shelters we also know quite a bit about what these people ate. By the time the Pecos River style suddenly appeared, roughly forty-two hundred years ago, the climate was far too dry for the buffalo, and the people mostly lived off wild food plants, the sotol and lechuguilla they cooked in earth ovens, native onions and oregano, wild fruits like persimmons and grapes. They ground acorns and mesquite pods in their rock mortars, several of which we could see right here in Fate Bell. Their fossilized feces, known as coprolites, reveal that grasshoppers were a staple, as were minnows, snakes, lizards, and any other small creatures they could catch. They organized group hunts in which rabbits and deer were driven into snares or natural traps, but meat was evidently not a large part of their diet. It was hard country, especially during the long dry spells.

"When I first started working out here," Carolyn said, "I was told that the paintings were graffiti, or that it was something that they did only in their leisure time. Well, if they were using animal fat, they were sacrificing food off their plates, because fat was a precious commodity. In the desert you're not going to find a lot of sources of fat, so that was a group sacrifice. When a deer was caught, which was rare, it was a communal sacrifice to make the paint. That shifts our understanding away from what you do in your leisure time to what you do before you do anything else." It's possible they spent all year collecting materials, making paint cakes that could be used for some special festival or ceremony when the whole community would come together.

But who were these people? And why did they consider these paintings so important? If Carolyn was right that the paintings were narratives, that they could be understood as North America's oldest surviving books, what were they communicating? Was it possible that we could decipher the messages?

For many years, archaeologists had little to offer in the way of an explanation. The pictures were beautiful and intriguing, but they were hard to understand, and no scientific methodology had been established for working out their meanings. One prominent theory was that the Pecos River–style pictographs were shamanic visions, records of hallucinogenic trances, journeys to the spirit realm. Others thought they depicted warfare. Ultimately, the meaning of the artwork was thought to be lost. Scholars claimed that it died with the culture that produced the paintings. Soldiers and railroad workers had little interest in what seemed to be primitive graffiti; often they simply added their own names to the wall or used them for target practice. Landowners, preoccupied with making a living, were usually content to leave the paintings alone.

When Carolyn first encountered these images in 1989, she was an amateur, a professional artist fascinated with Indian paintings, but she was unable to reconcile what she was reading about the pictographs with what she was seeing in the shelters. As an artist, she thought it obvious that the panels were conceived and executed as compositions. They weren't just random indigenous graffiti or an anthology of individual shamanic visions, but she was equally sure that the archaeology profession would never listen to an outsider like her. So she went and got her doctorate in archaeology from Texas A&M and wrote her dissertation on the rock art of the Lower Pecos. Since then, she and her colleagues at the Shumla center, which she founded in 1998, have transformed the study of these astonishing paintings.

Carolyn's methods are painstaking. She and her team have recorded the pictographs in dozens of sites, drawing them herself and repainting them to scale, quantifying their motifs, then comparing her data and the iconographic patterns that she has identified with the ethnographic record. Her research has led to the discovery, after decades of hard work, that the Pecos River pictographs seem to be depicting certain archetypal myths of the great Mesoamerican civilizations, the Aztecs and the Mayans, and especially the Huichol, a culture whose religion has remained remarkably free from Christian influence to this day. Linguists and anthropologists have long surmised that some common linguistic and cultural ancestor must have existed to account for the profound similarities of language and religion among the Mesoamerican civilizations. They call the original cultural strain Proto-Uto-Aztecan. (Uto-Aztecan languages include those of the Aztecs, the

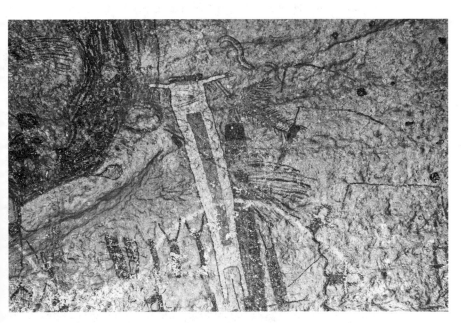

White Shaman Shelter

Mayans, and the Huichol, as well as those of northern cultures such as the Ute, Hopi, Shoshone, and Comanche.) Many scholars believe that the Proto-Uto-Aztecan culture would have originated in what is now the southwestern United States, possibly in the Great Basin region, before spreading outward across the continent. One strand of that migration seems to have passed through the Trans-Pecos, leaving behind paintings that represent the archaic core of what eventually developed into the Mesoamerican religions. It may very well be the case, Boyd surmised, that "the origins of those belief systems are first documented in the rock art here on the Lower Pecos, four thousand years ago."

Carolyn received powerful confirmation of her thesis in 1999, when she took one of her renderings of the White Shaman panel to Real de Catorce, in northern Mexico. She showed the painting to a Huichol man there, and "he became very quiet, and he said, 'That's our pilgrimage,' and proceeded to tell the story of the peyote hunt using that panel as the storytelling device." Years later, in 2010, a Huichol shaman came to Shumla and told Carolyn that his people had traveled along the body of the great serpent and that the serpent passed through this place.

The central ritual of the Huichol religion is the peyote hunt, a pilgrimage to Wirikùta, the Huichol spiritual homeland near Real de Catorce, that reenacts the birth of the sun and the creation of the peyote cactus. The Huichol say that their ancestors, wolf people who were neither human nor fully animal, were led out of the cold dark west and through the underworld by the deer, who sacrificed himself when they reached their destination in the east, Dawn Mountain. When the wolf people slew the deer, his body became peyote, which they ate, and the sun rose for the first time. According to Huichol traditions, peyote still grows in the tracks of the sacred deer, and they believe the life-giving rains follow the deer as well. Indeed, for the Huichol, deer and peyote and water are all symbolically indistinguishable. Other stories tell of a Sacred Deer Person who flew down from the sky with peyote in his antlers. When the sun sets in the west, he then rides through the underworld on the back of the deer, gathering water as it goes, water that the sun will give to the people and the land when he reaches his zenith, during the summer rainy season. When the Huichol perform their pilgrimage today, they do so to ensure that the sun will rise anew each morning and that he will gather up rainwater from the underworld, without which the world will surely die.


Later that first day, after settling into our tents on the Shumla campus, we hiked past the remains of prehistoric earth ovens on the uplands, to a small shelter known as Javelina Grid. On the way, Elton showed us how to recognize the signs of middens resulting from those ovens, the mounds of earth and the fractured and heat-darkened limestone. Cooking sotol and lechuguilla for several days to make the plants digestible required a huge investment of time and labor in return for a meager amount of nourishment. And yet for thousands of years these foods were a staple. Stories I've heard, from my father and others who lived through the hard times of the 1950s, when livestock were obliged to eat ground sotol, appear somewhat differently when considered in that light.

We picked our way along the slope of the canyon. Wild oregano grew thick and unbelievably fragrant alongside native tobacco. Javelina dung carpeted the ground inside the shelter. We found room for just two or three people to crouch below the smoke-blackened ceiling. Several moments passed before I was able to grasp what I was seeing: an abstract grid pattern had been incised everywhere, all across the ceiling and walls of the shallow depression. Elton pointed out that similar sites are found up and down the Pecos. No one can say for sure who made these carvings, or when, but the same patterns were found on incised stones at the Gault Site in Central Texas, an important source of artifacts from the Clovis culture, once believed to have been the first to inhabit North America. Jim Keyser, a rock art specialist from Oregon, spoke cautiously about "entoptic phenomena," visual patterns that reflect the structure of the optic nerve. They show up in the early stages of a hallucinogenic trance. Unlike the massive figures we saw at Fate Bell, which were very public, communal, and probably required the construction of scaffolding, this art was private, best experienced by one or two individuals, perhaps as part of a vision quest.

Over the next week, as we hiked into shelters on the Devils River, the Pecos, and neighboring canyons, we saw much of this odd scratching, both on its own and among the more dramatic large-scale murals of the Pecos River style. Many of the paintings had been deliberately scarified, as if someone were trying to collect chips of paint. In some sites the chipping, scratching, incising, or rubbing was everywhere; at others it was highly selective, as if the figure that was singled out were a special source of power or an object of fear. Often it was the antlered figure of the Sacred Deer Person, his tines adorned with peyote buttons, who was scratched most aggressively. Perhaps those chips of paint were used in rituals to summon the rain, or to start new batches of paint, to be used in rituals to ensure the sunrise.

One day, after a harrowing night of thunder and wind threatened to carry off our tents, we all climbed into pickups and headed out on Texas 163 north of Comstock. Leaving the blacktop, we drove through one ranch after another, carefully unlocking and locking gates as we bounced down fourteen miles of dirt roads, until we came to the magnificent canyon of the lower Devils River, just above its confluence with Dead Man's Creek. We waded the river, stepping over deeper channels cut in the smooth bedrock as monstrous carp coursed up and down the swift stream at our feet. Our destination lay miles upriver, so we walked carefully along the eroded limestone, among shapely grooves and terraces and overhangs. We examined veins of chert, and Jim Keyser explained the techniques used by the Indians to mine that glassy silicate mineral used for knives, scrapers, and projectile points.

Julius Froebel described this stretch of the Devils River valley in ecstatic terms:

> Here, where the road again approaches the river, this valley displays the truly classic beauty of the wilderness. The river now a broad crystal stream, flowing over flat, polished, yellowish-white limestone slabs, is here surrounded by noble trees, wreathed by vines, above which the enclosing rocks lift their towering heights. The river-bed is very remarkable, and the transparency of the water such as to make every line and crevice in its marble floor visible. Here and there, where a flaw has occurred, mud has collected, in which high reeds have taken root. The contrasts in these particulars are uncommon, and the harmony in which they are composed is equally rare.

Luxuriant vegetation in the valley surmounted by naked rocks, lofty trees shading a brilliant water surface, islands of reeds on the flatbed of a rapid stream, a feature seldom united in one picture. A picture truly of wild and brilliant beauty.

We turned from the riverbed and climbed through a jumble of boulders and faulted caprock to the upland, where we encountered a ranch road and signs of a more contemporary economy: a small shed, several deer blinds, and dozens of spent shells. Resurrection plants, dormant until the recent rains, were sprouting up along our trail. Prickly pear and strawberry cactus blooms vied for my attention with delicate yellow, red, and blue wildflowers. We picked our way down the canyon rim and entered the shelter in silence as the roar of a passing military jet drowned out the melodic calls of wrens and sparrows in the thick brush nearby.

As the sound of the jet faded into the distance, I began to discern the patterns of imagery on the wall. Small delicate depictions of felines and humans and deer—often with exquisitely drawn antlers, sometimes with puckered lips—were intertwined with a thick fabric of somewhat larger figures, men carrying atlatls and spears, a mountain lion spitting blood or speech or medicine, ghostly outlines of humans or gods, strange ambiguous designs resembling something from Klee or Kandinsky or Miró. Almost all the larger images bristled with hair-like protrusions. Many were impaled with spears. Carolyn told us that the paintings here had been dated to thirty-eight hundred years before the present, and she zeroed in on one particular image that shows up repeatedly across the landscape. Tall, painted in red, yellow, black, and white, and heavily incised, it was a vaguely triangular figure with arms protruding from the upper corners and a small head with an open mouth resting on the line between them. A pair of deer antlers emerged from the head, and two long, serpentine lines projected from the shoulders encompassing an enigmatic black square and linking up to a yellow circle. A field of radiating lines filled the space between the circle and the square. Almost everything in the panel, in one way or another, seemed to be connected to this figure. This, Carolyn said, was "the point of intersection between this world and the other world," the *axis mundi*, the mouth of the gateway serpent.

Sacred Deer Person

Years ago, Carolyn was camping out here one summer with students from A&M, recording this site, when a fast-moving thunderstorm blew in. They had been swimming down by the river and had to run for cover, just making it to the shelter when the skies opened and sheets of water poured over the edge of the cliff. "It was like being behind a waterfall, the thunder was rolling, and the bedrock was just shaking," she recalled. "You could feel it through your entire body." Sitting there, behind that sudden wall of water, protected from the rain and the wind and the lightning, in a place that had been sacred to the people of this desert for thousands of years, Carolyn and her students simply drifted off to sleep. When they awoke, the ancient basin below the paintings was full, holding water just as it evidently had done thousands of years before. Desert sunlight reflected off the precious water onto the walls, and the paintings came alive with a motion of limbs.

No one knows exactly what happened to the great artists of the ancient world who left us these pictographs. It remains unknown why or even when exactly they left the area. Their tradition persisted for more than a thousand years, and then one day they put down their brushes, gathered their children, and left. That mystery was on my mind as we hiked down into White Shaman, a few miles above the mouth of the Pecos. The site lies in a steep gorge that feeds into the main channel of the river among massive limestone cliffs. We picked our way up and down a steep trail and eventually arrived at the shelter, surrounded by a very high fence topped with three strands of barbed wire to discourage vandals. Days of clambering up and down limestone cliffs had begun to take a toll on my knees, but all my exhaustion fell away when I saw the paintings.

All the main characters from the Huichol creation stories were there: impaled deer covered with black peyote dots; five black ancestor figures spread across the panel, carrying ten candles as offerings; a headless white moon goddess, sometimes known as Mother West Water, facing due west; an antlered figure emerging from Dawn Mountain; and Grandmother Growth, an earth monster who appears as a combination of serpent and catfish. There was even a figure of the first man, who was saved by the moon goddess from a great flood, a tiny human figure, directly below the great white goddess (the so-called white shaman), suspended above a tiny canoe. Peyote buttons, which grow close to the ground along these canyons, were ritually impaled in the pictographs, just as the Huichol continue to do on their pilgrimage today. It wasn't hard to imagine that the artists who painted this panel, like today's Huichol pilgrims, believed that their own sacrifices—of precious deer marrow as well as energy and time that might otherwise have been invested in gathering food—were necessary to guide the sun through the underworld each night, riding on the back of a deer to be reborn in the east, so that the rains might follow and bring forth the desert's fruits, among them the sacred peyote.

But perhaps one spring the painting failed. Perhaps the rains did not come for several years or more. And if, like the Huichol today, the Pecos River people believed that the existence of the world depended on their actions, perhaps they came to see a long drought as a sign to move on, to the south, where Grandmother Growth was more generous, where the Sacred Deer Person was more reliable. We don't know exactly what happened. "What we're learning from studying the rock art," Carolyn said, "is that they followed the rain, they followed the water." Nothing was more important to these people than water. In that sense, the experience of the Pecos River people was probably really not so different from our own. Like us, they faced violent weather and climate change and drought. They felt hunger and thirst. "Everything follows the rain," Carolyn said. "Everything follows the water."

Some things don't change. Thousands of years after the paint dried on the rock art of the Pecos River people, restless souls like my Wilson ancestors grazed their livestock along the Devils River, because the land was open and the water was good. Eventually, some of them settled and raised their families. They were neither the first nor the last to arrive, and soon a town appeared nearby, with saloons and hotels, a post office and a school. Time passed and most people moved away. Little remains of that brief episode but a handful of scattered ranches that haven't been sold to tobacco lawyers or oil tycoons. Compared with the long tenure of the Indians, the European presence here has been as brief as a cloud of dust.

Painted Shelter

At Painted Shelter, on a ranch owned by Missy and Jack Harrington, who donated land for the Shumla campus, a stream flows along the base of walls on which I could see the faint remnants of Pecos River–style pictographs, ancient and faded and almost illegible, underneath large red monochrome-style paintings, younger but still old. Graffiti from 1911 looked as if it were painted yesterday. Just up the hill lay the ruins of a small house constructed from native flagstones that was already present when Missy's great-grandfather settled there. Inside that old structure, near the floor, Frank Greenwood carved his name and his family's brand in 1891, possibly while working as a U.S. marshal, waiting for smugglers to pass through the canyon on their way to Mexico. Greenwood's granddaughter Frankie Lee was one of my grandmother's oldest friends. Missy Harrington told me that she used to picnic along the bank and swim in that stream when she was a child. For uncountable generations, people have been drawn by the water to the cool shadows of this place. They came, rested, and passed on, leaving their marks, their signs and symbols, on the shelter walls.

# ACKNOWLEDGMENTS

This book began long ago as an essay in *Harper's*, and I am grateful to Lewis Lapham, Ben Metcalf, and Jennifer Szalai for helping me craft that first attempt to reckon with the landscape and history of the southwest borderlands. Over the years, many others have provided help and editorial guidance, including Jake Silverstein, Christian Lorentzen, and Luke Mitchell. I am especially grateful to Jin Auh, who first saw the germ of this book, and to Jonathan Segal for giving me the opportunity to write it. Eliza Borné, Maxwell George, Caitlin Love, and my other colleagues at the *Oxford American* cheered me on when the writing was hard, and John Jeremiah Sullivan's friendship, example, and encouragement helped me through the dark times. A special thanks to Jamie Quatro, whose suggestions improved the manuscript immeasurably.

I am deeply grateful to Rudy Garcia, Art Garcia, and the other members of the Mount Cristo Rey Restoration Committee. Jack Skiles, Carolyn Boyd, and Elton Prewitt were extraordinarily generous with their time and knowledge.

To my family I owe more than I can ever express. My grandmother Anale Hodge and my father, Byron Hodge, both sat with me for untold hours as I pestered them with questions. Patricia and Grant Clothier welcomed me into their home and generously shared their genealogical research. They gave me invaluable insights into our family's history. Merily and Tom Keller, Luralee and Tom Wallace, Ann Hodge, Shay Scruggs, Jessica Hodge, and my mother, Joanna Heller, all gave aid and comfort and encouragement. I am grateful for the love and support of my sons, Sebastian and Wriley, who rode shotgun on more than one long journey through West Texas. And, finally, my darling Deborah, who listened patiently as I read hundreds of pages aloud, who read multiple drafts of the manuscript, without you this book would not exist.

# BIBLIOGRAPHY

Audubon, John Woodhouse, and Maria Rebecca Audubon. *Audubon's Western Journal, 1849–1850: Being the MS. Record of a Trip from New York to Texas, and an Overland Journey Through Mexico and Arizona to the Gold Fields of California*. Cleveland: Arthur H. Clark, 1906.

Aulbach, Louis F. *The Devils River*. Houston, Tex.: CreateSpace, 2011.

Austerman, Wayne R. *Sharps Rifles and Spanish Mules: The San Antonio–El Paso Mail, 1851–1881*. College Station: Texas A&M University Press, 2000.

Bancroft, Hubert Howe, and Henry Lebbeus Oak. *History of Arizona and New Mexico, 1530–1888*. San Francisco: History, 1889. http://archive.org /details/historyofarizona00banc.

Barry, Tom. *Border Wars*. Cambridge, Mass.: MIT Press, 2011.

Bartlett, John Russell. *Personal Narrative of Explorations and Incidents in Texas, New Mexico, California, Sonora, and Chihuahua, Connected with the United States and Mexican Boundary Commission, During the Years 1850, '51, '52, and '53, by John Russell Bartlett, United States Commissioner During That Period*. New York: D. Appleton, 1854. http://archive.org/details/mobot31753000248002.

Bell, Horace. *Reminiscences of a Ranger; or, Early Times in Southern California*. Los Angeles: Yarnell, Caystile & Mathes, Printers, 1881. http://archive.org /details/reminiscencesofroobellrich.

Bell, James G., and J. Evetts Haley. "A Log of the Texas-California Cattle Trail, 1854, I." *Southwestern Historical Quarterly* 35, no. 3 (1932): 208–37. http:// www.jstor.org/stable/30237292.

———. "A Log of the Texas-California Cattle Trail, 1854, II." *Southwestern Historical Quarterly* 35, no. 4 (1932): 290–316. http://www.jstor.org/stable /30235405.

———. "A Log of the Texas-California Cattle Trail, 1854, III." *Southwestern Historical Quarterly* 36, no. 1 (1932): 47–66. http://www.jstor.org/stable /30235419.

Benavides, Alonso de. *The Memorial of Fray Alonso de Benavides, 1630*. Translated by Mrs. Edward E. Ayer. Chicago, 1916. http://www.williamreesecompany

.com/pages/books/WRCAM21602/alonso-de-benavides/the-memorial-of
-fray-alonso-de-benavides-1630.

Bender, A. B. "Opening Routes Across West Texas, 1848–1850." *Southwestern Historical Quarterly* 37, no. 2 (1933): 116–35. http://www.jstor.org/stable /30240524.

Berlandier, Jean Louis. *The Indians of Texas in 1830*. Washington, D.C.: Smithsonian Institution Press, 1969.

Black, Steve, and Susan Dial, eds. "Texas Beyond History: The Virtual Museum of Texas Cultural History." University of Texas. https://www.texasbeyond history.net.

Bolton, Herbert E. "The Jumano Indians in Texas, 1650–1771." *Quarterly of the Texas State Historical Association* 15 (July 1911).

Bourke, John Gregory. *On the Border with Crook*. New York: C. Scribner's Sons, 1891.

Boyd, Carolyn E. *The White Shaman Mural: An Enduring Creation Narrative in the Rock Art of the Lower Pecos*. Austin: University of Texas Press, 2016.

———. *Rock Art of the Lower Pecos*. College Station: Texas A&M Press, 2003.

Brandimarte, Cynthia. " 'We Have Our Fingers Crossed': Mining in Big Bend's Fresno Canyon." *Journal of Big Bend Studies* 22 (2010). http://cbbs.sulross .edu/jbbs22.php.

Brigandi, Phil. "The Southern Emigrant Trail." *Overland Journal* (Fall 2010).

Cabeza de Vaca, Álvar Núñez. *The Account: Álvar Núñez Cabeza de Vaca's Relación*. Translated by Martin A. Favata and José B. Fernández. Subsequent ed. Houston, Tex.: Arte Publico Press, 2001.

Campbell, Randolph B. *Gone to Texas: A History of the Lone Star State*. New York: Oxford University Press, 2012.

Castaño de Sosa, Gaspar. *A Colony on the Move: Gaspar Castaño de Sosa's Journal, 1590–1591*. Annotated by Albert H. Schroeder. Translated by Daniel S. Matson. Santa Fe, N.M.: School of American Research, 1965.

Chamberlain, Samuel. *My Confession: Recollections of a Rogue*. Edited by William H. Goetzmann. Austin: Texas State Historical Association, 1996.

Chandler, Charlena. *On Independence Creek: The Story of a Texas Ranch*. Lubbock: Texas Tech University Press, 2004.

Chipman, Donald E. "In Search of Cabeza de Vaca's Route Across Texas: An Historiographical Survey." *Southwestern Historical Quarterly* 91, no. 2 (1987): 127–48. http://www.jstor.org/stable/30240015.

Chipman, Donald E., and Harriett Denise Joseph. *Spanish Texas, 1519–1821*. Austin: University of Texas Press, 2010.

Clothier, Patricia Wilson. *Beneath the Window: Early Ranch Life in the Big Bend Country*. Marathon, Tex.: Iron Mountain Press, 2003.

Coleman, Marion Moore, and Kalikst Wolski. "New Light on La Réunion: From the Pages of *Do Ameryki i w Ameryce* (Part I)." *Arizona and the West* 6, no. 1 (1964): 41–68. http://www.jstor.org/stable/40167092.

———. "New Light on La Réunion: From the Pages of *Do Ameryki i w Ameryce* (Part II)." *Arizona and the West* 6, no. 2 (1964): 137–54. http://www.jstor.org/stable/40167807.

Connell, Evan S. *Son of the Morning Star: Custer and the Little Bighorn.* San Francisco: North Point Press, 1984.

Conover, Ted. *Coyotes: A Journey Across Borders with America's Illegal Aliens.* New York: Vintage, 1987.

Considérant, Victor. *Au Texas.* Philadelphia: Porcupine Press, 1975.

———. *European Colonization in Texas: An Address to the American People.* New York: Baker, Godwin, Printers, 1855.

———. *The Great West: A New Social and Industrial Life in Its Fertile Regions.* New York: Dewitt & Davenport, 1854.

Davidson, Rondel V. "Victor Considerant and the Failure of La Réunion." *Southwestern Historical Quarterly* 76, no. 3 (1973): 277–96. http://www.jstor.org/stable/30236775.

Dearen, Patrick. *Crossing Rio Pecos.* Fort Worth: Texas Christian University Press, 1996.

———. *Devils River: Treacherous Twin to the Pecos, 1535–1900.* Fort Worth: Texas Christian University Press, 2011.

DeCordova, Jacob. *The Texas Immigrant and Traveller's Guide Book.* Austin, Tex.: DeCordova and Frazier, 1856.

DeLay, Brian. *War of a Thousand Deserts: Indian Raids and the U.S.-Mexican War.* New Haven, Conn.: Yale University Press, 2009.

Dering, J. Philip. "Earth-Oven Plant Processing in Archaic Period Economies: An Example from a Semi-arid Savannah in South-Central North America." *American Antiquity* 64, no. 4 (1999): 659–74.

Dixon, Ben F. *Lost Creek Memories: A Book About Two Quaker Families of Tennessee and How They Got Together in the Little Log Meeting House at Lost Creek.* San Diego, Calif.: Family Historians, 1966.

Egan, Ferol. *The El Dorado Trail: The Story of the Gold Rush Routes Across Mexico.* New York: McGraw-Hill, 1970.

Ely, Glen Sample. *Where the West Begins: Debating Texas Identity.* Lubbock: Texas Tech University Press, 2011.

Fehrenbach, T. R. *Comanches: The History of a People.* New York: Anchor, 2003.

———. *Lone Star: A History of Texas and the Texans.* New York: American Legacy Press, 1987.

Foreman, Grant. *Down the Texas Road: Historic Places Along Highway 69 Through Oklahoma.* Norman: University of Oklahoma Press, 1936.

———. *Pioneer Days in the Early Southwest*. 1923. Repr., Lincoln: University of Nebraska Press, 1994.

Froebel, Julius. *Seven Years' Travel in Central America, Northern Mexico, and the Far West of the United States*. London: Richard Bentley, 1859.

Gallaway, B. P. *Texas, the Dark Corner of the Confederacy: Contemporary Accounts of the Lone Star State in the Civil War*. 3rd ed. Lincoln: University of Nebraska Press, 1994.

Gelo, Daniel J. "'Comanche Land and Ever Has Been': A Native Geography of the Nineteenth-Century Comanchería." *Southwestern Historical Quarterly* 103, no. 3 (2000): 273–307. http://www.jstor.org/stable/30239220.

Greene, A. C. *900 Miles on the Butterfield Trail*. Rev. ed. Denton: University of North Texas Press, 2006.

Gregg, Josiah. *Commerce of the Prairies; or, The Journal of a Santa Fé Trader, During Eight Expeditions Across the Great Western Prairies, and a Residence of Nearly Nine Years in Northern Mexico . . .* New York: H. G. Langley, 1845.

Gwynne, S. C. *Empire of the Summer Moon: Quanah Parker and the Rise and Fall of the Comanches, the Most Powerful Indian Tribe in American History*. New York: Scribner, 2011.

Haley, James Evetts. *The Diary of Michael Erskine: Describing His Cattle Drive from Texas to California Together with Correspondence from the Gold Fields, 1854–1859*. [Midland, Tex.]: Nita Stewart Haley Memorial Library, 1979.

Haley, James L. *Sam Houston*. 2nd ed. Norman: University of Oklahoma Press, 2004.

Hall, Roy F., and Helen Gibbard Hall. *Collin County: Pioneering in North Texas*. Bowie, Md.: Heritage Books, 2009.

Hämäläinen, Pekka. *The Comanche Empire*. New Haven, Conn.: Yale University Press, 2009.

Hammond, William J., and Margaret F. Hammond. *La Réunion, a French Settlement in Texas*. Dallas: Royal, 1958.

Harris, Benjamin Butler. *The Gila Trail: The Texas Argonauts and the California Gold Rush*. Edited by Richard H. Dillon. N.p.: Write Thought, 2012.

Hawley, Greg. *Treasure in a Cornfield: The Discovery & Excavation of the Steamboat* Arabia. Edited by Debra Shouse. Kansas City, Mo.: Paddlewheel Press, 1998.

Hernandez, Kelly Lytle. *Migra! A History of the U.S. Border Patrol*. Berkeley: University of California Press, 2010.

Hickerson, Nancy Parrot. *The Jumanos: Hunters and Traders of the South Plains*. Austin: University of Texas Press, 1994.

Hicks, John Edward. *Early Days on the Missouri River*. Kansas City, Mo.: Indian Creek Books, 2000.

Holmes, Kenneth L., ed. *Covered Wagon Women*. Vol. 9, *Diaries and Letters from the Western Trails, 1864–1868*. Lincoln, Neb.: Bison Books, 1999.

Horgan, Paul. *Great River: The Rio Grande in North American History*. Vol. 1, *Indians and Spain*. Vol. 2, *Mexico and the United States*. Middletown, Conn.: Wesleyan University Press, 1991.

Hyde, Anne F. *Empires, Nations, and Families: A New History of the North American West, 1800–1860*. New York: Ecco, 2012.

Irving, Washington. *A Tour on the Prairies*. Edited by John Francis McDermott. Norman: University of Oklahoma Press, 1985.

———. *The Western Journals of Washington Irving*. Edited by John Francis McDermott. Norman: University of Oklahoma Press, 1944.

James, Marquis. *The Raven: A Biography of Sam Houston*. Austin: University of Texas Press, 1988.

Jarrett, T. J. *Kin, Cowboys, Outlaws & Friends*. Austin, Tex.: Nortex, 2004.

Johnson, Frank White. *A History of Texas and Texans*. Chicago: American Historical Society, 1916.

Jones, Daniel W. *Forty Years Among the Indians*. Springville, Utah: Council Press, 2004.

Kagay, Donald J. "Icaria: An Aborted Utopia on the Texas Frontier." *Southwestern Historical Quarterly* 116, no. 4 (2013): 358–85. doi:10.1353/swh.2013.0045.

———. "The Utopian Colony of La Reunion as Social Mirror of Frontier Texas and Icon of Modern Dallas." *International Social Science Review* 85, no. 3–4 (2010): 87. https://www.questia.com/library/journal/1G1-247971689/the -utopian-colony-of-la-reunion-as-social-mirror.

Kavanagh, Thomas W. *The Comanches: A History, 1706–1875*. Lincoln: University of Nebraska Press, 1999.

Kelley, J. Charles. "The Historic Indian Pueblos of La Junta de los Rios, Part 1." *New Mexico Historical Review* 27, no. 4 (1952): 257–95.

———. "The Historic Indian Pueblos of La Junta de los Rios, Part 2." *New Mexico Historical Review* 28, no. 1 (1953): 21–51.

———. *Jumano and Patarabueye: Relations at La Junta de Los Rios*. Ann Arbor: Museum of Anthropology, University of Michigan, 1986.

Kendall, George Wilkins. *Letters from a Texas Sheep Ranch*. Edited by Harry J. Brown. Urbana: University of Illinois Press, 1959.

———. *Narrative of the Texan Santa Fé Expedition: Comprising a Description of a Tour Through Texas, and Across the Great Southwestern Prairies, the Camanche and Caygüa Hunting-Grounds, with an Account of the Sufferings from Want of Food, Losses from Hostile Indians, and Final Capture of the Texans, and Their March, as Prisoners, to the City of Mexico; with Illustrations and a Map*. New York: Harper and Brothers, 1844.

Kenmotsu, Nancy. "Seeking Friends, Avoiding Enemies: The Jumano Response to Spanish Colonization, A.D. 1580–1750." *Bulletin of the Texas Archeological Society*, no. 72 (2001).

———. "Who Were the Jumano?" Texas Beyond History. http://www.texas beyondhistory.net/trans-p/peoples/who.html.

Kirkland, Forrest, and W. W. Newcomb Jr. *The Rock Art of Texas Indians*. Reprint, Austin: University of Texas Press, 1999.

Krieger, Alex. *We Came Naked and Barefoot: The Journey of Cabeza de Vaca Across North America*. Edited by Margery Krieger. Austin: University of Texas Press, 2002.

Lammons, Frank Bishop. "Operation Camel: An Experiment in Animal Transportation in Texas, 1857–1860." *Southwestern Historical Quarterly* 61, no. 1 (1957): 20–50. http://www.jstor.org/stable/30240788.

Lecompte, Janet. *French Fur Traders and Voyageurs in the American West*. Edited by LeRoy R. Hafen. Lincoln: University of Nebraska Press, 1997.

Lehmann, Herman. *Nine Years Among the Indians, 1870–1879: The Story of the Captivity and Life of a Texan Among the Indians*. Albuquerque: University of New Mexico Press, 1927.

Lundwall, Helen. *Copper Mining in Santa Rita, New Mexico, 1801–1838*. Santa Fe, N.M.: Sunstone Press, 2012.

MacLeod, William. *Big Bend Vistas: A Geological Exploration of the Big Bend*. Alpine: Texas Geological Press, 2003.

Magoffin, Susan Shelby. *Down the Santa Fe Trail and into Mexico: The Diary of Susan Shelby Magoffin, 1846–1847*. Edited by Stella M. Drumm. Lincoln, Neb.: Bison Books, 1982.

Maril, Robert Lee. *Patrolling Chaos: The U.S. Border Patrol in Deep South Texas*. Lubbock: Texas Tech University Press, 2004.

Martin, Mabelle Eppard. "California Emigrant Roads Through Texas." *Southwestern Historical Quarterly* 28, no. 4 (1925): 287–301. http://www.jstor.org /stable/30241775.

Mary of Agreda. "City of God: The Divine History and Life of the Virgin Mother of God, The Conception, Book 1." http://www.stjosephpublica tions.com/book_manuscripts_pages/page_templates/book7_ENG_1_page .htm.

McCarthy, Cormac. *All the Pretty Horses*. New York: Alfred A. Knopf, 1992.

———. *Blood Meridian, or, The Evening Redness in the West*. New York: Modern Library, 2001.

———. *Child of God*. New York: Peter Smith, 1994.

———. *Cities of the Plain: A Novel*. New York: Alfred A. Knopf, 1998.

———. *The Crossing*. New York: Alfred A. Knopf, 1994.

———. *No Country for Old Men.* New York: Alfred A. Knopf, 2005.

———. *Outer Dark.* New York: Random House, 1968.

———. *The Stonemason: A Play in Five Acts.* New York: Vintage, 1995.

———. *Suttree.* New York: Modern Library, 2002.

Miles, Elton. *Tales of the Big Bend.* College Station: Texas A&M University Press, 1987.

Miles, William. *Journal of the Sufferings and Hardships of Capt. Parker H. French's Overland Expedition to California: Which Left New York City, May 13th, 1850, and Arrived at San Francisco, Dec. 14.* [New York]: Cadmus Book Shop, 1851.

Neeley, Bill. *The Last Comanche Chief: The Life and Times of Quanah Parker.* New York: Wiley, 1996.

Neville, Joyce. *Tin Cups and China Saucers.* Joyce Neville, 2011.

Newcomb, W. W. *The Indians of Texas: From Prehistoric to Modern Times.* Austin: University of Texas Press, 1972.

Olmsted, Frederick Law. *The Cotton Kingdom: A Traveller's Observations on Cotton and Slavery in the American Slave States.* 2 vols. London: Sampson Low, Son, 1861.

———. *A Journey Through Texas; or, A Saddle-Trip on the Southwestern Frontier.* New York: Mason Brothers, 1860.

Ormsby, Waterman L. *The Butterfield Overland Mail: Only Through Passenger on the First Westbound Stage.* Edited by Lyle H. Wright and Josephine M. Bynum. San Marino, Calif.: Huntington Library Press, 2007.

Pancoast, Charles Edward. *A Quaker Forty-Niner.* Philadelphia: University of Pennsylvania Press, 1930.

Parkman, Francis. *The Oregon Trail: Sketches of Prairie and Rocky-Mountain Life.* Boston: Little, Brown, 1904.

Paxton, William McClung. *Annals of Platte County, Missouri, from Its Exploration down to June 1, 1897; with Genealogies of Its Noted Families, and Sketches of Its Pioneers and Distinguished People.* Kansas City, Mo.: Hudson-Kimberly, 1897.

Pearce, J. E., and A. T. Jackson. *A Prehistoric Rock Shelter in Val Verde County, Texas.* Austin: University of Texas Press, 1933.

Pike, Zebulon M. *Exploratory Travels Through the Western Territories of North America: Comprising a Voyage from St. Louis, on the Mississippi, to the Source of That River.* London: Longman, 1889.

Pingenot, Ben E. "The Great Wagon Train Expedition of 1850." *Southwestern Historical Quarterly* 98, no. 2 (1994): 183–225. http://www.jstor.org/stable/30241458.

Reid, Mayne. *The Scalp Hunters; or, Adventures Among the Trappers.* New York: G. W. Dillingham, 1891.

Romo, David Dorado. *Ringside Seat to a Revolution: An Underground Cultural History of El Paso and Juarez, 1893–1923*. El Paso, Tex: Cinco Puntos Press, 2005.

Sanderlin, Walter S., and M. H. Erskine. "A Cattle Drive from Texas to California: The Diary of M. H. Erskine, 1854." *Southwestern Historical Quarterly* 67, no. 3 (1964): 397–412. http://www.jstor.org/stable/30241960.

Santleben, August. *A Texas Pioneer: Early Staging and Overland Freighting Days on the Frontiers of Texas and Mexico*. New York: Neale, 1910.

Shafer, Harry J. *Ancient Texans: Rock Art and Lifeways Along the Lower Pecos*. Austin: Texas Monthly Press, 1986.

Shaw, Albert. *Icaria: A Chapter in the History of Communism*. New York: G. P. Putnam's Sons, 1884.

Skiles, Jack. *Judge Roy Bean Country*. Lubbock: Texas Tech University Press, 1996.

Smith, David Paul. *Frontier Defense in the Civil War: Texas' Rangers and Rebels*. College Station: Texas A&M University Press, 1994.

Smith, Ralph Adam. *Borderlander: The Life of James Kirker, 1793–1852*. Norman: University of Oklahoma Press, 2000.

———. "The Scalp Hunter in the Borderlands, 1835–1850." *Arizona and the West* 6, no. 1 (1964): 5–22. http://www.jstor.org/stable/40167089.

Sowell, Andrew Jackson. *Early Settlers and Indian Fighters of Southwest Texas*. Austin, Tex.: B. C. Jones, 1900.

———. *Life of "Big Foot" Wallace: The Great Ranger Captain*. Austin, Tex.: State House Press, 1989.

———. *Rangers and Pioneers of Texas: With a Concise Account of the Early Settlements, Hardships, Massacres, Battles, and Wars, by Which Texas Was Rescued from the Rule of the Savage and Consecrated to the Empire of Civilization*. San Antonio, Tex.: Shepard Bros., 1884.

Stephens, A. Ray, and Carol Zuber-Mallison. *Texas: A Historical Atlas*. Norman: University of Oklahoma Press, 2012.

Texas Bureau of Economic Geology. "The Big Bend of the Rio Grande: A Guide to the Rocks, Geologic History, and Settlers of the Area of Big Bend National Park (Geology, Place Names, and Legends)." https://www.nps.gov/parkhistory/online_books/geology/publications/state/tx/1968-7/sec2.htm.

Thrapp, Dan L. *The Conquest of Apacheria*. Rev. ed. Norman: University of Oklahoma Press, 1975.

Truett, Samuel. *Fugitive Landscapes: The Forgotten History of the U.S.-Mexico Borderlands*. New Haven, Conn.: Yale University Press, 2008.

Turpin, Solveig A. "The Lower Pecos River Region of Texas and Northern Mexico." *Bulletin of the Texas Archeological Society* 66 (1995): 541–60.

———. *Papers on Lower Pecos Prehistory.* Studies in Archeology 8, Texas Archeological Research Laboratory, University of Texas, 1991.

———. "Seminole Sink: Excavation of a Vertical Shaft Tomb in Val Verde County, Texas." Memoir 22, *Plains Anthropologist* (1988).

———. *Shamanism and Rock Art in North America.* Rock Art Foundation, Special Publication 1 (1994).

Tyler, Ronnie C. *The Big Bend: A History of the Last Texas Frontier.* College Station: Texas A&M University Press, 1996.

Vulliamy, Ed. *Amexica: War Along the Borderline.* New York: Picador, 2011.

Wade, Maria F. *The Native Americans of the Texas Edwards Plateau, 1582–1799.* Austin: University of Texas Press, 2003.

Way, Phocion R., and William A. Duffen. "Overland via 'Jackass Mail' in 1858: The Diary of Phocion R. Way." *Arizona and the West* 2, no. 1 (1960): 35–53. http://www.jstor.org/stable/40167007.

Webb, Walter Prescott. *The Texas Rangers.* Austin: University of Texas Press, 1965.

Wilbarger, J. W. *Indian Depredations in Texas.* Austin, Tex.: Eakin Press, Statehouse Books, 1889.

# INDEX